CIVIL WAR JOURNAL™

The Leaders

CIVIL WAR

JOURNAL™

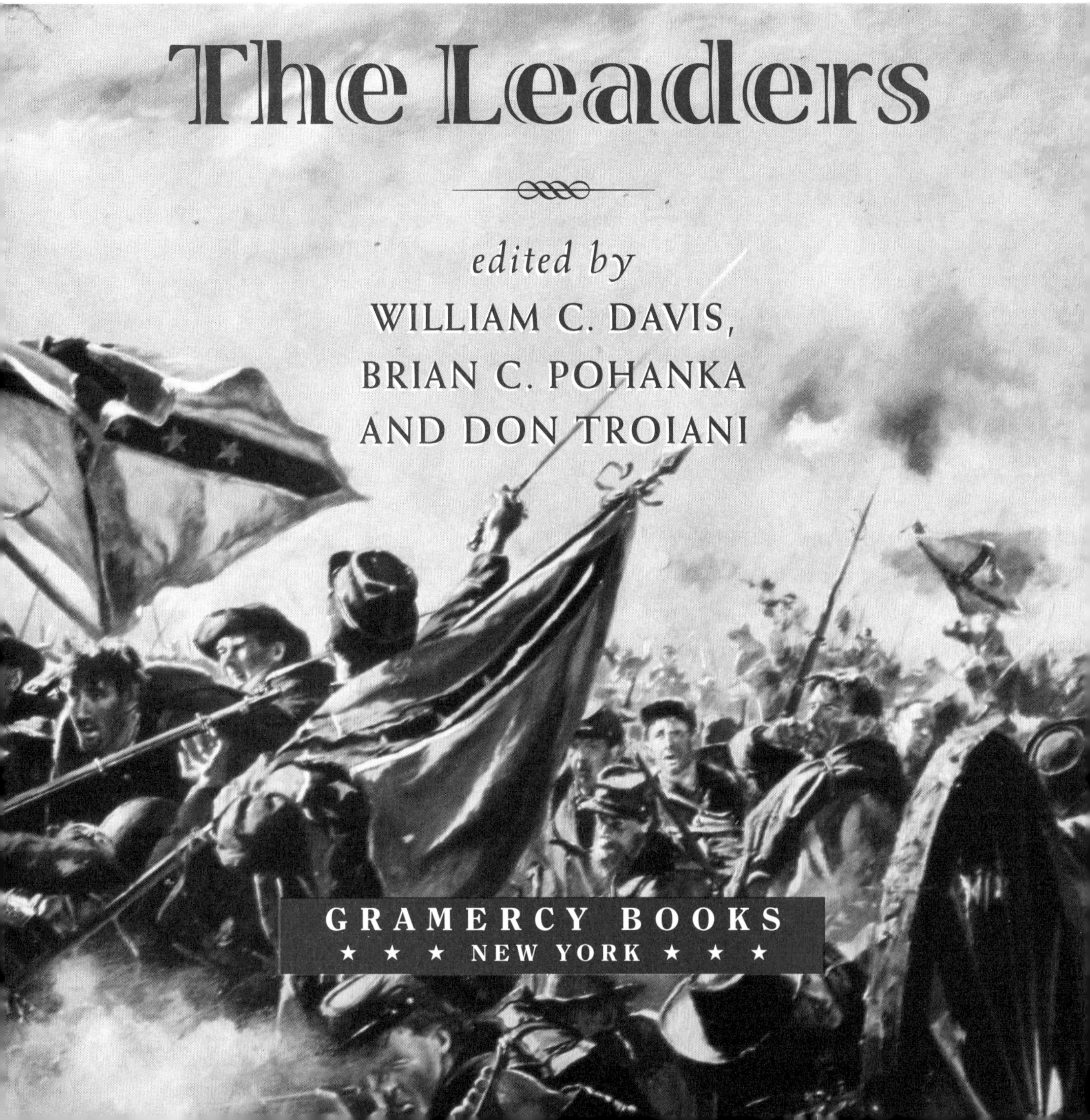

The Leaders

edited by

WILLIAM C. DAVIS,
BRIAN C. POHANKA
AND DON TROIANI

GRAMERCY BOOKS
★ ★ ★ NEW YORK ★ ★ ★

This 2003 edition is published by Gramercy Books, an imprint of Random House Value Publishing, a division of Random House, Inc., New York, by arrangement with Rutledge Hill Press, Nashville, Tennessee.

Gramercy is a registered trademark and the colophon is a trademark of Random House, Inc.

Typography by D&T/Bailey Typesetting, Inc., Nashville, Tennessee.

The maps on pages 9, 282, 285, and 291 were adapted by Janet Brooks.

Pages 446-51 constitute an extension of this copyright page.

Random House
New York • Toronto • London • Sydney • Auckland
www.randomhouse.com

Printed and bound in the United States of America

Library of Congress Cataloging-in-Publication Data

Leaders
Civil War journal : the leaders / edited by William C. Davis,
Brian C. Pohanka, and Don Troiani.
p. cm.
Originally published: Nashville : Civil War journal, 1997. As v. 1 of the
original three volume work. Includes bibliographical references and index.
ISBN 0-517-22193-4
1. United States—History—Civil War, 1861-1865—Biography. 2. Generals—
United States—Biography. 3. Generals—Confederate States of America—Biography.
I. Davis, William C., 1946- II. Pohanka, Brian C., 1955- III. Troiani, Don.
IV. Civil War journal (Television program)
E467.L428 2003
973.7'3'0922—dc21
2003048342

10 9 8 7 6 5 4 3 2 1

Contents

Foreword

THE SEED FOR *Civil War Journal* was planted in 1961. At the age of nine I discovered the American Civil War in a grocery store in Portland, Indiana. *Life* magazine was starting its famous series on this landmark conflict and the artwork on the front cover had done its job. I could not stop looking at it—I had to have a copy.

That magazine became item number one in my treasured history library. It stimulated my imagination and sparked a quest that has taken me through hundreds of books and to dozens of historic sites. As I pursued a career in television and film, my dream was to create projects based on the Civil War era.

In 1985, while working at ABC Television, my first opportunity presented itself. I wanted to produce a weekly series on the Civil War and was given the chance to produce a pilot episode. My production team created a documentary on the battle of Gettysburg. The creative concept was a simple one. The battle served as an epic panoramic background with the main focus on individuals, military and civilian, who had experienced the event firsthand. Although it was a ratings and critical success, five years elapsed before I had another opportunity to expand this effort.

History- and so-called period-based projects have never been an easy sale in Hollywood. Two events, however, gave *Civil War Journal* another chance: the growth of the cable television industry and the success the Public Broadcasting Service achieved by scheduling its eleven-hour Civil War special as a week-long event.

In the fall of 1990 I made a presentation to the Arts and Entertainment Cable Television Network for a weekly series on the American Civil War. The original treatment presented a blueprint for an ambitious project. It proposed 130 episodes whose subjects would include battles, leaders, followers, home fronts, weapons, symbols, and more.

Each was to be able to stand on its own so if viewers missed one week, they could still view the following week's show without a problem. Hallmarks of the series would include a distinctive and memorable main-title montage with an original theme, an all-star list of historians and authors, original and period music, state-of-the-art graphics, accurate re-creation footage, thousands of period photographs presented with computer enhancement and recorded by an animation camera, and a well-known personality as host who shared this love for history.

There was good news and bad news. The good news was that A&E liked the project and wanted to buy it. The bad news for an anxious producer was that the network wanted to wait. That wait ended in 1993, and *Civil War Journal* premiered with host Danny Glover to critical and ratings success.

Having now produced fifty-two episodes, a one-hour special on battlefield preservation, and a two-hour special on the Lincoln assassination, *Civil War Journal* continues on A&E's second cable service, The History Channel. Dozens of dedicated people have worked thousands of hours to create this award-winning series. I am proud to be a member of this production family we call Greystone and thank you for your continued support.

CRAIG HAFFNER
Executive Producer
Greystone Communications, Inc.
Studio City, California

Preface

THE CULT of the personality was every bit as strong in the Civil War as in our own time, and the men included in *The Leaders* are the personalities upon whom American imaginations were most fixed between 1861 and 1865. Some were controversial, some were adored, and a few were reviled, but all were newsmakers and at least a few of them had the opportunity or ability to affect the outcome of the conflict. In short, while most were important in their own right, some were important chiefly because the public believed they were. Even today the mention of their names still stirs debate in some corners, making the war alive to each generation. Was McClellan ever going to act? Was Longstreet one of the South's greatest generals? Did Jackson ever falter? Moreover, the public has never lost interest in these men during the ensuing century and more, testimony to their central role as legendary figures of the war.

The men who led were those who defined the war. They determined how it was fought, where it was fought, and who fought it. They controlled directly the destinies of more than three million men under arms and indirectly the lives of every American. More than six hundred thousand paid with their lives for their decisions, and the remainder bore the scars of the conflict for as long as they lived. What these men did, how they did it, and where they did it have had a residual effect on every American since.

These men were not all cut from the same cloth. They were not all trained at the same school. They were not all from the same region of the country. They were paragons, paranoids, and profligates. Yet they became the best this country—the Union and the Confederacy—had to offer because the times demanded that of them. Some had outstanding reputations before the war that were enhanced by what they did during the war. Some came out of nowhere and became household names. Some were despicable and found a kind of redemption in their duty. There was no formula for success. Each man defined it for himself. Their stories made this book possible.

As the war progressed, the demands for leadership also shifted. Thus we have arranged the material in a way that follows the impetus of the war itself. These men did not just burst all at once onto the scene. There was interaction and development. The oratory of Frederick Douglass balances John Brown's fanatical dedication to a single goal. A soldier who ranked at the bottom of his class became one of the most successful cavalry commanders in history, while another who ranked second in his class never seemed to learn to fight.

In the treatment of the classmates at West Point, some of the romance of the period comes through, especially the camaraderie that predated and survived the battlefield. Certain individuals stand out. So many of these men knew each other from the classroom. So many of them had fought together in Mexico. So many of them recognized the band of brotherhood that Lee described during his superintendency of the academy.

Joshua Lawrence Chamberlain, whose story is part of this book, said, "History is not a Dead Sea, it is a flowing River." History is not merely a record of events, names, dates, or facts. To reduce it to such is to, in a sense, mummify it—to make it dry as dust and, heaven forbid, boring. History is in a very real sense biography: the interaction of hopes and dreams and passions and lives. No period in the American saga is more illustrative of the willingness of human beings to grapple with their destiny than the fiery crucible of the Civil War.

These Americans confronted head-on, not only their own destinies, but the destiny of the nation itself. Be they great or humble, successful or failure, noble or rascal, they were idealists who realized that upon their personal and cumulative exertions rested the fate of generations yet unborn. By telling some of their stories, we hope that *Civil War Journal* has not only served to commemorate their service and sacrifice, but to touch the idealism inherent in Americans in our own time.

THIS UNIQUE PORTRAYAL of the Civil War began for us—William C. Davis, Brian C. Pohanka, and Don Troiani—when Craig Haffner of Greystone Productions contacted each of us to join in the venture of creating a video series on the war that would be broadcast eventually on the A&E Network. We signed on because of Greystone's commitment to authenticity and accuracy. We are historians.

William C. Davis is a writer and lecturer who has written more than thirty books on the Civil War. Brian C. Pohanka is a writer, a consultant, and a reenactor with insight into the life of the common soldier during the war. Don Troiani is one of the leading historical artists whose works have been added to the collections of the Smithsonian, the National Park Service, and the U.S. Military Academy at West Point. Participating in the creation of *Civil War Journal* gave us an opportunity to contribute from our varied backgrounds to the telling of the story of the Civil War by means of television to a larger audience than we had been able to do previously.

A generation ago, around the centennial of the war itself, people became interested in the Civil War by watching Walt Disney's *Great Locomotive Chase* and *Johnny Shiloh* or *The Gray Ghost* series. Through television the children of the late 1950s and early 1960s were influenced to read about the war and to visit the battlefields. Through this project, we believed we could develop in another generation an interest in the war using the same medium. The success of *Civil War Journal* has borne that out.

There were several features in *Civil War Journal* that distinguished it. With the indispensable assistance of a dedicated cadre of "living historians"—a group of reenactors carefully selected for their attention to detail and specialized knowledge of tactics, military and civilian clothing, and mid-nineteenth-century society— we produced probably the most accurate Civil War reenactment footage ever filmed. We were given access to some very important sites, including Jefferson Davis's office in the White House of the Confederacy. No other film crew had ever been allowed there.

Another hallmark of the series was the distinctive tone established by the scholars who were filmed in office settings or as voice-overs. Each episode called for the leading authorities on that topic. Thus we were not limited to using only academic experts. We also brought in descendants and museum curators, people who lived and breathed on a daily basis the topics they discussed. Their contributions have made the episodes stand out as one of the most comprehensive treatments of the war, covering the well known and the almost known.

Here one aspect of television production worked to enhance the series as a whole; namely, the episodic treatment of each subject precluded our having a specific bias. Hence, there is no narrative thread connecting the first episode to the last. Nor are pronouncements made. For example, this is particularly true of Nathan Bedford Forrest and the Fort Pillow incident. Rather than decide for the viewers, a reasoned presentation of the battle described what happened and avoided one-line truths. The viewers were allowed to draw their own conclusions.

Although most of the episodes have been shown many times, there were a few that have never been broadcast. They are, however, reproduced in this printed version in their entirety. Thus the enthusiasts for *Civil War Journal* finally have the complete series in hand in these books.

For the printed version of *Civil War Journal* we arranged the fifty-two episodes into three volumes under the categories of leaders, battles, and legacies. We admit the structure is artificial, but we grasp history better when we create points of reference among persons, events, and things. We began with the leaders because people were never more central to a conflict than they were to this one.

The text for each chapter was taken from the script for the corresponding show and only slightly embellished to enhance readability. An effort was made throughout to maintain the voice, nuance, and inflection conveyed by the many experts who made this a distinctive body of work. Their words are set off in the text with superscript bullets; open bullets (°) mark the beginning of a speaker's words and solid bullets (•) indicate the conclusion. Attribution is indicated by initials in the left margin, and these initials are identified on the first page of each chapter.

WILLIAM C. DAVIS
BRIAN C. POHANKA
DON TROIANI

Acknowledgments

WE WOULD be remiss in acknowledging the many people involved in this project if we did not express appreciation to the following writers whose scripts undergird this book. They are Lisa Bourgoujian (Stonewall Jackson, Frederick Douglass, Joshua Lawrence Chamberlain), Yann Debonne (Daniel E. Sickles), Arthur Drooker (West Point Classmates, Ulysses S. Grant), Kellie Flanagan (The Boy Generals), Linda Fuller (Nathan Bedford Forrest), Martin Gillam (Jefferson Davis), Greg Goldman (William T. Sherman), Martin Kent (The Union Cavalry and Philip H. Sheridan), Steve Manual (Winfield Scott Hancock), Chris Mortinsen (James Longstreet), Carolyn Neipris (George B. McClellan [with Rhys Thomas]), Scott Paddor (John Brown), and Rhys Thomas (Robert E. Lee, George B. McClellan [with Carolyn Neipris], John S. Mosby, Jeb Stuart and the Confederate Cavalry). James A. Crutchfield aided in the writing of the captions.

Of course an adaptation such as this would not have been possible without the assistance of Craig Haffner and Donna Lusitana of Greystone Communications. Without their help, this project would have been unthinkable. Similarly, Thomas Heymann, Jonathan Paisner, and Jennifer O'Neil of A&E Television Networks have been invaluable in their guidance.

A book such as this is dependent on the willingness of archives, museums, historical societies, universities, and private collectors to allow us access to their collections for photographs. We cannot be profuse enough in our thanks to the many people and institutions involved. The list of photograph credits appears on page 446.

We are particularly happy to have had the opportunity to work with Rutledge Hill Press in the production of this volume and look forward to the two remaining books in this series.

The Contributors

ONE OF the distinctive elements of *Civil War Journal* is the authority conveyed by the fifty scholars, historians, curators, and descendants who infused each topic with something of themselves, bringing the leaders alive for a television audience. Their comments have been marked throughout the text, with an open superscript bullet (°) indicating the beginning and a solid superscript bullet (•) marking the conclusion of direct quotations from the television script. Initials appear in the left margin designating attribution. Each chapter's opening page includes a list in the lower right hand corner of the experts whose voices can be heard on the pages that follow. Their names are reproduced here in two lists, one arranged by last name and another by initials (page xvi).

TCB *Thomas C. Battle*, director, Moorland-Spingarn Research Center, Howard University

ECB *Edwin C. Bearss*, chief historian and special assistant to the director for military sites, National Park Service

DWB *David W. Blight*, author

CB *Catherine Bragaw*, historian

NB *Nat Brandt*, historian and author

CMC *Chris M. Calkins*, historian

TC *Tom Clemens*, associate professor, Hagerstown Junior College

WC *William Cooper*, professor of history, Louisiana State University

WCD *William C. Davis*, historian and author

JD *John Divine*, historian, Loudoun County, Virginia

JRE *Col. John R. Elting*, associate professor of history, U.S. Military Academy, retired

WEE *W. E. Erquitt*, former curator, The Military Collection, Atlanta Historical Society

DE *David Evans*, author

GE *Gwen Everett*, author

TJF *Thomas J. Fleming*, historian and author

DEF *Dennis E. Frye*, historian

GWG *Gary W. Gallagher*, professor of history, Pennsylvania State University

KEG *Lt. Col. Keith E. Gibson*, executive director, Virginia Military Institute Museum

WGG *William G. Gwaltney*, historian and author

CBH *Clark B. Hall*, Brandy Station Foundation

JLH *Joseph L. Harsh*, professor, George Mason University

JJH *John J. Hennessy*, author

PAH *Paul A. Hutton*, professor of history, University of New Mexico

JMJ *Col. James M. Johnson*, history department, U.S. Military Academy

DMJ *David M. Jordan*, historian and author

DMK *D. Mark Katz*, author

RKK *Robert K. Krick*, National Park Service, author and historian

EGL *Edward G. Longacre*, historian and author

MAL *Michael Anne Lynn*, director, Stonewall Jackson House, Lexington, Virginia

WSM *William S. McFeely*, author

JMM *James M. McPherson*, professor of history, Princeton University

JFM *John F. Marszalek*, professor of history, Mississippi University

EGM *Edna Greene Medford*, historian, Howard University

WEM *Wayne E. Motts*, Gettysburg battlefield guide

AM *Agnes Mullins*, curator, Arlington House

CN *Chris Nelson*, historian

SBO *Stephen B. Oates*, historian and author

JCO *Julia Colvin Oehmig*, curator, J. L. Chamberlain Museum, Pejepscot Historical Society

GAP *Gerard A. Patterson*, historian and author

BP *Brian Pohanka*, historian and film consultant

WJR *William J. Rasp*, historian and curator, Nathan Bedford Forrest Collection

JIR *James I. Robertson Jr.*, Alumni Distinguished Professor of History, Virginia Tech, Blacksburg, Virginia

ALR *Armstead L. Robinson*, historian

MES *Mary Elizabeth Sergent*, historian and author

JYS *John Y. Simon*, director, Ulysses S. Grant Association, Southern Illinois University, Carbondale, Illinois

JEBS *J. E. B. Stuart IV*, great-grandson of Jeb Stuart

WS *Wiley Sword*, historian and author

JST *James S. Trulock*, historian

JDW *Jeffry D. Wert*, historian and author

BSW *Brian S. Wills*, assistant professor of history, Clinch Valley College

ALR	Armstead L. Robinson		JJH	John J. Hennessy
AM	Agnes Mullins		JLH	Joseph L. Harsh
BP	Brian Pohanka		JMJ	Col. James M. Johnson
BSW	Brian S. Wills		JMM	James M. McPherson
CB	Catherine Bragaw		JRE	Col. John R. Elting
CBH	Clark B. Hall		JST	James S. Trulock
CMC	Chris M. Calkins		JYS	John Y. Simon
CN	Chris Nelson		KEG	Lt. Col. Keith E. Gibson
DE	David Evans		MAL	Michael Anne Lynn
DEF	Dennis E. Frye		MES	Mary Elizabeth Sergent
DMJ	David M. Jordan		NB	Nat Brandt
DMK	D. Mark Katz		PAH	Paul A. Hutton
DWB	David W. Blight		RKK	Robert K. Krick
ECB	Edwin C. Bearss		SBO	Stephen B. Oates
EGL	Edward G. Longacre		TC	Tom Clemens
EGM	Edna Greene Medford		TCB	Thomas C. Battle
GAP	Gerard A. Patterson		TJF	Thomas J. Fleming
GE	Gwen Everett		WC	William Cooper
GWG	Gary W. Gallagher		WCD	William C. Davis
JCO	Julia Colvin Oehmig		WEE	W. E. Erquitt
JD	John Divine		WEM	Wayne E. Motts
JDW	Jeffry D. Wert		WGG	William G. Gwaltney
JEBS	J. E. B. Stuart IV		WJR	William J. Rasp
JFM	John F. Marszalek		WS	Wiley Sword
JIR	James I. Robertson Jr.		WSM	William S. McFeely

CIVIL WAR JOURNAL™

The Leaders

JOHN BROWN

Traitor to HIS COUNTRY, martyr for freedom, murderer—all were titles given to a gray-eyed man from Connecticut whose passion for freedom and human dignity in the mid-1800s ignited Americans into a sectional explosion that ultimately destroyed slavery. The man's name was John Brown. Although his moral commitment to freedom was truly righteous, it spread into a violent action that remains mired in controversy. It was one man's solution to the hated institution of slavery, which is remembered as John Brown's War.

His last words on December 2, 1859, rang with prophetic overtones: "I, John Brown, am now quite certain that the crimes of this guilty land will never be purged away but with blood. I had, as I now think vainly, flattered myself that without very much bloodshed it might be done."

WCD °Anyone meeting Brown would have seen in him the makings of a fanatic: tall, gaunt, dark sun-bronzed skin,
DEF and piercing, deep, burning eyes.• °He probably was best known for his eyes. His eyes looked through a person and captivated him. His eyes magnetized his followers. Once caught in his glare, a person could not escape him. When Brown looked a man in the eye, that man's eyes did not move, rather his mind opened and Brown would pour in his thoughts.•

SBO °He was truculent, even furious about slavery in this country. He called it the sum of villainy and "a rotten whore of an institution." Usually anyone who engaged Brown in conversation eventually talked about one of

TCB	Thomas C. Battle
CB	Catherine Bragaw
WCD	William C. Davis
GE	Gwen Everett
DEF	Dennis E. Frye
WGG	William G. Gwaltney
SBO	Stephen B. Oates

3

The heavy weight of slavery can be seen in the sadness and worry on the faces of these children in Natchez, Mississippi, and in the painful resignation of this couple in Savannah, Georgia, who have become well acquainted with the demands of their owner. These were the faces that fueled the passion of John Brown for abolition.

two things: slavery or the Bible and theology.• In 1854 he stated: "God commanded that thou shalt not deliver unto his master the servant which has escaped from his master unto thee. He shall dwell with thee, even among you in that place which he shall choose. Thou shalt not oppress him. Every man's conscience says 'Amen' to that command."

DEF °Slavery had come into existence in this country in 1619 when slaves were brought to Jamestown, the first English settlement of Virginia. Over time it grew to become the cornerstone of the dominant economic system of the South.• In the mid-nineteenth century the southern slave states kept at least four million African Americans in bondage. Brown would not accept this or the romantic descriptions white slave owners, such as Jefferson Davis, wrote of life on the plantation: "Out of a mild and genial climate of the Southern states, the African slaves have grown in number from four hundred thousand to four million in moral and social conditions. They have been elevated into docile and intelligent and civilized agricultural laborers. They are supplied with bodily comforts, careful religious instruction. Under the supervision of a superior race, they have helped make this land prosper."

WGG °Slavery was more than just working hard and not getting paid for it. Slavery limited a person's dreams, his hopes, whom he could and could not marry. It was a system encompassing everything from the federal government to the slave owner that kept a slave from having a personality, from having a human life. Slavery was, in a phrase, hopelessness condensed.•

WCD °When a man like Brown looked at slavery, he saw unrelenting, unrewarded toil by men and women who had no control over their own lives. To be a slave was to be born and to live one's life and die without ever having had control over one's destiny, while at the same time living within a society that had been founded on the principles of individual freedom and liberty. How much more difficult, how much more cruel than being whipped was it to live in a society where a person could see freedom all around and not touch it!•

IT WAS IN the North in 1800, far from the southern slave system, that John Brown was born in a frame house in Torrington, Connecticut. His father, Owen Brown, was a

SBO tanner and shoemaker °who inculcated into his children a strict Calvinist understanding of Scripture and way of life. All people were mortal sinners in the hands of an angry God. His father also taught him to hate slavery. When John was just a child, his father told him that slavery violated God's commandments and was a violation of the Scriptures.•

Owen Brown inculcated in his son John a devout Calvinist faith and an absolute hatred for slavery. An ambitious man from very humble beginnings, Owen's business ventures made him almost an absentee father. When his wife died, he married a much-younger woman, which was a pattern that his son would later follow. The boy proved to be an indifferent student, and so he joined his father's work and quickly learned the rudiments of tanning and developed a profound interest in fine livestock.

By 1812, when John was twelve years old, Owen

DEF Brown had moved his family to Ohio. °The boy's first exposure to slavery occurred when he was helping to move some cattle and he encountered a slave. According to his autobiography, Brown actually saw the slave being whipped. He never forgot that someone roughly his own age had been whipped by another person because he was property and because he was of a different color.• He wrote: "This brought me to reflect on the wretched, hopeless condition of fatherless and motherless slave children. For such children have neither fathers nor mothers to protect and provide for them. I sometimes would raise the question, 'Is God their father?'"

Twenty-five years later, in 1837, after the murder of an abolitionist newspaper editor at Alton, Illinois, protest meetings were held across the North. At one of

The strict, disciplined lifestyle of the Brown household can be seen in this photograph of Brown's second wife, Mary Ann Day, and two of their daughters, Annie (left) and Sarah (right). Mary Ann was a perfect wife for Brown. Physically, she was able to endure the rigors of the life he chose to live, and temperamentally, she had been trained that a wife's role was to bear children, maintain the household, and obey her husband. Chief among her virtues was that she never complained.

these meetings in Hudson, Ohio, Brown committed himself to oppose slavery, saying, "Here, before God, in the presence of these witnesses, I consecrate my life to the destruction of slavery."

THE MAN WHO dedicated his life to the freedom of God's enslaved children also had a family of his own. °When he was twenty years old, he married Deanntha Lusk, a woman he described as being remarkably plain. She gave Brown seven children, dying in the birth of the last child.•

°After her death, Brown knew he could not rear seven children by himself. He needed a wife, so he married a sixteen-year-old girl named Mary Ann Day. She was twenty years his junior, but she turned out to be an excellent wife for him because she was a strong woman capable of enduring the most grueling hardships.•

°Brown traveled from place to place for much of his life, becoming almost a transient. It was difficult for him to make a good living or to have sufficient income to make his family comfortable, so he went wherever he thought his prospects were best.• In Ohio, he owned a tannery but had little success. He worked as a farmer, a postmaster, and a shepherd. The family settled briefly in Springfield, Massachusetts, where Brown tried his hand at the wool business, but his work in Springfield was not limited to wool.

SBO °A new, stringent fugitive slave law, part of the Compromise of 1850, had an enormous impact on the blacks that Brown knew in Springfield, because it meant that those who had run away from slavery and even free blacks could be seized and returned to slavery in the South.• °Brown acted by organizing a group of men in DEF Springfield whom he referred to as the League of Gileadites, named after the Gileadites of the Bible. The group encouraged former slaves, runaways, and free African Americans living in New England to bond and to protect themselves against those who were seeking them out to send back to the South.• "Should one of your number be arrested," Brown instructed his followers, "you must collect together as quickly as possible so as to outnumber your adversaries who are taking an active part against you. Whosoever is fearful or afraid, let him return and depart early from Mount Gilead."

It was also in Springfield that Brown was inspired by GF a man named Douglass. °Frederick Douglass was an escaped slave. He had been born in Maryland and had escaped first to Baltimore and finally to New York. He

In 1849 Brown moved his family to North Elba, New York, to join an experimental community of black families. He approached Gerrit Smith, the philanthropist behind the project, and offered to turn one of the farms into a model for the others, to employ members of the community as best he could, and to assume a paternalistic role for the families that would settle there. In 1855 the Brown family moved into this frame house, but letters from his sons who had gone to Kansas turned their father's eyes westward.

This is the earliest known photograph of John Brown, taken at Springfield, Massachusetts, in 1846, where he had gone into the wool business. A stubborn nonconformist, Brown accepted no one's counsel regarding his business practices and, as he came in closer contact with abolitionists, he declined to join any antislavery society or participate in the Underground Railroad. He would assist fugitive slaves in his own way, and he became obsessed with a violent resolution to the problem of slavery.

met Brown in 1847, when Brown apparently invited him to visit Springfield.•

WGG   °Douglass was perhaps the most important public speaker of the nineteenth century. His words, his books, and his very presence made the reality of slavery come home to thousands, if not millions, of people in the United States and across the globe.• Finding sponsorship with several antislavery societies, Douglass reminded his audiences: "I appear this evening as a thief and a robber. I stole this head, these limbs, this body from my master and ran off with them."

The horror of the fugitive slave law also inspired
GE author Harriet Beecher Stowe. °Her book *Uncle Tom's Cabin* enraged and enlightened people by making them aware of the atrocities that were being done against escaped blacks in America. Her narrative vividly described how individuals were hunted down and treated like animals. Brown gave a copy of this book to his daughter, Annie, telling her that it was his favorite book and that she should read it and reread it to become aware of the things that were being done against blacks in America.•

In 1849 philanthropist Gerrit Smith had offered black settlers free farmland in the Adirondack Mountains of New York, at a community called North Elba. GE °Brown moved there in the early 1850s with his family, hoping to prove that blacks and whites could live together peacefully. He also went there to help the blacks work the land because he realized that many of the blacks who had escaped from the South did not have the skills necessary to live in the North or to work the land there.• War clouds, however, were gathering to the south.

THE ISSUE OF slavery had been fiercely debated in the halls of government and specifically addressed in the Missouri Compromise of 1820 and the Compromise of 1850. For the first half of the nineteenth century the pattern was set for admitting one free state and one slave state to the Union simultaneously so as not to upset the balance of there being an equal number of each in the U.S. Senate. The 1854 Kansas-Nebraska Act, however, allowed for "popular sovereignty" in these states, so that the territorial populations would determine whether a state was admitted free or slave. There was little question that Nebraska would enter as a free state, but the status of Kansas was debatable.

THE UNITED STATES BEFORE SECESSION 1860

Free States
Slave States
Territories
Public Land Strip (Status undefined until 1890)
Indian Territory (Land restricted to Indian ownership and use)

Passage of the Kansas-Nebraska Act of 1854 marked the failure of a half-century of political compromises struck over the issue of the great unsolved dilemma of the Constitution—slavery. By allowing the settlers of Kansas and Nebraska to determine if their territories would be open or closed to slavery by popular vote, Kansas became a battleground for the two sides. Proslavery Missourians, known as Border Ruffians (above left), harassed free staters and voted illegally in the elections. Free staters, however, united to protect their homes and communities and some were organized into militia-like units with outdated artillery, such as the six men (above right) gathered around this Mexican War–vintage field piece. Ultimately Kansas was admitted as a free state, but only after five constitutions had been drafted and two hundred lives had been lost in "Bleeding Kansas."

DEF °Self-determination brought settlers, both pro- and anti-slavery, into the territories,• and it appeared that slavery might be forced on the free Kansas settlers by either vote or violence.

Brown's son, John Jr., went to Kansas bent on resisting the imposition of slavery. °Brown himself was not planning on going to Kansas until he received a letter from his son that said, "We need guns more than we need bread; every slave state from Texas to Virginia is trying to fasten slavery upon this glorious land." He appealed to his father to come to Kansas to fight, and eventually Brown decided to do that.• Arriving in 1856, he announced: "I have only a short time to live. Only one death to die. And I will die fighting for this cause. There will be no more peace in this land until slavery is done for."

SBO °Brown entered Kansas in a wagon loaded with weapons, including artillery broadswords—heavy, brutal, machete-like weapons. He was there to fight against "Satan's legions," his term for the proslavery Missourians that the Kansas free-staters had labeled Border Ruffians.•

CB °They were there to fight or to crash the polls to affect the election of a proslavery legislature.•

DEF °As individuals and families moved into Kansas, they gathered according to their similar beliefs. Those who were of the proslavery faction settled together; those who were abolitionists clustered together. They formed their own villages and communities, and they took steps to protect themselves. Lawrence, Kansas, for instance, was an abolitionist community.*

Not far from Lawrence, at a rise along Pottawatomie Creek, was a settlement called Osawatomie. It was here that Brown and his sons set up their operation to prepare for war in 1856. Two events precipitated the following conflict.

SBO °The Border Ruffians despised the town of Lawrence because it was the center of all free-state activity. In May an army of them—in reality a drunken rabble—entered Lawrence and shelled the hotel with an artillery piece and burned several free-stater homes. As the smoke filled the air, Brown and a group of volunteers from the Pottawatomie-Osawatomie area marched to the defense of Lawrence,* but they were too late to intervene.

In the wake of the attack on Lawrence, disturbing
SBO news came from Washington. °Sen. Charles Sumner of Massachusetts, the leading antislavery voice in the U.S. Senate, had been beaten brutally by a southern congressman, Preston Brooks of South Carolina. In fact, Brooks almost killed Sumner on the Senate floor itself, in the hallowed sanctuary of the legislative body, beating him senseless with a cane.*

Within a month of his arrival in Kansas, John Brown erected this structure and began building other cabins for his sons and their families. The activity might better be described as fortifying the area, especially when it is noted how well armed Brown was when he arrived in the area—revolvers, rifles, knives, and artillery broadswords. While each town or village organized its own militia unit, the Browns formed their own unit and waited for the crisis to explode.

SOUTHERN CHIVALRY — ARGUMENT versus CLUB'S.

Charles Sumner of Massachusetts was the leading abolitionist voice in the Senate during the 1850s. He opposed the Kansas-Nebraska Act and condemned popular sovereignty as a deceit. In May 1856 he delivered a speech on the Senate floor denouncing the crimes perpetrated against Kansas and in so doing drew the offense of several fellow senators. Later Congressman Preston Brooks of South Carolina approached Sumner's chair and assaulted him with a cane, delivering more than thirty blows before his weapon broke. A northern cartoon (above right) depicts southern senators approving Brooks's action and even restraining those trying to come to the aid of Sumner.

CB
DEF
°When news of this incident reached Brown, one of his sons recalled later, Brown just went crazy.• °He wanted vengeance, and this would be vengeance at its SBO bloodiest and most vicious.• °So Brown gathered his sons and a small group of men who had been loyal to him and told them that they were going to the proslavery settlements along Pottawatomie Creek to retaliate CB for what had happened at Lawrence.• °On May 24, as night fell over the smoking Kansas landscape, the group, calling themselves the Army of the North, began its mission. They came to the cabin of James Doyle.•

SBO
°Doyle and his two grown sons had been active in CB the proslavery party.• °They and their families were sleeping when Brown's men invaded the cabin, took the men outside, and mutilated them with the broadswords WCD Brown had brought with him to Kansas.• °Not only did Brown and his men murder these proslavery men, but they did it in an especially barbaric fashion, hacking them to death. Worst of all, much of it was done before the eyes of their families.• Immediately, Brown became both feared and hated by the slave-staters. "The demon which those border forays had awakened is destined never again to sleep," wrote journalist David H. Strother. "Old Brown, Osawatomie Brown, Brown of Kansas, the Dread of Border Ruffians, the Moses of Higher Law cannot descend into the vulgar stagnation of common life."

Now notorious in Kansas, Brown set about raising money from the North to acquire weapons to pursue °his "principal object": the overthrow of the institution of slavery. He planned to utilize the slaves themselves in this great revolt that would start in the Upper South and then continue down through the mountains to encompass the entire South. If successful, he would have accomplished his task before God.•

WGG

°Brown wanted to create a revolutionary state. He even drafted a constitution for the new government he intended to install in the southern mountains once he had invaded the South with the guerrilla army he was gathering.• In part it read: "Whereas slavery throughout its entire existence in the United States is none other than a mad, barbarous, unprovoked, and unjustifiable war of one portion of its citizens upon another portion, in utter disregard and violation of those eternal and self-evident truths set forth in our Declaration of Independence."

SBO

°Brown's tiny army was comprised of very diverse individuals, all committed to abolition, all prepared to

DEF

On May 21, 1856, proslavery forces attacked Lawrence, Kansas, destroying the Free State Hotel (pictured below) with cannon fire and plundering the town. They met little resistance. As the alarm was spread from village to village, several local defensive units feared that something might happen to their homes if they departed for Lawrence. The groups that did move on Lawrence, including Brown and his sons, learned that the oppressors had abandoned the town to the U.S. troops sent to restore order. Messengers were sent to the advancing abolitionists, advising them to return home, particularly since their arrival in Lawrence would accomplish nothing and their presence would only deplete the town's very limited supplies. Brown, however, was determined to strike a retaliatory blow.

The Pottawatomie massacre triggered guerrilla warfare throughout Kansas, with each party claiming an eye for an eye and vengeance. Brown went into hiding and eventually decided to leave the territory, but he gathered a dedicated core of followers nonetheless. In October 1856 he departed for New York and Boston to raise funds for his next enterprise and visited Charles Sumner, still recuperating from the assault in the Senate chamber. Brown returned to Kansas in disguise, having grown a white, Moses-like beard, because the battle against slavery was still not finished.

die for the cause, all willing to follow Brown.• In 1859, he announced, "I expect to affect a mighty conquest, even though it might be like the last victory of Samson"—the biblical Samson had vanquished his enemies but had died in the process.

BY 1859 THE MAN who would electrify the nation and edge it closer to the brink of civil war had planned a truly audacious attack. Brown's horror and hatred of slavery made its destruction the principal objective of his life. He carefully chose a target as the beginning of his revolution. Neither a plantation nor a seat of government, his target was the small Virginia town of Harpers Ferry.

SBO   °Harpers Ferry was a remote town with a population of some two thousand, situated at the confluence of the Shenandoah and Potomac Rivers with a hill right in back of it. It was as remote a place as one was likely to find.•

WGG   °Brown selected Virginia for the site of his raid for two reasons. First, it was close, he thought, to large populations of slaves who would rise up and help him in his revolt. Second, it was at the junction of two rivers, and he could then go down the Shenandoah Valley, spreading his revolt to plantations in Virginia and throughout the South.•

Harpers Ferry was also the site of a U.S. Army armory, arsenal, and rifle works. There were sufficient weapons stored there to outfit an army, and Brown hoped to capture these weapons and use them to wage war on slavery and begin his new country.

DEF   °Prior to his raid, Brown had an advance scout there. John Cook had arrived in the area almost one year before the attack on the arsenal. He worked as a lock tender on the Chesapeake and Ohio Canal opposite Harpers Ferry, and he scouted the area, learning the terrain. He rode through the neighborhoods, noting when people came to work, what buildings were where, how many watchmen there were, and where the estates were and where the slaves were.•

SBO °By the summer of 1859, Brown arrived in the Harpers Ferry vicinity with some of his sons. He rented a farmhouse on the Maryland side of the Potomac River from a family by the name of Kennedy, giving his name as Smith and saying that he was a cattle buyer from New York. He had grown a flowing, white, Old Testament beard—a disguise so he would not be associated with the Pottawatomie massacre in Kansas.•

WGG °Brown had pikes made using long staffs. These large-bladed, Bowie-type weapons could be used by untrained slaves DEF unaccustomed to firearms.• °For a slave to even hold a weapon could be a capital offense. So Brown knew that he had to provide a simple means of defense until the slaves could learn to use the sophisticated weapons of the time.• The manufacturer of the pikes, Chet Blaire, explained, "In the year 1857, I made a contract with John Brown to make one thousand pikes, which he said were to be used by the settlers in Kansas to protect themselves from intrusions by the so-called Border Ruffians." Brown's true plans for the crude spears, however, lay far from Kansas.

His arsenal would also include powerful and accurate Sharps carbines. Some were brought with him from Kansas, but he hoped that more would arrive along with the army of followers he expected to join him.

CB °All summer and into the fall Brown waited for men in arms to come to the rented farmhouse in Maryland. His daughter Annie and his daughter-in-law Martha came down to join them, becoming the watching eyes to forestall discovery of what Brown intended to do.•

Annie Brown knew what was expected of her and declared later, "I was there to keep the outside world from discovering that John Brown and his men were in the neighborhood. I used to help Martha with the cooking,

PROVISIONAL

CONSTITUTION

AND

ORDINANCES

FOR THE

PEOPLE OF THE UNITED STATES.

PREAMBLE.

Whereas, Slavery, throughout its entire existence in the United States, is none other than a most barbarous, unprovoked, and unjustifiable War of one portion of its citizens upon another portion ; the only conditions of which are perpetual imprisonment, and hopeless servitude or absolute extermination ; in utter disregard and violation of those eternal and self-evident truths set forth in our Declaration of Independence : Therefore,

We, Citizens of the United States, and the Oppressed People, who, by a recent decision of the Supreme Court are declared to have no rights which the White Man is bound to respect ; together with all other people degraded by the laws thereof, Do, for the time being ordain and establish for ourselves, the following Provisional Constitution and Ordinances, the better to protect our Persons, Property, Lives, and Liberties ; and to govern our actions :

ARTICLE I.

QUALIFICATIONS FOR MEMBERSHIP.

All persons of mature age, whether Proscribed, oppressed and enslaved Citizens, or of the Proscribed

A

While he was in New York, Brown stayed in Frederick Douglass's home for almost a month. When he was not trying to recruit the great orator for his next mission, Brown was drafting a provisional constitution for the revolutionary state he planned to create in the southern highlands. There had been slave revolts before which had been quashed when they fell into chaos after initial successes. This could be avoided, Brown believed, by determining the shape and course of the revolution in advance. The provisional constitution was adopted on May 8, 1858, in Chatham, Canada, during a secret convention called by Brown and attended by none of the notables he had invited.

Harpers Ferry, the first target in Brown's war for slave liberation, stood on a narrow neck of land at the confluence of the Shenandoah and Potomac Rivers, amid the Blue Ridge Mountains of northern Virginia. The town of 2,500 included 1,251 free blacks and 88 slaves. The majority of the remaining 1,212 inhabitants were skilled workers and government employees from the North. There were no large plantations in the region, and whatever slave owners there were tilled farms in the surrounding countryside; their slaves were mostly house servants. From a distance it looked like a cramped cluster of homes and shops. The shops were the factories of the federal armory, employing several hundred people and producing 10,000 stands of arms per year.

all she would let me. Father would often tell me that I must not let any work interfere with my constant watchfulness. He depended on me to watch."

°Brown had twenty-one followers, most of them young, five of them black. Among the blacks was a forty-eight-year-old former slave, Dangerfield Nubie, who had been freed by his master but had had to leave Virginia because it was against the law for a free black to stay there. Nubie had to leave his wife and six or seven children in slavery. He had joined Brown in hopes of liberating his family.•

That summer of 1859 passed quietly at Harpers Ferry, but the huge volunteer force for which Brown waited at the Kennedy farm never arrived. Finally, the long period of inactivity gave way to climax.

°Shortly before midnight on October 16 Brown determined the time was right. He gathered his men and told them to get their weapons and to proceed to the ferry.°

SBO °The group descended the mountain road from the Kennedy farmhouse. Harpers Ferry came into view just across the river. Quiet, remote—not a single inhabitant had any idea that history was about to explode suddenly in their midst.°

WGG °Brown and his provisional army crossed the Potomac River on foot over an old railroad bridge. As they approached the railroad station, someone came out to see who they were. Someone called out, "Halt!" The silence was broken by a rifle shot, and a body thudded to the ground.° Ironically, the first man killed in Brown's raid was a free black, a baggage master named Haywood Shepherd.

DEF °Several of Brown's men fanned out into the estate area west of Harpers Ferry, toward Charles Town, to seize several estate owners—primarily Col. Louis Washington, the great-grandnephew of George Washington.° With hostages taken, Brown's men continued on to their primary target.

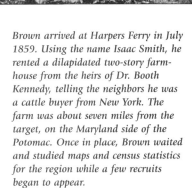

Brown arrived at Harpers Ferry in July 1859. Using the name Isaac Smith, he rented a dilapidated two-story farmhouse from the heirs of Dr. Booth Kennedy, telling the neighbors he was a cattle buyer from New York. The farm was about seven miles from the target, on the Maryland side of the Potomac. Once in place, Brown waited and studied maps and census statistics for the region while a few recruits began to appear.

Brown summoned seventeen-year-old Martha, Oliver's wife (left), and his fifteen-year-old daughter Annie (right) from North Elba to keep house and divert suspicion from the increasing number of men gathering at the Kennedy farm. The girls were to cook meals, wash clothes, work in the garden, and talk cheerfully with whatever neighbors visited, and they were almost always visited around mealtimes. At all times either Martha or Annie was posted at the kitchen window to keep a constant vigil. A barefooted old woman and her numerous children were particularly annoying, dropping by at all hours of the day and possibly suspecting that the "Smiths" were involved with the Underground Railroad.

John E. Cook (above) was Brown's advance scout in Harpers Ferry, entering the area almost a year before the raid. He studied the layout of the armory, made friends, and took an interest in a woman that led to their marriage in April 1859 and the birth of his son a few months later.

SBO °The raiders dashed across the intersection to the government armory and arsenal, where a night watchman was on duty. Suddenly surrounded by armed men and confronted by a man with blazing eyes and a flowing white beard, this unfortunate man had no idea what was happening to him.• "I came here from Kansas, and this is a slave state," Brown said. "I have possession now of the United States Armory. And if the citizens interfere with me, I must only burn the town and have blood."

WCD °With the seizure of the armory and arsenal, the first part of the plan had succeeded brilliantly. What Brown did not count on was that the alarm would go out to the townspeople and that they would react defensively. Brown had expected no opposition from the townspeople. Instead, very quickly they began to besiege Brown. Shots rang out.•

Journalist D. H. Strother described what happened next: "The outlaw chief had by this time perceived that instead of hundreds of allies, he was hemmed in by thousands of infuriated enemies. He retired into the fire-engine house within the public grounds. He next appeared in the street. One of the outlaws was shot down."

The dead man was former slave Dangerfield Nubie. WGG °He had been shot through the neck with an iron spike

On Monday morning, October 17, 1859, just before noon, a battle raged around the fire engine house as armed farmers and militia poured into Harpers Ferry in answer to the alarm that slaves and abolitionists were murdering townspeople and looting the armory. The speed with which the people mustered in defense of their town took Brown by surprise, and he was at a loss for what to do. Quickly his avenues of escape closed. He tried to negotiate his withdrawal in return for the thirty hostages he had taken, but the mob was not interested in a cease fire. They seized one of the raiders and shot two others who were trying to convey terms.

from one of the guns of the townspeople. Nubie's body was hauled off and mutilated. Later his body was fed to hogs in a local alley.•

WCD °Once the siege began, the scene inside the fire engine house where Brown and his men were holed up quickly turned to bedlam. They could not see out very well. They did not know what was going on around them. When they did fire on the townspeople, the brick walls in the confined, small building, which was only about thirty feet square, echoed tremendously with the loud reports of their weapons.•

WGG °Brown had expected the slaves in the plantations nearby in Virginia to come to his aid, take the pikes and weapons that he had acquired, and help him succeed in this revolt. But when the time came, such help did not materialize.•

DEF °Pulley Leaman, a nineteen-year-old raider, realized that things were not going well and decided to escape. He scurried down the armory wall, jumped into the river, and swam north toward Maryland in an effort to get away from the militia and the town citizens. He became exhausted.• Under fire from twenty militiamen, Leaman crept to a rock in the Potomac and became the next raider to die.

DEF °Since this was an attack on a federal installation, the president, James Buchanan, called in the nearest

Forty-eight-year-old Dangerfield Nubie was the oldest of Brown's raiders and the least fortunate. A freeman, he hoped to free his wife and children from a plantation at Brentville, Virginia. Nubie, however, was the first raider killed. Someone removed his ears as souvenirs. Then his body was beaten and thrown to the hogs.

On the morning of the second day, marines under the command of Lt. Col. Robert E. Lee stormed the engine house. The assault lasted only a few minutes, but one marine died in the fighting. The leader of the storming party, Lt. Israel Green, confronted Brown and struck him with his sword before the old man could fire his rifle. A second thrust caused the sword to double, and the lieutenant knocked Brown unconscious with the hilt. When it was over, Brown and five raiders had been captured. The rest were dead or had fled.

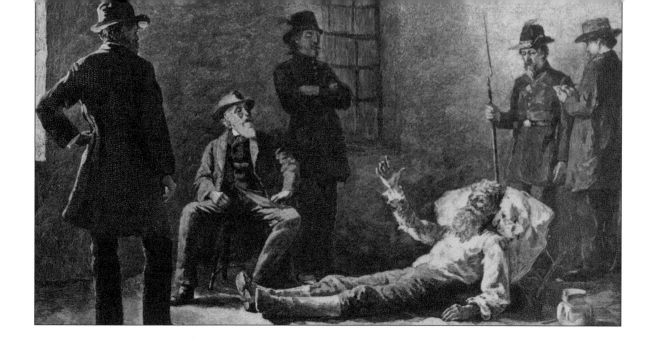

Early on Tuesday afternoon, as a small group that included Robert E. Lee, Jeb Stuart, former hostage Louis Washington, Virginia governor Henry A. Wise, and Virginia senator James M. Mason looked on, Brown endured a three-hour interrogation "to make himself and his motives clearly understood."

It was not many years before the fire engine house (below), where Brown and his raiders had defended themselves, became something of a tourist attraction.

U.S. troops—the marines at the Washington Naval Yard. Placed under the command of Lt. Col. Robert E. Lee, they were brought to Harpers Ferry via train.° °Arriving too late to do anything that day, Lee planned to wait until morning before storming the engine house.°

During that terrible night Brown paced the engine house, surveying the scene. His son Watson had been shot that day and lay beside his dying brother Oliver. °When the sun came up, Brown saw that he was no longer facing just farmers and townspeople but men in the sky blue uniform of the U.S. marines.° From Lee, he received a message requesting his surrender: "If they will peaceably surrender themselves and restore the pillaged property, they shall be kept in safety to await the orders of the President. Colonel Lee represents to them in all frankness that the armory is surrounded on all sides by troops. And that if he is compelled to take them by force, he cannot answer for their safety."

°Lee had brought with him as his aide, Lt. J. E. B. "Jeb" Stuart, who

approached the engine house doors and there began to discuss Lee's terms with Brown. Brown, however, refused to negotiate. With that, Stuart backed away from the door, waved his hat in the air, and gave the marines the signal to attack.•

Col. Louis Washington, one of Brown's hostages inside the engine house, described the scene during the attack, noting, "Brown felt the pulse of his dying son with one hand and held his rifle with the other. And he commanded his men with utmost composure to be firm and sell their lives as dearly as they could."

SBO ° The marines broke down the door, charged inside, and went after the other raiders. Lt. Israel Green came upon Brown. As Brown was about to shoot him, Green lunged toward Brown with his sword. The lieutenant stabbed forward and hit Brown in the belt buckle, but his sword doubled.•

DEF ° The entire attack, once the doors of the engine house had been penetrated, took three minutes. All the hostages were freed unharmed, and all of Brown's men were captured or mortally wounded. Brown himself, badly wounded and bleeding profusely around the head and the neck, became a captive of the marines.•

THE *Baltimore American* reported: "When the insurgents were brought out, some dead and others wounded, the lawn in front of the engine house presented a dreadful

Although Brown had attacked and seized federal property, Governor Wise of Virginia decided that he should be prosecuted in a Virginia court rather than be surrendered to the federal authorities. He argued that federal prosecution would take too long, and if the law did not act swiftly, Brown would be lynched. A grand jury was already in session in Charles Town, and Judge Richard Parker had just opened the term of the county circuit court. Thus John Brown stood trial for murder and treason only one week after his capture. Wounded, he endured the sessions from a makeshift bed. On October 31, the jury returned a guilty verdict after forty-five minutes of deliberation.

A fanatic in life, in death Brown became a martyr. His bearded visage was exploited in images that evoked both the Old Testament—Moses showing the way for others—and the New—a Christ figure dying for the sins of others and at their hands. Brown's heroic pose in his last month never failed to impress anyone who saw him. He remained composed and unrepentant and in doing so inspired his followers who faced the same fate. Brown was allowed to correspond with his family and sympathetic northerners. His letters contained some of the most eloquent statements to come from the pen of a condemned man, even causing his jailers who read them as a matter of duty to wipe tears from their eyes.

sight. The wounded father and his son Watson were lying on the grass, presenting a gory spectacle. One of the dead was Brown's son, Oliver."

WCD The war for slave liberation lasted only thirty-six hours. °Brown and his men, several of whom were desperately wounded, including Brown, were incarcerated in nearby Charles Town for several weeks awaiting trial.•

WGG °The trial was highly publicized, and people crammed the courtroom to get a glimpse of Brown the WCD madman.• °Because of his wounds he went through most of the trial lying on a stretcher, but he was feisty enough that he could still speak eloquently from his prone position.•

DEF °In the courtroom Brown abandoned the sword and took up the power of the word. He put, not just slavery on trial, but the country for allowing slavery to exist. Brown resumed the role of preacher,• defending his actions, saying, "I believe that to interfere, as I have done, in the behalf of God's despised poor is not wrong but right. Now, if it is deemed necessary that I should mingle my blood further with the blood of my children and the blood of millions in this slave country, whose rights are disregarded by wicked, cruel, and unjust enactments, I say let it be done."

SBO °He described the wrongs of slavery. He talked about how much the country needed to abolish it. Looking beyond that court, he addressed the citizens of the North. His actions had been the first step. His raid on Harpers Ferry was the signal that slavery was doomed to be ended by violence. Since he had failed it was now the responsibility of the northerners to accept and complete his mission to rid the country of slavery.•

Newspapers carried the news of the insurrection, and throughout the South support for secession grew.

Brown was driven from the courthouse steps to the gallows in the back of a wagon that also carried the coffin in which he would be placed following the execution. His arms were bound and he sat on the coffin as the wagon made its way to the hangman. The streets around the jail were filled with soldiers and militia because of rumors that some desperate attempt would be made to save Brown from execution. The Richmond Grays (below) were one such unit that rushed to secure the site. One of their number was an actor named John Wilkes Booth, who viewed the old man with contempt, believing all abolitionists were traitors.

Former President John Tyler, a Virginian, observed, "Virginia is arming to the teeth. More than fifty thousand stands of arms are already distributed and the demand for more daily increasing."

DEF °On November 2, 1859, only three weeks after the abortive raid, the trial concluded, and Judge Richard Parker sentenced Brown to be hanged—executed because he had committed treason, committed murder, and committed insurrection.• Prominent people spoke out on Brown's behalf. The social reformer Wendell Phillips said, "History will date Virginia emancipation from Harpers Ferry. John Brown has loosened the roots of the slave system. It only breathes; it does not live hereafter." Ralph Waldo Emerson wrote, "Brown is a new saint awaiting his martyrdom. Who of ye shall suffer will make the gallows glorious. Like the cross."

WGG °On the morning of his execution, the town of Charles Town was quiet. People were expected to stay in their homes. Fifteen hundred soldiers from as far away as Richmond were there expecting a last-minute attempt to free Brown.•

More than fifteen hundred militia lined the road from the courthouse to the gallows and encircled the platform. Brown wore slippers, a low broad-brimmed hat, and his ragged Harpers Ferry clothes. It was almost eleven o'clock, and a balmy wind blew from the south. From his perch in the wagon Brown commented on the beauty of the countryside until he saw the scaffold. His eyes fixed on it, and he moved quickly up the steps to the platform. A jailer removed Brown's hat, adjusted the halter around his neck, and placed a white linen hood over his head. The sheriff positioned him over the trap door, attached the halter to the beam overhead, and tied Brown's ankles together. There was a ten-minute delay as the troops tried to find their assigned places. Finally, the rope was severed, the trap door sprung, and Brown's body fell, convulsed, and then hung limply.

CB °Leaving the jail, Brown came down the steps to a wagon carrying a coffin on which he sat, his elbows bound, his back to the driver. The gallows was about a block and a half away, surrounded by soldiers and people.° Among the witnesses was a professor from the Virginia Military Institute, Thomas Jonathan Jackson, whom history would remember as Stonewall.

CB °Brown climbed the thirteen steps to the gallows and stood on the trap door as his death cap was fitted. When the signal was given, a hatchet severed a rope springing the trap door, and John Brown's body hung between heaven and earth.° Of that moment, the poet Henry Wadsworth Longfellow predicted: "This will be a great day in our history. The date of a new revolution. Quite as much as needed as the old one. Even now as I write, they are leading Old John Brown to execution in Virginia for attempting to rescue slaves. This is sowing the wind to reap the whirlwind, which will soon come."

Church bells tolled in the stillness of North Elba, New York, as Brown's body was carried to a simple

SBO grave. °Two years after he died on the gallows attempting to free the slaves, Union troops marched into the South, singing "John Brown's Body."•

TCB °John Brown predicted the American Civil War by his pronouncements that slavery would only be abolished through bloodshed. Yet not Brown, nor any of those soldiers who stood at his execution, nor any Americans of his day had any idea how much blood would be spilled in the war to come.• Six hundred thousand men and boys alive on the day that Brown was executed would be gone six years later.

In 1859 the public recognized John Brown as a fanatic with a readiness to sacrifice his own life for the freedom of others. But the story of John Brown did not end with the silent grave in the mountain stillness. It was slavery that was put on trial, not Brown. His raid and subsequent execution did not directly cause the Civil War, but his ideals and beliefs became the standard under which thousands upon thousands of men and boys marched off to do battle in their own land.

Brown was buried on December 8, 1859, in North Elba, by a large boulder on the family farm. He became a Northern legend, a symbol of noble idealism and self-sacrifice. The man himself, however, was all but forgotten.

WEST POINT CLASSMATES

A select FEW AMONG THE more than three million men who fought in the Civil War formed a unique fraternity. Although they came from very different backgrounds, they had in common the military training they received at an elite school—the U.S. Military Academy at West Point. At this institution they were transformed from boys into the kind of men who would become heroes and legends.

MES °They had a bond that started when they were very young, and for some reason the fires of battle against BP each other only strengthened it.• °Only through military professionalism could the Civil War be waged to a successful conclusion, and the West Pointers represented the pinnacle of that concept of military professionalism.•

TJF °Even though they did all that they could to kill each other, none of these men forgot that they were Americans. That was what West Point had taught them.• Morris Schaff of the class of 1862 wrote in *The Spirit of Old West Point:* "There are two West Points—the actual West Point and the overarching spiritual one, of which the cadet only becomes conscious about the time he graduates. He hears no voice, but there is communicated in some way the presence of an invisible authority—cold, inexorable, and relentless."

The first West Point is easy to define. It stands fifty miles north of New York City and since 1802 has been the home of the U.S. Military Academy. But the second WCD West Point, the spiritual one, is intangible. °More than anything else, the spirit of West Point was one of comradeship. None of the cadets expected to die fighting

WCD	William C. Davis
JRE	John R. Elting
TJF	Thomas J. Fleming
JMJ	James M. Johnson
GAP	Gerard A. Patterson
BP	Brian Pohanka
MES	Mary Elizabeth Sergent

For entering cadets approaching the academy from the east, Garrison's Landing provided their first glimpse of West Point. From the landing a ferry conveyed them to the south dock from which they made their way to the stables and the riding hall and then to the back of the library before entering the plain on which the academy stood.

one another, but that comradeship was what got so many of them through the war. One of the shining glories of West Point was that this comradeship survived the divisiveness of war.• William Woods Averell of the class of 1855 explained: "My most unfading memories of West Point are of my classmates. We were harmonized by identical work and concurred habits of mind and body during four long years. Together we obeyed the same commands and signals and were exalted by the same triumphs and strained by the same trials. Naturally, we turned to each other and loved and helped each other."

°West Point produced a sense of male bonding, of belonging to an entity that defied rational analysis. It was a mystique, and it was a powerful and effective mystique.• The bonding that created the spirit of West Point began with admission to the academy. The first step for a prospective cadet was to secure one of the two coveted appointments allowed each congressman.

Successful application in some cases tested the resourcefulness of the applicant. °In the 1840s an ingenious cadet managed to get an appointment despite keen competition by others in his state. Many young men in Virginia aspired to military careers, so George Pickett moved to Illinois where he asked a prominent former Virginian living there to write a letter to his congressman, Abraham Lincoln. Lincoln recommended Pickett, and the transplanted Virginian was accepted into West Point.• One wonders if Lincoln remembered Pickett twenty years later, following the Confederate general's famous charge against Union troops at the battle of Gettysburg.

Appointment by a congressman, however, did not guarantee admission. The cadet-candidate also had to pass an entrance exam, °although the standards were fairly straightforward and simple. Education was not universal in the United States then, and an uncomplicated entrance exam was an attempt to give the

The cadet barracks were built in eight sections, four stories high, with four rooms on each floor. Each section could be entered from either the front via a short flight of steps or the rear, where a door entered onto a stoop. The companies were housed in order from A to D. Tall cadets, known as flankers, were placed in A and D, and shorter cadets comprised B and C and were known as runts. D Company had a reputation for being southern, western, casual scholars, and proficient at accumulating demerits. This photograph is probably the earliest known depiction of the corps of cadets. It appears in the 1863 class album but was probably taken as much as two years before the album was assembled.

unlearned the advantage of an education at this national institution.•

One of the unlearned who benefited from this approach was a simple youth from the backwoods of Virginia—Thomas Jackson, later to be known as Stonewall, the brilliant Confederate general. °He was probably one of the most poorly prepared of any incoming cadets. It was only his earnestness and absolute sincerity that prompted the examining board to pass him.•

JRE

The bonding at West Point intensified as the raw youths began the transformation into soldiers. George B. McClellan of the class of 1846 confided: "You can't imagine how much more spirited I feel since I have acquitted myself handsomely at this morning's drill. It is strange how some little circumstance like that can make so great a difference in one's feelings. Before the drill, I felt in low spirits, homesick, and in doubt as to my competency to go through here with credit, but now, how different!"

The curriculum was demanding, the classes rigorous, and the dropout rate high. °The cadets did not study such things as Latin and Greek, which were taught in civilian colleges. Instead, they concentrated on engineering and mathematics. They studied tactics, ordnance, and gunnery; they learned to be soldiers from the ground up.•

MES

With advances in photography, the artillery pieces around West Point, both monumental and functioning, provided suitable backdrops for cadet pictures, even attracting a feminine presence (top of next page).

Dennis Hart Mahan was professor of mathematics and engineering at West Point from 1832 to 1871. A graduate of the military academy, he ranked at the head of the class of 1824. Mahan studied military theory in France for four years, returning to West Point in 1828 and being appointed a full professor two years later. He had a profound influence on most of the men destined to command in the Civil War. His stellar career ended tragically in 1871 when he accidentally drowned near Stony Point, New York. A chronic nasal infection led cadets to nickname the distinguished professor "Old Cobbon Sense," referring to his most frequent admonition.

In classes taught by Dennis Hart Mahan, they were inspired to emulate Napoleon, the preeminent military genius of the era. °Mahan's key word, which he adopted from Napoleon, was *celerity*, which means "rapidity of action." West Pointers were trained to make speed the essence of their military operations.° According to Averell, "We were trained down to the physical limits with rapid infantry and artillery drills, active fencing, engineering labor, and riding—sometimes overtrained until boils would afflict us."

At the heart of this intense study and training was a clearly defined purpose: °to turn out men of character and skill.° Schaff recalled: "West Point is a great character builder, perhaps the greatest among our institutions of learning. The habit of truth-telling, the virtue of absolute honesty, the ready and loyal obedience to authority, the display of courage—to establish these elements of character, she labors without ceasing."

The importance of character was rigorously enforced by adherence to a strict code of conduct. °For each breach of regulations, the cadets received a penalty in the form of demerits.° Ulysses S. Grant of the class of 1843 complained: "They give a man one of these 'black marks' or demerits for almost nothing and if he gets 200 a year they dismiss him. To show how easy one can get these, a man by the name of Grant got eight of these marks for

not going to church today. He was put under arrest so he cannot leave his room for a month. All this for not going to church!"

At the risk of accumulating even more demerits, many cadets sought relief from the pressures of their training by sneaking off campus to Benny Haven's, the local tavern. This was a favorite pastime of the future president of the Confederacy, Jefferson Davis. °In fact, he was once court-martialed for being caught there off duty. On another occasion he almost killed himself when he lost his footing as he was returning drunk to the Point and went rolling down a steep bank, breaking several bones.•

WCD

°Conduct demerits were an important element in determining a cadet's class ranking and were factored in with his academic performance.• Davis's conduct demerits contributed to his low class ranking. One's class standing at graduation, however, was not always an indicator of future performance. Ulysses S. Grant, the man who would lead the Union troops to victory, ranked only twenty-first out of thirty-nine in his class. °Grant did not distinguish himself as a student. He was good at mathematics and at drawing and was one of the finest horsemen the Point ever produced, but otherwise, as in all things in his life, it was hardscrabble from the start.•

JMJ

WCD

On the other hand, George McClellan, the Union general who failed to end the war early when he had the chance, graduated second in his class of fifty-nine. JRE °McClellan was an example of the intellect that learns but the character that does not deliver. People such as these make useful staff officers or instructors, but they always want to lead armies, and therein lies disaster.°

If there was one graduate whose class ranking foreshadowed the greatness to come, it was Robert E. Lee, the legendary commander of the Army of Northern Virginia. TJF °Lee was known as "the Marble Model" at West Point. He had a perfect record in conduct. He never received a single demerit, an accomplishment that remains unmatched,° and he graduated second in his class.

Lee briefly served as superintendent of West Point in the 1850s. As sectional differences arose, he reminded the corps that they were "a band of brothers." That band would reach the breaking point on the eve of the Civil War.

WCD °WEST POINT REFLECTED the political and social complexion of America itself. Thus when the country began to come apart in the late 1850s, especially after John Brown's raid on Harpers Ferry and later following the election of 1860, the cadet corps was just as divided as the people whom it represented.°

Perhaps no other group of cadets reflected the nation's divisions as sharply as the classes of May and June 1861. MES °With the outbreak of war in April, the class of 1861 was graduated six weeks early, at the beginning of May. The class that would have graduated in 1862 was allowed to graduate six weeks later, at the end of June 1861, thus confusing historians for the rest of time.°

BP °Although these men were friends, there were political differences that could not be avoided. Sometimes

At its best, life at West Point was spartan. Downriver, however, stood a tavern known as Benny Haven's (far left), and cadets patronized it almost nightly and always surreptitiously. While liquor was an attraction, good food tantalized the cadets almost as much. At one time the proprietor had been employed on post, but he had been fired and forbidden to return, despite the fact that he was a trustee of the local Presbyterian church. A portion of the mural in the officers club at West Point (lower left) depicts cadets enjoying Benny Haven's.

The illustration above depicts the three uniforms of the cadets at West Point. The far left character wears the on-post uniform, the center models the full-dress uniform, and the figure on the right shows fatigue dress. Full dress was always worn in class and for parade and informal dances.

The class of 1863 was one of six classes to see action in the Civil War. Yet even during the war there had been significant controversies over the fate of West Point, including arguments in Congress for its closing. The high number of defections from the classes at the beginning of the war, the poor performance of the Union armies in the East, and the perceived aristocratic demeanor of West Pointers in general found numerous critics. The successes of Grant, Sherman, and other graduates of the school, however, dispelled much of the controversy and fueled the successful passage of the appropriations needed to continue the school.

this would lead to violent altercations,• the most noteworthy of which was a fistfight between Emory Upton, an outspoken abolitionist from New York, and Wade Hampton Gibbes, a cadet from South Carolina. Morris Schaff recalled: "It was the most thrilling event in my life as a cadet, and, in my judgment, it was the most significant in that of West Point itself. It was really national and prophetic for it duly represented the issue between the states."

BP   °The two fought it out, but neither won. They were both standing and battered at the end of the fight. It was not a fight that ended with a shaking of hands, a pat on the back, and a positive sense of sportsmanship. Instead it represented the tensions that had grown at West Point and across the country.•

Tensions grew even further as the southern states
GAP   began seceding from the Union. °Whether to remain loyal to the U.S. government or give up their careers and go south was, of course, a tortuous decision for the officers who were serving in the Regular U.S. Army and also for the cadets at West Point.•

West Point taught that duty was the essence of an officer and a gentleman, but now it was a question of duty to whom. °Was it duty to the United States? Duty to the army? Duty to Virginia or Alabama or Tennessee? Was it duty to family or duty to the flag? This was the terrible test that these cadets faced.°

Resigning from the academy on April 22, 1861, John Pelham wrote: "It would be exceedingly gratifying to me and to the whole family to receive a diploma from this institution, but fate seems to have wielded otherwise. I don't see any honorable course other than that of tendering my resignation when Alabama leaves the Union and offer my services to her."

°At least one indecisive cadet sought guidance from P. G. T. Beauregard, a Louisiana native and briefly the academy's superintendent. The cadet came to Beauregard and asked, "Should I resign now or wait until my state secedes?" Beauregard supposedly replied: "Well, watch me and jump when I jump. There's no sense in jumping too soon." Stories like this got back to

The library's holdings impressed many incoming cadets who had never seen so many books. In 1856 its shelves contained twenty thousand volumes, but the regimented structure of the curriculum limited general library use. Students had access to the library only on Saturday during times allotted for recreation and were allowed to take books to their rooms only on Sunday. Circulation records indicate that most cadets read a balance of fiction and nonfiction, with James Fenimore Cooper and Sir Walter Scott being read with as much frequency as books on Napoleon and George Washington. The facility was also used during enrollment and for examinations.

The library building cemented the Tudor-Gothic architectural style at West Point. Construction began in 1839 and was finished two years later. The east wing contained the library, the west wing housed administrative offices, and the upper story held the lecture hall and the "apparatus" of the natural philosophy department. The telescope in the center tower was mounted on twenty-four large cannon balls, which served as bearings for the traverse. For decades the observatory was considered one of the finest in the country. While the general impression about West Point was that its purpose was to train command-quality officers, in reality the science-laded curriculum of mathematics, physics, and astronomy generated almost all the nation's civil engineers.

Washington, and the new secretary of war promptly relieved Beauregard of the superintendency.°

°Deep emotions ran through West Point during this period as cadets started to resign and leave.° Among the more emotional partings was the one between Morris Schaff of Ohio and his roommate from Georgia. Schaff described the scene: "He threw his arms around me and almost sobbed: 'God bless you, Morris.' 'Farewell, dear John.' Soon he disappeared down the roadway to the landing. The little ferry boat set out for Garrison's, and soon I saw a figure waving a handkerchief, and I fluttered mine. And those little colors of boyhood's love floated till the river was crossed. I wondered whether I should ever have so close a friend again."

In an effort to keep the remaining cadets from resigning, the school made a pointed observance of Washington's birthday. °It was almost a climactic moment in many ways. The cadets were marched to the chapel where they were read Washington's farewell address, which stressed the importance of the federal union°: "It is of infinite moment that you shall properly

36

estimate the immense value of your national union to your collective and individual happiness—watching for its preservation with jealous anxiety."

Later that day the school band played "Washington's March" as it crossed the campus, but as it approached the barracks, the band switched to "The Star-Spangled Banner." °Suddenly all the cadets were at the windows of all the barracks. George Armstrong Custer's best friend, Tom Rosser, a Virginian, began to lead the southern cadets in singing "Dixie!" Custer, in another set of windows across the way, countered by leading the northern cadets in singing "The Star-Spangled Banner." The two groups shouted each other hoarse while the band continued to play the national anthem. After that, nobody had any doubt that West Point was a divided school.•

On April 12, 1861, Confederate forces fired on Fort Sumter in Charleston Harbor, signaling the beginning of the Civil War. °The firing on Sumter itself was very much a West Point event. The commander of Fort Sumter, Maj. Robert Anderson, was a West Point graduate and had been an artillery instructor at the Point. The commander of the Confederate forces opposing him, P. G. T. Beauregard, had been one of Anderson's students. Even during the crisis, as tensions built up to the firing, the two men exchanged courtesies and

Pierre Gustave Toutant Beauregard ranked second in the class of 1838. After twenty-two years of military service he was appointed superintendent of West Point in January 1861. He held the position for only five days before he was relieved of duty for his outspoken southern sympathies. Beauregard resigned his commission in February 1861, faced Robert Anderson, his former West Point artillery instructor, at Charleston Harbor's Fort Sumter in April 1861, and then opposed Irvin McDowell, his West Point classmate, on the plains of Manassas in July 1861.

The food in the mess hall was neither plentiful nor well cooked. Some cadets complained that the diet was only a little above prison rations. Potatoes and boiled meat made up most meals, and fish was served every Friday. The light dinner menu often consisted of nothing more than bread and butter, coffee (water for the noncoffee drinkers), and seasonal fruits.

37

Throughout the nineteenth century West Point pitched summer camp on the extreme eastern edge of the plains. Logically, tents were cooler than barracks, and practically, an army lived and worked in the outdoors. The tents were arranged in eight rows along four company streets. Cadets slept on blankets laid over a wooden floor, their lockers served as their desks, uniforms were hung from a pole, and a mirror was placed on the front tent pole. The only furniture was a gun rack. It was said that in the first summer an entering class learned to be soldiers, the second they learned to be noncommissioned officers, and the third they were finally officers.

MES

pleasantries. It was with some anguish that Beauregard gave the order to fire the first shot.°

"When the news of the firing on Fort Sumter was received at West Point, the effect was instantaneous," Tully McCrea of the class of 1862 recalled. "Every Northern cadet now showed his colors. One could have heard us singing 'The Star-Spangled Banner' in Cold Spring. It was the first time I ever saw the Southern contingent cowed. All of their Northern allies had deserted them, and they were stunned."

The day after the firing on Fort Sumter, the secretary of war ordered that everyone at West Point take a new oath of allegiance. °Previously, officers and cadets had taken the oath as citizens of individual states. The rules were now changed, and the oath was altered so that the cadets and faculty swore fealty to the United States over any other state, county, or other political entity whatsoever.°

"The oath was administered in the chapel in the presence of the military and academic staff in full uniform," Cadet McCrea remembered. "Ten of the class refused to take the oath and, of course, will be dismissed. When the first one refused, a few Southern cadets tried to applaud him by stamping on the floor, but he was immediately greeted with such a unanimous hiss that he could clearly see the sentiments of the great majority present. Never before did a cadet refuse to take the oath of allegiance."

Of the 278 cadets at West Point on the day that Lincoln was elected, 86 were appointees from the South. Of them, 65 were discharged, dismissed, or resigned because of their loyalty to their native states.

"I cannot look forward to graduation with the pleasure I did formerly," lamented Henry DuPont of the class of May 1861. "And if it is to be our lot to be employed in cutting our countrymen's throats and fighting our dearest friends and classmates, I am very sorry that I ever came here."

Before they were sent off to war, the remaining cadets gathered in the chapel to sing "When Shall We Meet Again?" a West Point tradition practiced on the Sunday before graduation.

> When shall we meet again,
> Meet ne'er to sever?
> When will Peace wreathe her chain
> Round us forever?
> Our hearts will ne'er repose
> Safe from each blast that blows
> In this dark vale of woes,
> Never—no, never!

In the final year of instruction the intricate ballet of artillery—swabbing, reloading, priming, and firing—was practiced on alternate afternoons. The other afternoons were given to riding instruction. There were inevitable accidents, sometimes involving the positioning of artillery by overtired horses or undertrained gunners. Premature firings were the greatest offense, earning each erring cadet a minimum of two demerits and possibly crippling one of the gun crew. Fatalities, fortunately, were almost unheard of.

"Everyone felt the truth of the words, 'Never—no, never!'" Tully McCrea recounted, "for in all probability in another year the half of them may be in their graves, the victims of war or disease. At any rate they will soon be scattered and will never meet together again as a class."

WITH THE OUTBREAK of the war, the men of West Point faced very different challenges, depending on which side they fought. Those who defended the Confederate cause had the enormous task of building an army from scratch, while their Union counterparts had to deal with the bureaucracy that denied them promotion. Either way, these men had to take what they had learned at West Point and put it to the ultimate test on the battlefield.

More than three hundred West Point cadets and graduates had affirmed their loyalty to the South, and the impact of their disaffection was enormous. The North responded with a general suspicion of all things related to West Point. In July 1861, Secretary of War

Looking north from Trophy Point and across the Hudson River, the siege guns used in the cadets' artillery training can be seen in the foreground. Artillery instruction followed a logical progression, training each cadet in the responsibilities of every position on the gun crew, the capabilities of each classification of artillery, the coordination of a battery in combat, and maneuvering several batteries in concert on a field of battle. The curriculum included the technical and theoretical aspects of heavy weaponry, from how munitions were manufactured to the desired effects of various shells and shot.

The cadet barracks suffered from several well-intentioned attempts at heating. A few cadets reported that ice formed in buckets of water kept in the rooms. The rooms themselves were furnished sparely. Each was occupied by two cadets and contained a table, two straight chairs, two iron bedsteads with very thin mattresses, a wash stand, and a lamp. Belongings were kept in four trunks that lined the walls, and four brooms were kept behind the door.

Simon Cameron noted: "At the national military academy, they were received and treated as the adopted children of the republic. The question may be asked in view of this extraordinary treachery whether its promoting cause may not be traced to a defect in the education itself!"

GAP °Both the North and the South were fighting the Civil War with basically volunteer armies. As small as the Regular U.S. Army was—fewer than ten thousand men in uniform—it did provide a nucleus around which an army could be built. The Confederate officers, however, had to start from scratch.°

TJF °Being a graduate of West Point himself, Jefferson Davis appointed West Pointers throughout his administration and as general officers of the Confederate army. This proliferation of West Point–trained commanders gave the Southern armies an edge in the first year or two of the war.°

WCD °It was out of this cadre of West Point–trained officers, whom Davis had known largely before the war, that he built the nucleus that would expand eventually into a million-man army.° To organize the Confederate army, West Pointers had the difficult task of quickly transforming largely illiterate farm boys into soldiers.

WCD °Some did not even know their left foot from their right. The West Pointers, among other things, had to

Cadet uniforms were designed to nurture a sense of equality and esprit de corps. Thus all cadets dressed alike for all occasions. Trousers were uncreased and either white or gray, depending on the season of the year. Shakos were worn while on parade, but those were replaced with dark blue forage caps in 1861. In a day of flourishing facial hair, cadets were forbidden to allow such growths, sometimes being written up for having "dirty faces." Capes were unlined so as to show no partiality to any branch of the service. This limited wardrobe was the great equalizer, making West Point one of the great democracies in microcosm.

give them instructions on how to march by tying hay to one foot and straw to the other. They could then chant out a cadence of "Hay foot, straw foot," and this would teach the boys to march.•

On July 21, 1861, the two armies collided at the railroad junction of Manassas, Virginia, also known as Bull Run, the first major engagement of the war. For many West Pointers, like the volunteers they trained, it was their first taste of battle and a rude awakening. George Armstrong Custer of the class of June 1861 recalled: "I remember well the strange hissing and exceedingly vicious sound of the first cannon shot I heard as it whirled through the air. Of course, I had often heard the sound made by cannonballs during my artillery practice at West Point, but a man listens with changed interest when the direction of the balls is toward instead of away from him."

WCD   °The battle of First Manassas is perhaps the best demonstration of just how ill trained West Point officers were for this kind of war. They had been taught to be lieutenants, and now these lieutenants were commanding armies and brigades and regiments with no further
TJF   training or experience.• °William Tecumseh Sherman, for instance, said that four days before the battle of Bull Run was the first time he had read about maneuver-

ing—or, as he called it, "evolutions"—an army of thirty to forty thousand men in the field. He had never even thought about it before.•

WCD   °West Point had taught its students to operate on the plains of Europe, not in the wilderness of Virginia where a man could not see thirteen feet in front of him. A West Point education also reflected the still prevalent Napoleonic ideal, which was exemplified by no one so well as P. G. T. Beauregard, who was second in command of the Confederate army at First Manassas. Beauregard wrote grandiose battle orders as if they had been written by Napoleon himself, but they were so complex no one could understand them— even Beauregard may not have known what they meant. The orders were so confusing that at one point he ordered one of his brigades to attack another of his brigades.•

Across enemy lines, Beauregard's West Point classmate Irvin McDowell, the commanding general of the Union army, was enacting his own Napoleonic battle

JRE   plan. °The trouble was that he needed Napoleon's *Grande Armée* to carry it out, and he had instead a group of partially trained, ill-disciplined ninety-day volunteers under an undistinguished bunch of generals.•

Often described as an encounter between two armed mobs, the battle of Bull Run was a victory for the Confederates, but it was a less than glorious debut for West

The curriculum at West Point was not easy. All cadets took the same courses; there were no electives. The method of instruction required a great deal of memorization, and in some instances cadets were required to recite entire books. Everyone recited every day and received a grade in every subject every day. Competition was fierce, and the reward for excellence was additional, more difficult assignments.

Cadet Philip H. Sheridan, flanked by recent graduates Bvt. 2d Lt. George W. Crook and Bvt. Lt. John Nugen, missed graduating with his friends because of misconduct demerits resulting in a year's suspension from the academy. This picture was probably taken before or immediately after graduation in 1852 because both Crook and Nugen wear lieutenant's uniforms and Sheridan, an 1853 graduate, wears a cadet uniform, making this is one of the earliest photographs of a cadet in full dress uniform.

Pointers from the North and from the South. In time, though, they would adapt and demonstrate the spirit that distinguished them and the school from which they came.

THE SPIRIT THAT bonded the men of West Point manifested itself in many ways throughout the war. One was in the display of their superior military talent. Of the war's sixty major battles, fifty-five of them were commanded on both sides by West Point graduates.

GAP °Both the Union and the Confederate officers were products of the same instruction. They had studied the same texts. They all followed the same rules. They knew each other, and this had a direct impact on how the war

BP was fought.* °It took professionalism to wage this war in such a way that through those concepts of strategy and tactics and military bearing, the veteran armies ultimately fought it out until one side won and one side lost.*

TJF °The series of battles that best exemplify West Point training are the Shenandoah Valley campaign of Stonewall Jackson,* which was launched to prevent his West Point classmate, George McClellan, from receiving

TJF much-needed reinforcements. °The Valley campaign of 1862 was a masterpiece of marching and countermarching at top speed, which enabled Jackson to defeat four other armies that outnumbered his forces four to one. To accomplish this incredible feat, Jackson put into action the lessons he had learned from Dennis Hart Mahan, the great West Point professor. Jackson demonstrated Mahan's ideas about celerity and boldness, which was another primary emphasis of Mahan's—that a general had to be a daring character.

Sherman was another great student of Mahan. His March to the Sea was a masterpiece of celerity. Sherman's sixty-two thousand men moved faster than the Confederates ever imagined an army of that size could move.• In an effort to break the South's will to continue the war, Sherman's army swept from Atlanta to the sea and up through the Carolinas in the winter of 1864.

TJF °The great thing about Sherman's army that is often overlooked is that it had all kinds of "modern" devices, such as pontoon bridges and huge signal poles that could be erected quickly. Sherman used the telegraph well. In fact, his use of technology on his March to the Sea can be traced directly to his West Point training.•

As dazzling as these examples of military talent were, the most evocative expressions of the spirit of West WCD Point were in the bonds of friendship. °Time and time again throughout the war this bond transcended the hatred engendered by the war itself. After the battle of Fredericksburg when Ambrose Burnside, the Federal commander, was thoroughly humiliated, Burnside—a man who was much beloved by his fellow cadets—was actually mourned by the Confederates who had beaten him because they loved the man himself so much. At Fort Donelson, when U. S. Grant captured Gen. Simon Buckner, the first thing Grant did was to offer Buckner his purse in case Buckner needed money.

Perhaps the most poignant moment of all came at Gettysburg on July 3 at the highlight of Pickett's charge when Gen. Lewis Armistead was mortally wounded leading his Confederates over the wall. Among his last acts was a wish that his effects be given to his close friend, Gen. Winfield Scott Hancock, against whose corps he had just attacked.•

This seemingly bulletproof bond was hard for non–West Pointers to comprehend. Confederate

Gouverneur Warren graduated second in the class of 1850 (top) and had returned to West Point just prior to the war to teach mathematics. The apex of his military career occurred on July 2, 1863, when he noticed the exposed Federal left flank from the unoccupied Round Tops at Gettysburg. His urgent action averted a Union disaster, and he was subsequently promoted to major general (lower).

Patrick O'Rorke (above) was ranked first in the class of June 1861 and died a colonel at the head of his troops, rushing to secure the crest of Little Round Top at Gettysburg.

Henry DuPont (below) came from a distinguished family and graduated at the head of the class of May 1861. Assigned to artillery, he spent the first two years of the war in New York and the remainder in the Shenandoah Valley. He came under fire for the first time at New Market, served with distinction at Cedar Creek, and received the Medal of Honor.

Gen. George Pickett tried explaining it to his wife when he wrote her about George McClellan, his classmate and enemy: "He was, he is, and he always will be—even were his pistol pointed at my heart—my dear, loved friend. You, my darling, may not be in sympathy with this feeling, but you cannot understand the entente cordiale between us old fellows."

Perhaps Mrs. Pickett had a better appreciation for the entente cordiale when she gave birth to a son while Grant's Army of the Potomac besieged Richmond. °Upon hearing the news, Grant honored his old school friend by ordering bonfires to be lit all along the Union lines as a way of congratulating the new father. A couple of weeks later, under a flag of truce, Grant and some of his officers sent a silver service through the lines with an inscription saying, "To our friend and classmate, George Pickett." It was a sign of how closely connected these men still felt.•

Yet even West Point bonds had their weak links. Prior to the war, A. P. Hill had sought the hand of Ellen Marcy, but she married George McClellan instead. Hill later proved that all was fair in love and war. °Whenever McClellan's troops were within range of Hill's division, Hill always attacked him with everything he had. There was a story that one day, after beating off three of Hill's attacks, the soldiers in McClellan's army slumped in their trenches. At dusk there was another rattle of musketry and Hill's men attacked again. An old soldier, pulling on his boots, allegedly said, "Oh, my God, Ellie, why didn't you marry him?"•

The Union's George Armstrong Custer and the Confederacy's Tom Rosser, however, conducted their school-bred rivalry on much friendlier terms. °At one point Rosser captured Custer's baggage and left a note for Custer advising him to come up with a slightly larger coat the next time around, because Rosser was a larger man than Custer and had a hard time getting into Custer's clothing. Custer later did the same thing with Rosser—capturing some of his baggage, some of his clothing, and sending a note to Rosser advising him to have his tailor take it in the next time so it would fit better.•

Custer expressed the West Point spirit perhaps the most flamboyantly. Although he ranked last in his class, he became, at age twenty-three, the youngest general—up to that time—in the Union army. He thought nothing of crossing enemy lines to be the best man at a Confederate classmate's wedding or in rejoicing in the successes of Rebel West Pointer John Pelham.

But Custer and West Point were at their best when his classmate Stephen Ramseur, a Southern general, was mortally wounded on October 19, 1864, at Cedar

MES Creek. °Ramseur was carried to Union Gen. Philip H. Sheridan's quarters, where there were two of his classmates, Henry DuPont from the class of May 1861 and Custer from the class of June 1861. Those men stayed with Ramseur as long as he was conscious and gave him their support. That's the only way to express it.• Custer was also among the many West Pointers present at the event that was the supreme expression of the academy's spirit—Lee's surrender to Grant at Appomattox.

Tully McCrea (above), class of June 1861, was a part of the Union artillery at Gettysburg that was battered while answering the Confederate barrage preceding Pickett's charge. He remained in the military after the war and rose to the rank of general.

WCD °JUST AS THE war began as a battle between West Pointers, in a way, it ended in the same fashion when Grant and Lee met at Appomattox.• After four grueling years of war, Lee surrendered to Grant on April 9, 1865, at the McLean

WCD house in Appomattox, Virginia. °Virtually all of the officers present in the parlor of the house, Union and Confederate, were West Pointers. It was almost a class

TJF reunion for some of them.• °It was here that the spirit of West Point played a significant part in the national healing, or at least in preventing this terrible war from becoming a permanent division in the country.•

WCD °West Point, among other things, taught that a foe was a foe while he was in front of you, but once the war was over, a foe was an enemy no longer. Unlike many soldiers in that war, Grant understood this.•

TJF °Confident in knowing that he shared a similar background with Grant, Lee said, "General Grant will *not* force us to surrender unconditionally. He will give this army the terms it deserves." This was a tremendous moment in the history of West Point and the country, because had Lee not believed that, he might have opted for a guerrilla war. Yet he knew that the South

John Pelham (below) resigned his appointment to West Point two weeks prior to his class's graduation in May 1861. He became the head of Jeb Stuart's horse artillery, rose to the rank of major, and was killed at Kelly's Ford in March 1863.

The West Point band was exercised almost daily. It was not comprised of cadets but of army regulars stationed at the military academy. In one of the defining moments of the sectional controversy at the school, following the observation of George Washington's birthday in 1861, the band paraded, playing the national anthem. The cadets either joined in or sang "Dixie!" There was no longer a question of where a cadet stood in his loyalties after that demonstration.

had fought almost to the last man and that Grant knew that. For those reasons he could expect honorable terms.•

Grant never mentioned unconditional surrender to Lee. In an unusual move, he honored Lee's request that the Southerners be allowed to keep their side-arms and horses. °When Lee told Grant that his men were starving, the Federal commander sent thirty thousand rations through their lines as soon as possible. Those gestures were definitely part of the spirit of West Point.•

The cadets formed the post fire department. At the first alarm they fell into ranks. One company pulled the pumper, another carried the hose to the nearest water source, another salvaged whatever it could, and the last stood ready to act as ordered. In freezing weather, if water could not be pumped, the cadets formed fire brigades and fought the fire bucket by bucket.

The cadet chapel was built in 1836. Cadets occupied the middle section, and other worshipers sat on either side. Attendance was, of course, compulsory. The order of worship was Episcopalian. All cadets were considered Protestant, and efforts were made at nondenominationalism. Roman Catholics, however, were required to march a mile from the post to attend mass at Buttermilk Falls. The organ was positioned in the balcony over the entrance and was powered by a plebe who operated a hand sweep. The cadet choir sat around the organ and sometimes threw spitballs at the congregants during dull sermons.

GAP

not just happen, nor were they the result of favoritism. They were successful because these were men who had been screened, tried, and found competent.°

°As a group, the 306 graduates of West Point who joined the Confederacy were probably most responsible for the fact that the Civil War was the costliest conflict in which the country has ever been involved. Certainly without their contributions, the Confederacy could never have fielded forces of the military caliber of the Army of Northern Virginia and the Army of Tennessee. In the course of the war more than a quarter of those men were killed in action. The fact that as their services were lost the Confederacy's fortunes declined attests to their importance.°

WCD °Of course, once the surrender took place, there was a general round of handshaking and backslapping, smiles even on the faces of the defeated Confederates who— besides being glad that it was all over at last—were rather relieved and pleased to see their old comrades once more. Several called on Gen. George Meade and commented on how gray he had become, to which he responded, "You have to answer for most of that."•

Among those reunited were James Longstreet, com- mander of Lee's First Corps, and an old West Point

GAP friend, U. S. Grant. °It was a very touching scene as Grant slapped Longstreet on the back and said, "Pete [Longstreet's nickname], let's go back to the good old times and have a game of brag as we used to."•

The war was over, and the men from West Point had

JRE made the difference. °The main thrust of West Point's influence on the Civil War was simply that the North would not have won the war without it. It was the West Pointers who organized and administered and generally led the armies that were victorious. Their successes did

This photograph of the rear of th[e] cadet barracks better shows the b[...] stoop. Rigid discipline was rarely [...] relaxed. Such demands were only [...] slightly offset by pranks. These, ho[w]ever, were best executed at night a[nd] were very low key. There were soldi[...] fights and other confrontations, but [...] demerits or suspensions always fol- lowed. The goal of the academy was [to] instill a sense of honor and duty into [...] men of character.

Ultimately though, the story of the men of West Point in the Civil War was really about the sharing of a bond that was more powerful than any weapon and a spirit that transcended any political cause. °Jesus said, "Love your enemies." In the midst of the most horrible war this country ever fought and in its aftermath, the sons of West Point did love their enemies, and they should be remembered in the context of that love.•

As Morris Schaff concluded *The Spirit of Old West Point:* "I view the classes now across the slumbering years. I see them with the flush of youth on their cheeks; and a mist gathers over my eyes as one after another their faces come into view. Oh! Let the dew fall and the stars shine softly where the dead lie; and when the last trumpet blows, may the gates of heaven swing open to all!"

It was not so much that the men of West Point deserve admiration for what they accomplished, rather they should be admired for something much more elusive, something that cannot be reduced to dates and statistics. Perhaps it can be traced to what those men learned and became at West Point. There they were imbued with an enduring set of ideals, a strong spirit, and a clear purpose that transcended even the most bitter of conflicts and inspired a unity for which many still long.

The bond created at West Point was demonstrated throughout the war. Here Lt. George Armstrong Custer (above, right), ten months out of the academy, poses with former classmate Lt. J. B. Washington, who had been captured on May 31, 1862, near Fair Oaks, Virginia. Custer was an aide on George B. McClellan's staff, and Washington was an aide to Joseph E. Johnston. Custer's friendships recognized no war, and he occasionally crossed the lines to attend a wedding or a birthday of a classmate.

JEFFERSON DAVIS

When the SOUTHERN STATES broke away from the Union in 1861, Jefferson Davis announced that he did not want to lead the new Confederacy, but the seceded states chose him anyway because he possessed every quality for which they were looking. He was a war hero, a former cabinet secretary, and, of course, a passionate defender of slavery who had said as late as 1861, "We recognize the Negro as God's book tells us to recognize him—our inferior, fitted expressly for servitude."

Davis was born in Kentucky, as was Lincoln, but he grew up in the Mississippi cotton fields where his family had purchased a plantation and slaves. Here young Jefferson inherited the attitudes that changed his life and that of the country.

WC °He believed that slavery was the best possible world for black people, because he believed that black people were inferior to white people. He believed that in Africa blacks had been savages, and he believed that the whites in the South had civilized and Christianized them.°

By the standards of the time, the slaves of the Davis plantation were treated leniently. They were educated, GWG fed well, and rarely if ever beaten. °The slaves on the Davis plantation had a great deal more autonomy than that experienced on most plantations. Many questions of discipline were handled by courts made up of the slaves themselves, and there were rules governing how Davis could change punishments. For example, he could make them more lenient, but he could not make them harsher.°

WC	William Cooper
WCD	William C. Davis
GWG	Gary W. Gallagher
JMM	James M. McPherson
JIR	James I. Robertson Jr.

Hurricane plantation was a refuge for WCD
Jefferson Davis in the years of solitude
that followed the sudden death of his
first wife, Sarah Knox Taylor. Several
former Davis slaves, recently owned by
either Jefferson or his brother, Joseph,
posed in front of the garden cottage at
Hurricane in 1865. Although free,
many remained and worked on the
plantation after the war, eventually
owning much of it.

°Unfortunately for Davis, he never fully understood what slavery was like elsewhere, because most of his experience was on his own plantation. He, therefore, had a notion that slavery was more or less that benign and enlightened everywhere, which certainly it was not.•

Like many planters' sons, he was sent to West Point to train for the military. His classmates in 1824 included Robert E. Lee, but Davis showed none of Lee's promise. °In fact, he did not have a distinguished career at the military academy. He finished twenty-third in a class of thirty-three, having shown a great deal of interest in sneaking off campus to Benny Haven's tavern and otherwise flaunting the rules of the academy.•

After barely managing to graduate, Davis spent the next few years as a frontier soldier trying to keep the peace between Native Americans and settlers. In 1828 he noted, "I cannot say that I like the army, but it's better than being a politician whose struggles are begun in folly and closed in disgrace."

He earned a reputation for arguing with his superior officers. One was Zachary Taylor, a future president. Their dispute, however, was personal. Lieutenant Davis had become engaged to Taylor's daughter, Sarah, °but the commanding officer did not want his daughter to marry a soldier. This caused tremendous tension between them. Jefferson Davis and Sarah Taylor carried on their love affair for several years virtually by correspondence, as Davis was stationed in remote posts on frontier duty.• When they married in 1835, Zachary Taylor did not attend the wedding.

Davis resigned from the army to start married life as a cotton planter. It was midsummer, and Sarah was worried about going to Mississippi during the fever season, but Jefferson persuaded her to go. In a letter to her mother, Sarah wrote: "Do not make yourself uneasy about me. The country is quite healthy."

An owner's financial fortunes often dictated whether slave families were separated. In 1862 photographer Timothy O'Sullivan found that the Smith family of Beaufort, South Carolina, had kept five generations of a slave family intact.

Five weeks later, Sarah was dead from malaria. Davis, who almost died himself from the disease, was crushed. He would spend the next seven years in virtual seclusion on the plantation. °Almost certainly he felt responsible for her death, and to avoid admitting it to himself, he adopted instead a position that stayed with him for the rest of his life. Davis chose to believe that he was never wrong about anything, because if he were wrong some years later about some minor event or minor happening, it might force him to admit he could have been wrong about something else. Maybe that included the greatest mistake of his life—persuading Sarah Taylor to go south that summer to her death.•

Davis graduated in the lower ranks of the class of 1828 at West Point and was thus destined to join the infantry. At the time, Congress limited the number of officers in the army, and so most graduates of the military academy held brevet, or honorary, ranks until vacancies opened. Davis waited three years to receive his commission and lieutenant's rank.

When Davis finally reemerged, it was as a politician. In 1845 he headed to Washington as a newly elected congressman. He took with him his new wife, Varina Howell, a Mississippi landowner's daughter. Only nineteen years old, she sized up Davis perfectly at their first meeting with the observation, "He has a way of taking for granted that everybody agrees with him when he expresses an opinion, which offends me."

As a congressman, Davis, like most southerners, was there to defend states' rights, which meant the right to keep slaves. °In the South slavery was much more than an economic institution. There were millions of black

WCD

GWG

A congressman when the war with Mexico broke out, Davis was elected to command a regiment of Mississippi volunteers and found himself under the command of his former reluctant father-in-law, Zachary Taylor. The highlight of his war experience was at the battle of Buena Vista in northern Mexico, when his Mississippians helped to thwart the last Mexican advance.

JMM

people living in the South, and, for the whites who lived there, slavery was a way of controlling that very large black population. In fact, it was crucial to social control in the South.•

°Southerners, of course, saw themselves as kindly masters. They saw the institution of slavery as a beneficent institution for both the slaves and their southern masters, and that was why they were prepared to fight for it. They regarded their society as better than that of the Yankees where the almighty dollar rather than the human sense of paternalism seemed to be the governing institution.•

From the start Davis argued against Washington's power to restrict slavery. As a freshman congressman in 1845 he warned: "The Union is a creature of the states. It has no inherent power. All it possesses was delegated by the states."

States' rights would eventually create its own battlefields, but in 1846 there was a war to fight with Mexico over disputed territory. Davis, the former soldier, GWG quickly volunteered to go back into the field. °This gave him an opportunity to lead men in battle and also to further the cause of southern expansion and the potential expansion of slavery.•

When Congressman, now Colonel, Davis arrived in Mexico, he found that his commanding officer was his former father-in-law, Zachary Taylor. Davis did not know what to expect until Taylor sent him a note: "I am anxious to take you by the hand, and to have you near me." For Taylor, the rancor of the past was now buried along with Sarah. During the war itself, Davis proved to WCD be one of Taylor's best officers and °a natural leader on the battlefield. He was a brave man, impervious to fear, daring, calm, and cool under fire.•

GWG °At a key moment in the battle of Buena Vista, Davis amassed his First Mississippians into a large V-shaped formation. The Mexican troops moved into that open V and were decisively driven back. It was one of the crucial moments and high points of the battle on the American side.•

Davis, who survived a bullet wound to the foot, was hailed by both Taylor and the American press. He returned home to find he had become a national hero.

At the age of thirty-nine Davis emerged from his self-imposed seclusion to pursue a political career. Mississippi came to know him as a champion of states' rights and a strict interpreter of the Constitution, the nation came to know him for his exploits in Mexico.

HAVING COME BACK a hero from the Mexican War, Davis found himself showered with political rewards. First, he was given a seat in the Senate, and then President JIR Franklin Pierce made him secretary of war. °Davis has since been considered by many to be the finest secretary of war in the nation's history. He doubled the size of the army in the short period of two years. He endorsed such things as breech-loading rifles and other revolutionary weapons that were being developed at this time. In short, he was an extremely active and productive secretary of war.•

While serving as secretary of war, Davis was also put in charge in 1853 of building a dome for the Capitol in Washington. By the time it was finished eleven years later, he would be leading another country in a war against Washington, but in the mid-1850s Davis wanted to do more than just complete the Capitol. He wanted to be on the inside, speaking for the southern cause. The issue of slavery and states' rights was consuming the nation, and in 1857 he returned to the Senate. He warned in 1858 that if an antislavery candidate like Lincoln were elected president in 1860, the Union would

Zachary Taylor emerged as one of the heroes of the Mexican War and won the White House in 1848. He welcomed Davis to his command during the war and as an adviser during his presidency. Davis did not disappoint Taylor politically or as a devoted friend.

be dissolved: "We would declare the government at an end, even though blood should flow in torrents throughout the land."

GWG °His actions in the Senate were a vigorous defense of the institution of slavery, especially on the question of whether slavery could expand into the territories owned by the United States. Davis was unrelenting in his insistence that slavery be allowed in any territory owned by the national government.•

JIR °Further compounding the sectional controversy was the fact that there was no United States in the 1850s. The United States existed in name alone, not in fact. People were Mississippians first, Virginians first, Pennsylvanians first, and Americans second.•

For all this bluster, Davis did not really want to see GWG the South leave the Union. °Many who have studied him believe that he would have preferred to stay in the Union with ironclad guarantees for slavery, rather than WCD be forced to resort to secession.• °Davis understood, as many southerners did not, that secession would not take place peacefully. The North was hardly likely to let half the nation pull away without trying to coerce the former states into remaining. Of course, having served

Ten years after his brief marriage to Sarah Knox Taylor, Jefferson and Varina Howell Davis were married. The marriage was a lively one, with Varina's strong independent spirit clashing frequently with Davis's arrogant, peremptory personality. She was frustrated by his lengthy absences, the deference paid to older brother Joseph, and the opposite life she expected to have as the wife of a planter. He viewed her objections as insolence. They separated quietly and briefly in 1848. Time allowed her to acquiesce discreetly, and they resolved their differences as they began to build a new home at Brierfield. The portrait at right was made in 1849 and hints at the obeisance required of Varina.

under the old flag, it was also a personal wrench for Davis to think of leaving Old Glory.•

But then came the spark that ignited secession: Americans elected a northern abolitionist, Abraham Lincoln, president in November 1860. °Lincoln's election precipitated the belief among southerners, including Davis, that perhaps the only way they were going to be able to enforce what they called "southern rights" would be as a separate nation, outside the Union. They could not remain in a Union that was now controlled by people whom they regarded as their enemies.•

Davis was ordered by Mississippi to resign from the Senate, which he did in a speech that his wife called

Montgomery photographer William W. Culver captured the inauguration of the president of the Confederacy on the front portico of the Alabama State House at one o'clock on the afternoon of February 18, 1861. Before an audience of five thousand, Davis spoke of the possibility of war with the North no less than five times. He warned, "If we may not hope to avoid war, we may at least expect that posterity will acquit us of having needlessly engaged in it."

Lewis Crenshaw offered the old Brock-enbrough house on East Clay Street to Davis as the new executive mansion of the Confederacy. It possessed a good view of the James River and much of the city and was just a short walk from the Virginia State House, which was to be the Confederate Capitol. The home was the scene of much activity related to the military planning of the war, political and formal entertaining, and a heart-rending tragedy for the Davis family.

There is no doubt that Davis chafed at being given a political role in the Confederacy rather than a military position. Nevertheless, he expended all his energy in encouraging and cajoling the states to send more regiments, exhaust their armories, and supply more provisions for the armies needed in the field.

"inexpressibly sad." To his former colleagues, he said: "I feel no hostility to you senators from the North. In the presence of God, I wish you well."

He was now fifty-three years old and tired of politics. Davis headed home to his plantation, making it known that he did not want to participate in the leadership of the new Confederacy. °If anything, he said that his inclinations led him more toward a military command. Given his preferences, however, he would simply have stayed at home at his plantation and tended to his crops, or at least that is what Davis said.°

On February 10, 1861, he and Varina were working in their garden when a messenger arrived with news from the Confederate convention. Varina noted: "When reading the telegram, he looked so grieved that I feared some evil had befallen our family. He told me [of his appointment] as a man might speak a sentence of death."

The new Southern nation wanted a well-respected moderate to present its cause to the world, and so its leaders had picked Davis. °He was stunned, but his sense of duty was such that he felt he could not decline the office, so he accepted.° That week Davis told a friend there would be a long and bloody war.

The inauguration was held in Montgomery, Alabama. The new nation had no anthem yet, so the band played the French national anthem, "La Marseillaise." The crowd

WCD

JMM

was full of patriotic fervor and oblivious to the problems facing it. From his vantage point during the ceremonies, Davis recalled, "I saw smiling faces, but beyond them I saw troubles and thorns innumerable." He knew that war was probable, but he was still trying for peace.

JIR °The Confederacy began with nothing. The North, at least, had a capital, a monetary system, a government infrastructure, and a machinery of administration. The WCD South had to start from scratch.° °For example, the Confederate treasury began in an empty room in a rented building that had no furniture, with a clerk handing out five dollars of his own money to an officer as the department's first disbursement.°

JIR °Davis spent the first six weeks of his presidency trying to deal diplomatically with Northern officials in Washington. He hoped that the whole question could be resolved diplomatically and peacefully.°

There was, however, an immediate problem. Northern troops still occupied Fort Sumter in Charleston Harbor, in Confederate territory. For Davis, this was an WC insult to the South. °It was as if a foreign power were to fly its flag over a military installation in New York Harbor. The obvious solution was to remove it.°

When negotiations with the Lincoln administration failed, Davis gave his soldiers the order to fire on Sumter. Within thirty-six hours the Union garrison surrendered. In Montgomery, bands played in the street, but Davis stayed in his office, smoking a cigar. One official described him as being suddenly weighed down by the responsibilities of his office. "Sumter's fall," the Confederate president noted, "is either the end of a political contest or the beginning of a fearful war."

WITH WAR AGAINST the United States probable, who would fight for the South? It had no established army and only one qualified general, David Twiggs, who was seventy-one years old. Davis knew he would have to create a whole new breed of generals almost overnight. WCD °In this task Davis revealed one of the unfortunate facets of his character, which was an addiction, a dependence upon old friends and cronies. Probably the worst appointment of his entire first year as president was that

As first lady of the Confederacy, Varina Davis endured the unforgiving scrutiny of Richmond's social scene, which both criticized her for entertaining at the Confederate White House at all and also for not entertaining lavishly enough. Some believed she had too much influence over her husband, challenged her loyalty to the Southern cause on the basis of her father's northern heritage, or denigrated her as ill-bred and unrefined. There was no question, however, that her primary concerns were her husband's well-being and that of her family.

Perhaps the greatest criticism of Davis lies in his cronyism. Two of the worst examples are Braxton Bragg (left) and Leonidas Polk (right). Bragg, fifth in West Point's class of 1837, had impressed Davis in Mexico. He left the army in 1857 for the life of a Louisiana planter but was among the first West Pointers around which Davis organized the Confederate army. While Bragg's field experience was dismal, he was one of Davis's most loyal officers, which Davis always rewarded with additional responsibility. Polk and Davis had been close friends at the military academy, but Polk had resigned his commission shortly after graduation to pursue an ecclesiastical career. At the time of the war he was Episcopal bishop of Louisiana. Davis appointed him a major general with the great responsibility of defending the vast western regions. Polk enjoyed brief success and then lost the initiative to his Federal adversaries, but Davis continued to give him critical assignments. On June 14, 1864, he was killed in central Georgia while reconnoitering Sherman's advance.

of Leonidas Polk to command virtually all of what was the northern Mississippi area, one of the most vulnerable areas of the Confederacy. Polk had befriended Davis when the latter was a junior classmate at West Point. Yet Polk, immediately after graduating from the military academy, resigned his commission and never served a single day in uniform. These many years later he was instead an Episcopal bishop. The loss of the Mississippi River in 1862 and 1863 can largely be traced to the mistakes made by Polk at the beginning of the war, and for those mistakes Davis was ultimately responsible.•

Davis made several other unfortunate appointments, but he refused to admit and correct his mistakes. A classic case was his old friend Braxton Bragg, who was given command of the Army of Tennessee. °In a short time the command structure of the Army of Tennessee was in total disarray. The staff devolved into a bunch of backbiters, drunks, and feuding personalities. Davis knew this. He even went to Tennessee to try to settle the situation, but he did not do anything. He did not make any changes even though he had seen firsthand that it was a bad situation.•

Further compounding such problems, Davis was always fiercely loyal to his friends and supporters. At the same time, he would punish those who criticized him, such as Gen. P. G. T. Beauregard, who questioned

Davis's leadership. In 1862, caught up in the pettiness of their personal quarrel, Beauregard said of Davis, "He is either demented or a traitor, a living specimen of gall and hatred."

JMM °The two men had similar personalities. They had an overdeveloped sense of honor, they were thin-skinned, and both of them had a tendency to see disagreement as an insult or as a challenge to their integrity. To rid himself of Beauregard, Davis sent him to the western

WCD theater.• °In so doing, Davis actually crippled the Confederate effort. Later in the war, when Davis was desperate to find a commander for his army in the West, he turned from one insufficient general to another to avoid giving the command to Beauregard.•

Davis's problems were not unique. In the North, President Lincoln was also plagued with egotistical generals, but he had a different way of dealing with them.

WCD °Repeatedly with some of his generals, and especially with George B. McClellan, Lincoln allowed himself to be embarrassed, humiliated, slighted, and snubbed, but he did not react to it. Instead, he kept trying to deal with McClellan diplomatically to get from him the action and the achievements that Lincoln thought

JMM might be there.• °Lincoln, unlike Davis, was willing to lose an argument if it would help him win the war. He once said that he would be willing to hold McClellan's horse if McClellan would only give him victories. One cannot imagine Davis saying that about Beauregard.•

While Davis entrusted the Confederate military to his friends and then suffered the consequences of their failures, he went out of his way to avoid assigning P. G. T. Beauregard (above) any significant command after April 1862. Beauregard was the conqueror of Fort Sumter, a hero of First Manassas, and an almost-victor at Shiloh. His ego grew proportionately, and he and Davis clashed. While Beauregard's reputation exceeded his abilities as a field commander, Davis nevertheless sought to keep him in a subordinate role.

In assembling his cabinet, Davis tried to represent each state of the Confederacy. This well-intentioned gesture sacrificed talent and ability for geography. During the brief history of the Confederate States, only two men maintained their appointment—John H. Reagan and Stephen R. Mallory—while there were four secretaries of state, four attorneys general, five secretaries of war, and two secretaries of the treasury. The original cabinet is depicted here: (from left to right) Attorney General Judah P. Benjamin (Louisiana), Secretary of the Navy Mallory (Florida), Secretary of the Treasury Charles Memminger (South Carolina), Vice President Alexander Stephens, Secretary of War Leroy Walker (Alabama), Davis, Postmaster General Reagan (Texas), and Secretary of State Robert Toombs (Georgia).

Initially, the Confederate Congress, at first a unicameral body, performed admirably. The fire-eaters and radical secessionists had played their role in launching the government and were then displaced by more moderate representatives. The congress then endorsed Davis's emergency war measures and appropriations requests and confirmed the cabinet. By late 1861, however, the good rapport between the chief executive and the legislature deteriorated and continued to do so until the end of the war. Davis was perceived increasingly as dictatorial, and the representatives turned contentious, but the problem devolved largely to the inherent conflict between states' rights and the need for a strong central government in wartime.

Yet Davis had successes, too. It was Davis who promoted and supported a Virginia general with whom he would form one of the greatest military partnerships of the war. WCD °Robert E. Lee bears most of the credit, because Lee excelled at reading the character of others. Lee could read Davis very well, and he knew how to get along with him. Lee never challenged Davis, and he always kept Davis informed.• JMM °Lee came from genuine southern aristocracy, going back to the seventeenth century. He was not a person who suffered from insecurity, and so he could afford to defer to Davis's need for deference and for flattery.•

Davis gave Lee all the men and support he could, and Lee gave Davis a string of victories in the East. After Davis moved his capital to Richmond, Virginia, he would visit Lee at the battlefront whenever possible. GWG °Clearly the Confederate president felt comfortable near the action, and he yearned to take an active part in military affairs.• One reason was that it took him away from other problems, such as the Southern economy, which was in shambles with shortages and raging inflation.

WC In Richmond in April 1863, Davis had to face down a mob of several hundred women who were rioting over the lack of bread. °He jumped up on a wagon and spoke to them, telling them that they had to go home, that they had to bear their share of the privations, and that he would do what he could for them. Just like the soldiers in the field, they had to bear up. He concluded by telling them they had five minutes to disburse or they would be fired upon.•

All the economic problems and the setbacks on the battlefields made Davis a constant target of the press and the Confederate Congress. In 1862, the *Richmond Examiner* exclaimed: "The Confederacy has everything necessary for success, but talent. We must get more talent into the government or be ruined."

JIR As the war progressed, Davis found himself in the impossible position of urging nationalism and unity to people who prided themselves on states' rights and a sense of individuality. °A plantation owner was master of all he surveyed. When the war came, to ask him to cooperate was an action with which he was totally unfamiliar. In the end this strong-minded individualism that had been the dominant force in the growth of the cotton kingdom was also the chief cause of the destruction of the Southern Confederacy.•

JMM Confusion characterized the South's legislative body. °There were a number of fistfights on the floor of the Confederate Congress as well as a number of challenges to duels, which made it an unruly and almost unmanageable body.• Of course, matters were not helped by Davis's assumption that he was always right.

WC °Davis often took disagreement with his views to mean disagreement with the Southern cause, because he in some way came to see that cause embodied in himself.•

In the face of severe food shortages, on April 2, 1863, a crowd of several hundred women and children marched from Richmond's Capitol Square to the city's business district where the leaders said they planned to demand bread from the bakeries. The crowd quickly became a mob of more than a thousand looters. Davis rushed to the scene and urged the women to withdraw and cease the lawlessness, but when that failed to alleviate the situation he ordered them to disperse or be fired upon. The mob scattered, several were arrested, and a few were convicted and sentenced. The Confederate government tried to downplay the incident and asked the newspapers not to report it at all. Instead every newspaper exaggerated the story and some even attributed it to Yankee instigation.

JEFF DAVIS'S LAST APPEAL TO ARMS.
"Fellow Citizens — the Victory is within your reach. You need but STRETCH FORTH YOU'R HANDS TO GRASP IT."—(Address of Jeff Davis to his Soldiers.)

Davis built few bridges politically and none with the press. He was savaged editorially and second-guessed repeatedly, with the most devastating criticisms finding eloquent expression through the art of newspaper cartoonists.

On April 2, 1865, the Confederate defenses at Petersburg collapsed, opening the way for the Union army to seize Richmond. Southern officials, troops, and civilians fled the city almost immediately. Davis was apprised of the news while at St. Paul's Episcopal Church. He met with his cabinet and then went to the Brockenbrough house to oversee the packing of his papers and the family's belongings. His overloaded train departed around 11 P.M. He left behind a city in near riot (facing page). A fire began in the early hours of April 3 and raged for hours with no one to fight it. Shortly after sunrise, Federal troops occupied the smoldering city.

WCD °On the street, if he passed a congressman who was one of his opponents, Davis would sometimes walk past without saying hello or even acknowledging the man's presence.• Recognizing some of his own limitations, Davis acknowledged, "It is strange that a man should be so much in public affairs who is so JIR averse to them as I am." °If he could have mingled in the street and called upon simple patriotism, he would have been eminently more successful. On the Northern side, Billy Yanks as well as civilians affectionately referred to "Father Abraham." Yet nobody called the Southern president "Father Jefferson."•

While Davis seemed aloof in public, those close to him called him a kind, compassionate man. For example, he pardoned nearly every soldier who was sentenced to be shot for desertion.

WC °Many of his biographers believe Davis's own memories of battle and the catalogs of casualties his armies were suffering daily may have influenced his leniency with deserters. His generals hated for appeals to reach his desk, because he usually granted them. The unending slaughter of young men bore down on him.•

That loss of life only grew worse as the war progressed. By mid-1863, the South had lost Mississippi, and Yankee soldiers had vandalized and destroyed Davis's home there. In the East, General Lee had faltered with the crushing loss at Gettysburg. Lee offered to resign, but Davis would not let him, saying, "My dear friend, to ask me to substitute you with someone more fit to command is to demand an impossibility."

Yet it was the Confederate president who bore much of the public blame for the failed campaigns. °Davis WCD being Davis, he maintained some involvement, and occasionally heavy involvement, in the planning of almost every major campaign of the Confederate armies. That done, he rarely interfered. With Gettysburg, for instance, he allowed Lee to plan the invasion. He gave Lee the permission to do it, but after that he stayed out of Lee's way. The fact that the invasion ended in disaster was not Davis's fault.•

GWG °There was probably nothing that Davis could have done that would have changed the outcome of the war. For a while the war could have gone either way. Davis certainly made mistakes, but no one can point to one thing or another that he could have done that would have changed the outcome of the war.•

As THE WAR continued to go against the South, the strain showed on Davis himself. A virus had blinded one of his eyes and badly inflamed the other. °During most of his life, the condition subjected him to occasional bouts of intense pain whenever his eye swelled. There were times when he could not bear to be in a room in which there was any light.• °He also suffered from what nineteenth-century physicians called dyspepsia, a digestive ailment. Frequently during the course of the war, Davis was prostrate in bed, physically incapable of performing his job.•

WCD

JMM

According to Varina, this is the only wartime photograph taken of Davis. It reveals little about the man whom Clement Clay called "the sphinx of the Confederacy."

WCD °Emotionally, the public front Davis showed never varied. He always remained stern, what his friend Clement Clay called "the Sphinx of the Confederacy." But inside, gradually, year after year, the heartache, the trauma, and the tension of the war and of seeing his cause losing slowly ate at Davis and took years off of his life.•

Tragedy visited Davis even more directly. In the spring of 1864 the war was entering its decisive phase. Grant's Union army was poised above Richmond, and Sherman's Federal troops were marching through the Deep South. At the Confederate White House, Davis was in a strategy meeting when one of his six children—six-year-old Joseph—fell off the balcony and was killed.

WC °Davis was overwhelmed. Messengers were bringing him news of the war at that very moment, and he said, "I cannot do it. I cannot. I cannot." He went upstairs WCD and stayed there all night with his son.• °While his wife was heard shrieking in agony inside the house, visitors heard Davis pacing back and forth overhead. The next

The rail line ended at Greensboro, North Carolina. Confronted with the sad facts of his armies' faltering in the face of superior numbers, Davis was forced to admit defeat. With the debris of the Confederate government in tow, he set off for Charlotte with Mallory, Breckinridge, Reagan, and a small military escort on horseback. Upon his arrival, he learned of Abraham Lincoln's assassination and discounted it, remembering the number of times he himself had been reported killed.

day, he was back on the job doing what he had to do as the Confederate president.•

The war would not wait for Davis to mourn. The Confederacy was being battered. Sherman took Atlanta, Grant was closing in, and Davis was forced to take desperate measures. He ordered the recruitment of black soldiers for the Confederate army, something he had said he would never do. °Using slaves as soldiers went against a basic philosophy of Confederate thought. One Confederate senator had said, "Once you make them soldiers, then you have destroyed all the reasons why we keep them as slaves."•

°Davis's willingness to put black men into uniform and give them freedom demonstrated his willingness to do anything to achieve independence. States' rights could go. Even slavery could go, if that was what had to happen to win independence.•

Black soldiers began drilling in the streets of Richmond in early 1865, but it was too late to have any effect on the war. By then, Richmond itself was threatened. Grant had pushed Lee's army so close that Lee

JIR

GWG

Davis and his entourage departed Charlotte with plans of escaping to the Lower South. Wherever the president's party paused on its way through South Carolina, Davis continued to conduct the business of government, and people came to see the dusty, worn, and somewhat noble remnant of the Confederacy. This area had been untouched by the war, and they saw the president as their revered leader, not as an agent of woe. In Georgia, Davis disbanded the government until he and his cabinet could find refuge across the Mississippi River. His first priority then became finding and joining his family, which he did in the predawn hours of May 5.

Federal troopers captured Davis on May 10 near Irwinville, Georgia. Awakened at the news that the Yankees were almost upon them, Davis had barely stepped outside his tent when Varina threw her black shawl over his head and shoulders. Thus the story was born that Davis had tried to elude capture by dressing as a woman. In time, more sinister elements were added to the story, such as the dagger included above.

In addition to trying to disguise her husband with her shawl, Varina also sent one of her servants after Davis with a bucket so that it would appear that the two figures might be going to fetch water. That, too, played well in the story of the fugitive president dressed in women's clothing and incorporated in the cartoon to the right.

could dine with Davis at the Confederate White House between battles. One visitor, the Reverend Charles Minnegerode, observed, "It was sad to see these two men with their terrible responsibilities upon them and the hopeless outlook."

Civilians began fleeing Richmond. Davis sent his own family farther south. On April 2, Davis was at St. Paul's Church when a message arrived from Lee saying that he could protect the capital no longer and that Davis and the cabinet should flee. The Confederate president and what was left of his cabinet headed for Danville, Virginia, leaving Richmond to the looters and the Federals. Davis, certain of his cause, called the move a temporary setback.

°Even though the Congress had left him, his vice president had fled, and the capital had fallen, Davis headed south still convinced that the Confederacy could win the war if it persisted, if it held out, if it kept the faith.° He had barely reached Danville when he learned that his finest army no longer existed. Lee had been forced to surrender to Grant at Appomattox. Again Davis moved his capital, this time to Greensboro, North Carolina, and again he vowed to fight on.

°Davis was on the verge of losing touch with reality. It was evident to everyone else that the Southern cause was completely lost, but Davis, by his very nature,

Davis and his party were taken to Macon, Georgia, where photographer A. J. Riddle made this May 13, 1865, image of the ambulance and wagon that carried the captives. Col. Benjamin Pritchard's troopers occupied the street in front of Gen. James H. Wilson's headquarters.

WC could not admit defeat.• °When he arrived in North Carolina and met with his generals there who were commanding the Army of Tennessee, he wanted them to keep fighting. They looked at him, however, as if he had lost his mind.•

At what would be his last cabinet meeting, everyone present told Davis the fight was over, that it would be a WCD crime to continue. °When Davis heard that, he slumped down in his chair, almost fainting, and said, "Then I suppose all truly is lost." He tried to leave the room but had to be helped up by his secretary of war, John C. Breckinridge. Because he was so dejected, so traumatized by the admission to himself of the situation, he could not stand on his feet.•

WC °Davis could not accept the fact that the war was lost. His own son had died. His older brother and surrogate father was a refugee. All that he had owned had been destroyed. And hundreds of thousands of young Southerners were dead. If all this sacrifice were for naught, Davis simply could not face that.•

Alone now except for a small guard, Davis headed farther south, still speaking of fighting on. In Georgia he caught up with his family. Finally, on May 10, Yankee troopers surrounded his camp. Davis tried to escape on foot. Varina threw a shawl over him to hide his face, but a trooper saw him, and the Confederate president was a prisoner. His captors carried him off singing, "We'll hang Jeff Davis from a sour apple tree."

James H. Wilson was one of the boy generals, an officer who had rapidly risen in command to the rank of general while still in his twenties. A protégé of sorts to U. S. Grant, he failed to impress Philip H. Sheridan and quickly found himself in the West. He distinguished himself against the legendary Nathan Bedford Forrest, and his command received commendations for capturing Jefferson Davis.

Davis was imprisoned at Fort Monroe in Casemate Number Two and placed under the care of Maj. Gen. Nelson A. Miles. Because he was in Virginia and because several Confederate commands were still in the field, there was a general feeling of anxiety over the possibility of Davis's escaping. With Washington's blessing, Miles had Davis placed in leg irons, but public outcry caused them to be removed after five days. Other indignities befell Davis, however, including letters from former slaves congratulating him on his new position or contributions to his defense fund in the form of worthless Confederate currency. In the name of security, a light was kept burning in his cell all night, guards were stationed inside the cell with orders not to speak to the prisoner, and an officer of the guard inspected the area at fifteen-minute intervals. Davis paid a physical price for these restrictions, and after several months the measures were relaxed and his health improved. In October he was moved from the casemate cell to regular quarters at the fort. The noted artist Alfred Waud sketched Davis in his casemate cell (above), but the press enjoyed ridiculing the former Confederate president's complaints regarding his early rough treatment (below).

AFTER HIS CAPTURE, Davis was taken from Georgia to Fort Monroe, Virginia. Davis and nearly everyone else expected that he would be tried for treason. In the meantime, he was given rough treatment: °his legs were chained together by manacles, he was confined to his cell, he was given limited food, very limited exercise, and no access to visitors. His health began to deteriorate accordingly.•

WCD

GWG °Here was a man who had owned slaves, who had been raised in a slave-owning society; for that man to be put in shackles carried with it a much deeper message than it would to someone put in shackles today. Being manacled was a tremendous humiliation for Davis, one that left deep scars on him.°

After public outcry in both the North and the South, the leg irons were removed, but it would be a year before Davis was allowed to see his wife. There were other punishments. He received letters from newly freed slaves congratulating him on his confinement and their freedom. The Northern press also spread the rumor that Davis had been captured wearing, not a shawl, but a petticoat, and that he had tried to escape in women's clothes. One editorial put it this way: "A peal of laughter goes ringing round the globe. Davis, with the blood of thousands of noble victims upon his soul, will go down to posterity cowering under a petticoat."

WCD °Northerners were very anxious to promulgate this notion because it humiliated Davis. It helped to dehumanize him. It turned him into a coward. It made him ridiculous.°

WC °The garments actually worn by Davis during his attempt at escape eventually arrived in Washington, and Secretary of War Edwin Stanton realized what they were. He had them kept under lock and key, and generations passed before anyone ever saw them again. The official position of the government was that Abraham Lincoln's adversary had been captured in women's clothes, because that was an appropriate way for the hated Davis to have been apprehended as far as the politicians were concerned.°

Davis's suffering, however, made him a hero in the South. He was more popular after the war than he had ever been as president. JJR °The southern people began to see Davis as representing all that was the embodiment of what they would later call the Lost Cause. And so, in their minds and

While Davis was imprisoned for the better part of two years, public opinion mounted to release him. Although he was anxious for a trial in which he believed he would prove that secession was not treason and that the war had been nothing but self-defense for the South, his captors vacillated. Secretary of war Edwin Stanton was one of the last impediments to Davis's freedom, and Varina approached him through friends. The matter was then allowed to shift from the military to civil authorities. Just over two years from the date of his capture, Davis was remanded to civil custody in Richmond's courthouse and released on bond. The case was never prosecuted.

*Four of the Davis children were pho-
tographed in Montreal after the war,
awaiting their father's release. During
the war, the youngest, Joseph, had
fallen from the balcony of the Confederate White House and died. Varina
had been inconsolable, but matters of
state and military strategy allowed the
president little time to grieve. A month
later Davis had the balcony torn down.*

WCD hearts, they flocked to him.* °He
became a martyr, almost a Christlike
figure—the one who was paying the
price for the sins of all by this very
public captivity.* Davis himself viewed
his captivity this way and wrote, "If I
alone could bear all the suffering of the
country, I trust our heavenly Father
would give me the strength to be a
willing sacrifice." The impression of
martyrdom was further reinforced by a
gift from the pope, a crown of thorns
to signify Davis's suffering. The pope
had made it himself.

As the months dragged on, Washington was not sure what to do with
Davis. Many other Confederates had been granted pardons, but Davis refused to ask for one. He wanted to go
on trial to prove that secession had been legal; the
WC issue had never been legally settled. °The reason he
never went to trial was that the federal government was
afraid that he would be found right. He would have
been tried in Virginia, before a jury, and the government was very nervous that a jury might, in fact, find
for Davis.*

*In 1877 the Davis family settled in at
Beauvoir, near Biloxi, Mississippi. This
photograph is from 1882 and shows
Davis and Varina on the front porch
with their daughter, Margaret Davis
Hayes, and her three children. Here
life for the mostly bankrupt Davises
settled down, the former president's
health improved, and their fortunes
seemed to improve.*

In his last years Davis found a sense of serenity and peace at Beauvoir. Old friends, including some Yankees, came to visit, and Davis proved to be a genial host. When he was not occupied with his task of writing his history of the conflict, he would position some chairs near the window of the parlor or take his guests onto the verandah to enjoy the sea breezes and talk amiably and charmingly.

When he finished writing his memoirs, his justification for all that he had done, the rambling, disjointed two-volume work contributed to several postwar controversies. Numerous petty quarrels arose from the offended sensibilities of his former generals and their counterparts, such as Johnston, Beauregard, Sherman, and Grant.

Pressure grew on Washington to simply free Davis. A group of wealthy northerners, including Cornelius Vanderbilt, offered to pay his bail. In 1867 a bail hearing was held in the same Richmond building Davis had used as his capitol during the war. It was a formality. Bail was granted, a crowd cheered, and WC Davis was free to go. °He came out of the courtroom and walked past the door to what had been his private office when he was president of the Confederacy as he left the building.•

In frail health, he traveled to Canada to stay with relatives. On a family outing in 1867 at Niagara Falls, he looked across the border and saw the Stars and Stripes. "Look there!" he said. "There is the gridiron we have been fried on."

Shortly afterward, Davis returned to Mississippi, to his plantation, which had been turned into a home for freed WCD slaves. °He found himself virtually a ruined man. His plantation was largely overgrown. His crops were gone. His house vandalized by Federal soldiers.

Davis fell ill en route to an inspection of Brierfield and returned only as far as New Orleans, where he died at the age of eighty-two on December 6, 1889. The funeral was perhaps the largest ever seen in the South, with possibly two hundred thousand mourners in attendance. Davis was interred in the Army of Northern Virginia tomb at Metarie. Three years later his body was moved to Richmond's Hollywood Cemetery to join his son Joseph, several U.S. presidents, Jeb Stuart, and nineteen other Confederate generals.

He had no money.• Viewing his former home, he lamented: "I found everything I had destroyed or scattered. It was new to be in debt and without resources."

Davis eventually received his plantation back, but he could never make a living from it. He tried the insurance business, but that failed. He was finally forced to accept the charity of an admirer, Sarah Dorsey, who allowed him to stay in her home, Beauvoir, near Biloxi, GWG Mississippi. °In spite of his service in the Congress and the cabinet, valiant performance in the war with Mexico, and dutiful execution of the office of presidency of the Confederacy—the man who did all that found himself essentially beholden to people who were kind enough to give him what he needed to feed and clothe his family after the war.•

Davis began writing his memoirs, in which he wc defended secession and apologized to no one. °He was very much opposed to those people in the South who were trying to put the war behind them and get on with their lives. He said that they were forgetting their heritage, they were forgetting what 1861—the decision to secede—had meant, and their attention and focus should be riveted on those things for which the South had fought.•

He would live to the age of eighty-one, long enough to see all of his four sons die and a daughter become engaged to a Yankee from New York. When he died in December 1889, Davis had outlived the Confederacy and Abraham Lincoln by twenty-four years. His funeral was the largest in southern memory.

JIR °Every age needs a romantic, and Jefferson Davis answered the South's call at that time. If his devotion to the South was unrealistic, it was also magnificent. It was a quality of mind one can call patriotism.•

WCD °Given that Confederate defeat was inevitable, it would have been impossible to find anyone else who could have made as outstanding an effort as Davis did. He probably kept the cause alive as much as a year longer than anyone else could have been

WC expected to.• °As a result, he was a very sad man, because the world that he had known and cherished and to which he had devoted himself disappeared and collapsed. Yet he could not bring himself to say, "I had responsibility for it."•

GWG °It was that contrast between Lincoln's tremendous abilities and Davis's lack of those abilities that has made many people criticize Davis even more than they might have. In truth, it is unfair in many ways to criticize Davis because he was not Abraham Lincoln; nobody else has been Abraham Lincoln either.•

Davis remained a die-hard Confederate to the end. Although he finally accepted the reality of the Union, he never apologized for either secession or for slavery. Just before his death, he said, "Were the thing to be done over again, I would do as I then did. Disappointments have not changed my conviction."

The southern people never loved Davis as they did Lee, nor venerated him as they did Jackson, but they came to respect him with a stubborn pride that mirrored his own. He possessed an uncompromising spirit that led to the shackles of Fort Monroe and, in a sense, an atonement for the South, symbolized in the crown of thorns (below) prepared by Pope Pius IX and sent to Davis while he was still imprisoned.

STONEWALL JACKSON

There is NO PERIOD in the history of the United States that compares with the four years between 1861 and 1865. It was an age containing all the necessary ingredients for the making of American heroes. It was a time when beliefs were strong, battles were bloody, and bravery was admired beyond all else. With the Civil War came a series of events that could sometimes transform even the most ordinary men into mythical figures. One such man was Thomas Jonathan Jackson, better known as "Stonewall."

Col. F. W. M. Holliday, commander of the Thirty-third Virginia Infantry, described Jackson, noting: "Most of the actors in the world's drama are those who come and go and perform their work without enchaining our highest intention and admiration. But now and then, an individual appears, marking his advent and stay with evidences of marvelous superiority to his contemporaries in some high sphere of human action. We cannot always define by name his splendid traits and, for want of a better term, we say he is gifted among mortals with genius. Such was Stonewall Jackson. He was the very genius of war."

RKK °Jackson was a quiet, cautious, thoughtful, family man of whom almost no one had heard or ever would have heard except for the fact that the American Civil War gave him an arena in which he became one of the leading actors.• JIR °He was Robert E. Lee's greatest lieutenant in the South's foremost army. That in itself would give him a certain status, a certain station in the affairs of the Southern Confederacy. But his campaigns in the

WCD	William C. Davis
KEG	Keith E. Gibson
RKK	Robert K. Krick
MAL	Michael Ann Lynn
BP	Brian Pohanka
JIR	James I. Robertson Jr.
ALR	Armstead L. Robinson

79

Jackson was born on January 21, 1824, in this house near Clarksburg, Virginia, now in West Virginia (right). He was an orphan at age six and was raised by an uncle.

Jackson's admission to West Point was based more on his potential than his scholarly experience, and he advanced steadily through the ranks of his class as he campaigned in the spirit of his favorite maxim: You may be whatever you resolve to be. Initially ranked with the Immortals—the bottom of the class—he graduated seventeenth of fifty-nine in 1846. Hanging his diploma (below) in his study in Lexington was the closest thing to pride of which Jackson could be accused.

field created the myth, the legend of a man who was in a hundred places at one time.•

WCD

°Jackson defeated three Yankee armies single-handedly, and all of them combined outnumbered him four to one. There was no way something like that could not have had a catastrophic, more like a cataclysmic, effect on the course of the war. The fear that Jackson's name came to inspire in some Yankee soldiers gave him an edge over them if they knew they were going up against the Mighty Stonewall.•

BP

°At the mention of his name there were immediate fears for the safety of Washington, and the earthen forts that ringed the city and safeguarded it would be manned to the fullest. Jackson was truly a legend in his own time, and the inscrutable nature of Jackson himself furthered the mythic image.•

JIR

°He was a complicated man because he looked at things with such incredible simplicity. One obeyed or one disobeyed. One was a God-fearing man or one was not a God-fearing man. Jackson's whole life was a rather simple life for a man who had very complicated inner workings.•

RKK °Jackson genuinely believed that God was watching his every step. God was on his side, guiding every one of those steps. Before the Civil War, and particularly during the war, because his steps were so often successful, he absolutely believed that he owed that to God and that he was God's instrument on earth.•

BP °In his style, in his persona, Jackson was certainly not the Napoleonic ideal of a dashing soldier. He was somewhat rumpled in his appearance and eccentric in his mannerisms. He would be missing a button on his coat and not think much of it. He rode a rather sorry-looking horse, not a prancing stallion, and yet the very fact that he was not given to that foofaraw and foppery enabled him to establish a rapport with the common soldier, with the man in the ranks that is perhaps the most important bond that can be formed in warfare.•

JIR °As Jackson led his men to success after success, giving all the credit to God, asking them to do the impossible but leading them to victories and, at the same time, leading them to fame, they responded with respect and a high esteem that they felt for him.•

WCD °Jackson was the necessary Greek hero of the war. He did all the right things. He had just enough oddity of

The class of 1846 had just graduated when war broke out with Mexico. Jackson was anxious to fight and saw action in the battles of Vera Cruz, Contreras, Molino del Rey, and Chapultepec. With eighteen months in the field, he had three brevet promotions. At Molino del Rey (above) he was mostly a spectator. His battery was positioned at the far left end of the line and saw only brief fighting when a column of Mexican cavalry threatened to charge his position, which underscored for Jackson another maxim of war—the futility of a blind attack against a fortified position.

81

When the picture above was taken of Jackson in Mexico City in 1847, he was the most celebrated member of the West Point class of 1846. His heroic performance on the exposed causeway leading into Mexico City had drawn the notice of his commanding general, Winfield Scott, who publicly commended him.

A war hero, Jackson returned to Virginia and accepted a teaching position at the Virginia Military Institute (below).

character to make him personally interesting. He was brilliant at what he did, and he died at exactly the right time. He set up the creation of the myth and the speculation of all the might-have-beens.•

Yet long before he became the Mighty Stonewall, long before he gained legendary status, and long before he was the physical embodiment of Confederate patriotism, Thomas Jonathan Jackson lived a life almost foreshadowing what was to come. For thirty-seven years he honed the tools he ultimately needed to help shape history.

Jackson was born in 1824 in what is now West Virginia. By his fifth birthday, both his parents had died. By the time he reached adolescence, all his siblings but one had also died. He had been placed with a relative, Cummings Jackson, who then became responsible for his upbringing.

°He was reared on a large estate that contained a gristmill, sawmill, racetrack, fields, and herds. It was a diverse agricultural enterprise, so he learned to do many things and to do them well. Like most farm boys of that era, he attended school three months out of the year, during the short period between planting and harvesting. There he picked up the rudiments of arithmetic, English grammar, and composition. Armed with that minimal education, he went to West Point.•

In 1851 Jackson settled into the lifestyle of a small college town, discovered the denomination for which he had been searching, and two years later married Elinor Junkin, the daughter of a Presbyterian minister. The marriage lasted but a year, ending when Ellie died trying to give birth to a son. The loss was devastating for Jackson, and he turned to his church for support. Rather than dwell on his own needs, he began teaching a Sunday school class for Lexington's black residents. Jackson became a member of the Lexington community in the fullest sense, and in the summer of 1856 he took a leave of absence from teaching and toured Europe.

MAL °In many ways admission to the military academy was an entrée into the world of gentlemen and respectability. Jackson made the most of that opportunity even though he was self-conscious in his efforts at self-improvement.•

JIR °Few people at West Point thought that Jackson could ever be a military genius. He entered as a poor orphan, deficient in the knowledge of social amenities, not even knowing which knife or fork to use in a meal. In the first year at the military academy, he was ranked solidly in what West Pointers today still call the Immortals: he was at the very bottom of his class.•

RKK °Jackson's experience at West Point was almost his life in microcosm: starting out a little bit behind, catching up, and then forging onward. His progress was not so much brilliance and intuitive learning ability as it was a remarkable sense of determination.•

JIR °At West Point he began keeping a book of maxims, and he jotted down whatever one-liners he heard that impressed him. One of his favorites was "You may be whatever you resolve to be." And he lived by that axiom.• One of Jackson's fellow cadets recalled: "All lights were put out at taps. And just before the signal, he would pile up his grate with coal, and lying prone before it on the floor, he would work away at his lessons by the glare of the fire, which scorched his very brain until a late hour of

Jackson returned from Europe with an appreciation of the art and architecture of the Continent, but he was also on a mission to remarry. He approached another minister's daughter, Mary Anna Morrison (above), whom he had known before his marriage to Ellie. She accepted his proposal after a brief Christmas campaign won the family's approval in which he demonstrated high Christian principles, never-failing politeness, and good humor. They courted through the mail, he in Lexington, she in North Carolina, and they were married in July 1857.

Their only surviving child, Julia (below), named for Jackson's mother, was born in 1862.

the night. This evident determination to succeed not only aided his own efforts directly, but impressed his instructors in his favor, and he rose steadily, year by year, until we used to say, 'If we had to stay here another year, old Jack would be at the head of the class.'"

When Jackson graduated from West Point in 1846, he was seventeenth in a class of fifty-nine. A combination of persistence, perseverance, and determination was the driving force behind the steady climb that landed him within the top third of his class. These same characteristics would later turn the ordinary man into a legendary general. But in 1846 a hero's reputation was still more than a decade away. War, however, was not. Fighting in Mexico had already begun, and Jackson, along with his classmates, was ordered to proceed to the scene of the action.

JACKSON ENTERED MEXICO as a second lieutenant of artillery. It was there that he first tasted the bitterness of war. For two years he played the part of soldier, engaging in battle after battle and arming himself with more of the necessary skills he would later use to lead Confederate soldiers to some of their most significant victories.

He found his character fortified in combat, and in Mexico he first established himself as Thomas Jonathan Jackson, the fighting man. °From the moment he arrived in Mexico, he was anxious to fight. There was no hesitation, no fear in him. He wanted to get into a battle to find out if he could fight and if he could do well at it. Within a year he had been in three major engagements and had received three breveted promotions for gallantry.•

°Out where the bullets were flying, Jackson was very much distinguished. In the assault upon Mexico City in September 1847, he was second in command of a battery on one of the causeways that approached the city. The site was a bad place to be, raised above the surrounding ground; the Mexican army swept the area with both musket and cannon fire. Jackson's guns were exposed on that causeway, but he stood to them and ignored the danger. Later he marveled to someone that he had not noticed the danger. He was not ignoring it so much as he was unaware of it.•

JIR °Jackson was certainly the most celebrated member of the class of 1846, and he came out of the Mexican War with the rank of brevet major. He had learned many things in the war, such as the value of flanking movements, the value of staff work, and the value of concentrated attacks. At the same time he learned orderliness and discipline and devotion to duty, and suddenly he realized he liked those kinds of things very much. He came out of the Mexican War committed to the military.•

His experience had given him recognition, but more importantly, he had armed himself with more of the necessary characteristics for which he would later become famous. Along with perseverance and determination, there was now obedience and devotion to duty, but the Civil War was not yet even a spark on the horizon. Jackson's battle experience, however, was still a valuable asset, winning him more than brevet promotions to major.

In 1851 he was offered a position at the prestigious Virginia Military Institute, better known as VMI, in Lexington. In accepting the position, Jackson wrote: "Colonel, your letter of the 28th informing me that I have been elected Professor of Natural and Experimental Philosophy and Artillery Tactics in the Virginia Military Institute has been received. The high honor conferred by the Board of Visitors in selecting me unanimously to fill such a Professorship gratified me exceedingly. I am, Colonel, very respectfully, your obedient servant."

RKK °He was admired because of his successes during the Mexican War, and VMI was a military school, but by and large the school viewed him as only a moderately WCD successful teacher.• °He did not have a teacher's instincts. His approach to teaching was the same as his approach to everything else: things were white or black, right or wrong. Everything was rigid. There were no shades of gray in Jackson's intellect. Just as he had learned by memorizing his lessons, teaching for him was exactly the same thing. He taught by rote.•

JIR °By now he had poor eyesight. As a result he could not or would not study at night, so on the afternoon before

Laura Arnold (above) was Jackson's only sister, and the two were very close. Shortly after their mother's death, Laura was claimed by an aunt who felt it improper for a young lady to be alone with so many bachelor uncles. Jackson was disappointed at the outbreak of the war to see her express Unionist sympathies, but that did not stop their communication.

In 1861 Jackson (below) had not yet let his whiskers grow, and the artist depicted him as he was when he led the cadet corps of VMI to Richmond for duty as drill instructors.

On July 21, 1861, Jackson was ordered to take a position on Henry House Hill on the Manassas battlefield. In the course of the fighting that occurred below that site, Gen. Barnard Bee, who had known Jackson at West Point and had seen him in action at Chapultepec in 1847, pointed to the Virginian and rallied his own forces with the immortal and somewhat enigmatic cry, "There is Jackson standing like a stone wall. Let us determine to die here, and we will conquer." Exactly what Bee meant by these words was lost when he was mortally wounded and died the next day. Nevertheless, the sobriquet of Stonewall became attached to Jackson from that day forward.

the next day's classes, he memorized his lectures. The next morning he would recite the information to his classes. This was fine for the A students, but if a C or D student asked for elaboration or expansion, that was beyond Jackson's ability. All he could do was repeat what he had memorized verbatim. The student had better not ask a second time for elaboration, because Jackson viewed that as insubordination and might place the student on report.•

Recognizing Jackson's shortcomings in the classroom, Col. Francis H. Smith, superintendent of the Institute, observed: "As a Professor of Natural and Experimental Philosophy, Major Jackson was not a success. He had not the qualifications needed for so important a chair. He was no teacher, and he lacked the tact required in getting along with his classes. Every officer and every cadet respected him for his many sterling qualities. He was a brave man, a conscientious man, and a good man, but he was no professor."

KEG

°It was in his other capacity, as a professor of artillery tactics, that Jackson, not only was more comfortable, but he had the undeniable respect and atten-

JIR tion of his cadet corps.• °There are innumerable instances of graduating or high-ranking cadets in their final year at VMI making statements, who dreaded the memory of Jackson's classroom but admitted that if they ever had to go into battle, they would want to go in with him.•

Many of those same cadets would later become his soldiers. They would also become the backbone of the artillery branch of the Confederate army. These cadets followed him in command at VMI as they followed him in war. In 1858 VMI cadet Lee Wilbur Reed commented: "There's something in his very mode of life, so accurate, steady, void of care or strife that fills my heart with love for him who bears his honors meekly, and who wears the laurels of a hero. This is fact. So here is a heart and hand of mine for Jack."

JIR While the cadets had placed their faith in Jackson, he placed his in God. °It was only after he came to Lexington that he finally found the denomination that he had been seeking for the past four or five years, the Presbyterian Church. Yet it is almost incorrect to say that he became a Presbyterian; Jackson became a Calvinist and practiced an old-line, hard-shell faith.•

WCD °His was a religion of the Bible and the Bible taken literally. Jackson probably would have been a fanatic at any religion he would have adopted, because it was the way his turn of mind worked and was characteristic of his single-minded dedication to a goal.•

Following the battle of Fredericksburg, Jackson and his staff were invited to stay at the Corbin home, known as Moss Neck. The general was not inclined to inconvenience the family, but an earache led him to ask for temporary lodgings, which they offered willingly and gladly to a hero of the Confederacy. The Corbins invited him to use a wing of the house for his winter headquarters, but Jackson declined, saying that the house was "too luxurious for a soldier, who should sleep in a tent." A compromise was reached, however, and the Stonewall Brigade's headquarters was established in the yard near the house. Jackson described the home as "one of the most beautiful buildings I have seen in this country."

Jackson's men adored him. The Valley campaign had made him a hero to the South, and his euphonious nickname inspired those around him and unnerved his opponents. He was himself a man of few words, but the impression he made on his troops evoked torrents. Artilleryman Robert Stile saw Jackson on the Virginia Peninsula and wrote: "He sat stark and stiff in the saddle. Horse and rider appeared worn down to the lowest point of flesh consistent with effective service. His hair, skin, eyes, and clothes were all one neutral tint, and his badges of rank so dulled and tarnished as to be scarcely perceptible. The 'mangy little cadet cap' was pulled so low in front that the visor cut the glint of his eyeballs."

Jackson became known for his strong beliefs, but it was not his faith that caused the people of Lexington to single him out. °He had the kind of a personality that attracted people who would be intrigued by his quirks precisely because he was eccentric. Jackson was certainly not unique, but among the general run of southern men in his class, he was a little peculiar.°

°Jackson was very much a hypochondriac. One of the most frequently told stories about him—and it apparently was true—was that he rode with one hand in the air because he thought that the limbs on one side of his body were larger than the other and the blood needed to drain out of one. He attributed this and some of his other woes to eating pepper and therefore eliminated it from his diet.°

°He tended to eat things he did not like, believing that they would be better for him than to eat the things he did enjoy; one had to be careful of earthly pleasures. He once ate bread with butter on it and decided he liked it so much that he ate bread without butter thereafter.°

Unlike many generals in the field, Jackson was not an impressive looking figure. One Union prisoner caught a glimpse of the infamous Stonewall and said, "Boys, he ain't much for looks, but if we'd had him we wouldn't have got caught in this trap." A correspondent for a Northern newspaper described him as "seedy" and declared that his "general appearance was in no respect to be distinguished from the mongrel, barefooted crew who follow his fortunes."

Despite his oddities Jackson was an accepted member of the community. In Lexington he had found his faith. In Lexington he had become a gentleman. And in Lexington he learned about love. In the early 1850s, he met Elinor Junkin, the daughter of a Presbyterian minister and the president of Washington College, Dr. George Junkin. Once again he was faced with a new experience.

JIR °Jackson did not understand what was happening to him in the early 1850s when he and Elly, as he called her, became close friends. It was up to a colleague who taught math at Washington College to laughingly tell Jackson that he was in love, that these pains and strange feelings were romance.•

In 1853 Jackson and Elly were married and lived happily in Lexington. Then, after only fifteen months, the marriage ended. Elly and their unborn baby died during childbirth, and Jackson was devastated. He relied on his faith to overcome his grief, later writing: "I frequently go to the grave of her who was so pure and lovely. But she is not there. When I stand over the grave, I do not fancy that she is thus confined, but I think of her as having a glorified existence."

JIR °Two years later, in 1856, he took a summer tour of Europe. He returned thoroughly fascinated by all that he had seen, but also Jackson had the idea that life might be more satisfactory if he had a companion. So he contacted another minister's daughter, Mary Anna Morrison, and renewed their friendship. In July 1857 they were married.•

It looked as if Jackson would spend the rest of his life in Lexington, but by the beginning of the 1860s, the dark clouds of war were looming over the nation. Jackson himself noted: "I am anxious to hear from the native part of my state. I am strong for the Union at present, and if things become no worse, I hope to continue so."

WCD °Jackson had very much a Virginian attitude, the border state attitude, which is that the Union was the Union and he was loyal to it as long as it was together. If Virginia, however, happened to join with the Confederacy, then that was where Jackson's allegiance would be.•

By 1861 the country was tearing in two, and Jackson believed it was not only his duty to defend JIR his home state, but a necessary fight of faith. °He believed that God had ordained a civil war on America for reasons neither he nor any other mortal had a right to question. This war was a scourge, Old Testament fashion, of the land. He believed

Jackson always credited God for his abilities and successes on the field. He fought desperately against the sin of ambition, and through fortitude, deep faith, and the asceticism that army life allowed, he seemed to win that struggle. The general frequently held prayer services among his staff in camp. One visitor noted, "He did not pray to men, but to God. His tones were deep, solemn, tremulous. . . . I never heard any one pray who seemed to be pervaded more fully by a spirit of self-abnegation. He seemed to feel more than any man I ever knew the danger of robbing God of the glory due for our success."

that the side that displayed the most confidence in and respect for the Almighty would ultimately triumph in this war.° In April 1861, Jackson marched into war, and soon the country was introduced to the legendary Stonewall.

FOR JACKSON, THE Civil War marked the beginning of a new era. For thirty-seven years, he had unknowingly prepared himself for his final twenty-three months. By the end of April 1861 Thomas Jonathan Jackson the fighting man had returned, and by the end of July 1861 Thomas Jonathan Jackson the Mighty Stonewall had emerged.

RKK   °A colonel at the beginning of the war, he was still Thomas Jackson—not yet having earned his nom de guerre—and he was posted to the frontier of Virginia, which was Harpers Ferry. His troops fought a little battle the first week of July 1861 at Falling Waters, really not much of an affair. Then commanding five Virginia regiments, he led them as a brigade to the battle of First Bull Run, or Manassas, as the Southerners called it.°

JIR   °Manassas was not so much a battle between armies as it was the collision of two armed mobs, with inexperience being the common factor.° Henry Kyd Douglas, an aide on Jackson's staff, described the anxiety that afternoon, saying, "Wavering had been the fortunes of the days, and the hours passed slowly to men who'd never tasted battle before."

JIR   °The key position was Henry House Hill, and Jackson and his brigade—with an artillery battery—were positioned there.° Obeying orders, he stood his ground while a brigade of Confederate soldiers under the command of Gen. Barnard Bee fought part of the bloody battle below.

WCD   °Bee's brigade was being annihilated by the Federals at this point, and Jackson's brigade was in position but

The daily, dreary administration of an army tested a commanding general in ways combat did not. Although he commanded his brigade efficiently, Jackson's administrative skills were not one of his strengths, but he never failed to learn from experience. His concern for details took him around his camps frequently, and the faded blue coat, slouched kepi, dusty boots, and Little Sorrel were familiar sights to everyone under Jackson's command. Those who saw him up close or spoke to him experienced the strength of his personality. A big man, standing close to six feet, his deep blue eyes maintained a steady gaze and conveyed an inner determination that could be frightening or encouraging, depending on one's circumstances.

Jackson demonstrated his strategic and tactical abilities in the Valley campaign. While he had not done particularly well on the Peninsula, his operations after that impressed his superiors in the South and heightened his notoriety in the North. Everything he did became legendary. His single-minded efficiency at Second Manassas, Harpers Ferry, and Antietam gave Robert E. Lee unqualified confidence in this hero of the Confederacy. Lee recognized Jackson's contributions in September 1862 with promotion to lieutenant general.

not really doing anything. Bee's Alabamians were in advance of the line and taking heavy losses when Bee said something to the effect, "Look! There stands Jackson like a stone wall. Let us resolve to die here, and we shall conquer."•

Shortly after that, Bee was wounded, dying a day later, but his words lived on, and a legend was born. It was in that instant that Thomas Jonathan Jackson became Stonewall. More than a century later, there is no question as to where and when Jackson was renamed, but the moment is not without controversy. There still remains the question of the meaning of Bee's words. Was Jackson standing strong as a stone wall, or was he merely frozen on the hillside while his fellow countrymen were being killed?

JIR   °There are writers who say that Bee was not referring to Jackson as a stone wall in a positive note. He meant that Jackson was dragging his feet at Manassas. The evidence, however, is too strong in Jackson's favor for that kind of argument to have any validity whatsoever. Jackson was holding the position he was ordered to hold.•

RKK   °When the Federals finally closed on those five regiments standing like a stone wall, Jackson, in fact, held them and proved to be the pivot of the day. He was the bulwark on which the Federal advance stopped and eventually was broken as more Confederates came to that position.•

The men of Jackson's staff were young, hard-working, and pious and possessed a good sense of humor. As Jackson's command enlarged, they were needed to address the difficult problems of supply and logistics. In 1863 his staff was composed of (clockwise) chief of staff R. L. Dabney, chief of ordnance W. Allan, assistant adjutant general Sandie Pendleton, aide Joseph G. Morrison, provost marshal D. B. Bridgeford, aide Henry Kyd Douglas, aide J. P. Smith, chief medical officer Hunter McGuire, topographical engineer Jedediah Hotchkiss, and chief of commissary W. J. Hawks. They were likable, energetic, and jovial. They were also capable and mirrored much of their general's personality.

Manassas was a Confederate victory, but more than a battle had been won. The South now had its first war hero. Jackson and the men he had trained left the field as symbols of the courage behind the Rebel cause. Together they represented the strength and protection of a stone wall.

RKK °The fame that followed became part and parcel of him and also of the brigade he led. The brigade that had stood on Henry House Hill was promptly called the Stonewall Brigade, and eventually it was the only unit in Confederate service that had a formal nickname. The rest were only numbered.°

WCD °Jackson had a tremendously motivated command under him. They were all Virginians. They were all fighting for their homeland since it was Virginia that had been

The two armies began skirmishing near Chancellorsville on May 1, 1863, but the Union army under Joseph Hooker withdrew to the crossroads as night fell. That night Lee and Jackson, sitting on cracker boxes, devised one of the most daring plans in military history. Defying conventional strategic and tactical thinking, Lee divided his force, sending Jackson on a flanking march around the right side of the Federal line.

invaded. The invader's heel was on their hearts, so they had the best motivation any man can have to go to war.•

JIR °Jackson had done an incredible job of taking a bunch of militiamen, old veterans, and young recruits and welding them into a reasonably efficient military machine. He drilled them in the typical Jackson fashion. He paid no attention to time, no attention to need, WCD no attention to meals or rest.• °His men came to average about twenty miles a day of hard marching. A person in good shape can easily walk twenty miles a day, but not carrying a forty- to fifty-pound pack and an eight-pound rifle and wearing a wool or heavy cotton uniform in a hot summer sun.•

Maj. Gen. M. C. Butler of the Army of Northern Virginia observed: "There was a charm about General Jackson which inspired all private soldiers under his command with a sublime, unquestioned confidence in his leadership. An indescribable something amounting almost to fascination on the part of his soldiers that induced them to do uncomplainingly whatever he would order."

JIR °Now when one thought of Jackson, one thought of long hard marches. His men became accustomed to them and took them as a challenge. Many of them thought that what he was asking was impossible, but they were determined to do whatever he demanded.° Marveling at this esprit de corps, General Butler noted, "It was not the inspiration of fear, but a deep and abiding devotion to his person, to his character, to his matchless and unerring leadership and self-sacrifice." To the South they were known as the Stonewall Brigade, but to each other, they were Jackson's foot cavalry. As for Stonewall himself, in 1861 he was promoted to general.

RKK   °The legend of Jackson was not only growing, but people took hold of it and made themselves part of it and basked in its reflective glory. This of course redounded to the military good of the Confederate states, because the more élan the units had, the better they would fight. Success breeds success in all human endeavors, and most especially, it seems, in military affairs.°

IN THE SPRING of 1862 the legend grew again when the Mighty Stonewall and his men began the campaign that cemented their reputations. Their symbolic structure of strength was hardened by the battles fought on the fields of their homeland in the Shenandoah Valley. Here Jackson truly became a legend by leading an operation that is still considered one of the most brilliant in military history.

The Shenandoah Valley was a lifeline to the South. It was a source of provisions and a possible Northern invasion route. The Union wanted the territory, and Jackson and his men were sent to help stop them. In battle after battle Stonewall led a small contingent of Confederate soldiers in defeating massive numbers of Federal troops.

RKK   °At the climax of the campaign Jackson headed a force of slightly more than fifteen thousand men. It was still a very small army considering the fact that the Federals had as many as eighty thousand men chasing him from one point or another in the Shenandoah. At least three Union armies came after him. In return, Jackson darted about using his men's legs and his grasp of the terrain and confused his pursuers, appearing almost at will anywhere in the valley.°

Sandie Pendleton (above) was perhaps Jackson's favorite staff officer. The two had known each other in Lexington, where Pendleton, as a student at Washington College, had been a member of the same literary society to which Jackson belonged. Jackson had tremendous respect for the young man's knowledge, saying once, "Ask Sandie Pendleton. If he does not know, no one does."

The portrait of Jackson below was made two weeks before his death. Mary Anna, his wife, said it was her favorite, and it was reprinted on Confederate five-hundred-dollar bills.

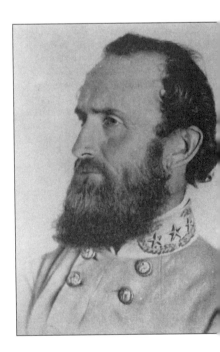

95

On the morning of May 2, Jackson watched his corps move out and then followed. When he reached an intersection of the Plank road he encountered Lee on foot. Jackson pulled up and spoke with him, then pointed ahead. Lee nodded and Jackson spurred Little Sorrel on down the road, but no one heard what passed between the two men. It was their last meeting. Although historically inaccurate, Everett B. D. Julio's heroic Last Meeting of Lee and Jackson *was conceived as the first of a series of paintings of the Confederacy. He failed to sell the original, but print adaptations were sold throughout the South, making it one of the foremost icons of the Lost Cause.*

ALR °He would attack in the morning, attack in the evening, attack at night. The Union commanders complained that he had to have more soldiers than they had been told; the same group could not possibly be striking here, there, and over there. The result was that the Federals had to keep large numbers of troops in the valley in a vain effort to defend against an army that was actually much smaller than it appeared.•

JIR °In about forty-eight days his men marched almost seven hundred miles, fought a dozen different battles, and defeated three Union armies. He was going up against four-to-one odds with the enemy coming at him from the north, east, and west, but he continued darting here, jabbing there, forming here, stabbing there. Coming out of that campaign, Jackson was arguably the most famous general in the world.•

BP °Generals on both sides of the war worshiped the memory, the tactics, and the legacy of Napoleon Bonaparte. Napoleonic tactics and strategy were what they sought to emulate: the ability to keep an opponent off balance, to strike him at one point and then move rapidly and strike him at another. Jackson lived up to that ideal. He was recognized as being the first Confederate general to flummox a succession of Union opponents, and his genius was recognized at

RKK the time.• °It was not that Jackson was doing things differently from other generals; he was doing them with more determination and better. When people looked at the whole war, they realized that Jackson had stood it on its ear. This fellow with the euphonious nickname, the fellow who had done so much in the valley, was on the threshold of fame, and he built on that with tremendous successes.•

ALR °He became a mythic figure who was alleged to sleep in the field with the soldiers, to eat soldiers' rations, to be able to stay in the saddle for days on end, to get men

to march as rapidly as cavalry could move, and to get them to fight with ferocity. Of course, he would be a feared person. How does one defeat him? How does one defeat a myth?•

RKK   °Jackson's reputation alone was worth a battalion or two. The Federals knew who he was, and they were afraid of him. Nannies in the North would try to hush crying children, saying, "Stonewall'll come get you." Part of being larger than life was that a person became a bogeyman to the enemy. When Jackson arrived, it was time to start worrying.•

MAL   °Stonewall Jackson became a household name in the North as well as in the South. He was a fearsome figure—and he won. His fame had to do with the fact that he was giving the Confederacy a sense of hope at a time when there was not that much to feel hopeful about.• The Mighty Stonewall had become the foundation of strength behind the wall of Southern beliefs, but for Jackson himself it was faith, not fame, that fueled the fire behind his success.

Jackson wore an oilcloth raincoat and was nursing a cold as his men moved closer to the Union flank. When Fitzhugh Lee's cavalry reported that the Federal right wing was farther north than anticipated, Jackson accompanied Lee to a point where he could observe the line. The cavalryman remembered that Old Jack's eyes "burned with a brilliant glow, lighting up a sad face." It took more time to get his men in place, but shortly before the sun began to set his troops were ready to attack. After consulting his watch, Jackson ordered his men forward. Sweeping aside the surprised Federal pickets, the Confederates announced their presence with what one of the general's aides described as "that peculiar yell characteristic of the Southern soldier."

Shortly after midnight on May 3 Jackson was returning to his own lines from an impromptu reconnaissance. Pickets of the Eighteenth North Carolina Regiment detected the sound of horsemen advancing on them and fired. Jackson was hit in three places: his forearm and upper left arm and his right hand. Uncharacteristically, Little Sorrel bolted. Branches whipped the general, knocking off his cap, and a limb almost unhorsed him. Finally he reined in Little Sorrel and moved back toward his lines until two other riders came alongside him. They helped him from his saddle, and a doctor from the North Carolina regiment assessed his wounds.

WCD   °He was, among other things, a man who regarded modesty as a great virtue, and he practiced it diligently. He ascribed every victory to the indulgence of a kind God; the Almighty gave him victories—Stonewall did not win them.° The general himself noted: "It chills my heart to think that many of God's people are praying to our ever kind heavenly Father for the success of the army to which I belong. Without God helping I look for no such success. My prayer is that all the glory may be given unto Him to whom it is properly due."

During the war it was as if his life's lessons had finally joined together. More than three decades of preparation had given him the dedication, determination, and devotion needed to win battles, and although the combination may have been the ingredients in the recipe for success, they may also be credited with creating the darker side of the Mighty Stonewall.

RKK   °Jackson's salient military shortcoming was his inability to get along with his subordinates. Subordinate after subordinate came under arrest for violating minor infractions of the military code. The men who answered directly to him, or just one layer below him, had an uncomfortable time.°

Despite his failings though, Jackson was still a leader among Southern men, but even the Mighty Stonewall had to obey orders, and beginning with the spring of 1862, the commands came from Gen. Robert E. Lee.

JIR   °The linking of Jackson and Lee brought together a military team that has no equal in the history of warfare. They became a model partnership. There is nothing in the Civil War that can compare with it. Lee had the vision of a great quarterback to see the game as a whole and what would work, and Jackson was his great running back with the ability to put that call into execution.° Together they were a locomotive of destruction.

In June 1862, during the campaign of Second Bull Run, Lee released Jackson, and the Mighty Stonewall struck the Union supply line, forcing the Federals under the command of Gen. John Pope to pull back. Then in the fall of 1862, during the Antietam campaign, the pair once again proved their power. Lee split his forces in two, and Jackson was in command of one. For three hours, the Mighty Stonewall resisted concentrated Union assaults while continuing to hold the Confederate line.

In battle after battle they took the country by storm. Then in May 1863 they began their most famous and what would be their last fight together during the campaign of Chancellorsville. °Here the Lee-Jackson partnership came to its apex. It was a battle that, on paper, Lee could not win, but he won it in great part because of Jackson.°

JIR   Lee and Jackson had their final meeting the evening of May 1. Together they devised a plan that is still considered a masterpiece. The Confederate army was

The oilcloth raincoat worn by Jackson at Chancellorsville has been preserved in the museum of the Virginia Military Institute.

A detail of the coat (below) shows one of the bullet holes in the garment.

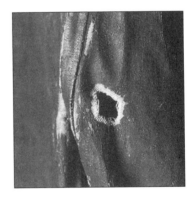

outnumbered more than two to one, but typical of the Lee-Jackson style, they were willing to make a bold move. By May 2, with their small force, they were ready to engage the Federals.

RKK °Jackson, with about thirty thousand men, marched a bit more than a dozen miles over wagon roads that were so primitive that the pioneer corps had to precede his army to cut the stumps low enough so that the axles of the artillery, ambulance trains, and ordnance trains could get over the stumps. At the end of all of that risk and endeavor, Jackson's corps had crossed the T of the Federals. They were facing one way; he was facing ninety degrees differently, overlapping them a mile on either side.•

By approximately 6 P.M. Jackson was in position. In the final moments before the attack, he looked at his men, many of whom he had known long before the war. JIR °At the moment of ordering them into action, he made the famous statement, "The Institute will be heard from today," because a number of the high-ranking officers of his corps were VMI graduates. Undoubtedly many of them had lambasted him as young cadets, and now they were going to their deaths to follow "Old Jack" into battle.•

WCD °He was on the verge of the greatest victory of his career, indeed the biggest victory in the Civil War in the

Jackson was cautiously borne by litter to an ambulance, then to the field hospital at Wilderness Old Tavern where his wounds were examined and the left arm amputated. He was encouraged to hear that the battle was going well for Lee and that Jeb Stuart had replaced him and was pressing the attack against the Union flank. Lee, however, was grieved over Jackson's wounding and feared that a sudden Federal advance might capture his fallen commander, and so he ordered that Jackson be moved farther to the rear. Given the choice of where he would like to recuperate, Jackson selected—with the approval of the family—the home of Thomas Chandler in Guiney's Station, near his former winter headquarters at Moss Neck. He anticipated a brief stay and looked forward to recovering from his wounds fully in Lexington and visiting with old friends.

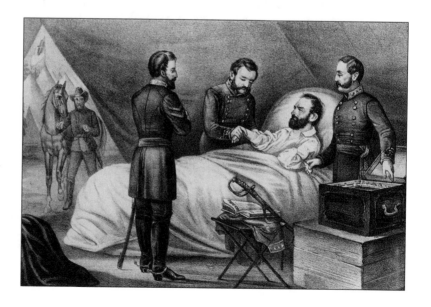

Jackson was taken to Guiney's Station by ambulance, and the twenty-five-mile journey was filled with what for the general was animated conversation. Uncharacteristically, he praised the brigade and his officers and discussed the strategy he had hoped to press had he still been at the head of his troops that day. When they arrived at the Chandler house, his entourage was taken to the little office building pictured to the left; the house itself was filled with wounded soldiers. Feeling instantly at home, Jackson discovered he had an appetite, and his doctor viewed that as a sign of recovery. Four days later, however, the general developed pneumonia and never recovered. His wife and child also arrived on that day, and the general's doctor began preparing her for the worst. On May 10, 1863, a Sunday, Jackson died. He had said that he had always wanted to die on the Lord's Day.

East. It was to be a tremendous crushing blow that sent almost half of the Army of the Potomac scurrying back toward safety.

JIR °When night fell, Jackson did not want to stop. He had a fury, a ferocity going, and he wanted to drive for the kill. In a totally unrealistic move on his part, he rode out personally through the woods to ascertain exactly where the Federal line was trying to stabilize.

WCD °He was between the lines, the sun had set, and the battlefield was full of smoke. Jackson's own people were badly disorganized because they had been running and pursuing the fleeing Yankees all day. So their own organization and command structure were tremendously disorganized. In the dark they could not discern friend from foe.

Among Jackson's last effects were his haversack and field glasses.

JIR °Jackson had issued orders for his men to be wary of Union troops still in the woods somewhere. As he concluded his reconnoiter and was returning to his lines, the sound of his accompanying staff and their horses carried to a line of Confederate soldiers. With the noise coming from the direction of the Union lines, the Southern soldiers logically concluded that these were Union horsemen galloping toward them, and so they opened fire.

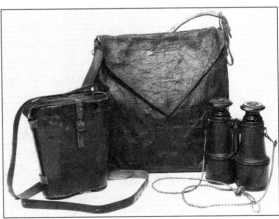

The general's body lay in state in Richmond before being transported to Lexington, where it was placed for viewing in his old classroom. Jackson's funeral was held in the Presbyterian Church and the body was interred in the city cemetery. The grave, that of a fallen hero of the Confederacy, was tended with loving care by students of Washington College and VMI.

The fog of war was upon the battlefield, and Jackson was caught in the confusion. With a volley of friendly fire came a pivotal moment in the war. The bullet from the gun of a Rebel soldier became the blow that ultimately shattered the Mighty, but mortal, Stonewall.

THE VOLLEY THAT struck Jackson's entourage also revealed the Rebel position to the Federal forces. An aide on Jackson's staff, Henry Kyd Douglas, recalled, "Suddenly, the enemy's artillery opened on the scene, and added to the confusion and horror of it, and verily, in the language of General Sherman, war was hell that night."

Several in Jackson's staff were dead, and the general himself lay suffering from various wounds. His most serious injury was a severed artery in his left arm. In 1863 amputation was the only option. Dr. Hunter McGuire performed the operation, and when it was over, Jackson's old friend, Beverly Tucker Lacey, took the hero's limb and

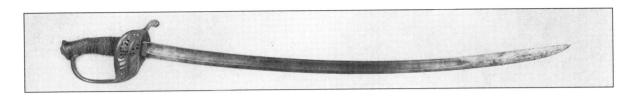

Jackson carried this sword throughout the war, but he rarely drew it from its scabbard, allowing it to eventually rust there.

gave it a proper burial a quarter of a mile from the field hospital. The limb lay buried, but the general lived on.

Word of Jackson's injury had spread quickly, but with the fragmentation of battle lines in the course of the battle came a break in communication. The forces of Lee and Jackson had been split for the fight, so it was six hours before the information reached Jackson's

RKK superior. °Two staff officers had ridden out to find Lee, and in the early morning hours of May 3 they gave him the message. When one of the men tried to describe the nature of the wounds, Lee said, "Stop. Stop. Don't go on. I don't want to hear any more about that. It's too

KEG painful."• °Lee wrote a brief note to Jackson saying, "You have lost your left arm. I have lost my right."•

Fearing a Union assault, Lee sent orders to remove Jackson from the area. After a twenty-seven-mile rocky wagon ride, the fallen general arrived at his final destination, Guiney Station. In a small structure, the general was left to recuperate. His wife joined him while a team of men kept a careful watch on his condition. It was soon clear that the wounds were healing, but Jackson was not. Within days, he was diagnosed with what was then a case of deadly pneumonia.

JIR °Physicians of that day were familiar enough with pneumonia that they could predict almost the hour of death. That morning Jackson's personal physician informed the general's wife that he would expire that day.•

RKK °Mary Anna and a group of his most intimate staff members were in the room with the physicians. Jackson's breathing became shorter and more labored as his lungs filled and ceased to function. Finally, at about 3:15, in the delirium that had him more and more under its control, he said, "Let us cross over the river and rest under the shade of the trees." And then, as he had done so many times, he led the way.• Henry Kyd Douglas recalled later: "This afternoon my watch

The valiant Jackson became one of the central figures of the lore of the Lost Cause. His faults were overlooked and his virtues emphasized until the legend of an unconquerable general emerged. With that legacy established, the questions that have tantalized the South since have been, What if Stonewall Jackson had not died in 1863? Would the fortunes of war have favored the Confederacy? Unanswerable, the children of the South have had to console themselves with the legend.

stopped at a quarter past three o'clock. At that moment the heart of Stonewall Jackson ceased to be and his soul departed for heaven."

On May 10, 1863, at the age of thirty-nine, the Mighty Stonewall died, and with him went the high hopes of the South. Jefferson Davis, the Confederate president, praised the fallen Jackson: "He fell like the eagle, his own feather on the shaft that was dripping with his own life blood. In his death, the Confederacy lost an eye and an arm. Our only consolation being that his summons could have reached no soldier more prepared to accept it joyfully."

At Chancellorsville, the site of Lee's greatest victory of the war, the South's foremost general fell. In an instant the man who protected the Confederate cause, the legendary war hero, the Mighty Stonewall was shattered. °The pall of misery that went across the South following Jackson's death was a major blow to the morale of the Confederate civilian population. They had regarded Jackson as invincible, just as they regarded Lee as invincible.• The *Charleston Courier* summarized the mood, observing, "Everyone feels as though he'd sustained a personal bereavement in the agony of this overwhelming sorrow. We exclaim would God I had died for thee."

°As soon as Jackson died, the South began to look for his successor. All future potential heroes were measured by the standard of Jackson. All failed to measure up, of course, but now and then, when some general was successful in a small campaign, he began to be called the new Jackson, but only briefly.• "Jackson died," wrote Brig. Gen. James H. Lane, "but his memory lived in the hearts of the soldiers, and on many a subse-

quent hard-fought field, I heard them exclaim: 'Oh, for
another Jackson!'"

MAL   °He became an embodiment of all the virtues, all
the hopes, all the aspirations for the Confederate
cause. In the years following the war, there rose the
enormous cult of the Lost Cause, and Jackson was central to that.° "I consider General Stonewall Jackson the
most extraordinary man as a soldier that I ever met,"
Maj. Gen. Henry Heth commented. "Never excited, he
was as cool under fire as he would have been if
attending to his devotions in his church. Had he been
spared to the Confederacy, during the years of 1863,
'64, and '65, it is my belief that matters would have
resulted differently."

Thomas Jonathan Jackson was truly one of the Civil
War's first heroes, and his symbolic strength lives forever
in the hearts of those from the South. What might have
been had the Mighty Stonewall lived, the world will
never know, yet one thing is certain: His death marked
the end of an era. Gone was the man, the physical
embodiment of the Confederate patriotism, but the
mythical figure, the legend, lived on.

GEORGE B. McCLELLAN

Few historical FIGURES inspire passions as powerful as Gen. George B. McClellan. He was the center of heated controversies during his lifetime and continues to evoke strong feelings to this day. By the time he was thirty-four, he was commander of the Army of the Potomac and general in chief of the entire Northern army. In 1861 the Union was confident that it could bring a victorious end to the war and that this dashing young Napoleon was the man to accomplish it. Managing the war, however, did not come easily to McClellan.

During the initial stages of possibly his greatest strategy, the Peninsula campaign, McClellan wrote on May 8, 1862: "It would have been easy for me to have sacrificed ten thousand lives in taking Yorktown. And I presume the world would have thought it more brilliant if they seek the view of the masses better as more bloody. I hope not and will make it as little so as possible."

DEF °McClellan was a man who had the potential to be an outstanding general, an individual who could have ended the war early. Yet the best way to brand McClellan as commander of the Union army is with the word *failure*. He failed time and again, and, as a result, the war continued three years longer than it should have.•

BP °The point should never be forgotten, however, that the soldiers in the ranks almost worshiped McClellan. Soldiers do not, by their nature, tolerate fools lightly. Can this devotion be dismissed lightly? "He was very popular with the men, but . . ." and then go on to the well-known litany of his failings? Or should it not be

TC	Tom Clemens
WCD	William C. Davis
DEF	Dennis E. Frye
JLH	Joseph L. Harsh
JJH	John J. Hennessy
BP	Brian Pohanka

The photograph above (left) is proba-bly the earliest known picture of McClellan, a daugerreotype dating from about 1846, the year of his graduation from West Point. With him are his father, Dr. George McClellan, and his sister, Mary. His uniform is no longer that of a cadet but of the regular army, and he was likely at home just prior to reporting for duty and shipping off for the Mexican War.

The photograph to the right was taken in 1855 in Warsaw during McClellan's assignment to a group sent to observe the Crimean War. McClellan stands to the far right in the picture, next to his unidentified Russian host and seated colleagues, Maj. Alfred Mordecai and Maj. Richard Delafield. McClellan returned with more than one hun-dred books and manuals in four lan-guages that ranged in subject matter from field rations to veterinary sci-ence. He had no problem reading the French and German writings, but for those in Russian he taught himself the language.

noted that he was more popular with the men in the ranks than any general who followed?•

McClellan may have been controversial as a general, but such was not the case in the events that mark the beginning of his life. George Brinton McClellan was born December 3, 1826, into a family that moved among Philadelphia's upper ranks and maintained the manners of that class. °Like a successful business execu-tive, he was someone who wore his confidence, his suc-cess, on his sleeve. Prior to the Civil War, McClellan was always successful.•

He was a young achiever. At the age of thirteen, he was admitted to the University of Pennsylvania, and in July 1842, at the age of fifteen, he entered the U.S. Mili-tary Academy at West Point.

°The general perception today of West Point before the Civil War is that it produced great military leaders. In the nineteenth century, though, the program of study was calculated to produce great engineers; West Point graduates did not know much about running an army. As one of the best and brightest in his class, McClellan became an engineer. In reviewing the way in which he

managed his campaigns, it is apparent that he brought an engineer's eye to almost everything he did.•

WCD ·McClellan was probably greatly influenced by the military legacy of Napoleon. Certainly all students of West Point had read Napoleon's memoirs and studied his campaigns, which were, up to that time, the most sweeping campaigns and the most exciting in what was then modern history. McClellan, in time, came to see himself as a young Napoleon. He did not call himself that, but he certainly did not discourage anyone else from making the comparison.•

McClellan learned the art of war as it was known at the time. His ideas were outlined in a speech he gave on the eve of his graduation, and they would be echoed in later years: "War is the greatest game at which man plays. And officers sustain the most important parts in it. And, as future officers, we must mitigate the miseries of the contest."

The Mexican War broke out in 1846, and McClellan, who had graduated second in his class at West Point, was immediately sent into action. He made use of his training in engineering and mapmaking. Although his

The battle of Contreras was memorable to McClellan for his many narrow escapes. He had two horses shot from under him, and he was knocked down by some grapeshot, with the force of the impact largely absorbed by the hilt of his sword. His commander, Brig. Gen. Persifor F. Smith, noted that "nothing seemed to [McClellan] too bold to be undertaken or too difficult to be executed." The young man from Philadelphia was commended and received promotion "for gallant and meritorious conduct."

Embarrassed by the Confederates at the first significant battle of the war, Irvin McDowell (above) lost his command to McClellan. Given a corps and charged with the defense of the capital at the beginning of the Peninsula campaign, McDowell lost the chance for field command for the remainder of the war when he failed to support John Pope at the battle of Second Manassas.

McClellan's appointment as general in chief was celebrated (below) in a ceremony that featured fireworks and a torchlight parade reviewed by the general at headquarters.

responsibilities were not great, he was noted for bravery. Following the war he was involved in surveying and exploring what was then the Wild West, and he quickly earned a reputation as one of America's brightest military minds.

JJH °In the eighteenth and nineteenth centuries America was not on the cutting edge of military developments, but Europe certainly was. France and Britain were both involved in the war in the Crimea, and presumably their armies would demonstrate the best technology, tactics, and strategy that modern war had to offer.° McClellan was privileged to be chosen to accompany a group sent overseas to observe the European war. Its assignment was to adapt the latest in military advancements for use in the American army.

BP °The fact that a young man in his twenties would be sent to Europe with a group of senior officers is some indication of McClellan's standing in the army of that time. He was in the forefront of some of the reforms in military tactics that were changing the way the American army would fight. He was a great proponent of light infantry tactics, the French approach to warfare, which was to loosen things up by rapid deployments. Freedom of movement was also emphasized. McClellan saw to it, to the extent that he could influence American military thinking, that the drill and even the uniforms were changed. Such emphases and improvements increased an army's potential on the battlefield.°

As a result of the ideas he would bring back from his travels, McClellan was marked as a leading man in the

BP military. °He proposed the McClellan saddle, which was a hybrid adapted from several European sources. He introduced the shelter tent, what later became known as the pup tent. The bayonet manual and drill that the army adopted was something McClellan had translated and modified from a French text.• He even evoked comments in the popular reading of the day. The reviewer for the *Atlantic Monthly* observed: "The author has given us in advance his repertory of instruments and principles. From the written word, we may anticipate the brilliant achievement."

Despite his successes, McClellan realized that promotion was a dull, slow process in the peacetime army, and so in 1857 he left the military. He entered the exciting new business of railroads, and by the time he was thirty-three in 1860, he had been named president of the Ohio and Mississippi Railroad. He also married Ellen Marcy, to whom he was extremely devoted and with whom he would maintain an extensive wartime correspondence.

WCD °McClellan was very much a man of his time. The mid-nineteenth century had a male ethic that many today would find repellent. Being essentially a loud-mouth and boastful blowhard was socially acceptable. It was a part of a kind of Sir Walter Scott, medieval knight-errant, cavalierish ethic that sounds silly today, but the American people lived it and McClellan epitomized it.•

McClellan and his wife, Ellen, were photographed (above) shortly after she joined him in the capital. He had arrived in Washington five days after the debacle at Bull Run. Following a day of conferences and inspections, he believed he knew the causes for the failure at Manassas and that he could rebuild the army and lead it to victory.

Below, he posed with his principal generals in August 1861: left to right, William F. Smith, William B. Franklin, Samuel P. Heintzelman, Andrew Porter, Irvin McDowell, McClellan, George McCall, Don Carlos Buell, Louis Blenker, Silas Casey, and Fitz John Porter.

Masses of volunteers had descended on Washington when the call first went out for soldiers to crush the rebellion. When they came straggling back to the city after the catastrophe of Bull Run, they were wounded and disheartened. McClellan dictated a rigorous training schedule and enforced strict military discipline, but he also mingled with the men so as to inspire confidence and raise morale. They drilled daily until they began to act like an army. They then staged reviews around Washington, and the people and the government began to look on them as an army. Finally, the expectation followed that this army of 150,000 men would not retreat again from another battlefield.

WAR BROKE OUT in April 1861 after the firing on Fort Sumter, which led Confederate Gen. Stephen Lee to comment: "The firing of the mortar woke the echoes from every nook and corner of the harbor. And at this, the dead hour of night before dawn, that shot was the sound of alarm that brought every soldier in the harbor to his feet."

WCD Soldiers across the country were in fact brought to their feet, and McClellan would not be left behind. °He was immediately commissioned a major general and put in command of Ohio's volunteer forces. Acting in concert with other volunteer forces in the East, McClellan began the first successful Federal campaign of the war. Success made him, almost overnight, the first Yankee hero of the war.• The *New York Times* trumpeted: "We feel very proud of our wise and brave young major general. There is a future behind him."

On July 21, 1861, however, the Union experienced a disastrous defeat in the first battle of Bull Run, the first WCD major engagement of the war. °Defeat at Manassas and the sight of leaderless soldiers running in panic through the streets had a tremendously demoralizing impact on the people of Washington and the government itself.

The capital was in danger of becoming a ghost town unless someone could make order out of chaos. Who else could the North turn to but its one heroic, successful general of the war thus far—George B. McClellan?•

On July 22 Lincoln telegraphed McClellan. Although he had not fought at Bull Run, he was to take command of the Army of the Potomac. McClellan would be the second-highest-ranking officer in the entire Union army. To his wife, Ellen, he wrote: "I find myself in a new and strange position here—president, cabinet, General [Winfield] Scott . . . all deferring to me. By some strange operation of magic, I seem to have become the power of the land."

McClellan was now faced with the difficult task of restoring confidence in the soldiers who had been brutally defeated at Manassas. °He began with a variety of actions. He issued grandiose, almost Napoleonic, edicts and proclamations. He demanded and received for his troops the best in arms and equipment. He saw to it that they were fully fed and fully paid. He had them well trained. He had them well clothed and fully housed. He took care of them in a very short period of time. McClellan had every man, right down to the lowliest private in his command, believing that the general in chief cared about him specifically—and indeed McClellan did. In the end, it might be that he cared about his soldiers too much.•

The men of the Army of the Potomac came from all over—from cities and mostly farms—but the majority

WCD

McClellan (below) came to identify with his army (above), and the army identified with him. "The Army of the Potomac is my army as much as any army ever belonged to the man that created it," he said looking back. He had seen that kind of relationship between Winfield Scott and the army in Mexico, and he wanted to emulate it in northern Virginia.

Military reviews around Washington had impressed everyone with the look of McClellan's army, but it was not long before the general found himself being pressured to engage the enemy. His reluctance was lampooned in the cartoon above that played on his diminutive height and placed him on a toy horse, going no where and in no hurry.

BP of them were not soldiers. °Not everybody in the nine-teenth century knew how to use a musket, how to load it, how to clean it, or what to do with it at night so it would not get rusty. These men were not born soldiers, and it took a lot of work to turn them into a function-ing army.*

McClellan set up schools of instruction and camps that circled the entire city of Washington. Volunteers entering the ranks quickly became familiar with the daily drills. In his diary, Warren Goss of the Second Massachusetts Artillery noted: "The first day I went out to drill, getting tired of doing the same thing over and over, I said to the drill sergeant: 'Let's stop this fooling and go over to the grocery.' His only reply was to address the corporal: 'Corporal, take this man out and drill him like hell.' I found that no wisdom was equal to a drill-master's right face, left wheel, and right oblique march."

BP °As the result of McClellan's efforts, the men of the Army of the Potomac began to see that they were becoming part of a coordinated military machine. In short, they *were* soldiers. That sense of accomplishment and pride had a lot to do with the feelings that the army had for McClellan.* On July 13, 1862, Pvt. Oliver Wilcox Norton of the Eighty-third Pennsylvania expressed his appreciation for McClellan, writing: "No general could

A small Federal force, at McClellan's suggestion, engaged a small Confeder-ate force at Ball's Bluff, Virginia, in October 1861. The result was disas-trous. The Federals moved on the bluffs without benefit of reconnais-sance, and the Confederates caught them in the open field and drove them into the river, maintaining a steady fire "as long as the faintest ripple could be seen" in the water. Of the 1,700 men, 49 were killed, 158 wounded, and 714 missing, of which as many as 100 had drowned—more than 50 percent casualties, including the Union commander.

ask for greater love and more unfounded confidence than he received from his men. He is everywhere among his 'boys,' as he calls them. And everywhere he is received with the most unbounded enthusiasm."

°At the same time McClellan felt that he was *the* leader of this army and this army was *his* army. That's how he referred to it almost to the day that he died. To some extent it was true. The soldiers of that army truly loved him.• "The soldiers were very enthusiastic and cheered him along the line of march whenever he appeared," Sgt. Augustus Meyers of the Second U.S. Infantry observed. "They had the greatest confidence in him and would have followed him anywhere."

°McClellan was capable and skilled in creating an army, but he had too much of a mother's instinct in him, too much of the protective instinct. He was creating an army, and he wanted that army to be as good as any that had ever taken a battlefield, but at the same time he wanted no harm to come to it.• On March 14, 1862, preparing for the Peninsula campaign, he announced: "Soldiers of the Army of the Potomac, I know I can trust you to save our country. Ever bear in mind that my faith is linked to yours. I am to watch over you as a parent over his children. And you know that your general loves you from the depths of his heart."

The disaster at Ball's Bluff led to the founding of the Committee on the Conduct of the War, a congressional body imbued with broad investigative powers over the entire war effort and dominated by Radical Republicans. It was a particular threat to conservative and Democratic generals in the Union army, which made McClellan suspect on both counts.

"MASTERLY INACTIVITY," OR SIX MONTHS ON THE POTOMAC.

McClellan was not alone in facing charges of inactivity. The Leslie's cartoon at left, published in February 1862, titled "Masterly Inactivity, or Six Months on the Potomac," pointed out that P. G. T. Beauregard and the Confederates were in no hurry to march on Washington.

WCD °ONE OF THE popular ideas of the time was the notion that warfare was somehow a grand pageant. That included the desire, indeed the demand, that once McClellan had made those volunteers into an army, he had to show it off.° To instill pride in the men, he staged grand reviews, but he did not realize that the image the army projected would lead others to press him to act.

BP °The impression given at those grand reviews was that the army was unbeatable. The people and the politicians were impressed with the way the soldiers marched, their confidence. They were obviously ready to be unleashed on the Rebels and to take Richmond. McClellan, however, was not willing to act at that time; he still wanted to train and discipline and supply, bring more troops down and create such a numerical advantage that he would be unbeatable.°

WCD °Throughout the summer and fall of 1861 the Union army literally did nothing. It was stationary in and around Washington. One small sideshow did take place though, a very small engagement at Ball's Bluff overlooking the Potomac, nine miles upriver from Washington. The result was that a small Federal force was virtually pushed back to the river, even into the water, by attacking Confederates. The defeat was humiliating, and the pressure increased greater than ever on McClellan to do something. Unfortunately, the year was advancing, so McClellan had the perfect excuse—winter—for again doing nothing but staying in his camps and continuing to build his army.°

While McClellan waited for good campaigning weather, political pressures began to build. In December 1861 the Committee on the Conduct of the War was created to investigate the fiasco at Ball's Bluff. One of the targets of its investigation was McClellan. BP °The committee had an almost French Revolutionary aspect to it in that it could make or break any officer's career. As soon as it was formed,

Finally faced with the need to act, McClellan proposed to attack Richmond by moving his army to the Virginia Peninsula and advancing on the capital from Chesapeake Bay. The army would face fewer natural obstacles than the direct route from Washington to the Confederate capital, and the navy would be able to render support from the three rivers on the peninsula. Lincoln had little problem endorsing the plan, but he withheld one corps to safeguard his own capital. Here McClellan posed with members of his staff, from left to right, Henry E. Clarke, McClellan, Stewart Van Vliet, and William F. Barry.

McClellan began to feel its shadow hanging over him. When one looks at the actions of the Committee on the Conduct of the War, some of what has been called McClellan's paranoia may well have been justified.• Brig. Gen. George Meade noted on March 9, 1862, "Public opinion in this country is so whimsical that I should not be surprised to see the same people who the other day called McClellan a demigod tomorrow applauding his removal."

McClellan believed in a slow but sure method to ensure success, but this was difficult to maintain in the face of the intense political pressure that surrounded him. °The press began to badger McClellan to move, to do something. The politicians began to badger McClellan to move, to do something. But he had bucked against authority all his life and had never learned to work with anyone, especially with his superiors, who disagreed with him. As the war progressed, those in authority over him came to disagree with him almost constantly.• After all, it was not as if he had not specified when and where he would attack. On October 6, 1861, shortly after his elevation in rank, McClellan had stated his position: "So soon as I feel that my army is well organized and well disciplined and strong enough, I will advance and force

For six months McClellan had been fashioning an army and stockpiling supplies. The Washington arsenal (above) was overflowing with artillery, caissons, and ammunition. The first step in implementing the campaign on the peninsula would be to transport this equipment and supplies to the staging area at Fort Monroe, on the tip of the peninsula and seventy-five miles from Richmond. Starting in March 1862, in less than three weeks, a parade of ships moved 121,500 men, 14,592 animals, 1,224 wagons and ambulances, and 44 artillery batteries. A British observer traveling with the army was so impressed with the operation, he called it "the stride of a giant."

JJH

The massive buildup of equipment at Cumberland Landing on the Pamunkey River was the most entertainment these troops could find one afternoon and was recorded by James F. Gibson. The camp extended two and a half miles along the river to White House Landing, an ancestral estate belonging to the Lee family. Rain was more of an impediment to the Federal advance than was the Confederate resistance.

WCD

BP

JLH

the Rebels to a battle on a field of my own selection. A long time must elapse before I can do that."

°During the Civil War a general had to be very much what an army commander is today. He has to be a logistician. He has to know how to look after supply. Most of all, he has to be a diplomat. He has to know how to get along with his superiors and his subordinates. McClellan, alas, as a diplomat was an utter failure.° Soon after his arrival in the capital in August 1861 he blasted the Washington politicians: "The president is an idiot! I only wish to save my country and find the incapables around me will not permit it."

°McClellan did not get along well with the Lincoln administration, partially because he was far more conservative in his war aims than Lincoln. McClellan was a Democrat; he was not fighting to free the slaves. McClellan was careful in the treatment of private property. He was very much a gentleman in his style of waging war.°

°He hoped to win the war with as few casualties as possible, in as little time as possible. While no professional soldier ever believes he can win battles without losing lives, the questions commanders have to face are, Are these lives wasted? Are they thrown away? That was the issue that concerned McClellan,° as he said, "I view with infinite dread any policy which tends to make this contest simply a useless effusion of blood."

McClellan had little respect for President Lincoln and his administration, whom he regarded as civilians with JJH virtually no military experience. °In retrospect, the degree of insubordination and insolence that McClellan showed the civilian authority—which technically governed his movements—was astonishing. At one point, in November 1861, McClellan spectacularly snubbed Lincoln. The president went to visit McClellan, who was out at the time, apparently at a wedding. Lincoln waited. When the general arrived home, he entered by the front door and casually walked upstairs. Lincoln continued to wait for half an hour. Finally, someone went up to get McClellan but returned with word that General McClellan had gone to bed. It was an unprecedented snub of the chief executive of the United States.°

WCD   °In time Lincoln grew increasingly exasperated with McClellan and had greater and greater difficulty in keeping quiet about it. After the end of 1861, especially after the spring of 1862, more and more often Lincoln

When the army began to move toward Richmond, progress was hindered, not only by swollen creeks and muddy roads, but also by the sheer mass of men and equipment and the limited number of primitive roads available to them. These men of the Second and Third U.S. Artillery, equipped with 10-pounders and horses for the cannoneers, formed a mobile "flying artillery" unit that was relieved to fight the enemy rather than the elements.

Just prior to the commencement of the campaign, McClellan was photographed at Upton Hill with members of his staff and two foreign observers. Gen. George Morell is at the left of the stump, and aide Albert Colburn stands behind it. To the right stands the Prince de Joinville, in civilian clothes, and his nephew, the Comte de Paris.

Facing a ten-thousand-man Confederate garrison at Yorktown, McClellan convinced himself that he faced a much larger force and chose to put the town under siege. Two weeks into the buildup he ordered an attack at Lee's Mill from this unpretentious headquarters (below). A Vermont brigade broke through but had no orders on what to do next, allowing the Confederates to counterattack and regain their lost ground.

began to utter the immortal quips about McClellan, such as "McClellan does not move. He has the slows."• The president wrote the general: "I think the time is near when you must either attack Richmond or give up the job and come to the defense of Washington. Let me hear from you instantly."

JJH

°In the end, General McClellan had very few friends in Washington because of his secrecy and his occasional arrogance. At the same time, he was one of the most charismatic military leaders and one of the best-loved army commanders this nation has ever had. The problem with McClellan is explaining how all of his good qualities ultimately resulted in failure on the battlefield.•

EVEN AFTER ALL of Lincoln's urgings, McClellan did not appear to be moving his troops anytime soon and did not divulge any of his plans for military action to the president. By the winter of 1862, with political pressures mounting, Lincoln ordered all arms of the military into battle with the declaration of General War Order Number 1. It addressed all military personnel, including the general in chief, McClellan: "President's general war order number one ordered that the 22nd day

The perception that the Union army faced equal or superior numbers on the peninsula was due to McClellan's own fears supplemented by the intelligence work of Allan Pinkerton. While Pinkerton's agents interview civilians and slaves at the general's headquarters at White House (left), the renowned detective can be seen seated in the background with a pipe in his mouth. Even though Pinkerton's projections of enemy strength were proved to be consistently wrong, McClellan believed him unquestioningly and pleaded for reinforcements from Washington. When his numerous requests were denied, McClellan anticipated defeat and even martyrdom. Thus his intent on the peninsula came to be less concerned with gaining victory in the coming battles and more focused on salvaging what he could from defeat.

of February 1862 be the day for a general movement of the land and naval forces of the United States against the insurgent forces. That the heads of departments and general in chief be held to their strict and full responsibilities for the prompt execution of this order."

JJH   °General War Order Number 1 was precisely the kind of meddlesome treatment that McClellan railed against most strongly. In this instance, however, it had an interesting effect in that it stimulated him to reveal finally to Lincoln what his plans were. Rather than march on Richmond directly from the north, McClellan wanted to use a seaborne route down the Potomac to the Chesapeake, all the way to the peninsula between Virginia's York and James Rivers. From there his army would approach Richmond from the southeast. The objective, after all, was to capture Richmond.•

The Peninsula campaign was launched in March 1862. Transports carrying more than one hundred WCD thousand men set sail on the Potomac River in °the largest water-borne military movement in American history, perhaps in all of world history, to that point. In truth, it was a very good plan.•

JJH   °McClellan moved his forces up the peninsula to Yorktown and laid siege to the Confederate line for a month, bringing up heavy siege guns. Still primarily an engineer, he tried, when he could, to make military operations into engineering operations.•

The Army of the Potomac spent a month preparing for the siege of Yorktown. The battery of 13-inch seacoast mortars above was one of fifteen erected south and southeast of the target. They never fired a shot. A day before the attack was scheduled to begin, the Confederates evacuated the town.

WCD   The commanding officer of the Confederate forces at Yorktown was Joseph E. Johnston. °He was a man exactly like McClellan—a man who was also very brave, but a man terrified of ultimate responsibility for leading an army and risking defeat. The only reason, in fact, that McClellan advanced was that Johnston continually pulled back. In the end Johnston pulled back almost to the environs of Richmond itself without a fight.•

McClellan, however, battled with the Lincoln administration in daily telegrams, calling for more troops when his attention should have been focused on the battlefield. In the battle of Seven Pines in late May, Johnston was wounded. He was replaced by Robert E. Lee, and that changed everything.

WCD   After its losses at Seven Pines, °almost immediately after Lee took command, the Confederate army was somewhat reorganized. Then began the famous Seven Days' battles, in which, day after day after day, Lee stymied McClellan.•

DEF   °Quickly McClellan proved himself incapable of destroying the Confederate army because he believed WCD that he was always, *always* outnumbered.• °A consistent pattern of overestimating the enemy's strength meant that McClellan always had an excuse for not advancing.• On June 25, 1862, he reported: "The Rebel force is stated at two hundred thousand. I shall have to contend against vastly superior odds if these reports be true. I regret my inferiority in numbers but feel that I am in no way responsible for it."

McClellan was aided by the famous detective Allan Pinkerton in gathering information to help estimate DEF what the enemy strength was. °Pinkerton and his detectives had designed a formula to estimate the numbers of Confederate forces in the area, but their presuppositions were so far off that their projections were grossly inaccurate and the purported enemy strength was a mirage. McClellan, however, accepted the Pinkerton numbers without question.°

JJH   °The Confederates under Lee were not inclined to allow McClellan to maintain his initiative on the peninsula. In late June, Lee launched an assault near Mechanicsville. The engagement was mismanaged at first, but eventually, on June 27, in the heaviest fighting of the war to date in Virginia, the Union troops were pushed back from Gaines's Mill, and McClellan was forced to conduct a retreat across the peninsula and down to the James River. The fundamental result was that McClellan was now twenty miles from Richmond, holed up along the James River, and Lee had the initiative.°

Throughout the Peninsula campaign, McClellan had wired Washington asking for reinforcements. He felt he needed more troops because he believed he was vastly outnumbered. The secretary of war, Edwin M. Stanton, did not fully comply with this request, which angered McClellan and prompted him to comment: "I have seen too many dead and wounded comrades to feel otherwise

Brig. Gen. William B. Franklin, commander of Sixth Corps, and his generals and staff posed for James F. Gibson on May 14, 1862. Seated from left to right, they are Col. Joseph J. Bartlett, Brig. Gen. Henry W. Slocum, Franklin, Brig. Gen. William F. Barry, and Brig. Gen. John Newton.

As the Peninsula campaign came to an ignoble end, McClellan found himself a general without an army. That did not last long, though. Field command had been entrusted to John Pope, and he had been defeated at Second Manassas. Despite Lincoln's frustrations with McClellan's cautiousness, his preference for maneuvering rather than fighting, and his political posturing, the president had no one else to turn to, and so he returned command of the Army of the Potomac to the general who had created it. "We must use the tools we have," he said. McClellan announced his return by appearing in as many camps as he could, eliciting cheers from the soldiers.

in that the government has not sustained this army. I tell you plainly that I owe no thanks to you or any other persons in Washington. You have done your best to sacrifice this army."

JJH   °By the spring and early summer of 1862, McClellan came to believe that elements of the Lincoln administration were scheming for his removal. Thus, with the army in the field engaging the enemy, the relationship between the army's commander and its government became perhaps one of the most acrimonious, adversarial relationships in history.•

After the failure of the Peninsula campaign, Lincoln was unsure of what he should do with McClellan. In early August he placed McClellan's army under Gen. John Pope's command to assist in the battle that would become Second Manassas. Only two of McClellan's corps arrived in time to fight, and the Union suffered another crushing defeat. As the defeated army streamed back to Washington, Lee quickly took advantage of the situation and moved north into Maryland. Lincoln, who feared the Confederates would capture the capital, became alarmed and realized he had to act quickly.

JJH   °On September 2, 1862, Lincoln did what was probably one of the most difficult things he ever did as president. With no one else available with the motivational ability or the organizational ability to rehabilitate the demoralized Union army, Lincoln offered McClellan his army back.•

BP   °McClellan rode out to meet the troops to tell them that he had again been called upon to reorganize and to command the Union armies, and they cheered him again. Caps flew in the air. Men clasped his hand as he rode past. He bred confidence in those beaten men, and morale improved.• Pvt. Charles F. Johnson of the Ninth New York described the effect on the army, noting: "I never knew a fighting spirit to rage so uniformly as it does now. McClellan seems to put new life into everything, and I hope we will only get a fair shake at the enemy."

BP   °The tragedy of McClellan, however, is that he failed to utilize his greatest strengths. His army would have done anything for him. His troops would have charged the untakeable hill for him. Yet he did not grant them that opportunity because it would mean that his beloved army would suffer. Successful generals cannot afford to be that humanitarian. Generals have to be willing to give the lives of their men if they are going to win.•

RETURNED TO HIS earlier position, command of the Army of the Potomac, the controversial McClellan prepared for one of the greatest battles in the history of the United States. It was to be a turning point for the Civil War as well as for McClellan.

He began by restoring the Union's demoralized troops with the sense of courage and enthusiasm they needed to march into Maryland to prevent Lee's Confederate forces from going any farther north. He took two days, September 15 and 16, to prepare for the battle of Antietam by putting his divisions and artillery in place. After a small skirmish on September 16, soldiers on both sides bedded down and waited anxiously for dawn to come. As the sun rose around 5:30 that next morning, the first movement began. Union troops

As McClellan departed Washington for Maryland, he wrote his wife: "I think we shall win for the men are now in good spirits—confident in their General & all united in sentiment. . . . I have now the entire confidence of the Govt & the love of the army—my enemies are crushed, silent & disarmed— if I defeat the rebels I shall be master of the situation." Some observers speculated there was some design in routing the departing columns of troops past the general's house, where he was cheered lustily, rather than past the White House to honor the president.

The fighting at Antietam lasted from the early predawn hours until the setting of the sun, and men fell in rows on both sides. Near the Dunker church, with the West Woods behind it, these Confederate artillerymen died attending to their duty. The picture was taken by Alexander Gardner on September 19, two days after the battle. It was among the first the public saw of a battlefield other than romanticized paintings, and it shocked all who viewed it.

Following the battle at Antietam, McClellan showed no signs of pursuing Lee's retreat into Virginia and remained near the battlefield resting and reorganizing. Ten days after the battle, he wrote the president, "This Army is not now in condition to undertake another campaign nor to bring on another battle." Lincoln decided to visit his general in the field and press him to action. He arrived on October 1, 1862, and remained for four days, reviewing troops, visiting hospitals, and touring the battlefield. The two spoke privately and at length about advancing the army into Virginia, but McClellan would not move until he judged his army to be recovered. Later the president looked over the army from the summit of a small hill. He turned and asked a friend what he saw, and the man responded that it was the Army of the Potomac. "So it is called, but that is a mistake," Lincoln corrected. "It is only McClellan's bodyguard."

marched through the north woods into the cornfield near Miller's farm toward the Dunker church.

°As the sun was beginning to rise over South Mountain, the Confederates knew that the Federals were advancing on their position. They could see the glistening, gleaming bayonets. They knew that that blue wave was about to bury them in the field of green corn. As the two lines collided in what became, in many cases, combat at very, very close range, the result was terrible carnage, terrible bloodshed.• Maj. Gen. Joseph Hooker, commander of the First Corps of the Army of the Potomac, lamented: "In the time that I am writing, every stalk of corn in the northern and greater part of the field was cut as closely as could have been done with a knife. And the slain lay in rows, precisely as they had stood in their ranks a few moments before. It was never my fortune to witness a more bloody, dismal battlefield."

The battle moved back and forth across the cornfield for more than three and a half hours, and neither side gained much advantage. As it raged, the battle escalated in the east woods and the west woods.

DEF °Just as the Federals started to walk into the west woods, the Confederates began to converge on that position, with the result that almost twenty-two hundred Union soldiers were cut down in about twenty minutes. Some of them were fired upon by their own men in the confusion, the paranoia, or the effort to escape from Rebel bullets as they were running backward.•

TC °McClellan rode up to the senior commander on the scene, Edwin V. Sumner, and asked whether, with the whole Sixth Corps there, they should charge again across that open field and into the west woods. Sumner pointed out that the field was like a hornets' nest and that the woods were filled with Confederates. "It would be foolish to send more troops into a trap like that," he said. McClellan acknowledged his commander's assessment, and the attack was never made.•

BP °Throughout the battle there was an odd sort of distance between McClellan and what was going on—a

In this photograph by Alexander Gardner, Lincoln towers over McClellan's staff, his height emphasized by his stovepipe hat. McClellan faces the president, and to Lincoln's right, his hand on his sword, is Fitz John Porter. To the far right, almost apart from the group, stands an aide on the general's staff, George Armstrong Custer.

In this rare pro-Democrat 1864 Currier and Ives cartoon, entitled "The True Issue or 'Thats Whats the Matter,'" presidential hopeful McClellan is portrayed as the intermediary of compromise between the extremism of Lincoln and Confederate President Jefferson Davis.

conceptual distance. He had lost control of the battle.° His headquarters had been set up at the Philip Pry house, where he could see some of the battle, but he could not monitor all the action.

DEF   °Battlefields have best been described as mass confusion: smoke, noise, yelling, screaming, men trying to maintain their courage but finding the individuals around them—perhaps a brother, perhaps a father—suddenly splattered with blood, parts of bodies being blown over their bodies, their faces. It was all part of a frightening, devastating, destructive war.° For raw recruits who had never seen action, the battlefield was a living nightmare, and some of McClellan's troops had only been in the army for one or two months and had never fired a rifle.

At about midmorning on September 17, two divisions of Union soldiers who had become lost on the battlefield, which stretched for three miles, stumbled directly into a Confederate line at a location called the
DEF Sunken Road. °The road had been formed primarily by farmers over the years and was simply a shortcut that had been eroded by wagon wheels and horses. Hence it was a natural position for the Confederates to be able to drop down into the earth and not be seen. Suddenly there was a blanket of smoke and a sheet of flame and the sound of rifle fire. Quickly, the Federals withdrew,

recaptured their senses, and again rose and prepared to assault. This happened time and time again for several hours, and each time the Federals were shot down. Hundreds of Union casualties piled up.•

Meanwhile, twelve thousand Union soldiers spent hours trying to cross a bridge that was being held by five hundred Confederate sharpshooters. After the Federals finally gained control of the bridge, they stopped to eat lunch and resupply their ammunition. In those two hours, fresh Confederate troops arrived and forced the Union men to retreat. As the sun set, the fighting slowly died out.

JJH   °It was a frustrating day for the Federals, but any frustration at the time was overawed by the magnitude of the horror that those armies left behind that day. The images of that day speak vividly of the price of this war.• °One out of every four men who marched into battle at Antietam was killed, wounded, or missing—about 23,210 total casualties. That number of Americans killed in a

Another cartoonist contrasted the Democratic candidates of 1832, Andrew Jackson, and 1864, McClellan. The earlier Democrat's staunch position regarding the preservation of the union is applauded while McClellan is presented as weak and conciliatory toward the South. In the left panel Jackson berates John C. Calhoun, the father of secessionism. On the right, McClellan and his running mate kneel on their convention's platform and offer an olive branch to a standing Jefferson Davis.

Presidential hopeful McClellan counted on his army's vote, but after three years of death and disease, the army knew that the road to peace lay with Lincoln. The incumbent defeated the challenger in the electoral race by a ten-to-one margin and in the popular vote by almost a half-million votes. The general told a friend that he was relieved not to have won the burden of the presidency: "For my country's sake I deplore the result—but the people have decided with their eyes wide open and I feel that a great weight is removed from my mind."

single day's time is still the highest number of casualties in a single day's time in the country's history.•

Reports came to McClellan with casualty figures that seemed endless. He also visited the battlefield where the dead and wounded still lay strewn on the ground. Any illusion that war was romantic was shattered.

BP °It had been a gentleman's war to him. He did not have a twentieth-century concept of warfare as "all hell." The sight of the battlefield legitimately shook him, seeing those soldiers who had cheered him and worshiped him, now torn apart and bleeding on the battlefield. He lacked the killer instinct that war demands, of that there was no question.• As he had commented in Virginia some four months earlier, the soul of George McClellan had no stomach for this kind of warfare: "I am tired of the sickening sight of the battlefield with its mangled corpses and poor, suffering wounded. Victory has no charms for me when purchased at such a cost."

On September 18 no action occurred on the Antietam battlefield. Both sides had regrouped, and on September 19 Lee's Confederate troops retreated back into Virginia. In October Lincoln came to Antietam to meet with McClellan to express his disappointment that Lee had been allowed to escape. By that time the war aims had changed, and everything McClellan had stood for was outdated. At Warrenton, Virginia, while moving southward with the Union army, McClellan was notified he was relieved of his duties.

BP °As part of his removal from command, McClellan conducted a farewell review of the army he had created. There are countless stories of the emotion that these troops expressed. It was something that no veteran who witnessed it could ever forget.•

Although McClellan left the army, it would not be long before he garnered the spotlight once again. The former general in chief became the presidential nominee of the Democratic Party in the election of 1864. He counted on the soldiers' vote, but by then the army itself realized that Lincoln and the Republican Party would bring a swift end to the war they wanted. Thus Lincoln was reelected.

BP °Soon after losing the election, McClellan decided to leave the United States. He traveled extensively in Europe. He had two small children, one of whom—George B. McClellan Jr.—later became a congressman and mayor of New York, an important figure in his own time. The general ultimately returned to the United States, and in 1878 he was elected governor of New Jersey. McClellan loved to speak to veterans organizations. He sensed that the bond that he had had with the Union soldier was still very strong, and indeed it was.°

McClellan died of heart failure on October 29, 1885, at the age of fifty-eight. His funeral was a tremendous affair held in Trenton, New Jersey, and was attended by the masses, including many of the soldiers who had fought under him.

Regarding his relief from command, on November 7, 1862, McClellan noted: "I have done the best I could for my country, but I must have made many mistakes, I cannot deny. But no one can judge of himself. Our consolation must be that we have tried to do what was right. If we have failed, it was not our fault."

There is no doubt that George B. McClellan was a complex man, and one thing is certain: McClellan brought forth a love and admiration from his troops that have remained almost unparalleled in American history. In turn, he respected and revered his troops and experienced a profound sadness at the loss of the lives of those who would never stand again. The traces of blood have long since faded away, and with the passage of time so too has the opportunity to understand McClellan fully.

McClellan resigned from the army and traveled extensively in Europe in a kind of self-imposed exile. He did not return to the United States until after the 1868 election. The general dabbled with some business dealings, and the family departed again for another two years in Europe, which allowed him to begin writing. He returned to the political arena in 1876, campaigning tirelessly for Samuel J. Tilden against Rutherford B. Hayes. In 1877 he was himself elected governor of New Jersey, serving three years and declining a second term. He hoped for a cabinet post under Grover Cleveland, but that failed to happen. Finally McClellan began to write his memoirs and speak to veterans groups and to visit the battlefields made famous by his army. He was working on an article for the Century magazine when he unexpectedly died at the age of fifty-eight.

ROBERT E. LEE

SINGLE word that is used
to ac___ ___ ___ soldier. It is *duty*. In the
Civil War, ___ ___ heav___ on many soldiers fighting for the North ___ ___ But throughout the
long, terrible conflict, no ___ man was called to
greater duty nor suffered the tug of all human struggles
more than Robert E. Lee.

On the afternoon of April 9, 1865, he waited half an
hour for Union Gen. Ulysses S. Grant in the parlor of
Wilmer McLean's house at Appomattox, Virginia. As
commander of the Army of Northern Virginia, Lee's
achievements were unequaled in the war, but that afternoon, as he waited for Grant, Lee contemplated the
hour of surrender.

GWG °His thoughts may have flashed back to scenes of the
men of the Army of Northern Virginia lying hungry,
tired, and exhausted in the fields around Appomattox.
He may have thought about their past triumphs, or he
may have replayed some of the moments where things
might have gone differently and taken him to some
place other than Appomattox in the spring of 1865.°

AM °A great many things were going through his mind
that afternoon, but chief among those had to be the fact
that all three of his sons had been reported missing.°

WCD °Perhaps he looked back upon all that had transpired in
the four previous years and asked himself how he came

BP to be at Appomattox.° °Above all, he must have felt a
tremendous sadness. Lee was a man who felt the
tragedy of war, and he wanted to spare his army any
useless bloodshed. He was a man who would have

WCD	William C. Davis
GWG	Gary W. Gallagher
RKK	Robert K. Krick
AM	Agnes Mullins
BP	Brian Pohanka
JIR	James I. Robertson Jr.
JDW	Jeffry D. Wert

Lee's father, Henry "Light Horse Harry" Lee (left), served in the Revolution, the Continental Congress, for three terms as governor of Virginia, and one term in Congress. A close friend and confidant of George Washington, Henry Lee eulogized the first president as "first in war, first in peace, and first in the hearts of his countrymen." His later years were spent in land speculation, accumulating debt, and political exile. He abandoned his family in 1813.

Anne Hill Carter (right) was Henry Lee's second wife and the mother of Robert E. Lee. In the absence of her husband she was left alone to care for five children and their finances, training, and education. Self-denial, self-control, and the strictest economy in all financial matters were part of the code of honor she taught them from infancy.

taken advantage of any military option that came his way, but there were no more options.•

Writing of those moments, Grant noted, "What General Lee's feelings were, I do not know. As he was a man of much dignity with an impassable face, it was impossible to say whether he felt inwardly glad that the end had finally come or felt sad over the result but was too manly to show it."

For Lee, the road to Appomattox began in Arlington, Virginia, on the night of April 19, 1861, when he resigned from the U.S. Army. That decision, like every decision in his storied life, was deeply rooted in the history of his family and his nation.

JIR   °He was born into Virginia aristocracy, the combination of two of the state's most venerated families—the Lees and the Carters. Two of his uncles had signed the Declaration of Independence. His father was Light Horse Harry Lee, a hero of the American Revolution and one of George Washington's most dependable compatriots.• Washington himself had commented, "I know of no country that can produce a family all distinguished

AM   as clever men as are Lee's." °His mother was Anne Hill Carter, whose family had a lengthy history of service to their communities.•

GWG   °Both of Lee's parents, for very different reasons, were strong influences on his later development. His father was audacious on the battlefield, willing to take risks—

a characteristic demonstrated by Lee as a soldier—but his father also had certain traits that Lee knew he did not want for himself. His father had not been able to exercise self-control or take care of his family, and so he abandoned them. That was a stark lesson for young Robert E. Lee.°

AM   °It was his mother who raised him to love and serve God and to serve his country. Because of her training and that of the Carter family, the idea of duty came to be a preeminent guidepost to Lee for all of his life.°

Robert Edward Lee was born on January 19 in the cold winter of 1807 at Stratford Hall, his family's ancestral home beside the Potomac River. Here he grew through infancy. In 1810 financial ruin sent his luckless father to debtor's prison, and the family was forced to leave Stratford. When it came time to go, young Bobby—all of three years old—showed his first true measure of devotion.

AM   °As the carriage was brought to the front door, he ran back to the nursery. A wonderful iron fireback in the back of the nursery had two little angels at the top, and the sensitive three-year-old kissed the angels good-bye. The angels are still there. Whether the story is accurate or not is unknown, but Lee's love for Stratford was rooted in his early years, and his love for this place would never die.°

Henry Lee had become the master of Stratford Hall through his first wife, Matilda. The Lees continued to live there until Henry's eldest son by his first marriage came of age and took possession of the estate. Robert was born in the house and was named after two of his mother's brothers, Robert and Edward Carter. He was three years old when the family moved to a small house on Cameron Street in Alexandria, but for the rest of his life he always thought of Stratford as home.

Mary Anna Randolph Custis married Robert E. Lee in June 1831. She was the daughter of George Washington Parke Custis, the adopted son of the first president. In 1838 the Lees were in Baltimore, and Robert decided to have his portrait painted by William E. West, the first portrait painted of Lee. After a brief period of indecision, Mary too chose to sit for West, although she preferred another artist.

Throughout his childhood, Lee was a model son, caring for his invalid mother in the absence of his disgraced father. She impressed him with the Christian tenets of duty, honor, and country. In 1825 his belief in these teachings culminated in his appointment to the U.S. Military Academy at West Point.

WCD °Lee attended the military academy at a time when a number of other future leaders on both sides of the Civil War were there. While he got along well with all of them, he never joined them in their evening revels. When they would go off post to Benny Haven's tavern to forget their studies and enjoy themselves, Lee always stayed behind; he was not one of the boys.°

JDW °He was a very studious young man who felt the need to restore his family's name. This desire compelled him in all that he did; thus his record at West Point was
JIR exemplary.° °In fact, it has never been equaled and probably never will be. In four years at the academy, Lee never received a demerit. That he did not get a mark for some small, inconsequential infraction of the rules is almost impossible to conceive. His record was perfect.°

In 1829 Lee graduated second in his class, and given a choice of assignments, he joined the elite Army Corps of Engineers. As he began his military career, Lieutenant Lee also courted the girl who would be his wife.

AM °Among the first families to be visited by Henry Lee's family when they moved in 1810 from their Stratford home on the Potomac to Alexandria was George Washington Parke Custis and his wife and their little girl. Lee probably knew Mary Custis from the time he was three. As a sign of their affection, the two planted trees on the front lawn of Arlington when she was ten and he was twelve.•

Mary Anna Randolph Custis was the great-granddaughter of Martha Washington. While her parents were fond of their daughter's suitor, her father was reluc-
AM tant to give her hand to a soldier. °It was not any disapproval of Robert that made him slow to approve the match; it was the fact that this young man would pursue a military career. George Custis finally blessed the union, and on June 30, 1831, the couple married at Arlington, surrounded by the relics of the nation's first president. Twenty-four-year-old Robert, however, was not so much concerned about the connection with the revolutionary past as he was about the girl whose hand he held.•

As he became a member of the Custis family, the responsibility for defending Washington's character
WCD devolved to Lee. °Any Virginian seeking a military career

The Lees had seven children, four daughters and three sons. The Lee daughters developed a special renown. Mary Custis (bottom left) was the oldest daughter and seemingly the most independent of the children. She enjoyed the distinction of being the last surviving Lee daughter. Mildred Childe (bottom center) was born just months before her father departed for duty in the war with Mexico. She was the youngest of all the children and managed her parents' household in their later years. Agnes (bottom right) was the fifth of the Lee children and was the most attractive of the Lee daughters. She tended to her mother's needs throughout the war years. No photographs survive of the fourth daughter, Annie Carter. She died of typhoid fever in 1862. None of the daughters ever married.

had to face living up to the example of Washington, which called for a very, very high sense of duty indeed.•

Over the next thirty years, Lee was a devoted husband, father of seven children, and distinguished himself as a dutiful servant of his country. He drew the highest praise from Gen. Winfield Scott in 1847, who said, "Robert E. Lee is the greatest soldier now living, and if he ever gets the opportunity, he will prove himself the great captain of history."

FOR THIRTY YEARS Robert and Mary Lee made their permanent home at Arlington, but his duty as a soldier always took him away. °He served in a variety of tasks as an army engineer. His best-known engineering duties were probably in the construction of a number of coastal fortifications that were underway at that time.•

Among his assignments, young Lieutenant Lee went to Saint Louis and performed a miracle. There in 1837, the Mississippi River threatened to wander away from the levee. Lee fought the river and a mountain of bureaucracy to keep the city from becoming a ghost town and oversaw the construction of levees that helped redirect the water flow, eliminating the sediment deposits that had menaced the harbor.

One of Lee's first assignments in the Mexican War was the placement of a naval battery at Vera Cruz only seven hundred yards from the city walls. He succeeded in masking the work of the sailors installing the six heavy pieces, and the enemy was unaware of what was happening until the battery opened fire on March 24, 1847. Gun crews from the fleet worked the cannon in shifts, and Lee directed the fire. Interestingly, one of the naval officers present with the gun crews was Smith Lee, Robert's older brother.

In this remarkable wartime daugerreo-type taken in 1847, Gen. John Wool, wearing a greatcoat, poses with his staff in the Calle Real in Saltillo. Because of the long exposure required by the daugerreotype process, the men had to halt their horses and pose in a stationary position so their image would be recorded. Lee, who scouted and oversaw road and bridge building for Wool's army, is reputed to be among the group. Another person believed to be in the picture is Irvin McDowell, later the ill-fated Federal commander at First Manassas.

A valuable aspect of his service as an engineer was that Lee developed an eye for and a sense of terrain, of topography, of the lay of the land. Such insight is a crucial ingredient for any commander in war.

By the time of the Mexican War in 1846, Lee was a captain and faced battle for the first time in his life. GWG °This was clearly a defining moment for Lee because he came in close contact with Winfield Scott, the great American soldier of his age. Lee saw Scott in action in JIR Mexico and learned a great deal from him.° °In turn, he performed so magnificently during the Mexican War that Scott went so far as to say that it was Lee's valor and skill that brought American success in that war.°

After Mexico, Lee was made a lieutenant colonel, and in 1852 he became superintendent of West Point. BP °At the military academy Lee began to develop those traits of character that enabled him to lead, to inspire, to criticize, or to reprimand without displaying anger, rage, or selfishness.°

RKK °He superintended a number of young men who would become important to him as subordinates and as significant foes. He became familiar, at the formative stages of their lives, with the whole panoply of people who would fight for and against him.° JDW °Two cadets would become essential parts of his army in the future. One was James Ewell Brown "Jeb" Stuart, and the other was the lanky, tall, long-faced John Bell Hood. One

Going into Mexico, Lee had been a captain. At Cerro Gordo he was brevetted a major, at Contreras-Churubusco brevetted a lieutenant colonel, and at Chapultepec brevetted a colonel. The photograph on which this engraving is based was probably taken in 1850 or 1851 and Lee was in civilian clothes. When this engraving was made in 1861 the uniform was substituted by the artist.

cadet Lee probably would not have surmised would become a future relentless enemy was a little Irishman by the name of Philip Sheridan.•

BP °Colonel Lee constantly gave good advice to these young men. He had weekly gatherings at his home where his wife and daughters hosted little receptions.• One of his daughters, Agnes, described these get-togethers: "We arranged for cadet suppers every Saturday evening. They were sure not very exquisite, but must be just right for Papa's scrutinizing eye."

Lee's duty at West Point was probably his happiest because there he could live with his wife and family. Born between 1832 and 1846, his children—three boys and four girls—were brought up with the strong Christian values of their parents and were largely influenced by the example of their father.

JIR °He molded his sons into military officers, and he
GWG was proud of the fact that they chose the military.• °Yet they were constantly reminded that they were Robert E. Lee's sons and that they would have to live up to certain expectations. It was an impossible standard to meet, and it was undoubtedly a very heavy burden for them.

Lee had a loving relationship with all of his children,
BP but in many ways their lives were not really normal.• °It must have been an awesome thing to knock on the door of the superintendent's house to court one of Lee's daughters. The four girls spent much of their lives in devotion to their father.•

AM °Agnes, the most beautiful of Colonel Lee's girls, fell in love with a cousin who drank, and so she turned him down. She never married.• Of her life at West Point, she wrote, "I have met a great many cadets but it frightens me so. I am so dreadfully diffident."

JIR °There are those who insist that Lee loved his four daughters so much that he did not want to see them marry. Whether or not he dominated them into becoming spinsters is argumentative, but they may well have thought that they could never find anyone who would measure up to their father.•

AM °Before the war, long before Lee was anything but an army officer at a very low grade and low salary, a cousin, watching him as he sat quietly reading in the parlor at

In 1857 Mary Lee inherited her father's estate, Arlington, which was in sad condition. Her father had died heavily in debt. Restoration of the estate and payment of these debts was left to Lee, and by 1859 he had paid all the debts of the estate except those owed to him. In May 1861 Federal troops occupied the estate (left), and in 1863 it was confiscated by the government for nonpayment of taxes.

Even though Mary Lee was hobbled by arthritis, she had seen more of the enemy by June 1862 than her husband. After leaving Arlington she had stayed with various relatives in northern Virginia, moved to a family home in White House until the Federal army began advancing on the peninsula, moved to a plantation owned by Edmund Ruffin, and then, against her husband's wishes, moved to Richmond. There she found a house to rent on Leigh Street before taking up residence on East Franklin Street in the two-story house below, which had been used earlier by her son Custis and several bachelor officers stationed in the capital. The home became as famous as the Confederate White House on Clay Street.

Arlington, said, "If I ever saw a great man, that certainly looks to me like a great man. Colonel Lee's children love him. His wife loves him. His dog loves him. There is no one who comes in contact with him who does not love him."•

At fifty-four years of age, Lee could look back on a long, dutiful career. In thirty years he had proved himself a capable engineer, a clever administrator, a brave soldier, a respected leader of young men, and a devoted husband and father. °He had done everything and done it well, both staff and field command. In 1859 he had led the contingent of marines that put down John Brown's raid at Harpers Ferry. There was little he had not done within the purview of a military career, and everything he had undertaken, he had performed superbly.•

In 1861 people looked to Lee for what was right, and many of them sought his opinion on the matters imperiling the nation. He was opposed to slavery, strongly pro-Union, and against civil war, but above all, he remained loyal to Virginia. °He was not caught up in the great political interpretation of how Virginia looked at the Union. Rather he viewed

Those people who encountered Lee in Richmond during the first year of the war remembered a noble person of manly grace and martial form. He was fifty-four years old but looked younger; moreover, he could look like an important person without affectation. Almost everyone who saw him for the first time remarked on his dignity, but few knew that his reserved manner masked a man who had trained himself to be proper instinctively when he met others. Most believed him to be a great commander, largely on the testimony of Winfield Scott, but Lee had never led troops in battle—he had performed well under fire in Mexico. He had led two expeditions in Texas, one against Comanches, the other against Mexican bandits, and the only time he had commanded in combat had been against John Brown at Harpers Ferry. Nevertheless, he was seen as a skillful soldier, and he gave the people of Richmond no cause to believe otherwise.

Virginia as his homeland, and he would go with Virginia wherever she went.[JDW] °There was a sureness about Virginia and its place in American history. As one of its sons, when Lee was called upon by this most dominant of all states in the nation's early history, he answered that call.•

On the night of April 19, after Virginia had quit the Union, Lee faced the most difficult question of his life.[JIR] °It was a momentous decision, a decision that kept him up all one night pacing the floors of the Arlington mansion, weighing one factor against the other, wrestling with his conscience, trying to make the right decision—morally, ethically, politically.•

[AM] °That night, Mary Custis Lee, one of Lee's daughters, said that Arlington was like a place where a death had occurred. The death they waited for was the end of a brilliant military career.• Her mother noted, "My husband has wept tears of blood over this terrible war, but as a man of honor and a Virginian, he must follow the destiny of his state. It was the severest struggle of his life to resign a commission he had held for thirty years."

Of his resignation, Lee explained, "With all my devotion to the Union and the feeling of loyalty and duty of an American citizen, I have not been able to make up my mind to raise my hand against my relatives, my children, my home. I have therefore resigned my commission in the army and, save in defense of my home state, with the sincere hope that my poor services may never be needed, I hope I may never be called upon to draw my sword."

ON MONDAY, APRIL 22, 1861, Lee left his home at Arlington never to return. Within two weeks, Union troops occupied his house. Mary and his daughters were vagabonds of war, his sons were soldiers in gray, and

Lee was in Richmond planning the defense of Virginia. While politicians boasted of a quick war, Lee felt differently. Two weeks after leaving Arlington, on May 5, he warned, "They do not know what they say. If it comes to a conflict of arms, the war will last at least four years. Northern politicians do not appreciate the determination and pluck of the South, and Southern politicians do not appreciate the numbers, resources, and patient perseverance of the North. Both sides forget that we are all Americans. I foresee that the country will have to pass through a terrible ordeal, a necessary expiation, perhaps, for our national sins."

Within six months, Lee was a general in the Confederate army and began to grow his whiskers. Although he held no field command, his beard quickly turned gray.

°For the first year of the war, Lee served as a combination troubleshooter and military adviser to the Confederate president, Jefferson Davis. As a troubleshooter, Lee was sent by Davis on several thankless tasks, few of which he admirably achieved. As a result, he received a

When Joseph E. Johnston (above) was wounded on May 31, 1862, Lee was named his successor. In four months he dramatically reversed Southern fortunes and seized the initiative.

At Antietam (below), Lee was absorbed with tactical decisions, and his success demonstrated his capacity to direct action on the battlefield, even with bandaged hands and his arm in a sling.

The Civil War artist Alfred Waud illustrated several significant moments in Lee's life for a biography of the general by John Esten Cooke. The illustration to the right depicts Lee at Fredericksburg on December 13, 1862. Standing with James Longstreet and others, Lee watched the Federal assault against Marye's Heights. At the crest of the heights was a stone wall that fronted a sunken road, a natural rifle pit for the Confederates. On either side, Lee had positioned artillery, herding the Union soldiers into the trap that lay in-between. The result was murderous. Turning to Longstreet, Lee said, "It is well that war is so terrible—we should grow too fond of it." Climaxing his six months of command, Lee's army of 75,000 had blocked the advance of 130,000 Federals, causing more than 12,500 Union casualties and losing around 5,000 of his own.

Five months later, the Federal army returned and trapped Lee between Fredericksburg and Chancellorsville. On the night of May 1, 1863, the general and Stonewall Jackson devised an unorthodox strategy to attack the right wing of the Union army at Chancellorsville. Their meeting was sketched by W. L. Sheppard (below), depicting the two men seated on cracker boxes.

JDW

JIR

variety of nicknames, none of them complimentary. They called him "Granny Lee," "Evacuating Lee," and "King of Spades" because of his penchant for earthworks and fortifications, but Lee knew that his efforts were vital to any defense of Richmond, the new Confederate capital.•

°As commander of Virginia's state forces, he wrought a miracle that has been largely overlooked. Lee's efforts were crucial in developing stockpiles of supplies, armaments, and other materials that would sustain the armies of the South in these advanced areas. He started to set the military boundaries for Virginia.•

°It was Lee's responsibility to put together an army, and although much credit is given to Gens. P. G. T. Beauregard and Joseph E. Johnston for winning the battle of First Manassas, much credit should also be given to Lee because it was he who put the army there. Still, it was not until June 1862 that Lee was called to lead an army.•

During George B. McClellan's Peninsula campaign, on the night of the first day's battle at Seven Pines near Fair Oaks, Joseph Johnston, commanding general of the Confederate Army of the Potomac, was twice

WCD   wounded while reconnoitering the battlefield. °John-
ston was everything that Lee was not. He would not
communicate with his commander, President Davis. He
politicked behind Davis's back. He never did anything
if he could retreat instead. By May 1862 Davis was
thoroughly sick of Johnston.

    The most propitious Yankee bullet of the entire war,
as far as the Confederates were concerned, was the one
that took Johnston out of the war for a while because it
gave Lee a chance to show his ability as a field commander.° Johnston himself conceded that Lee was more
fit to command, adding, "The shot that struck me down
is the very best that has been fired for the Southern
cause yet. While possessing no degree the confidence of
our government, now they have in my place one who
does possess it."

JDW   °When Lee took command of the Army of Northern
Virginia in June 1862, one of Jefferson Davis's aides
told a friend, an officer in Lee's army, that in time he
would find out that Lee was audacity personified. And
Lee was.°

*Waud's depiction of Lee at Chancel-
lorsville (above) places the general on
a dark horse rather than the gray
Traveller. To meet the threat on his
right and left, Lee divided his army to
address the Federals taking positions
near the Chancellor house, and then
he divided that force again, so that
Jackson could maneuver to the far
right side of the Union line and attack
from the rear. When his forces were in
position, the Confederates struck from
the west, south, and east, and the Federals withdrew into a tight perimeter
around Chancellorsville. Lee then
turned his attention to his right and
stymied the advance of the left wing of
the Union force, which withdrew. His
victory had been unlikely and his casualties were high, but the hardest blow
struck at Chancellorsville was the loss
of Jackson, critically wounded by his
own troops. Privately, Lee lamented, "I
do not know how to replace him."*

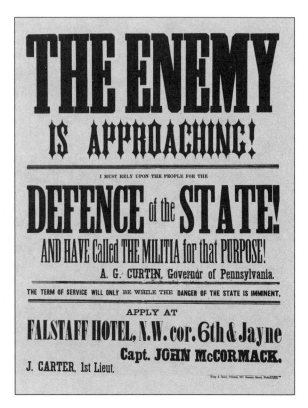

THE ENEMY IS APPROACHING!

I MUST RELY UPON THE PEOPLE FOR THE

DEFENCE of the STATE!

AND HAVE Called THE MILITIA for that PURPOSE!

A. G. CURTIN, Governor of Pennsylvania.

THE TERM OF SERVICE WILL ONLY BE WHILE THE DANGER OF THE STATE IS IMMINENT,

APPLY AT

FALSTAFF HOTEL, N.W. cor. 6th & Jayne

Capt. JOHN McCORMACK.

J. CARTER, 1st Lieut.

King & Baird, Printers, 607 Sansom Street, Philadelphia.

Lee, in the words of one staff officer, was "audacity personified." Within weeks of his victory at Chancellorsville he again led the Army of Northern Virginia across the Potomac and into the North (above left), moving into the Pennsylvania countryside.

Lee's successes caused widespread panic, and on June 12, 1863, Pennsylvania Governor A. G. Curtin issued a broadside (above right) calling out the state militia. Lincoln followed suit on June 15 with an appeal to the governors of Maryland, Ohio, and West Virginia as well as Pennsylvania for one hundred thousand men to repulse the Confederates. By June 22, portions of Lee's army had reached the Susquehanna River, and shops and businesses in Philadelphia closed. When action finally exploded, however, it was at the crossroads town of Gettysburg.

JIR °The opportunity to command was something for which Lee had been waiting. He found in the Army of Northern Virginia a great military machine by which he could demonstrate all the brilliance that had been building up in him and was now ready to demonstrate itself in the field.•

GWG °The situation in June 1862 was dire in the extreme for the Confederacy, with the mammoth Union Army of the Potomac within a few miles of Richmond when Lee

RKK took over.• °The Federals who were besieging the city were close enough to see the spires of Richmond and hear the bells in the church towers chiming the hours.•

GWG °What Lee accomplished was remarkable. He reoriented the war in a matter of just a few weeks from the outskirts of Richmond back to the Potomac River. He seized victories in the Seven Days' battles and then gained a follow-up victory in the campaign of Second Manassas.•

JIR °Within three months Lee had cleared Virginia of all major Union threats and was about to launch his own

At one time Lee's staff was composed of (clockwise from top) Walter H. Stevens, Charles Marshall, James L. Corley, B. G. Baldwin, Lafayette Guild, H. E. Young, William N. Pendleton (whose son served on Jackson's staff), H. E. Peyton, G. B. Cook, Walter H. Taylor, R. G. Cole, and Charles S. Venable.

invasion of the North. It was one of the greatest turn-abouts in military history.*

RKK   °Lee won because of his audacity and because he had skilled subordinates in James Longstreet and Stonewall Jackson. Lee did not interfere with them at the tactical level. Rather, he placed Jackson in positions where he could launch a mighty attack and smash an army, and he placed Longstreet in situations where he could fight with unparalleled tenacity on the defensive. His strategies worked wonderfully well.*

GWG   °Under Lee's leadership, the Army of Northern Virginia was one of the great field commands in American history. By providing victories on many battlefields, he infused this army with an expectation of victory.*

Between June 1862 and March 1864, Abraham Lincoln searched for a general who could beat Lee. Time after time, Lincoln sent new generals to the field, and time after time, Lee defeated them. He beat McClellan on the Peninsula, John Pope at Second Manassas, McClellan again in the bloody stalemate of Antietam, Ambrose Burnside at Fredericksburg, and Joseph Hooker at Chancellorsville. But these victories did not

GWG   come without great human cost. °The scale of the slaughter during the war bothered Lee as it would

The meeting of the two armies at Gettysburg was not what Lee had planned. A Confederate brigade had entered the town in search of supplies and clashed with a Federal cavalry division. Thus the two armies were brought together. Timothy O'Sullivan took this photograph of Union casualties. Because the Southerners were short on supplies, the Confederates removed the shoes from these fallen soldiers.

bother anyone with normal feelings, but that was part of being involved in a war.•

RKK   °Lee genuinely believed he was doing God's will and that God was watching out for him and for his cause. That belief, of course, was a grounding on which highs and lows could be evened out readily.•

By the spring of 1863, Lee's army was operating at its peak, but at this moment of impending triumph, Lee and the Army of Northern Virginia suffered an unrecoverable loss—the death of Gen. Thomas "Stonewall" Jackson.

WCD   °A GREAT DEAL of Lee's success came from the simple fact that he was a brilliant battlefield commander. There is no greater example of Lee's classic tactics than the battle of Chancellorsville where his army was outnumbered more than two to one, and yet he still divided his forces in half in the face of the enemy.•

JIR   °It was a battle that Lee could not possibly win. Yet he won it in spectacular fashion. His biographer,

Not wanting to squander the gains made on the first day at Gettysburg, Lee planned to attack the left side of the Federal line. Awaiting a report, an informal war council convened near the general's headquarters (above). Lee decided to press the attack, but by the time his soldiers were ready, a Federal corps had moved into position in front of the Union line. This corps absorbed the brunt of the attack, and a valiant defense of the Round Tops frustrated Lee's plans. On the third day the Confederates attacked the Federal center but failed to break through. Lee was forced to relinquish the field and retreated, never to invade the North again.

149

The situation was dire on the second day at the Wilderness, and then Longstreet's corps arrived. At its head were eight hundred men of the Texas brigade, and they were brought into the battle quickly. When Lee learned what brigade this was, he warned its commander that the enemy would only be dislodged by a charge, concluding, "Texans always move them!" Caught up in the moment, Lee rode through their ranks and prepared to lead the charge himself. Concerned for his safety, the Texans tried to stop him, shouting, "General Lee to the rear!" With a soldier clinging to Traveller's bridle, he was convinced to retire. The attack continued, and the Texans, at great cost, moved the enemy in a pivotal moment of the battle.

JDW Douglas Southall Freeman, called it Lee's greatest victory.° °At the moment of this great victory, however, Stonewall Jackson was mortally wounded, shot accidentally by his own men on the evening of May 2, 1863. He died of pneumonia eight days later, on May 10.°

RKK °Lee's immediate reaction was that Jackson's death was God's will, and he felt that God would raise up another to take Jackson's place. God, however, never did raise up anyone else in Jackson's place, and so Lee did the best that he could.°

JIR °Lee knew he had lost his most dashing lieutenant. He had made the comment that Jackson was his right arm, that Jackson was irreplaceable, but Lee did not realize just how irreplaceable Jackson was until subsequent campaigns. At Gettysburg, for example, he continued to direct his army as if Jackson were there. Lee had come to believe that his army was invincible because his soldiers were so capable, so self-sacrificing, so gallant in battle that they simply could not be beaten if they were properly led.•

GWG   °After Gettysburg, Lee admitted that he had asked too much of his men. That admission helps explain why he
JDW continued the offensive for three days.• °On the third day, as the troops were stringing back from Pickett's charge, one of the great moments of the war occurred. Lee rode out among his men, trying to cheer them, trying to restore some sense of morale, and admitting to them, "It was all my fault."• When he later submitted his report and resignation to Jefferson Davis, he explained, "No blame can be attached to the army for its failure to accomplish what was projected by me. I am alone to blame."

BP   °Gettysburg was Lee's greatest disappointment militarily during the war. He was not given to wearing his heart on his sleeve, but the fact that he would offer to tender his resignation in the wake of the Gettysburg campaign may be an indication that he saw the ulti-mate defeat of the Confederacy.• To Davis he confessed, "Mr. President, no one is more aware than myself of my inability for the duties of my position. I cannot even accomplish what I myself desire. How can I fulfill the expectations of others? In addition, I sensibly feel the growing failure of my bodily strength."

JIR   °It should be remembered that the war broke Lee physically and shortened his life appreciably. There is a

This graphic engraving illustrates the Union bombardment of the Confeder-ate lines during the siege of Peters-burg in June 1864. The battle pitted 110,000 Federal troops against 50,000 Southerners, and both armies settled in for the siege. Here Lee was at a dis-advantage. His successes had been facilitated by his great ability to out-maneuver his enemy, but confined to a defensive ring around Petersburg, he had no room to maneuver. His army could only wait out the inevitable.

Few pictures were made depicting Lee in the field. One of these (above) was by Frank Vizetelly of the Illustrated London News, *which shows the general watching the Federal bombardment of Petersburg during the summer of 1864.*

good reason to believe that just before the battle of Gettysburg he suffered a heart attack.•

After the losses at Gettysburg, Lee retreated across the Potomac, never to invade the North again. The following spring, a new Yankee general came to the field to fight him.

JIR °When Lt. Gen. Ulysses S. Grant took command of all Union armies and traveled with the Army of the Potomac, the situation became one of the best encountering the best.• °Although Grant quickly showed that GWG he was not cowed by Lee, he did underestimate Lee. He found out that Lee was different from the other opponents he had faced, just as Lee discovered that Grant was different from the other opponents he and the Army of Northern Virginia had faced.•

Immediately upon taking command, Grant issued orders to George Meade and the Army of the Potomac: "Lee's army will be your objective point. Wherever Lee goes, there you will go also."

Grant relentlessly pursued Lee from the Wilderness to Spotsylvania, across the North Anna River, and then to Cold Harbor, where horrible carnage ruled the day.

Throughout the bloody campaign and in spite of heavy losses, Lee gallantly led his army.

GWG °On May 6, 1864, when the Confederate line was wavering, Lee rode to the front, set an example of himself and in effect demanded that his men stand their ground in those very difficult circumstances with thousands of Union soldiers bearing down on them. He did the same thing in the Muleshoe at Spotsylvania.°

WCD °By the time of Cold Harbor, Lee had already seen enough of Grant to know that even a bloody setback was not going to stop the man. After June 1864, Lee's Army of Northern Virginia had been pushed back into the defenses of Richmond and Petersburg. He had been effectively taken out of the war. He was not able to maneuver. There was nowhere for him to go. All he could do was sit and react as Grant acted around him.°

BP °It must have been tragic for Lee to find himself ultimately bottled up at Petersburg because he loved the open fight and the war of maneuver. With his army pinned down and besieged, he realized the end was in sight.°

In the dark days of 1864 Southern soldiers were still fighting for their states, their homes, and their honor, but in Petersburg the Army of Northern Virginia also fought for Lee. Below is a Julian Vannerson photograph, probably taken in 1863. It was Lee's custom to wear the collar insignia of a full colonel rather than the wreath and stars of a Confederate general.

153

AM °Lee's anguish that summer was heightened by news that his home, Arlington, had been confiscated by the Union government. It was seized for unpaid taxes in 1864, and in June of that year it was made into a national soldiers cemetery. Montgomery Meigs, the quartermaster general of the Union army, directed that the graves be placed as close to the house as possible to GWG preclude its use as a private dwelling after the war.• °It was a cruel blow to Lee because he knew that his son would not inherit the estate as he would have in the normal course of affairs. Still the cruelest blow was yet to come. Through the winter of 1864, Lee's army lacked forage, rations, and supplies, but somehow his men retained their fighting spirit. That, however, disappeared in April 1865.•

As the lines collapsed around Petersburg in 1865, the Army of Northern Virginia began a desperate retreat. On April 3 Grant reported to Lincoln, "The mass of Lee's army was whipped badly south of Petersburg, and to save their remnant, he was forced to evacuate Richmond." Lincoln responded on April 7, "General Grant, [Gen. Philip] Sheridan says that if the thing is pressed, Lee will surrender. Let the thing be pressed."

That Friday, Grant sent a message across the picket lines to Lee. With the Army of Northern Virginia starving and on the run, the Union commander knew it was time to begin his dialog with Lee: "General, the result of the last week must convince you of the hopelessness of

When his defenses collapsed at Petersburg, Lee moved the remnants of his army toward Appomattox, where he hoped to find supply trains (below left). Instead, he found himself surrounded with little chance for escape. Thus he negotiated a meeting with U. S. Grant at the home of Wilmer McLean (below right).

further resistance in this struggle. I regard it as my duty to shift from myself the responsibility of any further effusion of blood by asking of you the surrender of the Army of Northern Virginia."

Lee answered, "General Grant, although not entertaining the opinion you express on the hopelessness of further resistance on the part of the Army of Northern Virginia, I reciprocate your desire to avoid useless effusion of blood, and therefore ask the terms you will offer in condition of its surrender."

On April 8, Grant wrote, "Peace being my great desire, there is but one condition I will insist upon, namely that the men and officers surrendered shall be disqualified from taking up arms against the government of the United States until properly exchanged. I will meet you at any point agreeable to you."

At midnight, Lee responded, "To be frank, I do not think the emergency has arisen to call for the surrender of the army, but as the restoration of peace should be the sole object of all, I should be pleased to meet you at 10 A.M. tomorrow."

In the early hours of the next morning, Grant eluded any misunderstanding, saying, "As I have no authority

On April 9, 1865, in the parlor of the McLean house, Lee and Grant met. They discussed everything but the surrender until Lee reminded Grant of the purpose for their meeting. The Federal commander's terms were generous, allowing officers to keep their sidearms and personal belongings and any soldier to keep his horse if it belonged to him (the late spring planting would be soon). Lee even received food for his starving army. When he returned to his camp, he told the men: "I have done the best I could for you. Go home now, and if you make as good citizens as you have soldiers, you will do well, and I shall always be proud of you."

On April 15, 1865, Lee returned to Richmond and his family, and shortly afterward Mathew Brady photographed him on the back porch of the house on East Franklin Street (left). Following the assassination of President Lincoln there was a cry for Lee's trial for treason. Grant interceded for his former enemy, threatening to resign if the government abrogated what Grant believed was his pledged word at Appomattox. Thus no charges were brought against Lee.

In August 1865 Lee was informed that the board of trustees of Washington College in Lexington, Virginia, had elected him president of the college. Two weeks later he accepted the appointment and began a brief five-year career as a progressive educator (right), reforming the curriculum and creating the nation's first departments of journalism and commerce.

Mary Lee had been confined to a wheelchair since 1864. Although her husband was silent, she was outspoken regarding the loss of Arlington and the harshness of Reconstruction policies.

to treat on the subject of peace, the meeting proposed for 10 A.M. today could lead to no good. Terms upon which peace can be had are well understood."

With no other recourse, Lee agreed to meet, writing, "I now request an interview in accordance with the offer contained in your letter of yesterday." To those around him, he said, "There is nothing left for me to do than to see General Grant, and I would rather die a thousand deaths."

That morning, Lee put on his best uniform and went to the home of Wilmer McLean. Grant described the scene he found, noting, "When I went into the house, I found General Lee. In my rough traveling suit, the uniform of a private with the straps of a lieutenant general, I must have contrasted very strangely with a man so handsomely dressed, six feet high, and of faultless form."

BP ° Grant, the mud-splattered, unostentatious, silent, little man; Lee the tall, immaculately uniformed, spotless, dignified, Washington-like man. In a sense, this was a meeting of the modern and the old-fashioned. ·

JDW ° The scene became an event of hugely symbolic importance. There were no demands by Grant for punishment.

GWG He allowed the Confederate soldiers to go home. · ° The terms proposed by Grant were far more generous than any rebel officer—which is what Lee was—had a right to

As part of his daily routine, Lee exercised Traveller almost every afternoon in Lexington. In the words of the general's foremost biographer, Douglas Southall Freeman, "That silent veteran of his campaigns had a place in the General's heart next after his God, his country, his family, his veterans, and his boys." The image on which the engraving is based was taken by Michael Miley of Lexington in 1866.

expect. It was a measure of Grant's respect for Lee that he handled himself and the terms the way he did.°

WCD °It was also characteristic of Lee that once he learned what Grant was going to give him, he found a diplomatic way of asking for more, of finding a way for his army to be fed. He could see by the tone of their conversation and by the terms as originally outlined that Grant felt no inclination to vindictiveness.°

Grant's terms were indeed honorable. Officers could keep their sidearms, baggage, and mounts. The enlisted men would be paroled after furling colors and stacking arms.

JIR °Lee signed not so much terms of surrender as he did the birth certificate of a nation, the United States, and the country was reborn in that moment. Afterward, Lee walked out of the parlor onto the front porch of the McLean house. Stopping, he inexplicably looked off into the distance and beat one hand into the open palm of the other and said nothing. History has always wondered what was going through his mind at that moment.°

AM °He was cheered by the Confederates and saluted by the Union army. Once the

General Lee's effects are preserved in the Museum of the Confederacy in Richmond.

157

The image that most often comes to mind when one mentions Lee is the stolid commander on horseback, leading a ragtag army against incredible odds and gaining unlikely triumphs. It is consistent with the other tenets of the Lost Cause that good people can lose wars, that might does not make right, and that virtue exists independently of victory.

surrender at Appomattox was over, Lee had one duty: to help reunite the country.•

After the war, Lee became president of Washington College in Lexington, Virginia, and dedicated his last years to education. On September 28, 1870, he went to a school meeting. On the way home, he caught a cold. Fourteen days later the general died at his post.

At his death, Mary, his wife, announced, "I have never so truly felt the purity of his character as now, when I had nothing left me but its memory. A memory which I know will be cherished in many hearts besides mine."

There was a huge funeral service in Lexington attended by thousands of Americans—not southerners, but Americans—and Lee was buried in the chapel.

Looking back, Lee had said, "I did only what my duty demanded. I could have taken no other course without dishonor, and if it all were to be done over again, I should act in precisely the same manner."

In life, Robert E. Lee used words like *gentleman*, *honor*, and *duty*. In legend, he defines them so completely that in Virginia they still tell the story of a little boy who came home from Sunday school and said, "Mama, I'm confused. Was General Lee in the Old Testament or the New?"

Lee died on October 12, 1870. Funeral services were held on October 15 in the Washington College chapel that he had helped design and construct, and afterward his coffin was placed in a vault under the chapel. Gray-clad students from the Virginia Military Institute occupy the center of the picture.

FREDERICK DOUGLASS

Abolitionist, ORATOR, jour-
nalist, and diplomat were names given to Frederick
Douglass, a tall and powerful man who would galvanize
the fight to overthrow slavery in the mid-1800s. He
became one of the noblest men in American history,
but he was born a slave—a slave who dared to steal
himself from his master and run away. He was armed
only with a vision of freedom and equality to save his
life and millions like him.

In 1863, while lobbying for the use of black troops
in combat, Douglass stated: "The day dawns. The morning star is bright upon the horizon. The iron gate of our
prison stands half-open. One gallant rush from the
north will fling it wide open while four millions of our
brothers and sisters shall march out into liberty."

In the war between the North and the South, Doug-
JFM lass was neither a soldier nor a politician. °Yet he was a
major figure in the coming of the Civil War and in the
way it was fought. It is fair to say that in many ways he
was the conscience of the nation because he kept before
the country the idea that this was a war, not just to
bring the nation back together, but it was a war to end
slavery, to bring equality to black people, and to make
them part of American society.°

TCB °Douglass projected an image of strength. Given his
visage and his mane of hair, he has sometimes been
characterized as "the Lion of Anacostia"° (the area in
WGG Washington, D.C., in which he lived). °He was certainly
striking in his appearance, with an aquiline nose, piercing eyes, and a strong chin. He was tall, about six feet

TCB	Thomas C. Battle
DWB	David W. Blight
WGG	William G. Gwaltney
JFM	John F. Marszalek
WSM	William S. McFeely
JMM	James M. McPherson
EGM	Edna Greene Medford

Enough slaves tried to escape their masters and find freedom in the North that the South sought federal sanction to curb the practice of free states becoming havens for fugitive slaves. As part of the Compromise of 1850, the Fugitive Slave Law allowed slave catchers to pursue escaping slaves beyond the boundaries of the slave states and to return them to their owners. The particularly galling aspect of the law required that the authorities within free states assist in the capture and return of any fugitive slave. For slaves, this meant that the horizon of freedom had been removed to the Canadian border, since Britain had outlawed slavery in its empire in 1833.

two inches, broad shoulders, and muscular. Douglass, in fact, purposely maintained a strong and forceful appearance.• °People who described his speaking style talked about the kind of power he presented and his deep, baritone, rich-toned voice.•

°Douglass's life stands across the expanse of the nineteenth century as a symbol of the worst and the best in the American character. He was a slave who saw most of the worst brutalities of slavery. He was a slave, however, who freed himself and by luck, pluck, and strength of character remade himself. Most importantly he had an enormous ability to capture in words the meaning of what America is about—freedom.•

Of his birth, he wrote in 1845: "I have no accurate knowledge of my age, never having seen any authentic record containing it. By far the larger part of the slaves know as little of their ages as horses know of theirs, and it is the wish of most masters within my knowledge to keep their slaves thus ignorant. I do not remember to have ever met a slave who could tell of his birthday."

It was along the Eastern Shore of Maryland, near a quiet creek called the Tuckahoe, that the life of the man who would inspire a nation began. °Douglass was born in Tolbert County. He thought he had been born in 1817,• but slave records tell of the birth of Frederick Augustus to a slave named Harriet in February 1818.

JFM °Douglass knew who his mother was, although she lived on another plantation and was a distant figure in his life. He never really knew who his father was, although he came to believe that his father was a white man, probably his master, Aaron Anthony.•

Anthony lived in a large white house on his planta-tion, which was part of a group of farms owned by Col.
EGM Edward Lloyd. °The Lloyd plantation was extensive by Maryland standards. Maryland was an Upper South state where large numbers of slaves could be found, similar to the massive plantations in some areas of the Deep South.•

Reared by his grandmother at the far end of the Anthony plantation, the tiny boy named Frederick led a carefree, playful life along the muddy shores of the
WGG Tuckahoe until he was six. °At that time Douglass found that his childhood had come to an abrupt end when he was assigned to act as the companion and caretaker of the child of the plantation owner. As a result, now that he had duties to perform, he could get into trouble for

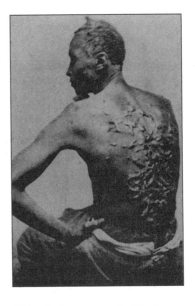

Although slaves were valuable proper-ties, many owners felt little compunc-tion about severely disciplining their more recalcitrant slaves. The photo-graph above was taken in April 1863 by a Union army surgeon.

The promise of freedom was enough to draw these slaves (below) toward Federal troops making their way toward Richmond in 1862.

Primitive methods of cultivation were frequent in southern agriculture. The rice empire of the Carolinas called for more painstaking cultivation than animals and machinery could provide, especially in small fields. Thus slaves pulled the plows through these rice fields near Savannah (above left).

Slave trading businesses were common throughout the South, including this enterprise in Alexandria, Virginia (above right). On the auction block, slaves were made to demonstrate their ability to work by dancing and jumping. To prove what little discipline was needed, they were often stripped to show what scars they had from whippings—an unusual measure of a compliant spirit.

things that he either had done or had failed to do. He was no longer a child, but rather a slave and a part of the institution of slavery.•

JFM °Slavery's basic premise was that black people were inferior and existed for the purpose of doing the heavy work so that the superior whites could spend their time doing more important things. Slavery was a "peculiar institution" where one human being had absolute control over another human being. A slave might be there one day and sold the next.•

WGG °Slavery was in many ways the epitome of hopelessness. Slaves could not control where they went, what they did, what they ate, who they could marry, or even how they would conduct their religious lives. For many, their existence was truly just a step above the grave.•

Into this inhuman system, young Frederick quickly
EGM came of age. °He witnessed the brutal beating of his Aunt Hester, beaten by Aaron Anthony because she had disobeyed him. She was strung up and brutally lashed.• Douglass recalled: "Her arms were stretched up at their full length so that she stood upon the ends of her toes.

He then said to her, 'Now you damned bitch, I'll learn you how to disobey my orders.' And soon the warm, red blood came dripping to the floor."

EGM   °Such discipline was terribly dehumanizing. In his first autobiography, Douglass commented: "I've often been utterly astonished to hear persons who speak of the singing of a slave as evidence of his contentment and happiness. This is a terrible mistake. The songs of a slave represent the sorrows of his heart." Douglass and slaves like him were aware that there were free people of color. He certainly wondered how it was that there were some people like him and his grandmother and his other relatives who were free and some people who remained slaves. When free people of color moved into close proximity to slaves it certainly made the slaves long for freedom even more.•

Young Frederick discovered his pathway to liberty after he was moved to the plantation owned by Hugh Auld, where he learned to read. °The fact that Douglass learned to read at all is amazing, because slaves were not supposed to read. It turned out that Auld's wife taught him despite the fact her husband was not happy that she was doing it.• °She treated Douglass as if he were an adopted child. It is possible that she herself was having trouble learning to read and that she was struggling to read the Bible. So she taught young Frederick to read the Bible. Then, still in his childhood, he tricked

JFM

WSM

Tobacco and rice had been significant cash crops in the South for more than a century before the American Revolution, but by the turn of the nineteenth century cotton was king. Eli Whitney's "gin" had given southerners the tool to perpetuate this agricultural system and also increase its profitability. Prior to the gin, a slave needed ten hours to deseed a pound of cotton, or "lint." A single gin, however, could deseed three hundred to a thousand pounds of lint a day. By 1850 the South was exporting a million tons of cotton annually. All of that began in the fields where three million slaves— men, women, and children like those pictured below—planted, tended, and picked cotton.

165

Sophia Auld, sister-in-law of Douglass's owner, taught him to read at the same time she taught her own children to read (above left). This went against one of the primary safeguards within southern society designed to keep slaves docile and subservient. The ability to read was the first step toward self-awareness and the development of an intellect that asked questions and expected answers. Curiosity, if it were encouraged, tended to begat dissatisfaction with fixed social structures—such as slavery.

Douglass was a voracious reader, and by 1850 he appeared as an articulate spokesman against slavery (above right), having memorized books of speeches and developed his own style of delivery.

his white child acquaintances into sharing their homework and their books with him, which was not something that would normally be accepted, but because it was among children, nobody thought much of it.•

Confessing later to his deceptions, Douglass explained: "From that moment I understood the pathway from slavery to freedom. It was just what I wanted, and I got it at a time when I least expected it."

AT THE AGE of fifteen the slave Frederick Douglass was moved across the Chesapeake Bay to become a laborer. No longer isolated on a plantation, he now had a view of urban life in Baltimore. In his autobiography he recalled, "I sat on Kenna's Wharf at the foot of Philpot Street in Baltimore, and I've seen men and women chained and put on a ship to go to New Orleans and I still hear their cries."

In a Baltimore shipyard Douglass was hired to learn JFM the trade of ship's caulker. °He was still a slave, but he was an urban slave. That is, he was rented out to

someone who paid his owner for his work.•
Allowed to keep a portion of his shipyard wages,

JFM Douglass eagerly saved to buy his first book, °the
Columbian Orator, a collection of famous speeches.
It is not really accurate to say he read it; he memorized it and practiced it. He would read one of
the speeches over and over again and then practice
it, experimenting with voice tone and delivery.•

WGG °Douglass also found a community of free
blacks, religious institutions, friends, and perhaps
even mentors that gave him a sense of social iden-
tity. All of these served him well in later life.• It
was also during this time in Baltimore that he

EGM courted Anna Murray, a free black woman. °She
was a pious, quiet, supportive African-American
woman. Douglass was attracted to her, and she
gave him the support he was looking for and
encouraged him to acquire his freedom.•

There were many schemes that slaves employed
to achieve freedom in the North. One slave even
mailed himself to Philadelphia in a box. Still others

JFM found freedom through the Underground Railroad, °a
series of places—houses, barns, sheds, tunnels, caves—at
strategic distances along several routes from slave territory to the North. Runaway slaves were hidden from their
pursuers by a variety of people, both black and white.•

WSM °Harriet Tubman was the most famous operator on
the Underground. A former slave, she would have been

TCB severely punished had she been apprehended.• °Tubman
took direct involvement in achieving African-American
freedom, returning to slave territory repeatedly and personally leading slaves to freedom by whatever means
were possible.• Douglass later met and admired Tubman,
but not before he had escaped on his own.

EGM °In 1838 Douglass devised a plan with Anna Murray
to escape to the North. She sold a poster bed and gave

WGG him the money to finance his journey.• °Douglass had
papers allowing him to pass as a sailor, and at that time
there were considerable numbers of black sailors
around the area shipyards. He went by train to Wil-
mington, Delaware, still a region where he could be
returned as a slave. Then he took passage on a

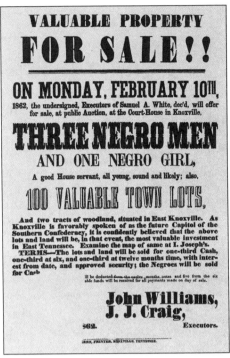

*This notice of an estate sale in Knox-
ville, Tennessee, illustrates the dispas-
sionate treatment of slaves as property
to be disposed of no differently than
furniture or kitchen utensils.*

This 1843 etching of Baltimore Harbor depicts the area as Douglass left it following his apprenticeship as an urban slave learning a shipbuilding trade. The city represented freedom to the young Douglass. Thousands of former slaves and descendants of slaves lived in the city. Even those who were slaves were allowed to hire themselves out, which meant that they determined when and where they worked. With this kind of enticement before him, Douglass was anxious to learn a skill that he could master and exploit in gaining his freedom and then enjoying the best that the city had to offer. He desperately wanted to be one of the respectable free people of color of Baltimore. Unfortunately, racism was used to pit workers against each other, and Douglass found himself on more than one occasion ambushed by co-workers threatened by his potential accomplishments.

steamboat for Philadelphia. In Pennsylvania he was in a free state.°

Douglass continued on to New York where he was joined by Anna. They were married and resumed the journey north to New Bedford, Massachusetts, a whaling and shipbuilding port. °He attempted to find work as a ship's caulker, a trade he knew well,° °but even in Massachusetts, Douglass found that racism reared its ugly head. There were white laborers who would not work alongside a black worker. Even though he was skilled in this particular line of work, he had to take a job as a common laborer, cutting wood and doing other odd jobs, to make enough money to survive.° Finding work, however, was not all that concerned him in Massachusetts.

°Douglass was not safe in New Bedford for one important reason: he was still a slave, a runaway slave. If a fugitive slave were discovered and captured, he could be returned to slavery no matter how long he had lived in a free state.°

Within months of his arrival in New Bedford, Douglass learned of the abolition movement. °William Lloyd Garrison was perhaps the most prominent abolitionist

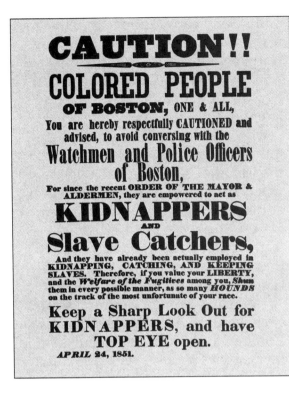

of that period, one of the group known as Immediatists—abolitionists who wanted slavery to end immediately.° In 1831 he had written: "On the subject of slavery, I do not wish to think, or speak, or write with moderation. Tell a man whose house is on fire to give moderate alarm. Tell him to moderately rescue his wife from the hands of a ravisher, but urge me not to use moderation in a cause like the present. I will not retreat a single inch and I will be heard."

WGG   °Douglass's interest in abolitionism directed him to the newspaper published by Garrison, called *The Liberator*. He became aware of the network of abolitionists that existed throughout the northeastern states.° Later Douglass declared: "*The Liberator* became my meat and my drink. My soul was set all on fire. Its sympathy for my brethren in bonds, its faithful exposures of slavery, and its powerful attacks on the institution sent a thrill of joy through my soul such as I had never felt before."

DURING THE SUMMER of 1841 a momentous event occurred in Douglass's life. He later recalled: "A grand

With the passage of the Fugitive Slave Law of 1850, slave catchers had license to cross state lines and recapture escaped slaves and could demand assistance from federal and state authorities. Some northern states enacted personal liberty laws as a defense against the slave catchers, terming their actions to be false imprisonment and kidnapping. Posters like this one (above left) from Boston were not rare.

Anna Murray (above right) was born a free woman on Maryland's Eastern Shore. She had lived in Baltimore since 1830, and there she met Douglass. The two never described how they met, courted, or came to marry, partly out of a natural reticence of the era to discuss such things. What is known is that she was a domestic servant, and it is believed that Douglass may have been moonlighting as a butler when the two met. They were not married until he had escaped to New York and she had followed.

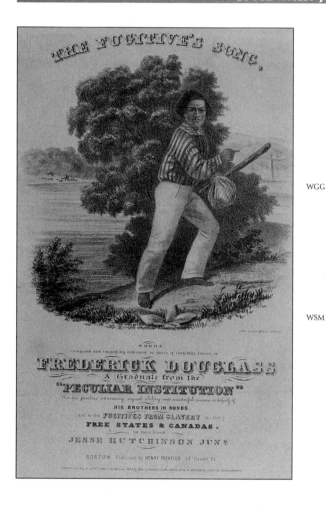

WORDS
composed and respectfully dedicated in token of confident esteem to

FREDERICK DOUGLASS
A Graduate from the
"PECULIAR INSTITUTION"
For his fearless advocacy, signal ability and wonderful success in behalf of
HIS BROTHERS IN BONDS.
(and to the FUGITIVES FROM SLAVERY in the)
FREE STATES & CANADAS.
by their friend
JESSE HUTCHINSON JUNR

BOSTON. Published by HENRY PRENTISS, 33 Court St.

The cover of "The Fugitive's Song" depicts Douglass's flight from slavery as he avoids two mounted pursuers and a pack a dogs. His escape was not so adventurous, since he took passage on a ship from Baltimore to New York and then moved on to New Bedford, Massachusetts, without any hounds in close pursuit. In fact, the greatest threat to his freedom was the high profile treatment he received following his first antislavery society meeting in Nantucket. Since his former owner knew where he was, slave catchers could be easily dispatched with the powers granted them by the Fugitive Slave Act of 1850.

anti-slavery convention was held in Nantucket under the auspices of Mr. Garrison and his friends. I had taken no holiday since establishing myself in New Bedford and I determined on attending the meeting."

He called it his holiday, but he journeyed to this new beginning on the island of Nantucket. °Douglass was electrified to hear Garrison speak at the meeting of the American Anti-Slavery Society. When Garrison learned that an escaped slave was in the audience, he asked Douglass to stand and say a few words.•

°Men and women were in a semicircle on the podium, and Douglass stood up at the lectern. Quietly he told them stories about having been a slave and what slave life was like. For two hours the audience hung on his every word, and Douglass worked the crowd like a skilled preacher:• "I stand before you this night as a thief and a robber. I stole this head, these limbs, this body from my master and ran off with them. I have seen this pious man cross and tie the hand of a young female slave and lash her on the bare skin and justify the deed with a quotation from the Bible."

°He became an overnight success speaking in the antislavery cause, not because of his oratorical powers, but because he was the genuine article—a former slave.• John Collins of the Massachusetts Anti-slavery Society observed: "The public had itching ears to hear a colored man speak and particularly a slave. Multitudes will flock to hear one of his class speak. It would be good policy to employ a number of colored agents if suitable ones can be found."

°Garrison too was impressed with Douglass and determined that he could be of enormous help to the antislavery cause. Soon thereafter Douglass was recruited to go around the country and lecture on behalf of the antislavery society.° By 1843 Douglass had embarked with Garrison on a one-hundred-convention project—a six-month tour of antislavery meetings in New England, Ohio, Illinois, and Indiana. As an abolitionist speaker, Douglass was regularly singled out for attack by proslavery supporters. Still the great speaker evolved into a persuasive writer.

EGM   °In 1845 Douglass published his first autobiography, *Narrative of the Life of Frederick Douglass.* In it he gave details, including information about his owners and the area from which he had escaped, and he did so at great risk to himself. He knew that his owner then knew where he was and could send a slave catcher to get him.°

JFM   °To protect himself from being returned to slavery, Douglass went to England, where he stayed for almost EGM two years.° °While in England, friends collected money for his purchase and made arrangements with Douglass's owner to have him sold to them. Thus Douglass gained his freedom,° and in 1847 he returned to the United States, not as a fugitive slave, but as a free man.

JFM   °Douglass then moved to Rochester, New York, and JMM began to publish a newspaper, *The North Star,*° °so-called because the North Star was used as a point of reference by escaping slaves as they fled northward toward what they hoped would be a better life. Douglass wanted his newspaper to be part of that process toward a better life for all black people.°

DWB   °It was also at this time in the late 1840s and early 1850s that Douglass experienced a kind of political awakening as well. He began to learn the art of politics, even though, like all black leaders before the Civil War, he would never be allowed to vote.°

In July 1852 the people of Rochester invited him to address their Independence Day festivities. For Douglass this was not a date to celebrate. To his fellow townspeople he said: "The character and conduct of this nation never looked blacker to me than on this Fourth of July. To drag a man in fetters into the grand illuminated temple of liberty and call upon him to join you in joyous anthems are inhuman mockery. My

Harriet Tubman had been a field slave on a Maryland plantation until she escaped in 1849. She became one of the most successful "conductors" on the Underground Railroad, a network of safe houses and sympathetic people who helped more than one hundred thousand slaves find freedom between 1830 and 1860. Tubman herself accounted for as many as two hundred escapes. Sometimes disguised as a man or as a frail old woman, she made fifteen covert missions to escort escaping slaves, each time risking her life and her freedom. She told her biographer many years later, "I never ran my train off the track and I never lost a passenger." In the North she enjoyed near mythic status among the abolitionists. In slave quarters across the South she was known as "Moses." In the South there was a $40,000 reward for her capture.

William Lloyd Garrison (left) battled for the abolition of slavery for almost four decades. In 1831 he began publication of The Liberator, *which never had more than three thousand subscribers and never saw a profit. Garrison wrote, printed, and mailed each issue with the help of only one other person. In the same year in which his paper appeared, a slave named Nat Turner led a brief slave revolt, which prompted South Carolina to offer $5,000 for Garrison's arrest. His voice extended beyond his paper because newspapers in the North and in the South picked up his stories. The outspoken Garrison was as dramatic as he was eloquent. On July 4, 1854, following passage of the Kansas-Nebraska Act, he burned a copy of the Constitution as a compromise with tyranny at an abolitionist rally.*

As controversial as Garrison was, the ultimate abolitionist propaganda appeared in 1852 in the form of a novel, Harriet Beecher Stowe's Uncle Tom's Cabin. *For many people it transformed slavery from an abstract legal question into a burning moral drama, winning converts to the abolitionist cause and arousing intense resentment—even being banned—in the South. On meeting Stowe in 1861, Abraham Lincoln remarked, "So this is the little woman who wrote the book that made this great war."*

subject, fellow citizens, is American slavery. This Fourth of July is yours, not mine. You may rejoice; I must mourn."

FROM THE BEGINNING of his public career, Douglass proclaimed to America that what was possible for him was surely possible for other black men and women. The Civil War would provide, not only a means to end the hated institution of slavery, but also a stage for Douglass to condemn more than two centuries of racial tyranny against the African people.

In the 1850s Douglass enjoyed a comfortable home life in Rochester, New York. He and Anna raised five children there, among them Charles and Rosetta. With their help he continued his newspaper, now called *Frederick Douglass' Paper*. It was also in Rochester that he met a man named Brown.

WGG °John Brown was an abolitionist dedicated to the
JMM overthrow of the institution of slavery.• °He claimed that slavery could be purged only by blood and overthrown only by force. By the mid-1850s Douglass was open to this message.•

EGM °Brown and Douglass established a close relationship because they shared the same mission. Brown was a white man who felt that it was immoral to hold slaves.

This rare daguerreotype made at a Syracuse, New York, meeting of the American Anti-Slavery Society during the 1840s shows Douglass seated at the left of the table. At the center of the image is believed to be philanthropist Gerrit Smith, who was a friend of both John Brown and Douglass. Smith had founded an experimental colony of free black landowners in North Elba, a community in the remote "high country" of the Adirondack Mountains, with the hope of settling three thousand blacks there with forty to sixty acres of land each. One of the recipients was Douglass. Nothing is known of what he did with the land, but some have suggested that he sold it since his work was centered in Rochester and he had little interest in farming.

He was determined to do whatever was necessary to free them and, if necessary, to lead the slaves in insurrection.• Indeed, Brown planned to foment such a revolt in Virginia at a place called Harpers Ferry.

°When Brown began to develop his plan for the attack on Harpers Ferry, he wanted Douglass to participate. Douglass considered it for some time, but he eventually decided against it and against joining Brown's army.• As a result of the unsuccessful raid, Brown and his men were hanged for treason. To Douglass and thousands of others, however, Brown had become a powerful symbol for the violent overthrow of the slave system. The former slave applauded Brown, saying, "Posterity will owe everlasting thanks to John Brown. Slavery is a system of brute force. It must be met with its own weapons. John Brown has initiated a new mode of carrying on the crusade of freedom."

The sectional dispute symbolized by men like Brown had reached grand proportions when in 1860 the

WGG Republican Abraham Lincoln ran for the presidency of the divided nation. °Lincoln the candidate made several non-committal remarks regarding slavery, but it was clear that he intended to limit the expansion of slavery by restricting
JFM it to those areas where it already existed.• °Nonetheless, as a result of Lincoln's election and the threat it engendered to slavery, the South seceded from the Union.•

On April 12, 1861, Confederate batteries bombarded Fort Sumter, a Federal installation in the harbor of Charleston, South Carolina. Douglass commented: "When the first rebel cannon shattered the walls of Sumter and drove away its starving garrison, I predicted that the war then and there would not be fought entirely by white men. The chance is now given you to end in a day the bondage of centuries, and to rise in one bound from social degradation to the place of common equality with all other varieties of men."
DWB °Once the Civil War erupted, Douglass interpreted its cause as unmistakable: the war was about slavery and its purpose ought to be the abolition of slavery. He saw Fort Sumter and the outbreak of war as more than reason for the federal government to commit itself to a war against slavery.•

The Narrative of the Life of Frederick Douglass was a powerful antislavery tract. The text is short and direct, from the "I was born" of the first line to the closing account of his Nantucket speech. It appeared in Boston in June 1845, priced at fifty cents a copy. Three European editions followed, and within five years thirty thousand copies were in circulation. While there were those who were skeptical that a former slave could have written such prose, anyone who heard Douglass knew that the voice of the narrative and the voice of the man were one and the same. Because his owner knew where to find him, Douglass was forced to flee the country. He found a highly receptive audience in England and even entertained the idea of not returning to the United States.

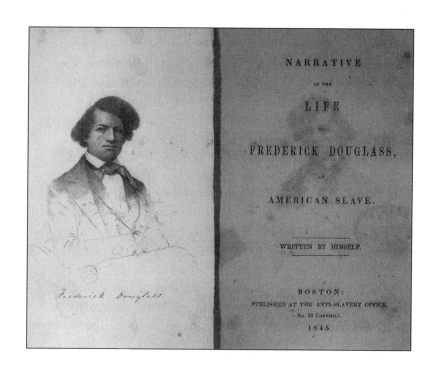

WGG °Douglass was glad to see the war come. He knew that it meant the freedom of millions of slaves in the South and a changed way of life for thousands of free blacks in the North. He constantly argued, lectured, wrote, and proposed that there should be a Negro army. His comments, however, fell on deaf ears. The War Department had no interest in recruiting black soldiers.•

By refusing to let blacks fight, the North deprived itself of thousands of willing and able soldiers. Meanwhile, the casualties that the Northern armies faced on the battlefield became alarming. September 17, 1862, was the worst day of fighting to date as the Union Army of the Potomac and the Confederate Army of Northern Virginia faced off along Antietam Creek in Sharpsburg, Maryland. The Union lost twelve thousand soldiers.

WGG °After the battle of Antietam, it was clear that this was going to be a long, bloody, difficult war. Politically, Lincoln used the perceived victory at Antietam as an opportunity to announce the upcoming Emancipation Proclamation:• "Whereas on the 22nd day of September, A.D. 1862, all persons held as slaves within any state, or designated part of a state, shall be then, thenceforward, and forever free, and the executive government of the United States, including the military and naval authority thereof, will recognize and maintain the freedom of such persons."

JMM °One of the provisions in the Emancipation Proclamation was that African Americans could be enlisted to help win the war in any way that the administration thought they could be useful, including as soldiers.•

WGG °Douglass was, of course, enthusiastic about this, and in 1863 he was approached by George L. Stearns, a Massachusetts philanthropist and businessman, who had been appointed to recruit a regiment of African-American soldiers. Douglass became one of his recruiting officers.•

When war broke out in 1861, Douglass lobbied Lincoln to make emancipation the primary goal of the conflict. In a speech in Rochester in June 1861 he said, "Not a slave should be left a slave in the returning footprints of the American army gone to put down this slave-holding rebellion." Calling for the North to enlist black soldiers, he said, "We are striking the guilty rebels with our soft, white hand, when we should be striking with the iron hand of the black man." After the Emancipation Proclamation was signed in 1862, Douglass served as a recruiting agent, and his two sons were among the first to volunteer for duty. For the rest of the war he campaigned against the Confederate policy of promising nothing but death to all black soldiers on the battlefield or if taken prisoner. Later he called for equal pay for black soldiers, which was what had been promised when blacks began enlisting in 1863.

Robert Gould Shaw (above), the son of a Boston abolitionist, was selected by Gov. John A. Andrew of Massachusetts to head the first regiment of black soldiers recruited in the North. Shaw was chosen largely because he believed that black troops could be trained to match the fighting skills of soldiers already serving on the front lines.

By war's end, more than 185,000 blacks were in uniform, although they fought as segregated units under white officers and did not always receive pay and benefits equal to their white counterparts.

°Douglass met with Lincoln at the White House in August 1863. He came away from that meeting and said, "I felt big there." Douglass also came away with a certain respect for Lincoln's intentions, if not a total respect for his policies.•

In churches and meeting halls across the North, Douglass spoke to crowds of young black men, convincing them to put on the uniform of the Union. He challenged his listeners to join the fight, saying: "From east to west, from north to south, the sky is written all over, now or never. I urge you to fly to arms and smite with death the power that would bury the government and your liberty in the same hopeless grave. He who would be free, themselves must strike the blow."

°Douglass recruited blacks particularly for the Fifty-fourth Massachusetts, an all-black unit with white officers.• Two of his first recruits were his sons Charles and Lewis, the latter of whom would achieve the rank of sergeant major.

°The Fifty-fourth Massachusetts became an outstanding example of the capabilities of black soldiers. Robert Gould Shaw, the white Massachusetts colonel of the Fifty-fourth, had been pleading for an opportunity to prove that his men would fight to prove their courage.

When he was given his chance—leading a July 1863 assault on Battery Wagner, one of the outposts defending Charleston Harbor—they did so, fighting heroically and suffering almost 50 percent casualties, including Shaw.° Douglass's son Louis reported: "This regiment has established its reputation as a fighting regiment. Not a man flinched though it was a trying time. I've been in two fights and am unhurt. The last was desperate and we charged a terrible battery on Morris Island, known as Fort Wagner. Men fell all around me. How I got out of that fight alive I cannot tell."

JFM   °The elder Douglass's role in the Civil War and in the victory for the Union was important. The fact that by the end of the war some two hundred thousand black soldiers and sailors had participated, about one-tenth of the entire Union force, is important. One could argue that they were pivotal as the war was coming to an end.°

Foreseeing the end in 1864, Douglass expounded: "I end where I begin. No war but an abolition war. No

The Fifty-fourth Massachusetts was the prototype for black regiments in the Union army, and the continued recruitment of blacks for combat service depended on how this unit fared under fire. After three months of routine garrison duty in South Carolina, the Fifty-fourth saw its first combat on July 16, 1863, at James Island and lost 46 men. On July 18 the Fifty-fourth spearheaded the assault on Fort Wagner on Morris Island (above) and reached the top of the rampart before being beaten back. The commander, Col. Robert Gould Shaw, was killed on the parapet, and the regiment lost 281 of its 600 men. Wagner never fell by force of arms, but the Fifty-fourth went on to perform well in expeditions to Georgia and Florida, most notably at the battle of Olustee in 1864.

Two years after he was widowed, Douglass excited controversy by marrying Helen Pitts, a white woman who had worked as his secretary. He defended the marriage by claiming it proved that whites and blacks could live in complete equality. His children, however, could not accept the idea of their father married to someone not their mother and certainly not to someone who was not black. It seemed to them a repudiation of the family and a statement that they, being darker in complexion than he, were of lesser value.

Both of Douglass's sons enlisted and served in the Fifty-fourth Massachusetts Regiment. Lewis Henry (left) achieved the rank of sergeant major and forever wondered how he survived the assault on Fort Wagner. He spent much of the war garrisoned on Morris Island, watching Union artillery pound Fort Sumter into rubble. Pvt. Charles Redmond Douglass (right) did not accompany his regiment to Morris Island but stayed in Boston due to illness. In March 1864 he was transferred to the Fifth Massachusetts Cavalry and promoted to sergeant. He was stationed at Point Lookout, Maryland, but never sent to the grim battlefields of the Wilderness or Cold Harbor. Again he fell ill, and his father successfully petitioned Lincoln in September to discharge him.

peace but an abolition peace. Liberty for all, chains for none."

STANDING IN SOLITARY grace in the hills above Washington, D.C., is a stately home called Cedar Hill. It was here, far from the plantation where he was born into slavery, that Frederick Douglass spent his final years. °The house had fourteen rooms, a white-columned porch, and it overlooked the Anacostia River and the nation's capital. It was reminiscent of the houses in which antebellum slave owners lived years before. So Douglass has an ironic place in the sun, in a setting representative of a Victorian gentleman.•

°By the end of the war Douglass was seen as a leader of black America. A fairly wealthy man, able to purchase this fine home, he still was not satisfied. To the end of his life, he kept looking for greater things. He wanted a governmental appointment, and eventually he did acquire several. He was made marshal of the District of Columbia.•

°Up through the 1890s he spoke at anniversary after anniversary, at GAR (Grand Army of the Republic) reunion after reunion, trying to forge a black abolition-

After the war, Douglass received presidential appointments to several high civil service posts, including minister and consul general to Haiti. Initially, the Benjamin Harrison administration had viewed Haiti as a peculiar little republic to which a loyal black supporter of the Republican Party could be sent to placate the black electorate. That changed in 1890 when the country came to be a prize in the game of international empire building because of the need for a Caribbean naval base to support efforts at canal building in Panama. Douglass did not succeed in gaining the lease for an American naval base in Haiti, but this failure was attributable to the State Department's choosing to allow the Navy Department to pursue the negotiations with Douglass as an onlooker.

ist memory of the Civil War but losing that struggle to the sentimentalized, romanticized Lost Cause meaning and memory of the Civil War. To his dying day Douglass insisted that what the war had been about was not just a fight between men of valor, but a struggle to establish a nation that could live up to its creeds.•

In the winter of 1882 Douglass published his last autobiography. The following summer, Anna, his wife, WSM passed away. °He grieved terribly, seeming to have had a nervous breakdown, but he pulled himself together largely through becoming involved in reform issues. One of these movements was equal rights for women.• Douglass never retired from public view in Washington. His lecture fee was then $150 plus expenses, and he remained in constant demand.

WGG °About seventeen months after the death of his wife, to whom he had been married for forty-four years, Douglass married a woman who had been working in his office. Helen Pitts was nearly twenty years younger than Douglass, and she was white. Their marriage in 1884 caused a tremendous sensation in the United States.•

TCB °One of the things that Douglass encountered in that new relationship was the realization that despite being the great Frederick Douglass, he was still another black man stepping across the bounds of American society's mores. If he thought that he had overcome the old prejudices or that America had overcome its own prejudices, his second marriage showed a different reality.° It also showed that well into his seventy-first year Douglass would not be stopped by bigotry.

°Late in Douglass's life, President Benjamin Harrison recognized him with an appointment as minister to Haiti, a black republic.° °His placement there as a representative of America was in a sense a crowning moment of his career.° It was a career that in many ways was a miracle—born a slave, he stood in his closing days a statesman. On February 20, 1895, Douglass suffered a stroke at his home on Cedar Hill and died at the age of seventy-eight.

°If Douglass's great voice had been silenced, it had, before he died, been heard.° Slavery was over, but more than that Douglass had insisted always that African Americans must have full equality. He never wavered

Douglass was extremely proud of his grandson Joseph, Charles's son, who became a concert violinist (below left). WSM

In 1877 Rutherford B. Hayes appointed Douglass U.S. marshal of the District of Columbia. It was the TCB *first appointment of a black man requiring approval by the Senate. In a move to limit the black presence in the White House, Douglass was excused from attending formal receptions in the mansion. His last act as marshal was to lead the inaugural procession through the rotunda of the Capitol, which is depicted below (right). Despite Douglass's campaigning efforts* WSM *for James A. Garfield, the new president made an old friend marshal and shunted Douglass off to the post of recorder of deeds.*

With his dog Ned asleep on the rug beside him, Douglass works in the book-filled study of his home in Anacostia. His violin, which he learned to play as a young man in Baltimore, rests at his elbow. Douglass was one of the giants of the nineteenth century. He possessed an unswerving commitment to human dignity and equality but confessed that he would likely be remembered as little more than a self-educated fugitive slave. In an age of oratory, some judged that he had the greatest voice. As a citizen, he struggled to rid his country of its most grievous social flaw, only to see it replaced with injustice and terror. In his last years he fought that, too.

from that. To all Americans he said: "To those who have suffered in slavery I can say I too have suffered. To those who have battled for liberty, brotherhood, and citizenship, I can say I too have battled."

From the long night of slavery, Frederick Douglass emerged a hero, a leader, and took his place in history. It was a history that began with a black man, a slave, the man furthest down who was driven by the spark of liberty, of humanity.

ULYSSES S. GRANT

He won THE CIVIL WAR and was twice elected president of the United States, yet Ulysses S. Grant remains largely unknown to most Americans. He was a mass of contradictions, difficult to understand, and hard to know. It is no wonder then that Grant is one of the most mysterious figures in American history.

One of his closest friends, William Tecumseh Sherman, said of him: "I knew him as a cadet at West Point, as a lieutenant of the Fourth Infantry, as a citizen of Saint Louis, and as a growing general all through the bloody Civil War. Yet to me he is a mystery, and I believe he is a mystery to himself."

JMM °Grant himself did not know the secret of his success. He was an unassuming man, in some ways a fairly simple man, but a man of iron will, a man of determination, a man who wanted to get things done and to do them in the shortest and most direct way possible.° That is consistent with what Grant himself said of his understanding of strategy: "The art of war is simple enough. Find out where your enemy is, get at him as soon as you can, strike at him as hard as you can, and keep moving on."

WCD °He is the great mystery of the Civil War. He is a man who should not have been. Nothing in Grant's background suggested he would become *the* pivotal general for the Union and perhaps the pivotal general of the war.° He had little interest in the military, confessing: "The truth is I am more a farmer than a soldier. I take little or no interest in military affairs. I never went into the army without regret and never retired without pleasure."

WCD	William C. Davis
TJF	Thomas J. Fleming
GWG	Gary W. Gallagher
WSM	William S. McFeely
JMM	James M. McPherson
BP	Brian Pohanka
JYS	John Y. Simon

Grant began his memoirs with the simple statement, "My family is American, and has been for generations, in all its branches, direct and collateral." The family had immigrated to America in 1630, first to Massachusetts and then venturing through Connecticut before ending in Ohio. Grant's father, Jesse, took the trade of tanner. In time he became interested in politics and even won a two-year term as mayor of Georgetown, Ohio. While Jesse was garrulous, his wife, Hannah, was reticent. There have been speculations about her health, but the best observation is that the family as a whole was very protective of her, shielding her from the public, especially after her eldest son's exploits drew the nation's interest.

JYS °Grant was a mystery because he had capabilities that were roused when the occasion arose, and then there were periods of what he himself called indolence. Once on the battlefield, once faced with an emergency, the essential Grant emerged and amazed the world.• The poet Walt Whitman perceived that about Grant and wrote: "How those old Greeks indeed would have seized upon him. A mere plain man. No art, no poetry, only a practical sense. Nothing heroic and yet the greatest hero. The gods seemed to have concentrated upon him."

WCD °His was a uniquely American story. He was Horatio Alger brought to life, the boy who through virtue, pluck, and luck—in Grant's case a great deal of luck—rose from obscurity to the very heights that American life can offer. It made him far and away the most interesting general of the war and far and away the one who was the most difficult to explain.•

GWG He was born Hiram Ulysses Grant on April 27, 1822, in the village of Point Pleasant, Ohio. °He was like his mother in that he was quiet but determined, and he was not very much like his father, who was much more outgoing and much more pushy than Grant ever was. He was very shy and reticent. Early on, Grant seemed almost more at home with animals than he did with people. He loved horses from the beginning,• and wrote: "I loved to train young colts. When old age comes on I expect to derive my chief pleasure from holding a colt's leading line in my hand and watching him run around the training horse ring."

JMM °In some ways that kind of symbiotic relationship with horses offers something of a key to Grant's character, to the simplicity and directness of his own personality. His ability with horses somehow also translated into an ability to command men.•

Grant's horsemanship distinguished him at West Point where he set a jumping record that held for decades, but riding horses was one of the few activities he enjoyed while attending the military academy. °The first thing to know about Grant and West Point is that he did not want to be there. The reason was very simple: His father sent him there. He did not like his father, so this guaranteed a certain antagonism between Grant and West Point.• In his memoirs, he explained, "A military life had no charms for me and I had not the faintest idea of staying in the army even if I should be graduated, which I did not expect."

When he was admitted to West Point in 1839, Hiram Ulysses Grant found that the congressman who had nominated him had gotten his name wrong. Consequently he was registered as Ulysses S. Grant. Academy rules prevented its correction, so U. S. Grant became his name from then on. °Naturally, with the initials U.S., his classmates and friends nicknamed him "Uncle Sam" Grant, and his close friends called him Sam.•

Soon after his arrival at the academy, Grant had an experience that foreshadowed his future stature. He recalled: "During my first year's encampment General Winfield Scott visited West Point and reviewed the cadets. With his commanding figure, his quite colossal size and showy uniform, I thought him the finest specimen of manhood my eyes had ever beheld. I believe I did have a presentiment for a moment that someday I should occupy his place on review, although I had no intention then of remaining in the army."

Like Scott, Grant would later be considered a consummate soldier, but no one would have known it from his academic performance at West Point. °He did not do well in a strategy course; the theory of war was not interesting to him at all. In retrospect, it was a good thing. When he did take an interest in strategy, he knew one thing that was absolutely crucial: Whatever the plan

In Robert Walker Weir's drawing class at West Point, Grant found an opportunity to engage his curiosity more than his creativity. The painting above shows an affinity for the subject, such as the simple sweep of the arms and shoulders of the nursing mother, and a certain lack of imagination, in that both the trader and the Indian brave bear a resemblance to Grant.

Grant had few positive impressions from his years at West Point, but one of these followed a review of the cadets by six-foot-five Gen. Winfield Scott. Afterward, Grant wrote, "I thought him the finest specimen of manhood my eyes had ever beheld and the most to be envied."

At age twenty-one, Grant (above left) graduated twenty-first in the West Point class of 1843. His love of horses led him to hope for assignment to the cavalry, but his ranking placed him instead in the infantry. Of his thirty-eight classmates, fifteen attained the rank of general during the Civil War.

In 1845 Grant (above right, in the background) and Alexander Hays of Pennsylvania were in Camp Salubrity, Louisiana, as part of Zachary Taylor's army of observation, awaiting the annexation of Texas. In September of that year they were moved from New Orleans to Corpus Christi as a three-thousand-man army of occupation. Camped along the shore, James Longstreet directed several plays in the evenings to entertain the troops. The baby-faced Grant "looked very like a girl dressed up," but one fellow actor noted that Grant's Desdemona "did not have much sentiment." In his memoirs, Grant noted that the army's presence in Texas had one intent: "We were sent to provoke a fight, but it was essential that Mexico should commence it." Three thousand men in Corpus Christi failed in that mission, and so they were moved to the Rio Grande and there found success.

was, it would all be gone by the end of the day and the next day would require the planners to start over again.° He noted, "I don't underrate the value of military knowledge, but if men make war in slavish observance to rules, they will fail."

Lacking enthusiasm for his military courses, Grant preferred reading novels in the school library and pursuing other activities that indulged his imagination. °Very few people knew, but he became a good artist at West Point. He had talent, and he did some beautiful drawings. Again, mystery was part of Grant's personality.°

In 1843 he was graduated from West Point, twenty-first out of thirty-nine in his class. His mediocre standing matched his modest ambitions. He later explained: "My idea then was to get through the course, secure a detail for a few years as an assistant professor of mathematics at the academy, and afterwards obtain a permanent position at a respectable college. But circumstances always did shape my course different from my plans."

AFTER GRADUATING AS a brevet second lieutenant, Grant reported to Jefferson Barracks near Saint Louis. While stationed there, he met Julia Dent, the sister of a classmate. °The relationship that grew between Grant and Julia, whom he later married, was a remarkable one; it was one of the pivotal relationships in Grant's life. Julia was the sort of woman many would have expected Grant to marry. Like him, she was mostly a face in the crowd. Yet she was steady, strong, dependable, and unyieldingly loyal to Grant, and these were the kinds of supports that he needed throughout his life.•

He wrote her: "You can have but little idea of the influence you have over me, Julia. If I feel tempted to do anything that I think is not right, I am sure to think, Well, now, if Julia saw me, would I do so? And thus I am more or less governed by what I think is your will." Grant's courtship of Julia, however, was interrupted by the outbreak of the Mexican War in 1846.

TJF   °If there is a place to penetrate the mystery of Grant, it is the war with Mexico. Reviewing his actions during that war, one can see him learning an enormous number of things that he later used, applied, or imitated in the Civil War.•

WCD   °Grant had the good fortune to serve under Gen. Zachary Taylor, known as "Old Rough and Ready," and to see one kind of general who had no pomp, no ceremony about him. Taylor was a rugged, down-to-earth

Fresh from victories at Palo Alto and Reseca de la Palmas, the Americans were confident as they approached Monterey. Grant, a quartermaster, rode to the front to see what was happening. Later he confessed, "I had been there a short time when an order to charge was given, and lacking the moral courage to return to camp I charged with the regiment." A third of the men were killed in the action. Grant later volunteered to resupply a unit trying to occupy the city's central plaza, but when he returned he encountered the remnants of this force withdrawing. The two armies negotiated a settlement and the Mexicans withdrew, but American newspapers hailed the taking of Monterey as a glorious victory for Taylor. Grant was near almost every significant action in the Mexican War, and few details of command escaped his attention. He studied every commander he saw in the field, later incorporating their strengths in his own actions when he had a field command.

Grant returned to his family in Missouri after he resigned from the army, borrowing money for travel from his classmate and fellow officer Simon Buckner. With no support from his parents and totally dependent on his in-laws, he took up farming. On land that his father-in-law gave them, Grant cut, hauled, and squared the timbers with which he built his own house. It was the only thing Grant had ever made, and he called it Hardscrabble (above). He struggled to provide for his family and had to supplement his subsistence farm by selling firewood on Saint Louis street corners.

fighter who got the job done.• The young lieutenant described him later, noting: "General Taylor never made any great show or parade either of uniform or retinue. In dress he was possibly too plain. Rarely wearing anything in the field to indicate his rank or even that he was an officer, but he was known to every soldier in his army, and was respected by all."

JMM °This became Grant's model for himself. He did not put on any airs, he did not like dress uniforms, and he did not wear a sword. He was direct and simple in the way he related to other men, and it was apparent that Grant learned such things from observing Taylor.•

TJF °Immediately he learned the basic principle that a general does not flinch. Grant was supposed to be a quartermaster, but whenever fighting broke out, he somehow managed to get into it.• The most dashing display of Grant's courage was during the battle of Monterey when he volunteered to be a courier to get more ammunition for his regiment. He described the affair later: "I adjusted myself on the side of my horse furthest from the enemy, and with only one foot holding onto the cantle of the saddle, and an arm over the neck of the horse exposed, I started at a full run. I crossed at such a flying rate that generally I was past before the enemy fired and got out safely without a scratch."

After Monterey, Grant was transferred to Vera Cruz to join Winfield Scott, the general who had so impressed GWG him at West Point. °Scott's campaign from Vera Cruz to Mexico City was a brilliant campaign in the course of which he cut loose from his supply lines and went toward the Mexican capital. Grant would do that in his Vicksburg campaign, and he must have had in the back of his mind how effectively Scott had carried out that kind of campaign.•

JMM °Under Scott, his men executed flanking maneuvers, penetrated deep into enemy territory, engaged the enemy, defeated him, and moved on. That became the hallmark of Grant's generalship: Seek the enemy. When you find him, fight him, defeat him, and keep on moving.•

In September 1847, Grant rode into Mexico City as a member of Scott's victorious army. The war was over, and it had provided Grant with an invaluable, wide-ranging education. He later noted: "Besides the many practical lessons the Mexican War taught, it brought nearly all the officers of the regular army together. The acquaintance thus formed was of immense service to me in the war of the rebellion afterwards. For instance, I had known General [Robert E.] Lee personally and knew that he was mortal, and it was just as well that I felt this."

WSM °The period between the Mexican War and the Civil War is a fascinating one in the Grant story, standing in sharp contrast to what happened to him during the wars. In short, things did not go well.•

TJF °One thing, however, did go right. He married Julia in 1848. That made him a happy man, but then he was ordered to the West Coast.• Thus, in 1852 Grant left his pregnant wife and son for two years to serve at forts in the Oregon Territory and California.

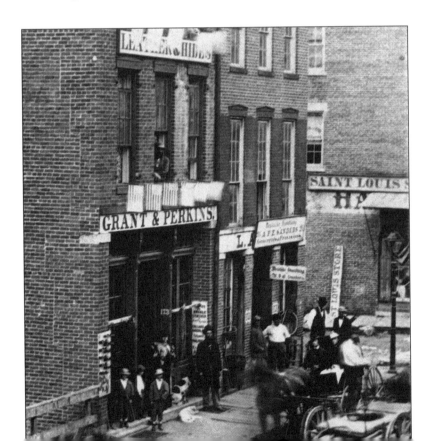

In 1858 the Grants gave up the farm. Whatever sustenance he had drawn from the ground, Grant had paid for with his health. He traded Hardscrabble for a house in town, took a job as a bill collector, and failed in a bid for the position of county engineer. Exhausted and humiliated, Grant finally asked for his father's help. While Jesse had been willing to help all along, he had always offered to do so only on his own terms. More than comfortable now, Jesse offered his eldest son a position in the family store in Galena, Illinois. In 1860 Grant moved Julia and the family to Galena and joined the firm. Grant and Perkins (by then Jesse had bought out his partner) sold harnesses and other goods and purchased hides from farmers. Grant made every effort to be a leather merchant, putting in tedious hours at the store. He also joined the Methodist church and made other adjustments to living in his father's town. Despite his best efforts, however, people noticed the vacant expression he wore throughout the days leading up to the outbreak of war.

When Confederate Gen. Simon Buckner asked for terms of surrender at
Fort Donelson, Grant replied, "Sir:
Yours of this date, proposing armistice
and appointment of commissioners to
settle terms of capitulation is just
received. No terms except unconditional and immediate surrender can
be accepted. I propose to move immediately upon your works."

In a time of great gentility, the
decisive nature of Grant's demand
surprised his opponents and sounded a
powerful positive note for the Union,
which had little to be proud of after a
year of war. Buckner had hoped that
his friendship with Grant would mediate the surrender circumstances. He
could only reply that the overwhelming size of the Union force required
that he "accept the ungenerous and
unchivalrous terms."

When this photograph was taken in
September 1861 in Cairo, Illinois,
Grant had only recently been made a
brigadier of volunteers. It is probably
the worst photograph ever taken of
him. Following the successes at Forts
Henry and Donelson, Grant found
himself under fire from his commander, Henry W. Halleck, who saw in the
battlefield successes of Grant a rival to
his own position. Grant's professionalism found support from the White
House, as Lincoln discovered he had a
general who knew how to fight.

JYS   °On the Pacific Coast he had a series of problems
with low army pay, an inability to earn money on his
own, poor health, and an unsuitable commanding
officer, one with whom he had quarreled before. He
encountered a sense of isolation and loneliness.° To
Julia, he wrote: "My dear wife, I sometimes get so
anxious to see you and our little boys that I am
almost tempted to resign and trust to providence and
my own exertions for a living where I can have you
and them with me. Whenever I get to thinking upon
the subject, however, poverty, poverty begins to stare
me in the face, and then I think what would I do if
you and our little ones should want for the neces-
saries of life?"

WCD   °He had little to do and nothing but time on his
hands. What that always meant in the old army was
either gambling or drinking or both. In Grant's case
almost certainly he found some solace in the bottle.°

JYS   °When he resigned in 1854, the old army gossip ran
that it was because of his drinking, that he had been
forced into resigning because he could not handle his
liquor. There is no way of knowing if that was the case
or not. He had plenty of reasons to leave the army; he
did not need to be drinking to get out, and many other
officers also resigned at the same time.°

JMM   °Returning from the West Coast, Grant tried to farm the sixty acres in Missouri that his father-in-law had given Julia as a wedding present. He called his farm Hardscrabble, and indeed it was hardscrabble. The most lucrative crop he raised was firewood, which he peddled in Saint Louis. Grant lacked the business ability to make a go of farming. He tried to sell real estate and collect rents in Saint Louis, but he lacked the temperament to succeed at either. Whatever he tried he seemed to fail at.°

WCD   °Although Grant would never have said so, for him probably the ultimate admission of his own failure was the fact that just before the war he had to come back to his father to ask for a job.° So, in 1860, Grant became a clerk in his father's leather goods store in Galena, Illinois.

TJF   °Grant did not think of himself as a failure; he had an inner self-confidence that was not always apparent to others. Julia was a wonderful source of encouragement

Whatever gains Grant had made in the field in Middle Tennessee were almost lost at Shiloh. The surprise Confederate attack on Grant's army came close to pushing it into the Tennessee River. A delaying action at a thicket known as the Hornets' Nest allowed Grant to regroup his forces at a strong position near Pittsburg Landing. The attack was suspended at nightfall, and Union reinforcements arrived during the night. The battle was joined the next morning, and the Southerners were forced to retreat. The victory more or less salvaged whatever prestige Grant had lost in the surprise attack, and it set back the Confederate cause in the West.

While Grant commanded thousands of soldiers in the field, the men who were with him in his command posts during the war were the most important to him. With the possible exception of William T. Sherman, no old friends from West Point, the Mexican War, or the peacetime barracks worked with Grant during his second war. Thus none were as close to Grant as the men on his immediate staff. Some have described them as "Galena men," that is, men who were new in their acquaintance with Grant. They were a nondescript gathering of ordinary men who provided the essential comradeship Grant needed in the small cluster of tents that were his headquarters. Their names were Orville E. Babcock, Adam Badeau, Theodore S. Bowers, Cyrus B. Comstock, William S. Hillyer, Clark B. Lagow, Ely S. Parker, Horace Porter, John A. Rawlins, William R. Rowley, and Joseph D. Webster.

for him, always believing that something good would happen and knowing that he was marked for greatness.•

On April 12, 1861, the war began when Confederate forces fired on Fort Sumter in Charleston Harbor. Shortly after hostilities commenced, Confederate Gen. Richard S. Ewell commented: "There is one West Pointer whom I hope the northern people will not find out. I mean Sam Grant. I knew him well at the academy and in Mexico. I should fear him more than any of their officers. He's not a man of genius. But he is clearheaded, quick, and daring."

AT THE OUTBREAK of the war, Grant announced: "I have but one sentiment now: that is we have a government and laws and a flag and they must be sustained. There are but two parties now: traitors and patriots. And I want hereafter to be ranked with the latter and, I trust, the stronger party." He made his mark early in the Civil War as a brigadier general of volunteers in the West.

JYS   °The war in the West received less attention than the eastern theater and seemed to be less vital, but the western theater provided a young commander like

Grant, who was still less than forty years old, a chance
TJF to mature and to learn by trial and error.• °He studied
the problems the Confederacy had defending itself in
the West and saw that one of the key points in its western defense was Fort Donelson in Tennessee. Grant perceived that if he captured Donelson he would disrupt
the entire line of Confederate forts. With a directness
that was a marvelous characteristic of the man, he
advanced on Donelson.•

JYS   °In the winter of 1862 Grant showed his audacity, his
daring, his willingness to take risks as he encircled
Donelson with an army smaller than the Confederate
garrison. He began to pound the fort, calling for the
assistance of gunboats. The Confederates launched a
successful attack that actually broke through the Union
line, but Grant assessed the situation quickly, closed the
gap in his line, and compelled the surrender of the fort
the next day.•

JMM   °The Confederates asked for terms of surrender, and
Grant's message in response made him famous: "No
terms except unconditional and immediate surrender
can be accepted." That gave new meaning to Grant's initials, U.S.—"Unconditional Surrender"
Grant. Overnight he became one of the
Union's most famous commanders
because he had won what was thus far
the biggest Federal victory of the war.
Lincoln recognized that there was a new
star rising in the West and promoted
Grant to major general.•

But fame nearly turned to infamy on
April 6–7 at Pittsburg Landing, Ten-
BP nessee, better known as Shiloh. °The
battle there was a near disaster for
Grant's career, just as it was a near disaster for his army. The fact that his
army had been surprised and routed
out of its camps could have ended
Grant's career then and there.•

WCD   °At Shiloh, however, Grant's imper-
turbable nature appeared for the first
time. The battle had been going against

The taking of Vicksburg was one of Grant's greatest achievements. Failing in his first attempt to seize the city, he encircled the town and laid siege to it. Both armies and the townspeople turned to living in caves and dugouts. The Forty-fifth Illinois Infantry encamped near the Shirley home (below), which was between the lines and miraculously survived the siege. When news of the twin victories of Vicksburg and Gettysburg hit Wash-ington, the perceived hero of the Union was Grant despite the contrast between the three-month siege and the three-day battle. Vicksburg was an inglorious starvation of a small river town, and Gettysburg was a massive confrontation of two armies with all the gory majesty of European lore. The difference was in the generals. George Gordon Meade was an aristocratic Pennsylvanian who had no words for the press. Grant, however, was more open with the press and more interest-ing for his vices—notably stories about his drinking.

A war-weary Grant with Julia and their youngest son, Jesse, posed for the camera late in the war (above). From City Point, Virginia, Grant directed the last ten months of the war. Lincoln twice visited him there, and on one occasion the triumvirate of Lincoln, Grant, and Sherman hammered out the terms for peace for what they hoped would soon be the South's surrender.

him all day on April 6, and his army was very nearly pushed into the Tennessee River. Yet all day long Grant stayed calm, steady, and just dealt with the situation as it unfolded. Grant would do that again, time after time.°

°Nevertheless, the Union forces had suffered such a beating that first day that some of Grant's subordinates advised retreat. "Retreat? No, I propose to attack tomorrow and whip them," Grant replied. He refused to concede defeat, and reinforced the next day with a reorganized army, he counterattacked and won the battle.°

Grant assessed the battle later, noting, "Shiloh was the severest battle fought in the West during the war, and but few in the East equaled it for hard, determined fighting." °It stunned people both in the North and the South because it took the war to a new level of slaughter. There was nothing in the American experience to prepare people for that kind of battle—a battle that brought more American casualties than all American wars to that point put together.°

Grant was severely criticized for the thirteen thousand Union casualties at Shiloh. Many congressmen urged Lincoln to replace him, but the president, frus-

Shortly after coming east to take on Robert E. Lee, Grant the horseman was photographed with one of his favorite mounts, Cincinnati, at Cold Harbor, Virginia. While Grant had been promoted to lieutenant general by then (the only man of such rank in the Union), the saddle blanket still signifies his major general's rank.

trated with the Union war effort, declared, "I can't spare this man—he fights."

The capture of the key Confederate stronghold at Vicksburg, Mississippi, on July 4, 1863, temporarily JYS silenced Grant's critics. °At Vicksburg the general was at the peak of his form. He was the man who broke all the rules, who did not maintain his supply line, who ran the batteries at Vicksburg with some daring and considerable success. He landed his men on the side of the river that he had tried to reach for so long and then, in effect, marched the wrong way—not toward Vicksburg, but toward Jackson. In doing so, he successfully drove a wedge between two Confederate forces in Mississippi, and they never coordinated again. He followed that action with a series of lightning-like blows that advanced his army from Jackson to besiege the enemy in Vicksburg. The siege completed an inevitable victory.°

GWG °Vicksburg presented the very best evidence to counter the notion that Grant was simply a hamhanded butcher who fed his troops into a meat grinder and won by sheer strength of numbers. Vicksburg was

The photograph above was taken at City Point in the spring of 1865 with the victory almost within Grant's grasp.

The photograph below was made at Lookout Mountain, Tennessee, about eighteen months earlier, following the culmination of the Union victory at Chattanooga that precipitated Grant's promotion to lieutenant general and placed all Federal armies under his command.

Ole Peter Hansen Balling's heroic painting Grant and His Generals *presents almost every general to serve under Grant's command. From left to right, they are Thomas Devin, George A. Custer, Judson Kilpatrick, Philip H. Sheridan, William Emory, George Crooke, Wesley Merritt, George H. Thomas, Gouverneur Warren, George G. Meade, John G. Parke, William T. Sherman, John A. Logan, Grant (bareheaded), Ambrose Burnside, Joseph Hooker, Winfield Scott Hancock, John A. Rawlins, Edward Ord, Francis P. Blair, Alfred H. Terry, Henry W. Slocum, Jefferson C. Davis, O. O. Howard, John M. Schofield, and Joseph A. Mower. The three great commanders— Grant, Sherman, and Sheridan— served in sequence from 1864 to 1888 as general in chief of all U.S. forces.*

a campaign of sheer brilliance on Grant's part, involving maneuvers and few casualties and leading to a decisive victory.°

JMM

°His capture of Vicksburg had several important consequences. It eliminated an entire Confederate army. It opened the whole Mississippi River to Union control. And because it occurred simultaneously with the great victory at Gettysburg, the capture of Vicksburg gave the Union cause a tremendous morale boost.°

JYS

°Lincoln sent Grant a remarkable letter saying that when the campaign began he had had his doubts. Now, with the capture of the river strongpoint, Lincoln realized that he had been wrong and Grant had been right. It was an exceptional letter to receive from the president of the United States. Grant had no idea how to reply; it simply humbled him.°

Grant's success at Vicksburg was rewarded with a promotion from major general of volunteers to major general in the regular army. He would validate that ranking at Chattanooga in November 1863.

GWG °Chattanooga was the capstone of Grant's service in the West. He arrived in a city that was under siege by Braxton Bragg's Army of Tennessee. Grant found the Army of the Cumberland demoralized after its defeat at Chickamauga two months earlier, and he pulled together a chaotic situation. He brought in his friend Sherman, he received reinforcements from the East, and he won a decisive victory at Chattanooga—a victory that became the springboard for his eventual command of all Union armies.•

WCD °Until the end of 1863, Grant and Lincoln had never met. All the time that the president's commanders in Virginia had been giving him one defeat after another, bad news after bad news, chewing up troops and achieving nothing, word had been coming from the West of the man Grant who had taken Fort Donelson and cut off the Tennessee and Cumberland Rivers. Of Grant who had stopped a Confederate invasion at Shiloh. Of Grant who had taken Vicksburg for him and given Lincoln the Mississippi River. And Grant who had broken this terrible stalemate siege at Chattanooga, turned it to his advantage, and sent the Confederate army retreating into Georgia. There was no question that when Lincoln looked for someone to turn the war around in 1864, there was only one direction in which

The photograph above was made shortly after Grant had been promoted to major general in the regular army and given command of the western theater. He was en route to Chattanooga and would be followed quickly by Sherman with reinforcements for the besieged Union army. Confederate President Jefferson Davis was also en route to Chattanooga to mediate a spat between the two Southern commanders, Braxton Bragg and James Longstreet, which he settled by sending Longstreet to attack Knoxville. Grant was grateful. While he believed Bragg and Longstreet would have been formidable foes, the division of their forces was, in his opinion, an example of Davis's poor military acumen.

Grant's headquarters were simple, consisting of a few tents. Those around him were opinionated and verbose, and the general listened to everything they said without commenting. One visitor described the two sides of Grant he encountered in this environment. The first was moody, dull, and unsocial, but the second was pleasant, genial, and agreeable. Grant smoked almost constantly and had a habit of whittling sticks into small chips,

Julia Grant posed with her two eldest children, Frederick Dent (named for her father) and Nellie. Two other younger sons are not pictured, Ulysses Jr. and Jesse (named for Grant's father). Frederick followed his father in camp and had seen five battles by the time he was thirteen years old. He later attended West Point and pursued a military career, but he was always seen as Grant's eldest son, not an individual in his own right. Nellie married an Englishman during her father's occupancy of the White House and moved overseas. The marriage was not a happy one, and the situation compounded the ache the Grants felt at her living so far away.

he could look, and that was to the West and to Grant.•

IN 1864 THE PRESIDENT promoted Grant to the rank of lieutenant general. With this new rank came new responsibilities. Grant now was in charge of all Union armies and came east to achieve what had seemed impossible for three years: the defeat of Robert E. Lee and the Army of Northern Virginia.

BP   °Grant was able to do what no other Union commander thus far had been able to do, and that was to accept the idea of working in concert with other armies, east and west, to launch a simultaneous offensive. On May 1, 1864, this unified offensive sent Sherman forth to strike at the Deep South while Grant struck against Lee's army. That was exactly the kind of strategy Lincoln most wanted to see put into action.•

The president approved the proposed offensive and said: "Grant is the first general I have had. You know how it's been with all the rest. They all wanted me to be general. Now it isn't so with Grant. He hasn't told me what his plans are. I don't know, and I don't want to know. I am glad to find a man that can go ahead without me."

At the heart of Grant's strategy was a simple belief held over from his youth. He later explained it, saying, "One of my superstitions had always been when I started to go anywhere, to do anything, not to turn back or stop until the thing intended was accomplished." The Army of the Potomac would find out what Grant meant by that when he led them into Virginia's Wilderness on May 5, 1864, for his first showdown with Lee.

JYS   °In the Wilderness, Lee struck before Grant was ready, and the army took tremendous casualties. Anybody but Grant would have turned back after that encounter.• In the heat of the battle a distraught Union officer came to Grant with concerns over what Lee would do next. The general's response proved without a doubt that someone new was in charge: "I'm heartily sick and tired of hearing what Lee is going to do. Go back to your command and think about what we're going to do to Lee instead of worrying about what he's going to do to us."

JYS   After the fighting in the Wilderness had ended, Grant achieved a moral victory when he ordered his army to move south. His men responded with cheers. °This was the turning point of the war. The army had been in the same area many times. It had been defeated there many times. It had pulled back to Washington for regrouping and reinforcement many times. This time, however, there was a determination that this would be the last campaign of the Civil War—no matter what it cost.•

JMM   °Grant sent a telegram to Lincoln at about that time, saying that whatever happened, there would be no turning back. Lincoln knew he could rely on Grant's word, and Grant never turned back.•

JYS   °The spring campaign of 1864 was a costly encounter for the Army of the Potomac from the Wilderness to Spotsylvania to Cold Harbor. At Cold Harbor, Grant made an unsuccessful assault on Lee's forces and then two days later launched a second assault. The second attack was the one that he regretted for the rest of his life. Many of his soldiers had pinned their names on their uniforms so that their bodies could be identified later. They had a sense of impending death as they went against tremendous odds, and in fact the second assault on Cold Harbor was nearly as awful and as disastrous as was Pickett's charge at Gettysburg.•

WCD   °It was at Cold Harbor that Grant acquired a reputation and the nickname of "Grant the Butcher" because of the tremendous and senseless losses incurred there out of an act of frustration. It is a reputation that has been expanded over the century or more since then, but it is a reputation that is undeserved. The fact is that in the three years prior to 1864 the Union armies in Virginia suffered more than one hundred thousand casualties and achieved nothing. In the six weeks after Grant took command and started the last campaign, his army

Successful officers in the field frequently received gifts from the public as well as from their own men. For example, Grant was inundated with cigars from admirers when his penchant for them was publicized following his victory at Shiloh. The presentation-grade light brass railroad latern (below) by Kelly & Co. of Rochester was a similar gift. The fixed hand-blown globe is engraved, adding to its value and indicating that the lantern was given to Grant following his elevation in rank to lieutenant general.

Grant's last campaign was a series of flanking maneuvers against Lee's Army of Northern Virginia. Following the fighting at Spotsylvania in May 1864, Grant made his headquarters at Massaponax Church. Aides pulled pews out of the church for an open-air council of war, and fortunately Timothy O'Sullivan set his camera in one of the church windows and recorded what followed. In the first picture (above left) Grant sits in the pew directly in front of the two trees. Meade occupies the corner of the pew at the far left. The man standing at the right seems to be reading something aloud. In the second picture Grant has moved to the far left pew to talk with Meade as they both review a map. In the third picture Grant has returned to his original position to write, presumably, orders of march.

removed Lee from the war by bottling him up in Petersburg and placing the city under siege. Grant accomplished this at a cost of sixty thousand casualties. The figure was high, certainly, but it was a much better tradeoff than one hundred thousand for nothing. That was not butchery. That was using an army the way it was supposed to be used.•

BP °Grant was a man who abhorred bloodshed, who felt deeply the horror of war. But the very fact that he realized the horror of war meant that he was going to try to end that conflict as soon as possible.

A telling, visual example of Grant's style of command in that desperate overland campaign can be seen in the remarkable photographs taken by Timothy O'Sullivan at Massaponax Church in Virginia.• In the first of O'Sullivan's photographs (top of page), which offers a rare behind-the-scenes look at a Union war council, Grant is seen smoking a cigar, lost in thought amidst a whirl of activity. In the second photograph Grant has moved to peer intently at a map over Gen. George Gordon Meade's shoulder. And in the last image, a resolute Grant has returned to his seat to

BP write his battle orders. °From those photographs, almost newsreel-like, one gets a sense of what Grant must have been like in action.•

By April 1865, Grant's strategy to keep moving south and applying continuous pressure on Lee had worked. Grant had broken the siege at Petersburg, Sherman had burned his way to Atlanta and the Carolinas, and Gen. Philip Sheridan had laid waste to the

Shenandoah Valley, the Confederate breadbasket. Lee had no choice but to surrender when his army was cornered at Appomattox.

GWG °The encounter at Appomattox offered the most graphic example of Grant's essential humanity. He stood at the brink of the greatest victory that any American soldier had ever achieved. He was in a position to humiliate his enemies if he wanted to, but he did not.•

WCD °Grant had experienced defeat in his life in ways that most never had. He had failed at almost everything he had tried. As a result, at Appomattox when he had imposed on Lee the ultimate failure any soldier can suffer, all Grant could think of were Lee's feelings.• He recalled, "I felt like anything rather than rejoicing at the downfall of a foe who had fought for so long and valiantly and had suffered so much for a cause, though that cause was, I believe, one of the worst for which a people ever fought."

TJF °Even though he was known as Unconditional Surrender Grant, he never mentioned the phrase "unconditional surrender." Instead, he gave Lee very generous terms,• allowing the Southern officers to keep their sidearms and all who owned their horses to take them home for the spring planting. Grant also shared his army's rations with the starving enemy troops, and

On April 9, 1865, the two commanding generals, Grant and Lee, met in the front parlor of Wilmer McLean's home at Appomattox Court House. Lee wore an immaculate uniform and arrived before Grant; Grant entered with his coat open and his clothes muddy and soiled. The two shook hands as Grant's staff filled the room. Rather than discuss the surrender, Lee and Grant talked about their experiences in Mexico during the war almost twenty years earlier, until Lee reminded Grant why they were there. The surrender terms were discussed and slightly modified; allowing any Southerner, not just officers, to take his horse with him for the late spring planting. When all was agreed upon, the two rose and shook hands again in parting. Grant made some allowance for rations to be delivered to the former Army of Northern Virginia. The two men met again the next day and then mingled with small reunions of West Point classmates of both armies.

President Andrew Johnson, a Tennessee Unionist, was caught between wanting to punish anyone who had been active in the service of the Confederacy and wanting to recognize the constitutional rights of the newly enfranchised black population. Congress, however, passed the severest Reconstruction policies it could devise. In a fallacious move, Johnson decided to take the issue to the people and tour the country with the great heroes of the Union to bolster his presence and bring out the crowds. It was a disaster. In this rare photograph (above left) Grant stands with Secretary of the Navy Gideon Welles and Johnson on the steps of former New York Governor Throop's home. To Julia, Grant wrote: "I have never been so tired of anything before as I have been with the political speeches of Mr. Johnson."

Johnson, meanwhile, gave Grant a fourth star (above right) and the title of general of the army, which had not been used since 1799 when a grateful Congress had given it to George Washington. A year after his promotion, Grant accepted the Republican nomination for the presidency and won the White House.

although the surrender was indeed unconditional, Grant allowed Lee to leave Appomattox with his dignity and his sword.

TJF °That was the end at Appomattox. The war ended there on a note of reconciliation, and it should never be forgotten that Grant was the man who struck that note.• As the general told his officers, "The war is over. The Rebels are our countrymen again."

BP °VICTORY OVER LEE propelled Grant into greatness. It placed him on a pedestal. He would never be able to escape the limelight. It gave him great honor, but it also propelled him into realms that it probably would have been best he never enter. He was a soldier; he was not cut out to be a politician.• Nevertheless, in 1868 Ulysses S. Grant was elected the eighteenth president of the United States. °Elected to that high position, the American people expected a great deal from the hero who had won the Civil War. With Lincoln's death, Grant had become the greatest living American hero. Unfortunately, Grant, who had been a great unmilitary general, now wanted to be a nonpolitical president, and this was not an effective tactic.•

JYS

WCD °Grant, who understood soldiers, had never understood politicians. As far back as 1863 his friend Sher-

man had warned him to avoid the political chicanery of Washington, describing the capital as a nest of thieves. What happened was exactly that when Grant moved into the White House in 1868 and found himself among men who were far more subtle than he, men whom he believed because he was naive, and men who disappointed him.•

As a result, Grant's presidency was plagued with corruption and scandal. Although Grant himself was never accused of wrongdoing, as a president, he is considered a failure. He left office after two terms in 1877.

°Even so, he was now only fifty-five years old and had no idea what he should do. While he was making up his mind, he embarked on a tour around the world that lasted more than two years. Although the Grants traveled as private citizens, they were welcomed everywhere and received a more than normal welcome for former heads of states. Everybody wanted to see the great American hero, and Grant rose to the occasion.• A reporter for the *New York Herald* covered the world tour

The inauguration of 1868 had one element of intrigue: Would Johnson ride with Grant to the ceremony? Grant had finally broken with Johnson over the president's nominee to replace Secretary of War Edwin Stanton. The acrimony between the two was never as great as it was made out to be in the newspapers, but on the morning of Grant's inauguration Johnson chose not to attend the ceremony and called his cabinet to meet in regular business session. In an effort to appear gracious, Grant had his carriage pull up to the gate of the White House, but he was told that the president was too busy to be disturbed. Johnson vacated the mansion while Grant took the oath of office.

JYS

Grant's cabinet had many men who had been with him in the field. While he proved to be an outstanding commander, Grant was no politician. The depiction of the cabinet in 1869 (right) correctly shows the president being ignored by (left to right) Secretary of the Interior Jacob D. Cox, Secretary of State Hamilton Fish, Secretary of War John Rawlins, Postmaster General John Creswell, Secretary of the Treasury George Boutwell, Secretary of the Navy Adolph Borie, and Attorney General Ebenezer Hoar.

The photograph below was made shortly after Grant's inauguration and was reported to be one of his favorites.

and wrote: "[Grant] liked Thebes better than Milan, the Pyramids than Cologne. The preference was typical. It was the colossal character that impressed him, not the artistic elaboration or effect."

Upon his return to America, Grant's popularity was such that he was nearly nominated for president a third time in 1880. The following year, he settled in New York City, where he hoped to live the life of a prosperous businessman by investing all of his money in Grant and Ward, his son's Wall Street firm.

°Suddenly, however, Grant and Ward was bankrupted. Ward, it turned out, was basically a swindler. Not only did he lose millions of dollars of Grant's friends, but all of Grant's money, too. The former president was literally broke. He had to borrow money to live from hand to mouth.•

Now as poor as he had been before the Civil War, Grant sought to provide for his family by accepting Mark Twain's generous offer to publish his memoirs. But writing them soon became complicated when he was diagnosed with throat cancer.

°The writing of his memoirs, in a way, was a final example of Grant's excelling as a soldier, because here his enemy was disease, and it was a battle he was not going to win. But he fought with all the grit and determination that he had shown at Donelson and at Shiloh and at Chattanooga and at Appomattox.•

On his doctor's orders, Grant moved to Mount McGregor, a resort in Upstate New York. He continued writing despite the pain that cost him his voice and the side effects of such medication as cocaine. As the end neared, he wrote to his doctor: "I think I am a verb instead of a personal pronoun. A verb is anything that signifies to be, to do, or to suffer. I signify all three."

On July 23, 1884, just four days after his memoirs were completed, Ulysses S. Grant died. He was sixty-three years old. He never had the chance to teach mathematics. He never had the chance to train horses. But as he wrote in his memoirs, "Man proposes, God disposes."

Of Grant, then General in Chief Philip Sheridan pronounced, "When military history is analyzed it will show that he was the steadfast center about and on WCD which everything else turned." °There was no other soldier in the world who demonstrated the ability to wield

When the Grants vacated the White House in 1877, they decided to vacation in England. They returned two years later having taken perhaps the grandest world tour ever made by an American couple. Unusually, the tourists themselves were on display, making the Grants ambassadors of American simplicity and American power. They were entertained constantly, and their travels were reported so that Grant's latest adventure could be enjoyed vicariously by every American. A correspondent for the New York Herald joined the Grant entourage and commemorated the venture in a two-volume work that sold well across the country. A cartoonist's view of the expedition (below) played on the ubiquitous cigar and the easily caricatured Grant.

This is the last photograph of Grant, taken four days before his death as he reviewed a newspaper on the porch of the Drexel cottage in Mount McGregor, New York. Dying of throat cancer, the former general of the army and president of the United States focused all his energies on the completion of his memoirs with the hope that its successful sales would provide financial security for his family. Following the book's publication, Julia never worried about money again and even recorded her own reminiscences that sold well, too.

Flags flew at half-mast over New York's city hall in memory of the former president (below left). Grant's body was escorted from Saratoga to Manhattan by a detachment of U.S. army regulars and a group of veterans of the Army of the Potomac, then known as the Grand Army of the Republic.

Grant's funeral (below right) was held on August 8, 1885, and the casket was escorted to a temporary tomb in Riverside Park overlooking the Hudson River. This photograph captured the procession as it neared the intersection of Thirteenth Street and Fifth Avenue.

such a huge machine as the Union army and to bend it to the mighty purpose of winning the war. That was Grant's great achievement.•

°His style of waging war—realistic, concentrate your strength, win as quickly as you can, go for the jugular, hold nothing back, work closely with your administration because "we are a democracy"—is what soldiers aspire to today, because it is the only way to wage war.• His West Point colleague and later adversary, Confederate Gen. James Longstreet, observed, "As the world con-

tinues to look at and study the grand combinations and strategy of General Grant, the higher will be his reward as a soldier."

Grant's body was taken by rail to New York City, where it lay in state at city hall for two days. Then the funeral procession made its way uptown to Riverside Park as thousands lined the route. There had been an enormous instinctive bond between Grant and the common people. They sensed that he was one of them and that he expressed something deep within themselves, especially his love of the Union.

He was buried in a temporary brick tomb. In 1897 his body was reinterred in a marble-and-granite memorial overlooking the Hudson River. Meanwhile, Grant's memoirs had been a tremendous success. More than three hundred thousand copies were sold, and Julia, his widow, received nearly $450,000 in royalties.

Grant's personal memoirs are a book much like Grant himself: simple, unpretentious, yet brilliant in its own way. It is one of the finest memoirs ever written in America. Mark Twain himself said, "It's a book I wish I had written."

The general and former president closed his memoirs with the statement: "I feel that we are on the eve of a new era when there is to be a great harmony between the Federal and the Confederate. I cannot stay to be a living witness to the correctness of this prophesy, but I feel it within me, that it is to be so. Let us have peace."

Ulysses S. Grant will always be something of a mystery, yet there is one clue to the man that serves as the best way to remember him. It came from General Sherman, who said: "Grant more clearly than any other man impersonated the American character of 1861 to '65. He will stand therefore as the typical hero of the great Civil War."

A decade after the funeral some of the same soldiers made the pilgrimage to the dedication of Grant's Tomb. Attendance was low, however, due to heavy rain, but the sentiment was expressed eloquently from Grant's own memoirs, both toward the nation and the man commemorated by the tomb, in the carved inscription over the entryway: "Let us have peace."

JAMES LONGSTREET

He was ROBERT E. LEE'S senior
lieutenant, and Lee called him "my old warhorse."
Outranking even Stonewall Jackson, he commanded
the legendary First Corps of the Army of Northern Virginia. A true Confederate hero, to many James Longstreet was the best corps commander on either side of
the war. Yet he is known as the man who argued with
Lee at Gettysburg and lost the war for the South. For
that reason, °Longstreet is the Confederacy's most controversial soldier.°

JMM

His recalcitrance peaked on the third day at Gettysburg when, in response to the order that would be Pickett's charge, he confronted his commander and said that
no fifteen thousand men ever arranged for battle could
succeed on that field and take the Federal position.

Afterward, with failure apparent, he said: "I would
prefer that all the blame should rest upon me. As General Lee is our commander, he should have the support
and influence we can give him. The truth will be known
in time, and I will leave that to show how much of the
responsibility rests on my shoulders."

WCD

°Longstreet is the great might-have-been of the Confederacy. If only Longstreet had been a better man, if
only Longstreet had been a better general, Lee might
have won the battle of Gettysburg, Lee might have
destroyed a Yankee army at Second Manassas, the South
might have won the war. He is one of the great scape-
goats of history.°

In the immediate aftermath of Gettysburg, one of
Longstreet's division commanders, Maj. Gen. Lafayette

ECB	Edwin C. Bearss
WCD	William C. Davis
GWG	Gary W. Gallagher
JMM	James M. McPherson
JDW	Jeffry D. Wert

The highlight of James Longstreet's service during the Mexican War occurred in the storming of Chapultepec on September 12, 1847. He was wounded as he carried the colors toward the crest of the wall and turned and handed the flag to his friend George Pickett, who bore the colors over the wall and into the fortress.

McLaws, assessed his corps commander's actions on the field and concluded, "I think the attack was unnecessary and the whole plan of battle a very bad one. General Longstreet is to blame for not reconnoitering the ground and for persisting in ordering the assault when his errors were discovered. During the engagement he was really excited, giving orders to everyone. I consider him a humbug. A man of small capacity, not at all chivalrous, exceedingly conceited, and totally selfish. If I can, it is my intention to get away from his command."

Years later, in 1938, a veteran of the war tersely noted, "Longstreet opposed Pickett's charge. Failure shows he was right. All those damnable lies about Longstreet make me want to shoulder a musket and fight another war."

GWG °A tremendous debate has raged through the years about just how good a general Longstreet was. Some say he was one of the best corps commanders produced during the entire war, North or South. Others argue that he probably did as much mischief on the battlefield as he did good for the Confederacy. The degree to which controversy swirls around Longstreet extends even to how different writers describe his height. Those who tend to be unfavorable to Longstreet say he was about five feet ten. In fact, he was about six feet two.•

James Longstreet was born on January 8, 1821, in Edgefield District, South Carolina, to James and Mary Ann Dent Longstreet. His mother brought him to the family's cotton plantation near Gainesville, Georgia, when he was just a few weeks old, and for the rest of his life he called Georgia his home. He once said, "My earliest recollections were of the Georgia side of the Savannah River, and my school days were passed there."

He was called Pete by his family. The boy spoke often of a military career, and childish dreams of glory filled his head as he read books about Alexander the JDW Great, Julius Caesar, and George Washington. °He loved the outdoors, and his body developed as one suited to outdoor activity, which in turn would make him well adapted to army life, a life he enjoyed.• Recalling his youth and these aspirations, he wrote: "My father was a planter. From my early boyhood he conceived that he would send me to West Point for army service. But in my twelfth year he passed away during the cholera epidemic at Augusta. Mother moved to North Alabama with her children, whence in my sixteenth year I made application to a kinsman, Congressman Rubin Chapman, for appointment as cadet. [I] received the coveted favor and entered with the class that was admitted in 1838."

To prepare for admission to West Point, Longstreet was taken to Augusta in the fall of 1830 to live with his Uncle Augustus and attend the Richmond County Academy. Augustus Longstreet was a talented, well-educated man who had served in the state legislature and who was a strong advocate for states' rights.

GWG °Four years at West Point was very tough for most young men. The life was extremely spartan, the quarters were spare, the food was terrible, the discipline was rigorous, and the classes were difficult because it was basically an engineering school. The cadets, especially those from the South whose schooling almost always was not as good as their northern counterparts, struggled with the math and the physics in the curriculum.• Longstreet later confessed: "As a cadet, I had more interest in the

Following a better service record in Mexico than his last-place ranking in the West Point class of 1846 portended, George E. Pickett received two brevet promotions and served throughout the interwar years in Texas, Virginia, and Washington Territory. In 1861 he resigned his commission to offer his services to his home state of Virginia. There he was again placed under Longstreet's command.

Longstreet first met Louise Garland in 1844 when she visited her father, Lt. Col. John Garland, Longstreet's regimental commander, at Jefferson Barracks in Saint Louis. She was slender, petite, and quite attractive, with high cheekbones and black hair. They married on March 8, 1848, and the couple had ten children, but only five survived childhood. Two died in infancy, and three died in a scarlet fever epidemic that raged through Richmond in 1862. The photograph of Louise and the two oldest children—twelve-year-old John Garland, left, and three-year-old James, right—was probably taken in 1860.

school of the soldier. Horsemanship, sword exercise, and the outside game of football than in the academic courses. The studies were successfully passed, however, until the third year when I failed in mechanics."

Many of the cadets Longstreet befriended at West Point fought at his side in the future conflict between the North and the South, and some of them faced him across the battlefield. JDW °His best friend was in the class behind him, a cadet from Ohio named Ulysses Grant. In contrast to Longstreet's enthusiasm for the life of a soldier, Grant was one of the more reluctant cadets at West Point.•

ECB °In 1842 Longstreet graduated fifty-fourth in a class of sixty-two, but class rankings rarely presage how good a general the graduate becomes. George B. McClellan was second in his class, but he failed to end the war when he had the opportunities.•

JDW °Longstreet's first assignment was one of the better posts in the army: Jefferson Barracks outside of Saint Louis.• He commented, "I was fortunate in the assignment to Jefferson Barracks for in those days the young officers were usually sent off among the Indians, or as near the borders as they could find habitable places."

At Jefferson Barracks, Lieutenant Longstreet met Louise Garland, the daughter of his post commander. After a long courtship, they were married in the spring of 1848. The marriage lasted more than forty years, and Louise bore ten children—only five of whom lived through childhood.

Longstreet's first military action was with the Eighth Infantry in the Mexican War. He served under Gen. Zachary Taylor and was cited for bravery and coolness under fire. JDW °After Taylor's operations ended in northern Mexico, the Eighth Infantry was assigned to Winfield Scott's army, which was marching on Mexico City. There, in the storming of Chapultepec, Longstreet carried the flag of the Eighth Infantry. As they were going over the fortress wall, he was wounded, shot in the leg, and fell back. In one of the touching moments of history, he turned and handed the flag to George Pickett,• °who then carried it across the Mexican defensive wall. Later Pickett became one of the principal division commanders under Longstreet in the Civil War.•

In November 1860, Abraham Lincoln was elected president, and beginning with South Carolina, the southern states left the Union. Longstreet was faced with the most important decision of his life, but he made it quickly.

°One of the great tragedies of the American Civil War, and one of the reasons it has been called "the brothers war," is that so many professional army men who had been close friends, classmates together at West Point and colleagues in the old army—the peacetime army and the Mexican War army—found themselves on opposite sides.• °A southern officer in the U.S. Army in 1861 had three choices. He could stay in the U.S. Army, resign and accept a commission in the Confederate army, or resign and go home and become a civilian. Very few men took the third choice because that would have meant standing by while their kin fought bloody battles against Northerners.•

Longstreet, a major in the U.S. Army, resigned and wrote, "I desire to tender through you my services to Alabama should she need a soldier who has seen hard service. I am the senior officer of the army from Alabama and should be the first to offer her such assistance in my profession as I may be able to render."

THE LAST TIME Longstreet had worn gray was as a West Point cadet. Now he wore it in defense of his homeland. In the spring of 1861, he had given twenty years of service to the Union blue, but he rode off to fight for the South. Recalling that day, he wrote: "It was a sad day when we took leave of lifetime comrades and gave up a service of twenty years. Neither Union officers nor their families made efforts to conceal feelings of deepest regret. When we drove out from the post, a number of officers rode with us, which only made the last farewell

There was little time for Longstreet to grieve for his lost children or worry over the prolonged illness of his eldest son when the Federals began moving en masse to the Virginia Peninsula. With mourning crepe on his sleeve, Longstreet moved with his division to meet the threat. He did not agree with the series of withdrawals he was ordered to make as the Union army advanced on Richmond, but he took heart when command of the army was given to Robert E. Lee. Following the successful Seven Days' battles, Longstreet emerged as Lee's most reliable subordinate commander, with Lee stating, "Longstreet was the staff in my right hand." In the photograph above Longstreet wears a short Austrian-style tunic that enjoyed a brief popularity in the Confederate army during the early months of the war.

Longstreet was never more composed than when in combat. At Sharpsburg, Maryland, on September 17, 1862, he found a strong defensible position in an eroded farm road and placed his men in the natural rifle pit. When the focus of the Union attack turned to the center of the Confederate line and Longstreet's men in the sunken road, the Federals were, in the Southern commander's words, "mowed down like grain before the scythe." Only through the force of numbers were the bluecoats able to breach the sunken road and turn the terrain against the Confederates who fell in turn, but the affair lasted for hours and depleted the attacking force so that it could not follow through on the break in the line. Thereafter, Antietam and the Bloody Lane were scorched into the American conscience as the bloodiest day in American history.

JMM

more trying. At every station old men, women, and children assembled, clapping hands and waving handkerchiefs to cheer the passengers on to Richmond, the spirit electrified the air. And the laborers of the fields, white and black, stopped their plows to lift their hats and wave us on to speedy travel."

°In 1861 the morale of the Confederate army was high. The Southerners were extremely confident, many of them actually believing the contemporary mythology that one of them could thrash at least three Yankees, maybe even as many as ten.• Thomas J. Goree, who would serve under Longstreet's command, observed: "The Yankees are not so keen to fight. In every fight that has taken place, they have ingloriously fled."

Finally Longstreet received an answer to the offer of his services, which were required almost immediately, as he remembered: "On the first of July I received notice of my appointment as brigadier general, with orders to report at Manassas Junction to General [P. G. T.] Beauregard."

GWG °Unlike many of his contemporaries who were cat-apulted into much higher positions, Longstreet clearly was up to the task, and he demonstrated that from the beginning. He moved easily into the position of being a brigadier general, although he had never commanded anything like that number of men before the war.•

Thrown into action a few days before the battle at Manassas, T. J. Goree noted: "On [July] 18th, a large body of the enemy made an attack, principally against General Longstreet's command, and it was with great difficulty that our men were persuaded to stand. Some of them started to fall back two or three times, but General Longstreet, amid a perfect shower of balls, rode amongst them with his cigar in his mouth, rally-ing them, encouraging and inspiring confidence among them."

WCD °Given the fact that Confederate soldiers were volun-teers, they were always somewhat skittish. Volunteers could be extremely brave, but at a moment's notice and for almost any reason, they could also turn and run. A general who stood his ground in front of them, a gen-eral who looked magnificent and acted magnificently, a general who played the role of the Sir Walter Scott storybook hero was the kind of man who gave them the confidence to put their own fears aside and to stand with him and fight.•

At Fredericksburg on December 13, 1862, Longstreet again took advan-tage of the topography to exploit a strong defensible position against superior numbers. Here he formed his men behind a stone wall that fronted a roadway at Marye's Heights and looked down over the sloping ground. For two days the Federals tried to breach the stone wall, but none came closer than thirty-five yards. One Union officer said, "[We] might as well have tried to take Hell." The photograph of the stone wall (left) was taken months later, after a second battle when the Union army had advanced on Chancel-lorsville, but it served as the model for A. C. Redwood's engraving of the fight at the stone wall for the Century magazine's four-volume work Battles and Leaders of the Civil War *(right). Redwood retained the dead soldier in the lower left corner and brought the house closer.*

The three-day battle of Gettysburg began with the collision of a Confederate patrol and Union cavalry on the outskirts of the town. It was a battle that neither side wanted to fight, but the skirmish led to both sides sending their armies en masse to the crossroads.

That was the image Longstreet projected. Moxley Sorrell, a captain and an aide-de-camp to Longstreet, elaborated on the general's demeanor, noting: "[He] was then a most striking figure. About forty years of age, a soldier every inch, and very handsome, tall, and well proportioned. Strong and active. A superb horseman and with unsurpassed soldierly bearing."

JMM °At first the Confederate troops, like the Union troops on the other side that volunteered en masse in 1861, were in fact nothing but an armed mob running around the countryside. They were civilians with no military experience; they had to be turned into an army.°

GWG °This need was what made a West Pointer like Longstreet so valuable early in the war. He was a professional soldier and at least knew the basics of military life, while many of his peers at that point did not.°

JMM °Longstreet was also an effective trainer of troops. He believed in drill and discipline. His troops may have disliked how hard he made them work, but it paid off, and Longstreet's brigade at First Manassas was one of the best drilled and best disciplined there. Those qualities continued to characterize his troops throughout the war.°

JDW °There were two critical standards for an officer in the Civil War, and Longstreet excelled at both. The first focused on how he took care of his men at camp, on the march, and, most particularly, in battle. The second

As the fighting escalated around Gettysburg, reinforcing Union infantry expelled Confederates from McPherson's Woods and took positions around a stone barn on the McPherson farm. They lost one of their corps commanders, John F. Reynolds, in the process. Without reconnoitering the fields, Gen. Henry Heth, whose Confederates were the first to arrive on the scene, called for Col. J. M. Brockenbrough's brigade to repulse the Federals from the farm.

standard was personal courage; officers had to demonstrate personal courage or they could not lead.•

WCD   °Longstreet was something of a man's man. He enjoyed the camaraderie of the campfire and a drink now and then, but he was by no means intemperate. He liked a good story, practical joking, playing pranks upon his fellow officers, and having pranks played upon him.•

During the Peninsula campaign in the late spring of 1862, Longstreet's commanding officer, Gen. Joseph E. Johnston, was wounded at the battle of Seven Pines. As his replacement, Gen. Robert E. Lee was appointed to command what would be called the Army of Northern Virginia. Thereafter, Lee and Longstreet would be forever linked in history. Lee evaluated his new lieutenant, noting: "Longstreet is a capital soldier. His recommendations heretofore have been good, and I have confidence in him."

GWG   °The first full year of the war, 1862, was a very good year for Longstreet as a soldier. He followed up his strong performance at the Seven Days' battles with an even better performance at Second Manassas, where he and his wing of the army delivered the decisive counterattack the last day of that fight, driving John Polk's Federal army from the field. Following Second Manassas, he and the Army of Northern Virginia went northward where they fought the battle of Antietam.• During the

Culp's Hill marked the extreme right end of the Federal line at Gettysburg, towering above Cemetery Hill and Cemetery Ridge. Had the Confederates seized this wooded summit, the Union positions on the lower hill and ridge would have been indefensible. The site was largely ignored by the Southerners on the first day, and so several Federal units were relocated to reinforce other positions on the line. Late on the afternoon of the second day, however, Confederates under Maj. Gen. Edward Johnson finally attacked. They met resistance from only one Union brigade under the command of Brig. Gen. George S. Greene, but the small Federal force successfully repulsed three Confederate brigades. Reinforcements were brought up that evening, and the fighting resumed the next morning. The Federals would not be dislodged, and the attack ended around noon. The focus of the battle then shifted to the center of the Union line.

battle he sent Lee a message saying: "I'm sending you the guns, my dear general. This is a hard fight and we had all better die than lose it."

GWG   °At Antietam, Longstreet showed his great strength as a tactical leader. His performance so impressed his commanding general that Lee bestowed the nickname "my old warhorse" on him,• saying: "Ah, here is Longstreet. Here is my old warhorse. Let us hear what he has to say."

On the same day in October 1862, the two finest brigadier generals in the Confederate army were each promoted to major general: Stonewall Jackson and James Longstreet.

GWG   °Perhaps Longstreet's most satisfactory moment as a commander came in December at the battle of Fredericksburg. It was his kind of battle. He had a strong defensive ground, and he had improved it with ample artillery support.• During the battle, Lee sent Longstreet a message, warning, "General, they are massing very heavily and will break your line, I'm afraid." But Longstreet replied: "General, if you put every man now on the other side of the Potomac on that field to approach me over the same line and give me plenty of ammunition, I will kill them all before they reach my line. Look to your right. You are in some danger there, but not on my line." Longstreet was correct.

GWG °Thousands of Federals were shot down in front of Longstreet's corps. It was a perfect victory as far as he was concerned. That was how war should be fought: pick your ground, smite the enemy, and then look for an opportunity to follow up your success.° Reviewing the field of the one-sided victory, Lee pronounced, "It is well that war is so terrible, lest we should grow too fond of it."

While 1862 had been good militarily for Longstreet, it was particularly tragic for him personally. In January 1862, Louise Longstreet cabled her husband to hurry to Richmond. All four of their children had come down with scarlet fever. Within a few desperate days three of them died. Neither Longstreet nor his wife could bring themselves to attend their children's funeral. George Pickett, now a longtime friend, saw to the burial of the Longstreet children in a Richmond cemetery.

JMM °Longstreet was never the same after that. Before that time he was talkative, and when he was in a good mood, he could enjoy a game of poker. After the deaths of his children, he was sometimes unapproachable. He suffered from depression and never fully recovered from that experience.°

On May 2, 1863, Stonewall Jackson was fatally wounded by his own men at the battle of Chancellorsville. Lee then needed to rely even more on

While Culp's Hill was under attack, the Federals on Cemetery Hill anticipated an assault, which finally occurred in the twilight as the fighting at the far left of the Union line subsided. At about 7:30 P.M. two brigades under Brig. Gen. Harry T. Hays and Col. Isaac E. Avery stormed up Cemetery Hill's eastern slope. Sixteen guns on the crest and six on Culp's fired on the charging Southerners. The Confederates, including Avery, fell in clumps, but they continued the charge, taking almost an hour to reach the top. A Union brigade collapsed as the fighting raged in the darkness around the guns. The attackers, however, were exhausted, and a Confederate division that was ordered to join the attack failed to appear. When a Union brigade counterattacked, the Southerners broke and withdrew, ending the fighting on the second day with the Union line intact.

On the afternoon of the third day at Gettysburg, George Pickett's three all-Virginia brigades spearheaded the last charge of the Confederacy across a mile of open field toward the center of the Federal line at Cemetery Ridge. The Southerners were decimated by Union artillery. Pickett tried valiantly to coordinate the ill-fated attack, but the task was impossible and his reputation was clouded. Following the withdrawal, Lee ordered him to re-form his division. A shell-shocked Pickett could only look up to his commander and reply, "Sir, I have no division left."

Battles tend to generate a lore of their own. On the first day at Gettysburg nineteen-year-old Lt. Bayard Wilkeson commanded a battery on the extreme right of the Federal line and impeded the progress of John B. Gordon's division. Confederate fire was concentrated on Wilkeson's battery and he fell, severely wounded, and died in a Confederate hospital that night. His father, Samuel Wilkeson, was a correspondent for the New York Times *and was in Meade's headquarters when his son was wounded. After the battle, he found his son's grave.*

Longstreet, his senior lieutenant, as he prepared for his summer campaign into Union territory, the campaign he hoped would bring victory at last to the South.

GETTYSBURG WAS A battle James Longstreet did not want to fight. When he arrived on the field on the afternoon of July 1, he found Gen. George Gordon Meade's Union army holding the high ground, and his own commander was planning an attack. Lee claimed, "If the enemy is there tomorrow, we must attack him." But Longstreet warned, "If he is there, it will be because he is anxious that we should attack him. A good reason, in my judgment, for not doing so."

JMM °The battle of Gettysburg was what military historians call a "meeting engagement." Neither commander had planned to fight at Gettysburg, but advance units of the two armies collided on the morning of July 1, 1863. Each of them called back to their commanders for reinforcements, and both sides continued to pour in reinforcements until the engagement escalated into a major battle.•

JDW °Longstreet did not want to fight on the battlefield at Gettysburg because of the superiority of the Federal position. It was the strongest position that the Union had held on any battlefield up until that time, and he saw that.• °Thus he recommended that the Confederates

JMM

shift their position to the south, find strong defensive ground of their own, and force the Union army to attack.• He argued: "We could not call the enemy to a position better suited to our plans. All we had to do was file around his left and secure good ground between him and his capital."

JMM °He reasoned that because a Confederate army was in Union territory, Meade, the Union commander, would be forced by political pressures to take the offensive to drive the enemy out of Pennsylvania. So he recommended to Lee that they find a strong position, wait for the inevitable Union attack, and then break it to pieces.•

GWG °Longstreet wanted ground of his own choosing. He believed he could hold a good position against anyone and then look for an opening to follow up a defensive victory. That was his ideal scenario: Make the enemy come to you, inflict heavy casualties on him, and then follow up with as powerful a counter-stroke as possible.•

JMM °The Confederacy was fighting a defensive war, a war to defend its independence. It did not have to invade and conquer the North to win that war, and so Longstreet believed that the Confederacy had to con-serve its manpower because it had fewer men than the North and fewer resources.• But Lee was in no mood for

James Walker's depiction of Pickett's charge from behind the Union line was "historically arranged" by Col. John Bachelder, the congressionally appointed historian of the battle. The work was five years in the making, with the artist surveying the ground shortly after the battle, while many dead still lay on the field, and inter-viewing Confederate prisoners and touring the battlefield with survivors. In the mid-foreground the wounded Gen. Lewis Armistead is depicted as he surrendered his personal effects to sol-diers with the request that they be given to his friend Union Gen. Win-field Scott Hancock. When the Federal commander George Meade saw the painting, he found it "wonderfully accurate in its delineation of the land-scape and position of troops." Longstreet saw it before its completion and announced that it was "a remark-ably fair and complete representation of that eventful scene. . . . That's where I came to grief."

Longstreet viewed the head-to-head engagement at Gettysburg as a mistake and verbalized his disagreement with Lee after the first day's fighting. On the morning of the second day, while Lee waited for a scouting report, an impromptu war council convened and Longstreet sat with John Bell Hood at his right. Noting that Pickett's division was not yet in the area, he told Hood that any attack would be premature, like going into battle "with one boot off." When the scouts returned, despite Longstreet's protestations, Lee ordered the attack.

defensive strategy on July 1, 1863. The successes of the first day had given him a taste of the prize he wanted so dearly—a great Confederate victory on Northern soil. He reasoned, "The enemy is here, and if we do not whip him, he will whip us." °Lee was combative. Some would say that his fighting blood was up. He had the enemy apparently on the ropes, and he was overconfident. He thought that his men could do anything he wanted.•

At eleven o'clock on the morning of July 2, against the advice of Longstreet, Lee ordered an attack against the strong Union position. °Longstreet, however, stalled, playing for time. He tried to persuade Lee to do something other than what Lee had already ordered. When Longstreet failed to get his way, he sulked.•

°Lee had a hot temper too, and some have argued that Longstreet was afraid of Lee's temper should he push him too far. But a lot of other officers would have pushed Lee harder.•

As the time to attack drew near, Maj. Gen. John Bell Hood, one of Longstreet's division commanders, requested permission several times to circle around and attack the Federals from the rear. Longstreet denied these requests. If General Lee insisted on a frontal assault, then that was what he would get.

°Longstreet was in a bad humor, even pouting, and he was going to do exactly as General Lee had ordered. He was going to follow those orders to the letter and not carry out his prerogative as a corps commander to make certain changes.• °He was going to do exactly what Lee had told him to do, to prove Lee wrong. As a result, many thousands of Confederate soldiers paid for that clash of wills in blood over the next three hours.•

Just after four o'clock, five hours after Lee had given the order, the Army of Northern Virginia began

The casualties both armies experienced were staggering. The Federals had lost 3,155 dead, 14,529 wounded, and 5,365 missing; the Confederates 3,903 dead, 18,735 wounded, and 5,425 missing. With Lee's retreat and Meade's army following but not anxious for another battle, the countryside around the little crossroads town in Pennsylvania was littered with the dead of both sides, and homes, shops, farms, and churches were filled with the wounded. These Confederate dead were interred near the Rose farm.

the attack. Although Longstreet had not agreed with Lee's decision to attack, he threw himself into it, personally leading the charge. One captured Union officer observed: "No wonder we are thrashed upon every field. There is not in the whole of our army a lieutenant general who would have risked his life in such a charge."

In his account of the attack, Longstreet reported: "We felt at every step the heavy stroke of fresh troops, the sturdy regular blow that tells a soldier instantly that he has encountered reserves or reinforcements. We received no support at all, and there was no evidence of cooperation on any side. To urge my men forward into these circumstances would have been madness, and I withdrew them in good order to the peach orchard that we had taken from the Federals early in the afternoon."

By the end of the second day at Gettysburg, four thousand of Longstreet's men lay dead or wounded. The Federals had fallen back to Cemetery Ridge, but they still held the high ground. The men

These three lean Confederate prisoners taken at Gettysburg portray a fierce sense of pride and fearlessness even after three days of battle. While the Army of Northern Virginia was depleted on the Pennsylvania field, the fighting spirit that pervaded its men was not extinguished and found expression in two more years of combat.

Disenchanted after the battle of Gettysburg, Longstreet was granted a transfer to the western theater. His timely arrival on the battlefield made Chickamauga a Confederate victory. Longstreet, however, could not work with Braxton Bragg, and he experienced defeat in trying to wrest Knoxville from Ambrose Burnside. He returned to Virginia in time to join Lee in his first encounter with the new Federal commander, U. S. Grant. Lee did not wait for Grant to attack him but struck first at the battle of the Wilderness. During the fighting, in an eerie parallel with Lee's unlikely victory at Chancellorsville, Longstreet was fired upon by his own men and wounded, very near the spot where Stonewall Jackson had been wounded the previous year. The wound knocked Longstreet out of the war for seven months. By then the end was in sight.

of the First Corps bedded down for the night on the bloody ground they had captured.

GWG   °Even though Longstreet had taken so long to get into position, he had come very close to breaking the Federal line. That must have given Lee a sense that if only they had attacked a couple of hours earlier, if only this or that had gone differently, they would have succeeded on the second day. He would have thought, *If we do it right tomorrow, we will succeed.*°

That night Lee ordered a morning attack against Cemetery Ridge, with George Pickett's division leading the charge. The agony of Gettysburg was not over for James Longstreet.

OF THE PROPOSED attack, Longstreet said: "I don't want to make this attack. I believe it will fail. I do not see how it can succeed. I would not make it even now but that General Lee has ordered it and expects it."

GWG   °By the morning of July 3, Lee must have been disappointed in Longstreet, his prime lieutenant. This was the man he had relied upon, the one among all his subordinates from whom he had expected great results. Yet Longstreet had not done well the preceding day, and now he was disagreeing again with what Lee wanted to do.°

ECB   °At Gettysburg on the third day, Longstreet told General Lee: "I have been a soldier all my life. I have commanded companies. I have commanded regiments. I have commanded divisions. And I have commanded even more. But," as he pointed toward Cemetery Ridge, "there are no fifteen thousand men in the world that can go across that ground." Lee replied, "There is the enemy, and there I mean to attack him."•

Crestfallen, Longstreet recorded: "Never was I so depressed as upon that day. I thought that my men were to be sacrificed and that I should have to order them to make a hopeless charge."

The attack that became known as Pickett's charge was preceded by a furious exchange of artillery fire. Explosions tore holes in the Confederate ranks as they waited for the order to advance. One of Pickett's brigade commanders, James Kemper, noted: "While this was going on, Longstreet rode slowly and alone immediately in front of our entire line. I expected to see him fall every instant. Still he moved on, slowly and majestically, with a repressed power in every movement and look that fascinated me."

Minutes later Longstreet was resting when Pickett came to him for the order to attack. "Shall I lead my division forward, sir?" he asked. Longstreet recalled: "The effort to speak the order failed, and I could only indicate it by an affirmative bow. He accepted the order with seeming confidence of success, leaped on his horse, and rode gaily to his command."

Pickett's charge was a failure. Lee's Army of Northern Virginia retreated. Never again would the entire army cross the Potomac River. One Southern soldier vowed, "I'm willing to fight them as long as General Lee says fight, but I think we're ruined now without going any further with it." Lee blamed himself, saying, "It is all my fault." Pickett too blamed Lee, charging, "That old man had my division massacred."

JDW °Pickett's charge is the great question of the battle. Why was Lee so adamant in his belief that this charge would succeed? When Longstreet told him the truth, Lee would not accept it. There is only one conclusion. Lee believed that his infantry was invincible, and if properly led and properly supported, they could have taken the center of the Federal line.•

Longstreet (front row, fifth from left) was a frequent visitor to the Gettysburg battlefield after the war. It was here that his reputation had been damaged and here that controversy arose over who was to blame for the defeat. Lee was above reproach, so the blame had to rest on one of his subordinates. Since Longstreet had dared to criticize Lee's decisions at Gettysburg, he came to be the most likely culprit. The Union was not without its own controversy at Gettysburg. Daniel E. Sickles (standing at Longstreet's left) had moved his men beyond the Federal line and lost a third of his command and his right leg. He maintained that had he not done so, Longstreet's attack on the second day would have broken through the Union line. Sickles found one of his greatest supporters in Longstreet himself, who said that he would have done just that had Sickles not hindered him.

WCD °Certainly a part of the chastening and the leavening of Longstreet's character in the war resulted from the constant loss around him. The death of his children naturally upset him. Additionally, in encounter after encounter he saw the men he had trained and led going into battle and not surviving. Most of all at Gettysburg, of course, when the attack was made on July 3 of which he did not approve and which he had no choice but to carry out, he saw two divisions shattered, never to be rebuilt again. Those visions and memories had to have a tremendous psychological impact on a man like Longstreet.•

In September, at his own request, Longstreet was sent with two divisions to report to Gen. Braxton Bragg GWG in Tennessee, °but his experience in the West in the fall of 1863 was a mixed bag. He was successful at the battle of Chickamauga where his troops launched the decisive attack. After that, however, he and Bragg quarreled. They were upset with each other during the siege of Chattanooga, and eventually Longstreet went off to lay siege to Knoxville, where he did very poorly against a Union force under Ambrose Burnside.•

In the grip of depression after his failure at Knoxville, Longstreet requested he be relieved of his command, explaining: "I earnestly desire that some other officer be sent to the command. It is fair to infer that the fault for Knoxville is entirely with me, and I desire, therefore, that some other commander be tried." The secretary of war refused to accept his resignation, and he was sent back to Virginia.

GWG °A tremendous reunion occurred when Longstreet and his men returned. As Lee and Longstreet cantered up and down the Confederate lines, wild cheering broke out among the troops at the sight of Lee and of Longstreet with Lee.• The joyous reunion was short-lived, however, for at the battle of the Wilderness, Longstreet was mistakenly shot by his own troops.

GWG °Longstreet was hit in the throat with a minié ball with such force that it lifted him out of the saddle. He was a large man, so it took tremendous impact to do that. As he was being taken from the field, Lee realized that it was Longstreet in the ambulance,• and a staff officer who was present said that Lee seemed almost overcome with emotion. Another soldier noted: "I never on any occasion during the four years of the war saw a group of officers and gentlemen more deeply distressed. They were literally bowed down with grief. All of them were in tears. It was not a lone general they admired who had been shot down, it was rather the man they loved."

LONGSTREET RECOVERED FROM his wound, but it required many months. He lost the use of his right arm, and his once clear voice became hoarse and raspy. By the time

After the war President Andrew Johnson proclaimed that former Confederates could apply for official pardons from the government. Longstreet (above) sought a pardon with the endorsement of his longtime friend U. S. Grant. Johnson, however, refused to grant the pardon with the statement, "There are three persons of the South who can never receive amnesty: Mr. Davis, General Lee, and yourself. You have given the Union cause too much trouble." The next administration was more benevolent, and in June 1868 Congress enacted a law granting pardons and restoring political rights to a number of former Confederates, including Longstreet.

Eight years after his wife's death, Longstreet, then seventy-six years old, married thirty-four-year-old Helen Dortch, a graduate of Brenau College in Gainesville, Georgia, and the assistant state librarian of Georgia. "Old men get lonely and must have company," he said.

he returned to his command, the war was winding down. Lee's army was fighting a holding action and was close to collapse, but the South would not surrender until the following spring at Appomattox.

GWG °Longstreet was with Lee to the very end. He made the long trek from the defenses of Richmond and Petersburg westward to Appomattox.° As Lee left camp to meet with Grant, Longstreet said, "General, if he does not give us good terms, come back and let us fight it out."

But the terms were generous, and the surrender reunited Longstreet with his old friend Grant, who approached him and said, "Pete, let us have another game of brag to recall the old days which were so pleasant to us all." Longstreet's feelings toward Grant had not changed during four years of civil war, and he observed, "General Grant was the truest as well as the bravest man who ever lived."

After the surrender, the officers of the Army of Northern Virginia bade farewell to one another. T. J. Goree, one of Longstreet's officers, recalled: "When General Lee was about to take his departure for Richmond, a great many of his old officers called at his headquarters to bid him good-bye. As General Lee passed around, he had some pleasant remark to make to each one whom he bade good-bye. I was standing next to General Longstreet and he warmly embraced the general, and then, turning to me and shaking my hand said, 'Captain, I'm going to put my old warhorse under your charge. I want you to take good care of him.'"

Longstreet never saw Lee again. After the war, he settled in New Orleans, where his published accounts of the war and his political views stirred up much contro-
JDW versy. °Longstreet had a very practical view of things:

The South had fought the fight, had lost, and had to move on and heal its wounds. It was time to get the country back together. Many southerners, however, did

WCD not feel that way.• °In their eyes, Longstreet had committed a number of sins. He became a Republican. He accepted a political patronage position from a Republican president. But his greatest sin was to speak critically of Robert E. Lee,• having written, "That General Lee was excited and off his balance at Gettysburg was evident on the afternoon of the first, and he labored under that oppression until enough blood was shed to appease him."

WCD °After he had dared to criticize Lee, his brother officers, who were largely trying to win with the pen the battles they had lost by the sword during the war, found in Longstreet a scapegoat and a culprit for many of their own failings.• Richard Taylor, the son of Zachary Taylor and a former brother-in-law of Jefferson Davis, had performed admirably during the war and took umbrage at Longstreet's assessment of Lee, noting: "A recent article in the public press signed by General Longstreet ascribes the failure at Gettysburg to Lee's mistakes. That any subject involving the possession and exercise of intellect should be clear to Longstreet and concealed from Lee is a startling proposition to those having knowledge of those two men."

JMM °In evaluating the war, somebody had to be blamed for the Confederate defeat at Gettysburg. One obvious candidate was Lee, who made all of the tactical decisions there; however, Lee was canonized after the war and could not be blamed for losing Gettysburg and

JDW therefore losing the war.• °If Gettysburg was the great "if" of the Confederacy, and if Lee was the commanding officer at Gettysburg, and if Lee was above reproach, then somebody else has to be at fault at Gettysburg—and that man would be Longstreet.•

As the years passed, Longstreet became increasingly involved in veterans activities. He visited battlefields and helped with the marking of unit locations. He spoke at the dedication of the Chickamauga-Chattanooga National Battlefield Park in 1895 and attended the dedication ceremonies of Grant's Tomb two years later. Even though he became a Republican after the war, which offended many southerners, Confederate veterans retained their respect and admiration for him. When they saw him, they cheered and offered the Rebel yell. Such responses gratified the elderly Longstreet and probably emboldened him even more in his outspokenness.

Longstreet died just six days shy of his eighty-third birthday. His funeral (right) was on January 6, 1904. A reporter for the Atlanta Constitution *described it as "the most impressive ceremonial ever held in Gainesville." A local guard unit and representatives of the Longstreet Chapter of the United Daughters of the Confederacy attended the body. The casket was accompanied to the cemetery by a long procession of state and local dignitaries, militia units, and Confederate veterans.*

Helen Longstreet survived her husband by fifty-eight years. Below she lays a wreath at the general's grave in Alta Vista Cemetery in Gainesville, Georgia. Following his death, she dedicated her life to perpetuating his memory and rehabilitating his reputation. She died in 1962.

WCD   °It probably would have been best for Longstreet's memory had he died during the war. His best opportunity for that, of course, was in the flush of victory, or what seemed like victory at the moment, in the Wilderness. Had he died there, he would not have been around for that last sad year of the war or those thirty sad years that followed the war, when everything he seemed to do intentionally or unintentionally outraged his fellow southerners. Had he been killed in battle, Longstreet's memory would have remained as bright and shining as Stonewall Jackson's, because he would have died where a general should die for the sake of posterity.°

JDW   °One compelling quality of Longstreet's generalship was the idea that he believed the lives of men should be spared. War was not a matter of how brave a man could be or how his character could be tested in combat. War was killing and maiming, and Longstreet saw it clearly and in a modern sense. He knew that the Confederacy could not continue to lose men as it did. Because Longstreet tried to take care of his men, they never forgot him. They might have disagreed with his politics after the war, but they never lost respect for him as a soldier, and that is how he should be remembered.*

Louise Garland Longstreet died in 1889. Eight years later, at the age of seventy-six, James Longstreet married thirty-four-year-old Helen Dortch. They were together until his death seven years later. Helen Dortch Longstreet outlived her husband by fifty-eight years, dying in 1962.

In the end, James Longstreet died a soldier. He had been a failure as a politician and a businessman, but to the men of the First Corps, he had no equal as a soldier and a general. To them, he was the best general in the army, and forty years after the war, at his funeral, they were there to honor him.

WINFIELD SCOTT HANCOCK

BP ° *A man* OF GREAT PRESENCE, Maj. Gen. Winfield Scott Hancock was all soldier. He was six feet two inches tall, barrel-chested, powerfully built, and possessed a loud, clear voice. Always well mounted, always wearing remarkably clean uniforms with a tall white starched collar, he was the nineteenth-century Victorian ideal of a military commander. A man of great charisma and great force, he was able to galvanize his troops on the battlefield.• Hancock, however, was more than an outstanding military leader of the Civil War for his life mirrored much of the American saga of the nineteenth century. He played a role in the Mexican War, western expansion, the Civil War, and Reconstruction.

He was referred to in admiration by his Confederate adversaries as "the Thunderbolt" of the Army of the Potomac. It was said that he never committed a mistake in battle for which he was responsible, and he saw many battles. From Williamsburg to Fredericksburg, from Gettysburg to the Wilderness and beyond, Hancock acted with resourcefulness and reserve, which assured his men and awed his enemies.

WEM °Hancock's finest moment in the Civil War was his arrival at Gettysburg on July 1, 1863. He had been sent there by George Gordon Meade, the recently promoted commander of the Union army. When he arrived, he found the condition of the army was probably the worst it had been in the previous two years of the war. Yet

WCD William C. Davis
DMJ David M. Jordan
WEM Wayne E. Motts
BP Brian Pohanka

By the time Hancock could play with his son, Russell, on his knee, he had seen action in the Indian Territory and in Mexico and had settled into the life of a regimental quartermaster in Saint Louis. The boy had an adventuresome childhood when the family moved to Fort Myers, Florida, in 1856 during the third Seminole war, to Fort Leavenworth, Kansas, in 1857 during the unrest of "Bleeding Kansas," and to Los Angeles, California, in 1859.

when Hancock arrived, an officer said that his presence was immediately felt on the battlefield. The mere sight of him on that field had an immense psychological impact on the soldiers who were there.• Assuming command at the direction of Meade, he pronounced, "Gentlemen, this battle is the turning point of the war. If we win this fight, the war is practically over."

It was appropriate that Hancock should triumph at Gettysburg for he was a son of Pennsylvania. One of twin brothers born February 14, 1824, to Benjamin and Elizabeth Hancock in Montgomery Square, north of Philadelphia, he was named after Winfield Scott, the preeminent military hero of the day. The name fit his disposition. WEM °Hancock was a born soldier with the ability to approach any situation and sum it up quickly. Bringing order out of chaos was a trait for which he would become well known.•

At the age of sixteen, Hancock secured an appointment to West Point. A colleague, Gen. Francis A. Walker, commented: "Hancock's career at West Point was in no sense distinguished. The qualities which made him powerful as a commander were not those which would give academic distinction. His ultimate success was to be preeminently through character."

Shortly after his graduation from the military academy, the Mexican War broke out. Hancock repeatedly wrote the War Department requesting a transfer from his desk job to the front, but his reasons were vague. One such appeal stated, "I am exceedingly anxious to go as I have not been there." Within a year, he found himself in Mexico, serving under his namesake, Gen. Winfield Scott.

WCD °In the Mexican War, Hancock saw limited but important action, especially for a developing soldier learning his craft. He learned a number of things: how to make men follow him in small-unit engagements;

how to lead by example, which became very important to him in the Civil War; and how to take care of his men. He learned that an officer does not just take care of his men by leading them in battle, but he makes sure they are provided for while they are behind the lines.°

DMJ

°After the Mexican War, Hancock was stationed in Saint Louis. Here he was introduced to Almira Russell. She was considered a great catch, and she considered Hancock a great catch. It was not long before they were married,° which occurred on January 24, 1850, amid great social interest. The bride noted: "The idle rumor at home and abroad that the bridal dress was made of spun glass had brought together a great crowd of the curious who were hoping for a glimpse of this phenomenal costume. This mob impeded every approach to the house, necessitating the assistance of a police force, which irritated the people almost to violence."

A son, Russell, was born to the Hancocks in Saint Louis. They remained there until 1856, when Hancock was posted to Florida where the Seminole Indians were stirring. While there, the Hancocks had a daughter, Ada, the only white infant girl born in that area before 1857. Her birth prompted Hancock to reflect: "Sole daughter of our house and home. Things had gone well for us and we had many inducements to make life worth living." With the Seminoles moderately contained, Hancock was transferred in 1857 to Fort Leavenworth,

Almira Hancock (above) was anxious about living in California. Her husband had gone with his regiment to Benicia and would return to collect the family in Washington. Hearing of her reservations, Col. Robert E. Lee took Almira aside and told her that her place was by Hancock's side, warning that the future happiness of young couples was often jeopardized "upon small provocation, to live apart," because "they ceased to be essential to each other." She followed his advice.

In 1860 Los Angeles (left) had a mostly Spanish-speaking population of four thousand. Ignoring the saloons and gambling halls, Almira Hancock decried that it was "too small to attract or sustain public amusements of any kind." There was no Protestant church in the area, and so a retired minister from Philadelphia held services in his home, and Almira led the singing from a small church organ.

Scion of an old, influential Virginia family, Lewis A. Armistead had been dismissed from West Point in his second year for breaking a plate over Cadet Jubal Early's head. Nevertheless, he joined the army and saw action in the Seminole War and was brevetted three times for service in Mexico. He and Hancock were kindred spirits, and the two became fast friends during the occupation of Mexico. As the southern states seceded, Hancock commiserated with his brother officers, including Armistead, whose loyalties led them to resign their commissions. When Armistead bade Hancock good-bye, he gave him a new major's uniform that he would no longer need and he gave Almira a prayer book with an inscription to "Trust in God and fear nothing."

Kansas, the starting point of the march of the Sixth Infantry across the plains to California.

DMJ °As a quartermaster at the time, Hancock was responsible for keeping the army supplied as it marched across
WCD the country, and he did this job well.° °Quartermasters were paper shufflers; they were administrators. In the massive war to come in 1861, heroic leadership alone was not enough to determine the outcome of battle; it also required an element of management. A good general had to be a good executive, and Hancock's experience as a quartermaster trained him to be just that.°

Upon arriving in California, he was joined by his family and was eventually stationed in Los Angeles, then a town of four thousand people, only a dozen of whom were English-speaking North Americans. Almira observed, "The little town of Los Angeles presented nothing of interest in itself, being too small to attract or sustain public amusements of any kind."

DMJ °While Hancock was in Los Angeles, the Civil War started, and there was significant talk in Southern California of secession. Hancock, through some speechmaking and the threat of ultimate army intervention, was able to squelch that movement. He was instrumental in keeping Southern California in the Union at the start of the Civil War.

Yet while the area remained in the Union, a number of Hancock's colleagues and friends who were southerners resigned their commissions. They gathered at a party in the Hancocks' home prior to their leaving to go east en masse to join the Confederacy.° Among those in attendance was Hancock's dearest friend, Virginian Lewis A. Armistead.

WEM °Hancock and Armistead were good friends because their characters were very similar. To cite the strong points of one would be the same as describing the other.° The parting of the two friends was very emotional, as Almira remembered: "The most crushed of the party was Major Armistead, who, with tears which were contagious streaming down his face and hands upon Mr. Hancock's shoulders, by looking him steadily in the eyes, said, 'Hancock, good-bye. You can never know what this has cost me. And I hope God will strike me

dead if I am ever induced to leave my native soil.' Turning to me, he placed a small satchel in my hand requesting that it should not be opened except in the event of his death, in which case, the souvenirs it contained, with the exception of a little prayer book intended for me, should be sent to his family. On the flyleaf of this book is the following: 'Louis A. Armistead. Trust in God and fear nothing.'"

BP °These friends who bade farewell to each other that day knew that they would be doing their best to kill one another in a matter of weeks, certainly in a matter of months. But that did not lessen their friendship for one another. They knew that as soon as the war was over, they would be friends again. There was no hatred in that room. Every one of those men had a sense of something more important than their own lives, something that was right, something that was just, something that was worth fighting for and, if need be, dying for. That is why the Civil War was so tragic, and that is why the friendship between Hancock and Armistead is such a powerful image of that fratricidal war.•

IN LOS ANGELES, Hancock had said, "The government resulting from the union of these states is a precious heritage that we intend to preserve and defend to the last extremity." Toward that end, he proceeded to Washington. There he was promoted in September 1861 to brigadier general by Gen. George B. McClellan.

DMJ °Hancock received his brigade command at a time when McClellan was trying to shape the Army of the Potomac into what he hoped would be an invincible fighting unit. The recently arrived officer from California was highly regarded by his soldiers; it could almost be said that they loved him. One of the reasons for this was that he respected the volunteer citizen soldiers. At the start of the war, some of the regular army officers were somewhat scornful of these volunteers. Hancock, however, knew that these men could be trained to be a great combat machine.•

Hancock possessed all the characteristics necessary BP for success as his first trial loomed ahead. °A soldier was supposed to be stalwart, and Hancock was. A

As soon as he heard of Fort Sumter's fall, Hancock requested a transfer to the East. Arriving in Washington in August 1861, he feared he would be consigned to quartermaster duty, although he desperately wanted a combat command. Fortunately, the new general in chief, George B. McClellan, remembered Hancock from West Point and the Mexican War. When he restructured the army in the wake of the Bull Run debacle, he reserved a brigade for Hancock. On September 23 Hancock was made a brigadier general of volunteers and given a command position under Gen. William F. "Baldy" Smith.

When the war came, Hancock was one of the most diligent officers in the regular army. After his first meeting with McClellan, he knew that his troops would not be thrown into combat immediately, allowing some time to train them. Hancock never ceased to give military instruction to his officers. He was a stern disciplinarian, but he was no martinet. In the army, one means of instilling discipline was through oaths, curses, and imprecations; Hancock's vocabulary was sulphuric. He was also a master of army regulations and knew how to acquire the supplies his men needed. His troops responded with respect and devotion and performed admirably.

soldier was supposed to be neat and orderly in his appearance, and Hancock was. A soldier was supposed to be brave or maintain a facade of bravery even though he might be terrified. Bravery can be contagious, just as fear can. Hancock had all these qualities without showing them off or being reckless. He possessed that almost unique combination of steadiness and what the French called élan.•

In the spring of 1862 Hancock's brigade was part of McClellan's Virginia Peninsula campaign. Its first major engagement was at Williamsburg. Interestingly, George Armstrong Custer, then a lieutenant on McClellan's staff, observed: "With that excessive politeness of manner which characterizes him when everything is being conducted according to his liking, Hancock, as if conducting guests to a banquet, rather than fellow beings to a life-and-death struggle, cried out in tones well befitting a stentor, 'Gentlemen, charge with the bayonet.'"

WCD °At Williamsburg, Hancock found an opportunity to strike an unprotected Confederate line and refused, on his own initiative, to have his brigade pulled out, in spite of repeated orders, until he had no choice but to follow those orders. He showed the initiative to realize a good opportunity when it presented itself. Beyond that, once he began to pull out, the Confederates turned and attacked him. Hancock, however, managed to make his brigade stand hard in battle, repulse that attack, and then led them in a devastating countercharge.•

On the battlefield at Williamsburg, Hancock earned his lifelong nickname—"the Superb." They were McClellan's own words as he reported: "Hancock was superb today. This was one of the most brilliant engagements of the war. And General Hancock merits the highest praise for the soldierly qualities displayed and his perfect appreciation of the vital importance of his position."

BP °Hancock *had* been truly superb. It was one of the few times when the name was genuinely applicable to the character. Williamsburg was a battle in which the Union lost heavily, but the Federals gained a competent general on the same field. By refusing to abandon his

position, by seeking a rationale to compromise with his superiors while urging them to hold this ground, and by holding his men to their duty when the attack did come against him, galvanizing them with his voice and presence and then launching them in a counterattack in which they inflicted many more casualties than they sustained, Hancock first demonstrated his ability to control large numbers of men in battle.°

Despite Hancock's success at the individual engagement at Williamsburg, the Peninsula campaign itself was a Union failure. Joined with the defeat at Second Manassas in late August 1862, the army returned to its camps around Washington. It did not remain encamped for long, however. In September 1862 Confederate Gen. Robert E. Lee mounted an offensive northward through Maryland that climaxed at Antietam, the bloodiest single day of battle in American history.

°At Antietam, Hancock's role was at first a peripheral one until Maj. Gen. Israel B. Richardson was mortally wounded and he was placed in command of the First Division of the Second Corps. This was the beginning

WEM

Lincoln had called for seventy-five thousand volunteers. Hancock was among the first of the regular army officers to recognize that a force of citizens under arms could become a formidable weapon of war. Many of his colleagues, however, sneered at the volunteers, compared them unfavorably to regulars, and bemoaned the fact that the army was cursed with such clods. Hancock knew how important it was for the volunteers to consider themselves the equals of any soldiers under arms. He wanted his men to know of his regard for them. As a result of the way he treated his regiments and the training he prescribed for them, Hancock's superiors noted that no brigade was more prepared for action than his. These volunteers from Vermont (above), though lacking weapons and uniforms, mastered the intricacies of the drill at Camp Baxter, near Saint Johnsbury, in the early weeks of the war.

On the Virginia Peninsula, Hancock (at left) conferred with his divisional commander, Brig. Gen. William F. "Baldy" Smith, and Brig. Gen. John Newton, who commanded another of Smith's brigades. During the wasted month in which McClellan made preparations to lay siege to Yorktown, Hancock's brigade participated in a number of skirmishes and reconnaissances, making itself as useful as possible in a basically useless endeavor.

of Hancock's relationship with the corps that he would carry the rest of his life, and he forged the First Division, and later the Second Corps, into something that would be the pride of the Army of the Potomac. Certainly the Second Corps was revered by Union and Confederate soldiers alike as being one of the finest combat units in the American Civil War.° Gen. Francis A. Walker noted, "An hour after Hancock rode down the line at Antietam to take up the sword that had fallen from Richardson's dying hand, every officer in his place and every man in his ranks was aware, before the sun went down, that he belonged to Hancock's division."

°The association of Hancock with the Second Corps was one of the strongest forces in his life, and these ties persisted even beyond death. Today when many think of Hancock, they think of the Second Corps. The two are intertwined. Their lives, their fates, their bravery, their sufferings on the battlefield, their legacies are inextricably linked.°

While the outcome at Antietam was tactically a stalemate but strategically a victory, McClellan was removed from command of the Army of the Potomac, largely for failing to crush Lee's weakened army after the battle. Although he had become a close personal friend of McClellan's, Hancock subscribed to a cause that transcended friendship and commented: "The army are not satisfied with the change and consider the treatment of McClellan most ungracious and inopportune. Yet I do not sympathize in the movement going on to resist the order. It is useless, I tell the gentlemen around me. We are serving no one man. We are serving our country."

Gen. Ambrose E. Burnside replaced McClellan. His first engagement—in December 1862 at Fredericksburg—proved to be his Waterloo, but Hancock's men displayed a courage that he had imparted to them. ᴮᴾ °How can one man's bravery—his coolness in the face of death—transfer itself to another? It is an intangible of command, and in Hancock's case, that was precisely ᵂᶜᴰ what happened.° °One need look no further for demonstration of this than the performance of Hancock's division at Fredericksburg in front of the infamous stone wall at the foot of Marye's Heights. His men came closer to the stone wall than any other Federal soldiers that day. Time after time, others had attacked only to be repulsed. Some came no closer than one hundred yards. After the battle, Hancock's dead were found seventy-five yards, fifty yards, even thirty-five yards from the wall. No one came closer. Those men paid with their lives in testimony to the kind of confidence they felt for Hancock and the way they followed him into fire and flame.°

Afterward, Hancock reported: "We went into action today, although we did not gain the works we sought. Out of the fifty-seven hundred men I carried into action, I have this morning in line but fourteen hundred and fifty. It was a desperate undertaking. And the army fought hard."

BURNSIDE'S FAILURE AT Fredericksburg cost him his command. He was replaced by Gen. Joseph Hooker, who

Hancock was a large man, standing six feet two inches tall and weighing more than two hundred pounds. U. S. Grant once described him as having "an appearance that would attract the attention of an army as he passed. . . . His genial disposition made him friends, and his personal courage and his presence with his command in the thickest of the fight won him the confidence of troops serving under him."

advanced his army to Chancellorsville, Virginia. Hancock recalled: "The day before the fight, Hooker said to a general officer, 'God Almighty could not prevent me from winning a victory tomorrow.' Pray could we expect a victory after that? Success cannot come to us through such profanity."

BP

°Despite the fortunes of war, Hancock most certainly had that ability to draw out from his men—be they generals or private soldiers—what it took to enable them to go beyond themselves, to transcend their own weakness. At Chancellorsville the best-laid plans of Hooker went tragically awry, and his brilliant plan, which for a time promised to frustrate Lee, collapsed in defeat. During the chaos that erupted on the battlefield, Hancock's clothing was torn with numerous bullet holes and his horse was struck, but he continued to return to the holocaust of battle. His men eventually covered the Union retreat from that disastrous battleground.°

The battle of Williamsburg was fancifully depicted in this contemporary print by Kurz and Allison. To Secretary of War Edwin M. Stanton, McClellan wrote, "This was one of the most brilliant engagements of the war and General Hancock merited the highest praise." To his wife, Little Mac wired, "Hancock was superb yesterday." The adjective was picked up by the press, which was anxious to find Union heroes, and applied regularly to Hancock thereafter.

WCD

°The battle of Chancellorsville created few Union heroes, but Hancock was one of them. Hooker, however, did not perform well. It was still uncertain whether he was drunk, disoriented, or simply lost his nerve, but the obvious fact was that Hooker exerted very little control over the battle. When the army was almost routed, when it was in retreat and about to be pursued by victo-

At Antietam, Hancock was a brigade commander in the Sixth Corps, which was ordered to take the ground east of the West Woods. The Confederates encountered them at the sunken road, later known as Bloody Lane. There the divisional commander, Gen. Israel Richardson (seated, center), was killed, and command was given to Hancock.

rious Confederates, Hancock's men held the tide. Hancock covered the withdrawal. Hancock acted as rear guard and stood his ground, ensuring the safety of the rest of the army.•

Hancock tersely summarized his actions, noting: "We have had tremendous fighting at Chancellorsville. The losses on both sides were very heavy. I am unhurt, though I was struck several times with small fragments of shells. My horse was shot twice. My division did well."

BP　　°The young soldiers of the mid-nineteenth century had been raised on stories of the Revolution and Napoleon. The idealized general on horseback was not a statue covered with pigeons in the town square or something to be scoffed at; he was a very real thing in those days. So when these soldiers saw a man like Hancock, who lived up to their idealized image of what a general on horseback should look like, and when they found that not only was it image but also substance in his case, it was no wonder that many of them felt almost a sense of worship toward him.• Capt. Charles King admitted: "Hancock was almost my idol. I swore by him and almost worshiped him."

Disgusted with Hooker's leadership, the commander of the Second Corps, Gen. Darius Couch, asked to be relieved of his command, and Lincoln transferred that

In fairly rapid succession, Hancock had served under three commanders. McClellan (above left) had trained the army and taken it to the outskirts of Richmond. Hancock had almost no role in the brief time the army had been assigned to John Pope (not pictured), but he was with McClellan again in Maryland at the battle of Antietam. When command passed to Ambrose Burnside (above center), Hancock was with him at Fredericksburg and saw his division mauled in front of the infamous stone wall. When command passed to Joseph Hooker (above right), Hancock was with him at Chancellorsville, holding the center of the Union line and covering the army's withdrawal.

BP command to Hancock. °The new commander found in the men of the Second Corps a sense of pride, a sense of reputation, a sense of honor that was not diminished by defeat but cherished for its numerous battle scars. As a result, their accomplishments would become singular. The Second Corps would experience more casualties than any other corps in the Army of the Potomac. The Second would capture more Confederate guns and flags than any other corps in the Union army. The division in the Army of the Potomac that suffered the greatest casualties would be the First Division of the Second Corps, the division that Hancock had led at Fredericksburg and at Chancellorsville. That implies a great deal about the relationship between the Second Corps and Hancock, and in that sense, as in so many other ways, Hancock's story was the story of the Second Corps and the story of the Army of the Potomac.°

Hooker's defeat at Chancellorsville also resulted in the command of the Army of the Potomac being given to Gen. George Gordon Meade. Most importantly, Lee's victory at Chancellorsville gave him the confidence to advance into Pennsylvania. What followed was to be a turning point of the Civil War, and Hancock's role there was to be conspicuous.

THE BATTLE OF Gettysburg began on July 1, 1863. "Beautiful as that landscape appears to the eye of the peaceful traveler," noted Gen. Francis A. Walker, "it is now a scene of terror strewn with the dead and dying and with the wreck of battle."

BP   °At first the Union was losing the battle. Not yet on the field, General Meade was trying to concentrate his army at Gettysburg to face Lee, but the battle seemed to have all the makings of a great disaster. Meade needed to make decisions, and he needed a man on the field who could assess the situation and who could restore an obviously disintegrating situation. He called on Hancock.•

DMJ   °When Meade ordered Hancock to Gettysburg to take command, Hancock pointed out that Gen. Oliver O. Howard, the commander of the Eleventh Corps, who was on the battlefield already, was senior to him. Meade said that he wanted Hancock to take command regardless.• "As soon as I arrived on the field," Hancock recalled, "I rode directly to General Howard and said to him that I had been sent to take command of all the forces present. He acquiesced in my assumption of command."

The impact of Hancock's presence was immediate.

BP   °He again exerted his extraordinary ability to bring order out of chaos. On a number of other significant occasions he had demonstrated that by riding into the chaos of the battlefield, into the disorganization that threatened to cross over into panic and collapse, his presence had a calming influence. That was exactly what he did on July 1, 1863, on Cemetery Hill at Gettysburg.• Hancock again lived up to his nickname, the Superb.

DMJ   °On the first day of the battle he rallied the defeated Union army on Cemetery Hill, put them back into a cohesive form, and formed a good defensive line. He also chose the site of the battle by sending word to

WEM   Meade that it was a good defensible position.• °After the first day's battle, Hancock's units were posted in the center of the Union line. They saw heavy fighting on the second day and sent reinforcements to the different parts of the line, Hancock himself personally leading some of those reinforcements.•

Lee's successes on the first two days at Gettysburg compelled him to proceed with the third. For the attack that day he chose, among others, Gen. George E. Pickett's division. The attacking force consisted of twelve thousand men under the direction of Gen. James Longstreet. This infantry assault was preceded by a two-hour artillery barrage that shook the Pennsylvania countryside. At Cemetery Hill, Hancock was in the very center of this Confederate storm of shot and shell.

BP   °The ground trembled and reeled during the barrage as if in an earthquake. It seemed like the end of the world to the Union soldiers hunkered down along Cemetery Ridge. As they hugged the earth and Confederate shells exploded above and around them or shrieked overhead, Hancock, accompanied by a single orderly carrying the corps flag, rode slowly up and down the line. This was the supreme example of his ability to spread a sense of, if not calm, at least determination through his soldiers who were about to face what they knew would be coming across that field.•

WCD   °On that third day of battle at Gettysburg, Hancock completed what had to be the three finest days' performance given by any corps commander in the Union army in the course of the Civil War. His corps held the

The Second Corps under Hancock was the best corps of the Army of the Potomac when George G. Meade assumed command in June 1863. While this photograph was taken almost a year later near Cold Harbor, the men pictured here had demonstrated their mettle earlier, especially at Gettysburg. Leaning against the tree is Francis Barlow, who began the war as a private and rose to the rank of general. Just to the right of the tree stands Hancock, and next to him are Maj. Gen. David B. Birney and Brig. Gen. John Gibbon.

center of the line against Longstreet's massive assault. Hancock himself was magnificent. His men said afterward that merely to be near him gave them the confidence to stand in the face of that terrible onslaught.•

Hancock's professional gain at Gettysburg came with enormous personal loss, however. Lewis Armistead, his best friend, commanded one of Pickett's brigades and was mortally wounded within yards of Hancock. It was the closest they had been since embracing each other in Los Angeles two years earlier.

Capt. Henry H. Bingham described his interview with the wounded Confederate general: "I dismounted from my horse and inquired of the prisoner his name. He replied, 'General Armistead of the Confederate army.' Observing that his suffering was very great, I said to him, 'General, I am Captain Bingham of General Hancock's staff, and if you have anything valuable in your possession which you desire to be taken care of, I'll take care of it for you.' He then asked me if it was General Winfield Scott Hancock. And upon my replying in the affirmative, he desired me to say, 'Tell General Hancock for me that I have done him and done you all an injury which I shall regret or repent—I forget the exact word—the longest day I live.'"

Hancock had been severely wounded, too. Lt. George G. Benedict recalled: "My eyes were upon

In the panic that characterized the first day at Gettysburg, Meade ordered Hancock to take command of the fighting and to be his eyes and ears. His first duty was to decide whether to fight at Gettysburg, and he pronounced it "the strongest position by nature upon which to fight a battle that I ever saw." Years later, veterans of the battle recalled the comforting and heartening view of Hancock on the field because his reputation as an accomplished fighter was well known.

By nightfall on July 1, the Union army was positioned south of Gettysburg and in possession of Culp's and Cemetery Hills, occupying a line that ended with two hills called the Round Tops. Just prior to leaving for the battlefield, Meade (above) addressed a message to Hancock, stating, "It seems to me we have so concentrated that a battle at Gettysburg is now forced on us, and that, if we get up all our people, and attack with our whole force tomorrow, we ought to defeat the force the enemy has."

Hancock's striking figure when he uttered an exclamation and I saw that he was reeling in his saddle. General [George] Stannard bent over him as we laid him upon the ground, a ragged hole an inch or more in diameter, from which blood was pouring profusely, was disclosed in the upper part of his thigh. Stannard had whipped out his handkerchief and as I helped to pass it around General Hancock's leg, I said to him, 'This is not arterial blood, General. You will not bleed to death.' From the use of the surgical term, he took me for a surgeon and replied with a sign of relief, 'That's good. Thank you for that, doctor.' We tightened the ligature by twisting it with a barrel of a pistol and soon stopped the flow of blood."

A long recovery period followed for Hancock in his father's house at Norristown, Pennsylvania, but he rejoined the Second Corps in the spring of 1864 for U. S. Grant's overland campaign in Virginia, his wound still unhealed. In the dark, tangled jungle of the battle of the Wilderness, Hancock found that his personal style of leadership and the grand maneuvers of Gettysburg were impossible. Then, from the Bloody Angle of Spotsylvania to the killing fields of Cold Harbor, Hancock saw the Second Corps bled white. Finally, at Reams's Station, Virginia, where railroad trains once had stopped, so too would Hancock's magnificent career as a commander in battle.

BP   °The tragedy at Reams's Station was that Hancock tried to use the Second Corps as if it were the same corps that had fought at Gettysburg. But it was not the same corps. The men at Reams's Station were either exhausted veterans or they were new men, draftees, or bounty men who had been paid to join the army in the place of another. When they were attacked, they did something the Second Corps had never done before— they broke and ran.

Hancock watched the Second Corps disintegrate before his eyes. Of course, he threw himself into the crisis as he had done in every other battle in which he had fought—personally leading, cajoling, cursing, trying to get those men to plug the hole in the line.

John Gibbon, commanding the Second Division, great general though he was, came up to Hancock and said, "My men can't do it. They just can't do it." Hancock, however, would not accept the fact that his corps could not succeed. But Gibbon was right; at Reams's Station the Second Corps could not do it.

Nor could Hancock. Shortly after the battle of Reams's Station, exhausted, he relinquished command of his beloved Second Corps. In leaving, he told them: "Soldiers of the Second Corps, I desire in parting with

Hancock made a dramatic appearance on Cemetery Hill when he arrived at Gettysburg at midafternoon on July 1. There was a brief animated conversation with Oliver O. Howard, who outranked him and interpreted Meade's order to mean that Hancock could give no orders to him. One of Abner Doubleday's staff officers recalled that Hancock solved the impasse by saying, "Very well, General Howard, I will second any order that you have to give," and then changed the subject to whether or not the fighting should continue at Gettysburg. Hancock then rode off to see to the deployment of troops.

The three days at Gettysburg climaxed with Longstreet's attack, a mile-long assault by three divisions, more than eleven thousand Confederates against the center of the Union line. The second wave of George Pickett's division was led by Lewis A. Armistead, a close friend of Hancock's. The two had not seen each other since the night they had said farewell in Los Angeles in 1861. Armistead placed his hat on the tip of his sword to guide his troops, taking them over the stone wall that defined the Union line. Standing next to the wreckage of a Federal battery, he was shot down by reinforcements rushing to fill the gap. Ironically, Hancock was also wounded and lay not far from Armistead, propping himself up to see the action and refusing to leave the field. Only later did he learn of Armistead's injury.

DMJ

you to express the regret I feel at the necessity for our separation. The story of the Second Corps will live in history, and to its officers and men will be ascribed the honor of having served their country with unsurpassed fidelity and courage."

WINFIELD SCOTT HANCOCK was one of only a handful of eminent Northern soldiers who possessed more than military skills. Courageous during the war, he was equally compassionate after it.

°Following Lincoln's assassination, Hancock was in charge of the military district that included the District of Columbia. One of those convicted of conspiring to assassinate the president was a woman named Mary Surratt, the mother of one of the other conspirators. Along with three others, she too was sentenced to death.° Although he had no particular knowledge of

250

her guilt or innocence, Hancock felt it was wrong in principle to execute a woman, but he could not prevent her hanging.

WCD Lincoln's successor, Andrew Johnson, had plans for Hancock in the Reconstruction South and appointed him military governor of Texas and Louisiana. °The state of Yankee Reconstruction in those two states was deplorable when Hancock took over. His first act was to issue his famous General Orders Number 40, a reaffirmation of the supremacy of the Bill of Rights. He promised, in short, to keep the military out of the lives of the former Confederate civilians in his command so long as they remained peaceful and law-abiding citizens.•

DMJ °While this sounded appropriate, it provoked a great controversy across the country. Southerners loved it, but the Radical Republicans in Washington and elsewhere in the North were infuriated by it and turned their severest criticism on Hancock.•

Hancock was forced to resign his office, but subsequent to George Gordon Meade's death in 1872, Hancock, as senior major general of the army, was given command of the Division of the East. While holding this position, he was nominated in 1880 as the Democratic presidential candidate.

Hancock required six months to recuperate from his wound. When he returned to duty, he led his corps in the Virginia campaigns until November 1864. The promise of an independent command led him to accept assignment with the Veteran Reserve Corps, which was to be made up of men who had two years of service and had been mustered out, had served their enlistments, or in some other way were not subject to conscription. Recruitment was slow, however, and Hancock was instead named commander of the Department of West Virginia and the Middle Military Division.

When Lee surrendered, Hancock anticipated some time with his family, but Lincoln's assassination was followed by a panic, and Andrew Johnson called him to Washington. Hancock was subsequently involved in the proceedings against the Lincoln conspirators and supervised their hanging (left), despite having reservations about hanging a woman—Mary Surratt. To her attorney, he said, "I have been in many a battle, and have seen death and mixed with it in disaster and in victory. I've been in a living hell of fire, and shell, and grape-shot and—I'd sooner be there ten thousand times over than to give the order this day for the execution of that poor woman."

During Reconstruction, Hancock (above) offended many Republicans by refusing to use military power to replace civil courts in Louisiana and Texas. He was reassigned to command of the Department of the East. In 1880 the Democratic Party was looking for a war hero to counter the Republicans and nominated Hancock for the presidency. He faced a fellow Union general, James A. Garfield, and lost the election by a narrow margin and fifty-nine electoral votes.

The legacy of Hancock's 1880 presidential campaign was a political phenomenon that came to be known as the Solid South. From 1880 to 1980, the former states of the Confederacy formed a consistent, dependable political base for the Democratic Party and tolerated few, if any, Republicans.

WCD °He very nearly won the White House. A few thousand votes cast differently in New York would have given him the election. But far more significant than whether Hancock would have won or lost the White House was the impact his candidacy had on the South. Every former Confederate state gave its electoral vote to Hancock—a Yankee general—a man who had been instrumental in their defeat. As a result, in the election of 1880, Hancock's candidacy created the political phenomenon that became known as the Solid South and would last for generations as a Democratic voting block.•

After the election, Hancock continued his command of the Division of the East, settling not only into administrative routines but also into a certain sadness. WCD °Like many of his old comrades, Hancock lived to see a somewhat tragic contrast between the days of his youth—his glory days leading the proud Second Corps across one triumphant battlefield after another—and the decades of peace that followed. He also endured one personal tragedy after another. He outlived his only son. He saw the death of his teenage daughter. He lived to be nearly penniless in his old age because of his generosity to old comrades from the Second Corps down on their luck.•

Hancock died on February 7, 1886, at his home in New York of diabetic complications. He was sixty-one years old.

BP °When most people think of a Union general of the Civil War, they think of Grant, not Winfield Scott Hancock. He is to a great extent a forgotten leader of that war. Grant was a modern man in the sense of how he waged war. For him war had no glory, no pageantry. Yet Hancock was caught up in all of that. He was of another time. His style was not the modern style of waging war, but he did have two key aspects that are important in war and in life: he had presence and he had strength. Those are timeless virtues, which he had in abundance.•

Hancock's death was met with a tremendous outpouring of public grief. WEM °When the public looked at him, they realized that he had been the kind of person they would most want to be like or would most want their son to be like.• Of the many eulogies given at Hancock's funeral, one serves all. Capt. J. A. Wattrous said: "I met General Hancock once. I think I grew about a foot and a half."

Never to be in command of the army, Hancock was second in war. Never to be in the White House, he was second in peace. Nonetheless, he was forever first in the intrepid hearts of the famed Second Corps, and until his death he bore with considerable grace the title of "the Superb."

DANIEL E. SICKLES

The Civil WAR PRODUCED some of the most colorful and controversial figures in American history, many of whose lives off the battlefield were every bit as fascinating as their heroic efforts during battle. One of the war's most intriguing characters was the fiery, storm-centered Union Gen. Daniel Edgar Sickles.

In 1872 John Forney, a newspaperman-politician and longtime friend, described Sickles, noting: "Here's a man, still in his prime, whose career has been as diversified and romantic as if you'd filled out a full century of endless action. Few characters in our country, or in our history have passed through so many ordeals."

BP °If history had not produced Sickles, a novelist would have had to invent him. He was a remarkable character, a fascinating mix of negative and positive characteristics. On the negative side, he was a philanderer, a womanizer, an unscrupulous politician, a man of violent passions who at times could not be trusted. On the positive side, he was fearless and devoted to his beliefs and principles—such as they were. There was no one like Sickles, not only in the era of the Civil War, but in all of American history.•

JIR Many people know of Sickles as a Civil War general, but that was only part of his story. °He also was a politician, seducer, diplomat, seducer, murderer, seducer, Civil War general, and seducer. He wore notoriety like a giant cape with a scarlet lining whether politicking, fighting, drinking, or wenching. Sickles was a man with the throttle wide open.•

NB	Nat Brandt
WCD	William C. Davis
GWG	Gary W. Gallagher
JJH	John J. Hennessy
JMM	James M. McPherson
BP	Brian Pohanka
JIR	James I. Robertson Jr.

Teresa Bagioli married Daniel Sickles when she was sixteen years old and pregnant. He was twice her age. Teresa was once described as a "beautiful, voluptuous siren, without brains or shame" whose "damning effect was a lust for men."

Sickles had ingratiated himself to James Buchanan when the latter had been named minister to Britain. Teresa had also charmed him, even playing hostess for Buchanan in London until his niece, Harriet Lane, arrived to assume that role. Thus when Buchanan moved into the White House in 1857, few social gatherings in the mansion did not include Sickles and his wife as guests.

Much of Sickles's reputation came from scandal. His most famous escapade occurred while he was a U.S. congressman, two years prior to the eruption of the Civil War, in an incident that stunned the Victorian era and captured the nation's attention for months, and it involved Sickles's beautiful young wife, Teresa.

JIR °She was impish, coquettish, and naive. Teresa came to Washington as the bride of a young congressman, but she never became a part of Washington society, and so she was left virtually alone as Sickles pursued his ambitions and his congressional career.•

NB °The social scene in the capital centered on a series of parties, and most congressmen were too busy to attend, occupied either with their work or traveling around the country for political reasons. Thus it was customary for congressional wives to attend these social functions escorted by any of the many bachelors in the city. At the time it was perfectly acceptable behavior.•

Teresa, being the beautiful young woman she was, had no problem finding escorts. Many sought her company, all with her husband's blessings. °In fact, Sickles

GWG would sometimes ask Philip Barton Key, a prominent Washington attorney, to accompany her to functions that he chose not to attend.•

WCD °Key was not unlike Sickles. He was tall and handsome, and he was also the son of Francis Scott Key,

author of "The Star-Spangled Banner."
Seeking to make a name for himself in
Washington, Key was very prominent
socially, and women tended to like him, as
they liked Sickles.

By this time Teresa had become a
very unhappy young woman. She had a
husband who appeared not to be interested in her, who instead preferred to
spend time openly with other women.
Key was drawn to her, and Teresa, perhaps anxious for any kind of affection,
transferred her affections to him, and a
love affair ensued.°

NB   °The two devised a signal to schedule
their meetings. When Key wanted a rendezvous, he would stride across Lafayette
Square with a white handkerchief in his
hand and wave it at the second-floor
window of the Sickleses' home—the bedroom window. Anyone in Lafayette Square Park could
see him and the ostentatious gestures. Key would then
walk to a house he had rented nearby. Ten or fifteen
minutes later, Teresa would arrive at the rented house,
the scene of their trysts.°

The arrangement went on for more than a year with
all of Washington aware of it, except, apparently, Sickles
himself. Perhaps he never would have known had it not
been for an anonymous note alerting him to his wife's
indiscretions. It read: "Dear Sir, With deep regret, there
is a fellow who rents a house for no other purpose than
to meet your wife. And sir, I do assure you he has as
much the use of your wife as you have. With these few
hints, I leave the rest for you to imagine."

NB   °On the last Saturday of February 1859 Sickles confronted Teresa, and she acknowledged that she had
been having an affair with Key. Sickles demanded that
she write out the confession. It was an amazing document for the time. During this era—the Victorian
era—people did not discuss body parts or describe
anything of a sexual nature. Yet Teresa detailed the
affair in astounding candor.° She wrote: "There was a

*When Sickles learned of the illicit affair
between his wife and Philip Barton Key,
he demanded that she write out a confession. It was an astonishing document
for its time and eventually appeared in
newspapers from New York to San Francisco. The first and last pages were
made up for* Harper's Weekly *and are
reproduced above: "I have been in a
house in 15th St with Mr. Key. How
many times I don't know. . . . This I
have written with my bedroom door
open, and my maid and child in the
adjoining room, at [half past eight]
o'clock in the evening. Miss Ridgeley is
in the house, within call.—Teresa Bagioli / February 26, 1859, Lafayette
Square / Mr. and Mrs. Pendleton dined
here two weeks ago last Thursday, with
a large party. Mr. Key was also here,
her brother, and at my suggestion he
was invited, because he lived in the
same house, and Mr. Sickles wished to
invite all those from whom he had
received invitations; and Mr. Sickles
said, 'do as you choose.'—Teresa Bagioli
/ Written and signed in the presence of
O. M. Ridgeley [a friend of the family]
and Bridget Duffy [nursemaid to six-
year-old Laura]. Feb. 26th."*

Harper's Weekly carried extensive coverage of the murder trial, including densely illustrated pages that juxtaposed Sickles (left) and Key (right), contrasting the dapper congressman with Washington's most sought-after man-about-town. More than one admirer had labeled Key "the handsomest man in all Washington society." A widower with four young children, Key was district attorney for the capital just as his father had been before him. Sickles had even interceded for him when it looked as if Key's lax performance might lead to his dismissal.

bed on the second story. I did what is usual for a wicked woman to do. An intimacy of an improper kind. Mr. Key has kissed me in his house a number of times. I undressed myself and he also, then went to bed together."

°The next day, Sunday, was a beautifully warm day for February in the capital. Key, who had no knowledge of Teresa's confession, appeared in Lafayette Square Park, waving his handkerchief. Sickles happened to be looking out the window, saw Key and the handkerchief, and went into a rage. He bolted downstairs, ran across the park, and started shouting at Key as he approached him.•

°Sickles accosted Key on the sidewalk on the east side of Lafayette Square, which is directly across Pennsylvania Avenue from the White House. As he shouted at Key, Key turned away. Sickles produced a pistol and fired, grazing Key. The two men briefly grappled, then Key tried to move away. Sickles dropped the gun in the scuffle but pulled another from his overcoat. Key threw a pair of opera glasses at Sickles, and Sickles fired a second shot that struck Key in the upper leg, knocking him to the ground. As Key begged for his life, Sickles approached him again and tried to shoot, but the pistol misfired. Standing over Key, he placed the gun against the man's chest and fired

The map of the murder scene vividly shows how Sickles murdered Key in the shadow of the White House. The legend to the markings is as follows: (A) the Sickles home, (B) the Maynard House, the scene of the murder, (C) the men's club to which Key was taken after the shooting, (D) the White House, (E) the Treasury Department, (F) the State Department, (G) the War Department, (H) the Navy Department, and (I) the Dolley Madison House.

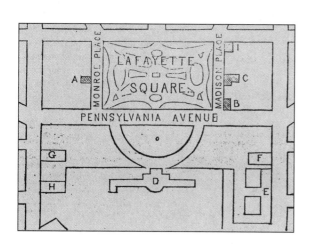

The Harper's Weekly artist depicted Sickles's final, point-blank shot at the wounded and pleading Key. The character in the background is Samuel Butterworth whose role in the slaying was never explained fully. Peculiarly, he was never called as a witness at the trial although he was an obvious witness to the murder. A friend of both Sickles and Key, Butterworth was visiting from New York, learned of the affair, and later claimed to have counseled Sickles to challenge Key. Consulting with an attorney before the trial, Butterworth said that he believed both men were armed and denied that he had conspired in any way to aid Sickles in the shooting.

again. As Key's body fell back to the ground, Sickles tried to fire once more, but the pistol misfired a second time.

Friends took Key to a men's club a short distance away, where he died on the floor of the parlor. Sickles, meanwhile, calmly walked to the home of his good friend, the attorney general of the United States, and surrendered himself.•

JMM °The trial of Sickles for murdering Key was front-page news in newspapers all over the country for several weeks. It attracted an enormous amount of attention because of the prominence of the people involved, because of the lurid details of the affair, and because of the way in which Sickles had murdered Key. It was one of the great news events of the spring of 1859.•

NB °The outcome was a foregone conclusion. This was the time of a double standard in American society. A man could be a rake, have affairs, and frequent prostitutes, but a woman's reputation was easily besmirched. It was clear from the newspaper coverage of the trial that most people believed Sickles had done the right thing to save his family's honor.•

JMM °Sickles's attorney, Edwin M. Stanton, devised—for the first time in the history of American jurisprudence—

the defense of temporary insanity. He argued that when Sickles had spotted Key outside his house, he temporarily went crazy, rushed out, and shot him. Stanton claimed that anybody under the influence of such powerful emotions was not fully responsible for his behavior. The jury accepted that argument, and Sickles was acquitted.•

JIR   °In the months immediately after the trial, Sickles emerged as a hero. He was mobbed by well-wishers when he left the courthouse. At a hotel reception that night, no fewer than fifteen hundred people stood in line to shake his hand and congratulate him on the successful outcome.•

JMM   °For a while Sickles's lifestyle was less flamboyant. It looked as if his political career had been ruined by the scandal. He fell out of the public limelight for a time as a consequence and seemed to settle down a bit,• but settling down was never on Sickles's agenda. Promoting himself was always his top priority, feeding his appetite for power and fame.

Tammany Hall, the home of all Democratic Party political dealings in New York City, stood on East Fourteenth Street in the mid-nineteenth century. Sickles had been involved in Tammany politics since the 1830s and was linked to stories of tampering and stealing ballot boxes, brawls, and generally any deceptive, politically motivated manipulation. At Tammany, Sickles learned to make and exploit connections with people on the rise. In this way he moved from New York to Washington, from the back rooms of Tammany to the floor of the Congress.

ALTHOUGH NOT MUCH is known of Sickles's youth, his tenacious temperament was apparent early on. He once noted, "I have said that I do not deem it a wise course, nor recommend it to any friend, but I have adopted it. It is mine and I will follow it, come what may."

GWG   °Sickles came from a comfortable background, his father being a prominent attorney in New York City. From an early age, Sickles showed an independent, strong-willed streak, and he frequently ran away from home. His parents tried to control young Daniel, but he proved to be uncontrollable. Finally, they sent him to live with another family, the Da Ponte family.•

BP   °The Da Pontes were Bohemian in temperament, their lifestyle and artistic background being far different from the typical Victorian household. Lorenzo Sr.

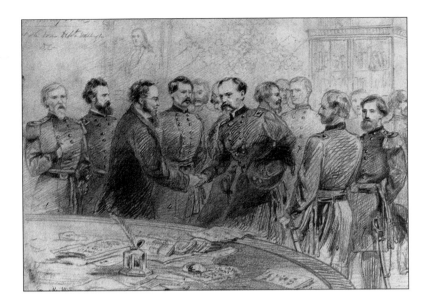

A War Department reception in January 1862 reunited Edwin M. Stanton, secretary of war, with Sickles, a brigadier general of New York volunteers. Stanton had been Sickles's attorney for the 1859 murder trial and had caused his client to be found not guilty on the grounds of temporary insanity, the first time such a defense had been used. In the early months of 1862 Sickles and his New Yorkers were in camp near Washington with little threat of battle against the Confederacy. Instead Sickles was in danger of losing his general's star because several senators were dubious about the former congressman's loyalties. In March the Senate negated his appointment, but in April Stanton endorsed it and encouraged the president to renominate Sickles for a brigadiership. This was confirmed by the Senate in May by a vote of nineteen to eighteen.

had been the librettist for some of the most famous operas of Wolfgang Amadeus Mozart, among them *Don Giovanni.* Thus the young and rather wild, headstrong Sickles moved in with this remarkable Italian-American family to prepare for New York University.•

He was not the only person taken under the wings of the Da Pontes. Another couple, the Bagiolis, joined the household. The young couple had just given birth to a baby girl, Teresa, when Sickles was nineteen years old. BP °She grew up to be a remarkably beautiful young woman, and by the time she was barely in her teens, Sickles, who was almost twice her age, was taking her out on walks, out riding, and generally spending a great deal of time with her.• To the shock of both families, he, then thirty-three years of age, married Teresa, who was sixteen and pregnant.

WCD °Sickles seemed to love her, and she undoubtedly loved him, but he had a very different idea of his role as husband compared to Teresa's role as wife. It was not long before Sickles began philandering—taking lovers and having one affair after another.• Along with his rather wide interest in women, he became obsessed with politics and law. As with everything in Sickles's life, he quickly became controversial in both pursuits.

NB °He was not so much interested in corporate law or litigation as he was in making deals. The deals he made, however, frequently caused him considerable trouble. He was accused of withholding funds and not paying off his debts, among other things, but he was never convicted of anything, although numerous charges were brought against him.•

BP

°As an up-and-coming young lawyer without the benefit of a full college education, Sickles saw politics as his entrée into the world of power. At this point he began to forge a connection with Tammany Hall, the Democratic Party machine of New York City.• °Tammany Hall taught Sickles a great many things, the foremost lesson being that the result was more important than the way in which it was achieved. Tammany officials looked the other way if rules were broken, and political hardball became a science at Tammany Hall.•

GWG

NB

°Sickles adjusted to Tammany politics remarkably well. He was, first of all, very congenial and had little difficulty in getting along with people. At the same time he was a brawler and joined into any fights when there were disputes at Tammany Hall. He was accused of stuffing ballot boxes, buying votes, anything an ambitious politico would do to support his leadership. His loyalty to Tammany Hall was beyond question.•

GWG

°Sickles began his state political career in 1847 as a member of the New York State Assembly. He subsequently aligned himself with James Buchanan, a

During the Peninsula campaign, as the Federals advanced within earshot of the church bells of Richmond, Sickles and the Excelsior Brigade were engaged at the battle of Fair Oaks, a furious Southern counterattack six miles from Richmond. For two days the Union army held its own, despite appalling casualty numbers, and many Federal commanders who perceived the action as a Union victory wondered why they were not allowed to press on to the Confederate capital. Sickles acquitted himself admirably in the midst of his troops, inspiring them with his presence and demonstrating a personal contempt for danger. He received a commendation from his commander, Joseph Hooker, who saw some promise in the lawyer-politician with a brawler's reputation. Below is William B. T. Trego's depiction of a Bucks County, Pennsylvania, regiment recapturing its battle flag during the fighting at Fair Oaks.

prominent Democratic figure, and accompanied him to England, where Buchanan was minister to the Court of Saint James. Sickles spent some time as Buchanan's private secretary, but after becoming embroiled in a number of controversies—including his refusal to toast Queen Victoria at an Independence Day celebration—he returned to New York and was elected to the state senate in the mid-1850s. He was finally elected to Congress in 1856 for the first of two terms.*

It was during this time that the Washington tragedy occurred. While Sickles was granted status as a hero, Teresa did
NB not fare as well. °After her confession, she returned to New York City with her daughter, Laura. They lived with her parents, but she was shunned by society. People in her neighborhood would not talk to her, literally turning their backs on her, ostracizing her completely.*

Sickles, however, pushed forward. With the Key affair behind him and with the full support of the public, his life and career resumed. But then he did the unthink-
NB able. °Several months after his acquittal, a story appeared in a New York paper indicating that Sickles had reconciled with Teresa. Suddenly, public opinion reversed itself. People wondered why, if he could forgive her now, had he not forgiven her several months earlier and not killed Key.

It was now Sickles who found himself ostracized, both in society and in the Congress itself. When the House was in session, he sat by himself. Nobody spoke to him. He neither addressed his colleagues nor voted on any legislation.*

JJH °Many wondered why he had taken Teresa back. Some claimed that he acted out of compassion. They noted that whenever he found people in travail, he invariably acted—or reacted—positively to them. He clearly loved his wife, or at least thought he did, and to him the act of forgiving her was the natural outcome of

Something of the huge numbers of men and equipment involved in the Peninsula campaign can be glimpsed in this photograph of Battery A of the Second U.S. Artillery near Fair Oaks. There was a three-week lull after the engagement during which military operations on the peninsula came to a standstill. On the Southern side, Robert E. Lee succeeded Joseph E. Johnston to command the Confederate army and began planning the offensive that would come to be known as the Seven Days' Battles. Northerners sensed that victory was within their reach and celebrated in their camps, an environment in which the gregarious Sickles thrived. When orders finally came to move toward Richmond, they were countermanded quickly despite the fact that sizable gains were being made. In the brief interlude before Union forces were ordered to advance again, Stonewall Jackson brought his troops into the area and stymied the Federal advance. Thus began the Seven Days and the retreat that ended the Peninsula campaign.

In October 1861 Sickles found himself attached to the command of Joseph Hooker (left), a West Point graduate with little regard for political generals. The two traveled a rocky road toward friendship, but Sickles excelled at demonstrating loyalty to someone in power with the expectation of reward later. In this case, he found promotion by supporting Hooker. When Hooker was elevated by Lincoln to command the army, he placed Sickles in command of the reinstituted Third Corps.

After the debacle of Chancellorsville, in the search for one person to blame for the defeat, Sickles supported Hooker in the contention that George Meade (right), commander of the Fifth Corps, had been a voice for retreat when the corps commanders were polled at a midnight counsel. Little came of the controversy itself other than personal grudges that lasted throughout the war. Within two months Hooker asked to be relieved of command, and Lincoln named Meade as his replacement. Sickles lost the prestige of being a confidant to the commanding general and had little respect for Meade, who viewed Sickles as a questionable corps commander.

the whole affair. The reconciliation, however, virtually ruined Sickles's career.•

In 1861 he quietly concluded his second term in Congress, returning to New York in shame, or so the public thought. With tensions growing between North and South, Sickles viewed the impending civil war as an opportunity for fame, fortune, and, of course, scandal.

WITH THE ELECTION of 1860, Abraham Lincoln entered the White House, ending all hopes of peace between North and South. Luckily for Sickles, with the nation in turmoil, one man's shame was quickly lost in the shuffle. °For a man interested in being in the public limelight, who craved attention and liked headlines, the war was a godsend. He saw the military as a way to carve out a new reputation and a new career for himself.•

°When Fort Sumter was fired upon in April 1861, a wave of resentment and anger rushed through the North, and Lincoln called for volunteers from all the states. The old ambitious Sickles very quickly emerged at this chance for advancement. He received permission from the New York governor to raise a regiment, which very quickly turned into raising a brigade that would be called the Excelsior Brigade. Sickles, in turn, acquired a state commission as a brigadier general. Suddenly, he had gone from being an obscure, embarrassed private citizen to being General Sickles.•

GWG

WCD

JIR °The first battle in which he led the Excelsior Brigade in action was at Fair Oaks, Virginia, in late May 1862. The men performed magnificently—"surprisingly so," as many of Sickles's detractors said. The brigade earned a prominent and heroic reputation, and that achievement demonstrated that Sickles had battlefield leadership qualities, a flair for leading men gallantly and dramatically—and it also kept his

JJH name in the news.• °Although other people noted it, most importantly for Sickles, his men noted it. Throughout the war, while he sometimes aroused the enmity and even hatred of other officers, it was hard to find a negative word about him from his men. They recognized that his boldness, his aggressiveness, and his concern for their welfare were genuine and that he was sincerely interested in contributing to the Union war effort.•

Sickles's brigade was attached to Joseph Hooker's division. Although Sickles was a political general and Hooker a West Pointer, it did not take long for the two

JMM to form a friendship. °They were similar both in their tastes and in their personalities. Hooker was a heavy

Sickles and the Third Corps were in position near Emmitsburg, Maryland, when word came of the Confederate presence at Gettysburg. In a quandary whether he should remain there or move toward Gettysburg, Sickles divided his corps and led two divisions to the Pennsylvania crossroads. He arrived at the battlefield on the evening after the first day's fighting, shortly before Meade.

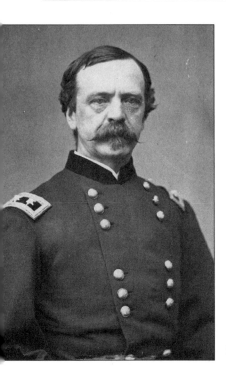

The restless aggressive nature of Sickles led him to interpret his orders quite freely at Gettysburg. Meade ordered Sickles to a position north of the two round tops on the left end of the Union line. Sickles saw similarities in this position to the tragedy he had endured at Chancellorsville two months earlier. He decided that he could best secure the area by placing his men near the peach orchard that served as a salient in front of the two hills. Advancing well beyond the Union line, the Third Corps was exposed with no supporting troops to cover its flanks. Before Meade could do anything to countermand Sickles's deployment, a Confederate attack led by James Longstreet slammed into the peach orchard. The fighting lasted for more than four hours, costing Sickles one-third of his twelve-thousand-man corps. Little ground was lost, though Sickles was wounded and lost his right leg. Meade remained highly critical of the deployment long after the battle, but after the war Sickles found support for his action from Philip Sheridan and, ironically, Longstreet.

drinker and notorious as a womanizer, and Sickles had the same reputation. They both had charismatic personalities, and so they developed a close friendship beginning in the latter part of 1861.•

JIR   °By the spring of 1863 Hooker had moved up to command of the Army of the Potomac, replacing Ambrose E. Burnside following the disaster at Fredericksburg in December 1862. One of his first acts as the new commanding general was to appoint Sickles as commander of the Third Corps, a position that brought him promotion to major general and placed him in the upper echelons of the army.•

BP   °The Army of the Potomac rested and refitted for several months during the winter of 1862–63, near Falmouth, Virginia. Sickles, Hooker, and their fellow officers did not allow that time to waste, giving a series of lavish parties. There was quite a bit of fast living JJH going on.• °Liquor flowed freely, women were available, and Sickles's men liked it.

The regular officers in the Army of the Potomac viewed such behavior with disgust. It was perceived as just more politicking, more of the same old immoral, on-the-edge Sickles.• Charles Francis Adams Jr., a captain of cavalry and the grandson of John Quincy Adams, commented: "[Hooker's] headquarters . . . was a place to which no self-respecting man liked to go, and no decent woman would go. It was a combination of barroom and brothel."

Meanwhile, Sickles and his men did not see much BP action on the battlefield. °After Fair Oaks in May 1862, it was not until the battle of Chancellorsville in May 1863 that Sickles again played a prominent role GWG in battle.• °His first big opportunity on the Chancellorsville battlefield occurred when the Third Corps detected Stonewall Jackson's flank attack on May 2 near Hazel Grove. He sent word to Hooker's headquarters that Jackson was retreating and he wanted to attack him. Aggressiveness was one of his key attributes as an officer, and this was another demonstration of his natural instinct on the battlefield. Attacking the enemy was his first impulse, and in this instance it meant attacking Jackson.•

JJH　°Hooker, however, saw things differently. Instead of reinforcing Sickles at Hazel Grove and trying to sustain his position there as a wedge between the two halves of the Confederate army, Hooker ordered him to relinquish that position, effectively giving up the high ground on the battlefield.°

GWG　°Hazel Grove was a plateau, a crucial piece of ground. Ordered to give it up, despite his own judgment, Sickles did so. The Confederates promptly crowded thirty-one artillery pieces onto Hazel Grove plateau and blasted the Union artillery near Hooker's headquarters at Fairview Cemetery, compelling a further retreat by the Union army.°

BP　°Sickles never forgot that defeat at Chancellorsville. He maintained that Hazel Grove should not have been abandoned, that if he had held the high ground, if he had lashed out at the Confederate column, then the outcome of the battle would have been different. All these what-if's haunted him.°

JJH　°After the Chancellorsville catastrophe, Hooker was occupied with finding a scapegoat for his own failure. One of those he targeted was George Gordon Meade,

Sickles was fascinated with the machinery of war. In his first months of military service, his regiment was encamped in Washington, a city he knew well. In addition to occasional appearances at the White House and the War Department and cajoling old friends, he toured installations around the capitol, including the Washington arsenal (above). Sickles also joined Thaddeus Lowe as a passenger in the latter's balloon, partly out of a sense of adventure, but also with the military objective of scouting Confederate positions across the Potomac.

After the loss of his leg, Sickles was removed from frontline command. Rather than be court-martialed for his action at Gettysburg, Sickles ultimately received the Medal of Honor and then proceeded to criticize Meade, especially for the benefit of the Committee on the Conduct of the War. During the remainder of the war he briefly acted as an ombudsman for the president and then fell into the role of a forgotten general. In December 1864 he wrote Lincoln from New York, begging for an assignment. The president responded with a diplomatic mission to South America rather than a military appointment. In Washington again, Sickles visited others like himself, former commanders without commands, such as Samuel P. Heintzelman, who had served previously under Sickles and was now overseeing a portion of the capital defenses.

WCD and although the attempt to assign the blame to Meade was ultimately unsuccessful, Sickles clearly sided with Hooker on the issue.° °He always defended Hooker's conduct of the battle, especially against the criticisms of Meade and others. Sickles once again was caught up in the pattern he repeated time and time again, identifying someone whom he thought was on the rise and attaching himself to that man.°

Regardless of why or how it happened, Hooker had retreated, and Lincoln was frustrated. He promptly replaced Hooker with Meade. The religious Meade and the wenching, rebellious Sickle made a volatile mix, and that mixture exploded in a tiny, unknown Pennsylvania town.

SICKLES'S ROLE IN the battle of Gettysburg seemed to fit the major general all too well—controversial, reckless, pompous, yet brave. This battle, more than any other event in Sickles's life, forever changed him. Personally, he suffered his own greatest loss. As the army marched toward the fateful encounter, tensions were high.

WCD °Sickles arrived on July 1, 1863, with the Third Corps. Late that night or early the next morning Meade gave him a simple assignment: occupy the left flank of the line. He was to stretch his corps between a point just below Little Round Top on the left and extend it onto Cemetery Ridge to join with the left flank of the Second Corps, commanded by Winfield Scott Hancock.•

JJH °Once Sickles was in that position, he discovered several things that he did not like. Most important was the high ground that stood in front of him. At Chancellorsville, he had given up the high ground on Hooker's order, and his men had suffered terribly for it. At Gettysburg, Sickles was determined that was not going to happen again.• °He requested permission to place his

GWG men where he thought the ground afforded the best position, and Meade replied that, within his broader orders, Sickles had that discretion.•

BP °If Meade was guilty of anything at Gettysburg, it was not fully explaining his strategy to his subordinates as the troops were taking position for the battle on July 2. Certainly Sickles felt that he had been vested with more latitude than Meade thought he had granted. In Sickles's mind, the best ground was the high ground that he could see to his front, toward the Emmitsburg Road. It was crested by a peach orchard.•

JIR °As events unfolded, Sickles realized that the battle was Chancellorsville all over again. This time, however, he saw that the Confederate troops were not

This photograph was taken at the fiftieth anniversary of the battle of Gettysburg on the headquarters site of the Third Corps. Sickles, seated to the left of the sign, was restricted to a wheel chair as the terrain was unforgiving to a ninety-four-year-old on crutches. Nothing shy of death would have kept him away. Woodrow Wilson spoke, and the old general sat on the porch of the Rogers house and watched the poignant reenactment of Pickett's charge by white-haired men in their seventies. Helen Longstreet, the young widow of the old Confederate commander and postwar friend, was there too, representing a southern newspaper.

THIS IS WHERE THE ROGERS HOUSE STOOD.

When surgeons removed Sickles's mangled leg, it was preserved for him. While he recuperated in Washington following the amputation, Sickles mused over his options. With a touch of gothic humor, he had it placed in a miniature coffin and sent to the Army Medical Museum. For many years following the war, Sickles escorted friends to the museum to visit the display.

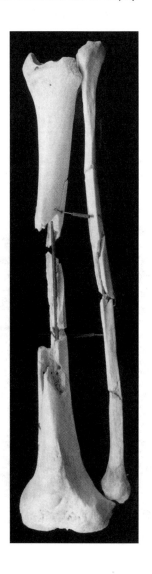

withdrawing from the field, as he had thought was the case at Chancellorsville; rather they were moving to attack. With that interpretation of the situation and without waiting for orders, Sickles pulled his men off Cemetery Ridge and moved them forward to the peach orchard on the hill a half-mile away.•

BP °This was a great surprise to Meade and the rest of the Union line. As the Federal troops looked down their line, they saw a beautiful deployment of the proud Third Corps marching as if on a parade ground, flags flying, every soldier in his place, moving toward the Emmitsburg Road and toward the hill and the peach orchard.•

WCD °James Longstreet's overwhelming assault on the left side of the Federal line crashed into Sickles's Third Corps in the wheat field, the peach orchard, and around the Devil's Den, forcing them to retreat. The fighting went on for hours, costing Sickles more than a third of his force in killed and wounded. The engagement felled several general officers, several colonels, and in fact destroyed the command structure of the Third Corps.•

It was not long before Sickles himself felt the effects WCD of Longstreet's deadly assault. °Around 6:30 in the evening, Sickles was on horseback, still trying to rally his men, trying to stop the impending rout that he feared would happen, when a Confederate cannonball crashed into his lower right leg and almost severed it, leaving it hanging by only a few shreds of skin. Men rushed to him quickly. He was conscious, but he feared that his men would lose heart if they saw him being carried to the rear, desperately wounded.

He engaged in an act of sheer bravado. Asking for a cigar, he placed it in his mouth, lit it, and began smoking it. Realizing that he might die at any BP moment, he never lost his composure.• °As he was being carried off the field, puffing on the cigar, Sickles occasionally lifted himself up on the stretcher to shout words of encouragement to his troops. It was a remarkable gesture on the part of a man who was terribly wounded, and it showed the grit behind the spirit of the man. Whatever they might think of his

Sickles visited the Gettysburg battle-field many times. Here he is flanked by Charles K. Graham and Joseph B. Carr. Graham was a longtime friend who had joined Sickles in recruiting the Excelsior Brigade and had fought with him on the peninsula and at Chancellorsville and Gettysburg. He had been wounded and taken prisoner at the peach orchard but was exchanged and reassigned to Benjamin Butler's Army of the James for the remainder of the war. Graham maintained his friendship with Sickles following the war and even served as a pall bearer for Teresa Bagioli Sickles. Carr had been active in militia affairs prior to the war and had recruited a regiment at the outset of the conflict. He had seen action at Big Bethel, commanded the Third Brigade of Hooker's division on the peninsula, and led the First Brigade of the Second Division of Third Corps at Fredericksburg, Chancellorsville, and Gettysburg.

morals, his scruples, or his honesty, almost everyone on that battlefield had to admit that Sickles was an amazing soldier, an amazing commander. Nothing intimidated him.•

JIR ○The doctors removed his limb early that evening. Sickles still had one card to play where his ambition and his status were concerned. A few days later, the Military Medical Museum in Washington received a wooden box. With it was a little card that said, "With the compliments of Maj. Gen. Daniel E. Sickles." Inside was the amputated leg that he had donated to the museum and to posterity.•

BP ○The loss of his lower right leg became a badge of honor for Sickles. He almost gloried in it. He learned to get about with an artificial leg, but he generally preferred not to use it. He chose to stump around on crutches, and he learned to move about fairly quickly on them. Sickles utilized his crippling injury from then on in such a way that his disability did not hamper him much at all. A man like Sickles would not be kept down by the loss of a leg.•

While the battle of Gettysburg ended with a Union JIR victory, a political battle promptly ensued. ○There was a strong undercurrent among the military that Sickles should be court-martialed for blatantly disobeying orders.•

271

Sickles campaigned for Ulysses S. Grant's bid for the White House in 1868 and received Grant's appreciation in the form of an appointment as minister to Spain. Achieving independence for Cuba was Sickles's foremost goal in Spain, but it did not overshadow his enjoyment of Spanish culture nor his philandering. In 1871 he married Caroline de Creagh (above), an attendant at the court of Isabella II before the monarchy had been deposed. Some whispered that the arrangement masked a more intense relationship with the former queen. Once married, Sickles spent little time with his wife, and the couple was estranged for almost thirty years, reconciling just before his death in 1914. Despite the reconciliation, Sickles ignored his wife and son in his will, saying, "She had means in her own right." Caroline returned to Spain, married, and died in 1919.

BP °To his dying day, Sickles insisted that by his putting the Third Corps in its precarious position, he slowed Longstreet's attack and broke up that series of sledgehammer blows into assaults that were individually dissipated. Had he not moved out there, he contended, the Confederates could have moved their artillery into position and blasted a way through the Union line. Once they had taken Cemetery Ridge, they could have split Meade's army in half and won the war for the South.•

JMM °It became known as the Meade-Sickles controversy. Sickles charged that Meade had been preparing to retreat on the second day rather than staying at Gettysburg and fighting it out. When Meade heard this he was infuriated. He went before the Committee on the Conduct of the War and won it to his side on that issue. The fallout from the controversy, however, went on for a long time after that, and there was nothing but enmity between the two generals.•

Meade ensured that Sickles was kept out of his army. Ironically, Sickles was awarded the Medal of Honor for his bravery at Gettysburg. His turbulent life was far from over, however. "When my services are no longer required in the army," the one-legged general wrote, "I shall prefer private life and remunerative briefs."

GWG °AFTER LEAVING THE military in the late 1860s, Sickles lived for more than forty years, and he filled those years with various activities. Yet he still seemed to lack any sense of scruples or morality. Sickles did what he thought he had to do to get what he wanted WCD to get.• °He was always, first and last, a public man, and somewhere in the shadows he had a private life that continued.

Sickles, as he did so often in his career, distanced BP himself from his wife, Teresa,• °to the point that he saw very little of her, and of course that reinforced her sense of isolation. There was talk that she was taking opiates because she could not sleep. She clearly had severe emotional problems, and this hastened her tragic death. Her health declined to the point where she died before she was thirty-two years old.•

WCD   °His daughter, Laura, gradually grew further and further away from him. She was strong willed, independent, and possessed a violent nature—rather like Sickles himself. In the end, when she was only about nineteen or twenty years old, she divorced herself from him entirely, and the two never saw each other again. When she died, a broken young woman, a victim of her own dissipation, he did not attend her funeral.•

BP   °Certainly his treatment of his family has to stand as one of the black marks against Sickles as a human being, but it did not end with Teresa and Laura. He would become engaged, marry, and later in life have two more children. The same kind of estrangement happened to them.•

Between 1864 and 1867 Sickles held various posts, including that of military governor of the Carolinas. Through political maneuvering, he found a high-profile

BP position as minister to Spain. °In that capacity, he became enmeshed in Spanish politics and pursued hopes for Cuban independence. While he was trying to convince the republican elements among the Spanish to free Cuba, he began to carry on a love affair with the exiled Queen Isabella, the hereditary ruler of Spain.•

Spain soon requested that Washington replace Sickles. Leaving his mistress, his second wife, and his two children behind, he returned to the national capital. To the surprise of many, he, then seventy-four years of age, was once again elected to Congress. His first task focused on Gettysburg.

BP   °Although he was controversial and often portrayed negatively by historians of the battle of Gettysburg, all Americans owe a debt to him, because he was the driving force behind the creation of a national park incorporating the entire Gettysburg battlefield.• He dedicated his every waking moment to this cause. He was also chairman of the New York Monuments

Isabella II was driven into exile after a series of violent revolutions in Spain. She presided over a court-in-exile in Paris and had a notorious reputation concerning numerous lovers. When Sickles arrived as minister to Spain, it was not long before rumors began to circulate about the queen and the one-legged American minister. Even after his marriage to Caroline, Sickles took advantage of any opportunity to visit Paris and spend time with Isabella. In 1875 Isabella's son returned to Madrid and was crowned Alfonso XII, which meant that his mother could return as well. Her affair with Sickles did not survive the restoration of the monarchy.

Even into the twentieth century Sickles still argued the wisdom of his occupation of the peach orchard. In 1902, in correspondence with Longstreet, who died in 1904, he received a reply that confirmed everything he had been saying for almost half a century: "I believe that it is now conceded that the advanced position at the Peach Orchard, taken by your corps and under your orders saved the battlefield for the Union cause." Sickles had the letter read and published at every opportunity. Thus he could not help but appear at the 1903 Gettysburg reunion in anything less than his most resplendent uniform.

Commission, which gave him considerable power to preserve the battlefield. °Realizing that the blood that was shed at Gettysburg, including his own, was something that really flowed from the heart of the country, he argued that the place should be sacred to all Americans. That was his shining moment as an American and as a human being.°

Sickles revisited the battlefield on many occasions, gallantly showing up at all the reunions with whatever mistress he had at the time, including the fiftieth anniversary celebration in 1913. °On the old general's last visit to Gettysburg, Joe Twichell, a regimental chaplain of the Third Corps and still in the ministry, was maneuvering Sickles in a wheelchair around the field. At one point he leaned over and commented that it was a tragedy that there was no monument to Sickles on the field. The former general responded in a booming robust voice, "Hell, the whole damn battlefield is my monument!" It was a typical Sickles remark.

He died the following year at the age of ninety-four. By then he had squandered a personal fortune of five million dollars in lavish fashion.°

°Sickles could have become a pitiful figure in his last years. He was a man crippled by wounds, shrunken with age, and yet there was a perverse nobility about him. There was so much about him that should be despised or scorned, but most people found it hard not to like him. He had a devilish charm, a sparkle in his eyes that won him many friends of both sexes—political supporters, soldiers who followed him into the jaws of death, and women who loved him. Sickles was a fascinating, intriguing figure.°

In 1863 one of the soldiers at Gettysburg, John Haley, observed: "The day was memorable because we

At the fiftieth Gettysburg reunion in 1913—his last—Sickles was restricted to a wheel chair but insisted on being pushed all over the battlefield. Among the many memorials on the field, none could be found to Sickles. He had an answer for that: The whole damned field was his memorial. He had fought there and paid the price of a leg for victory—a victory, Sickles contended, that had preserved the Union. If anything needed to be preserved, it was that field and that leg.

received General Sickles at night. As he passed along our line, he was greeted with such rounds of applause as to convince any man of his unbounded popularity. The best of it was that it was genuine. For if ever a general was idolized, it was Sickles."

JEB STUART AND THE CONFEDERATE CAVALRY

As Civil WAR STORIES GO, none are more romantic than those of the cavalry, and of those cavaliers, no one is more storied than Confederate Gen. James Ewell Brown Stuart. His glorious record earned him recognition and lasting fame, and throughout the nation he was best known by just one name—Jeb.

He was a hero to the South, a terror to the North, and the idol of his men. From First Manassas in 1861 to Yellow Tavern in 1864, he fought in every major battle in the eastern theater of the war, and more than that, he led by example at the front of every charge. A master of deception and an architect of the deep raid, he embarrassed enemy generals, frolicked among friends, and rode circles around the Union army. His scouts and spies gathered intelligence that led to victory after victory. With courage, wit, and dash, he brought honor and glory to his men, his country, and his cause.

Describing Stuart, John Esten Cooke, a cousin of Stuart's wife and author of *Wearing of the Gray*, wrote, "There was about the man a flavor of chivalry and adventure which made him more like a knight of the Middle Age than a soldier of the prosaic nineteenth century, and it was less the science than the poetry of war which he summed up and illustrated in his character and career."

Lt. Col. W. W. Blackford, chief engineer of the cavalry corps of the Army of Northern Virginia, was one of Stuart's biographers. In describing his commander, he declared, "Superficial observers sometimes made the

WCD	William C. Davis
JD	John Divine
GWG	Gary W. Gallagher
CBH	Clark B. Hall
JMM	James M. McPherson
BP	Brian Pohanka
JEBS	J. E. B. Stuart IV

Stuart (above left, center) posed with George Washington Custis Lee (left) and an unidentified classmate shortly after their graduation from West Point in 1854. Robert E. Lee had been the superintendent of cadets during Stuart's last two years at the academy, and Stuart had become better acquainted with the Lees than any other cadet on post. He liked all the Lees, male and female, young and old, and cultivated their friendship.

Stuart was initially assigned to a post in Texas, but a year later he was sent to Fort Leavenworth, Kansas, a second lieutenant in the First U.S. Cavalry. There he met Flora Cooke (right), daughter of Lt. Col. Phillip St. George Cooke, commander of the Second Regiment of dragoons. The two were married on November 14, 1855, less than four months after their first meeting.

mistake of considering him frivolous, but this was not so. I have never seen his superior on a battlefield." As a colonel of cavalry at the beginning of the war, a confident Stuart noted: "I regard it as a foregone conclusion that we should ultimately whip the Yankees. We are bound to believe that anyhow, but the war is going to be a long and terrible one first. We've only just begun it and very few of us will see the end. All I ask of fate is that I may be killed leading a cavalry charge."

GWG °Stuart made one of the most striking physical impressions of any leader on either side during the Civil War. He filled the eyes of everyone who saw him. He was colorful from the plume in his hat to the sash that he wore to the entourage that followed his headquarters. If Stuart were in the area, everyone would see him and everyone would hear him.•

CBH °The scarlet-lined cape, the rose in his lapel, the upturned hat with the plumed feather flowing behind made him appear to be somewhat superficial and irrelevant, but he was none of that.• °He was a fun-loving

JMM character, exuberant, and always optimistic, which may

have been one of the secrets of his strength. He was also confident that he could ride rings around the enemy, and in the early part of the war, at least, he did.•

JEBS •Some men are born to be authors, sculptors, painters, or statesmen. Stuart was born to lead cavalry.•

At the outset of the war, Stuart—a young, robust career officer in the U.S. Army—found himself a Confederate colonel in command of the newly formed First Regiment of Virginia Cavalry. With orders to pull this unit together, he imposed strict army discipline, battle readiness, and his own image of what cavalry should be.

WCD •Most of his men were volunteers, and this was their first experience with a professional, West Point–trained soldier as Stuart tried to make them

JEBS into cavalrymen.• °They quickly learned that life in the First Virginia Cavalry consisted of training, training, and more training. This had been part of their

On the afternoon of July 21, 1861, things were not going well for the Southerners at Manassas. Stuart, having resigned his commission in the U.S. Army, was a colonel of Virginia cavalry and received orders from P. G. T. Beauregard to "bring your command into action at once and . . . attack where the firing is hottest." In one of the decisive actions on the field that day, Stuart led two companies of horse soldiers to the left of the Confederate line and charged twice through the Eleventh New York Fire Zouaves, ending their effectiveness on the field and helping to ensure the final Southern victory.

Stuart's cavalry made national head-lines, both in the North and in the South, by riding around George B. McClellan's army in June 1862 during the Peninsula campaign. One of his pursuers was his father-in-law, Gen. Phillip St. George Cooke. Following the ride around McClellan, Stuart was given a hero's welcome in Richmond and even addressed a small crowd from the steps of the capitol building.

colonel's West Point experience, where training and repetition produced the kind of quality performance expected of a combat unit.•

JD °He drilled them unmercifully,•

WCD °and they did not like it. Some regarded him as a martinet; others considered him a lunatic.

He set the men to what seemed to them ridiculous exercises: running up hills, running down hills, running around screaming, hiding. On one occasion, Stuart took his men within range of a Federal battery and had them pose there. He later said that he had done this to entice the Federals to fire—which they did—so his men would know what it was like to be under fire and to show them that the Federals would fire high. He predicted the Federals would not be accurate, and he wanted to give his men the same confidence he had.•

George Cary Eggleston, a member of the First Virginia Cavalry and another Stuart biographer, noted: "We learned to hold in high regard our colonel's masterly skill in getting into and out of perilous positions. He seemed to blunder into them in sheer recklessness, but in getting out he showed us the quality of his genius. And before we reached Manassas, we had learned, among other things, to entertain a feeling closely akin to worship for our brilliant and daring leader. We had begun to understand, too, how much force he meant to give to his favorite dictum that the cavalry is the eye of the army."

WCD °The results of all this training, hard work, and seemingly incongruous drilling came together on the plains of Manassas on July 21 during the battle of Bull Run.• About two o'clock that afternoon, Stuart received orders from P. G. T. Beauregard to join the raging battle, directing him to "bring your command into action at once and that you attack where the firing is hottest."

The ride was not without casualties. During a skirmish between the Confederate Essex Light Dragoons and Cooke's cavalry, Capt. William Latané charged a Union officer who managed to fire two shots before being wounded by the Southerner's sword. Latané, a twenty-nine-year-old physician, was Stuart's only fatality.

The firing was hottest where Stuart found a regiment of colorfully dressed New York Zouaves. Boldly, he led a saber charge and slashed through them, creating panic in their ranks. His action sparked the Confederate rout of the Union army in the first significant battle of the Civil War.

WCD °The men of Stuart's cavalry behaved well. They went where he told them. They did what he told them. They charged through the enemy line, turned around, and charged back. They demonstrated the discipline that he had instilled in them.•

GWG °Stuart's reward for his visible and acclaimed role at First Manassas was promotion to brigadier general. He was given command of more troops, and after a fairly quiet late 1861 and early 1862, he found himself on the Virginia peninsula, southeast of Richmond, as Union Gen. George B. McClellan's army moved toward the Confederate capital.•

WCD °He was already a hero in the Confederacy by the spring of 1862. What cemented that more than anything else and also cemented the confidence of Robert E. Lee in Stuart was his first ride around McClellan.•

JMM °As soon as Lee took over command of the Army of Northern Virginia in June 1862, Stuart emerged as his right-hand man as a cavalry commander. One of Lee's first orders was to direct Stuart to carry out a reconnaissance to find out where the Union right flank was north

281

of the Chickahominy River. That led to Stuart's first Chickahominy raid when he rode around McClellan's army and sent back precisely the intelligence that Lee

JEBS needed.• °That one stroke, that one-hundred-mile ride around the Army of the Potomac, did more to unsettle McClellan than any other event that took place in the early stages of the Seven Days' battles.•

"It was not indeed so much a military expedition as a raid of romance—a 'scout' of Stuart's with fifteen hundred horsemen!" commented John Esten Cooke. "It was the conception of a bold and brilliant mind, and the execution was as fearless."

WCD °Stuart's name was in the headlines of every newspaper, making him a greater hero even than Stonewall Jackson for a time.• The *Richmond Daily Dispatch* of June 16, 1862, pronounced: "History cannot show such another exploit as this of Stuart's! The whole country is astonished and applauds. McClellan is disgraced. Stuart and his troopers are now forever in history."

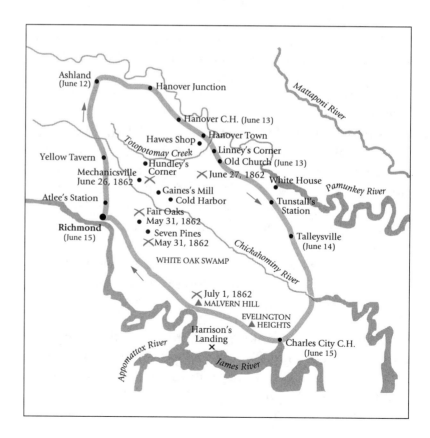

The route of Stuart's first ride around McClellan, June 1862

AFTER HIS FIRST ride around McClellan, Stuart began to cultivate fame. In July 1862 Lee promoted him to major general and placed him in charge of the army's new cavalry corps. As men flocked to his command, he assumed the trappings of glory.

BP °Stuart was fond of military pageantry, which he demonstrated in his own wardrobe—a plumed hat, short jacket, gold sash, high-topped boots with large spurs, and red-lined cape. He was always magnificently mounted on a superb horse, always projecting that sort of jingling, jangling, swashbuckling aspect of the cavalryman.•

GWG °The costume belied a hard-headed, professional soldier who knew exactly what cavalry should do and who was as good at those tasks as anybody on either side. When it came to screening his own army, gathering information about the opposing army, and controlling the middle ground between the two armies, Stuart was unexcelled.•

The men under him were no less colorful. He attracted soldiers who were as entertaining in camp as they were gallant in the field. °He hand-picked every WCD one of his staff officers and had tremendous confidence in them and felt tremendous loyalty for them: men like Channing Price; an eccentric like Heros von Borcke—a Prussian who stood six feet tall or more and carried arguably the largest saber of the Civil War; colorful characters like William Blackford, who was reputed to have eaten a whole frog, and Union Gen. George B. McClellan's cousin, Henry McClellan—both of whom later became Stuart biographers; and, of course, the beloved horse artilleryman John Pelham—the Gallant Pelham, as Stuart and others would call him. These people fought like Stuart and acted like Stuart, and they obeyed instantly when Stuart spoke. They formed a highly effective team.•

JEBS °Included in the ranks of the First Virginia Cavalry was a gentleman by the name of Joe "Banjo" Sweeney. He was a good cavalryman, but he also played the banjo very well. Stuart used Sweeney around the campfire to strike up a tune and get the troops to join in; this again added to the spirit, the camaraderie, and the pride

The full force of Stuart's cavalier personality comes through in this photograph. Those who met him were impressed by his ruddy complexion, full beard, and sparkling eyes; his broad shoulders and powerful build projected a seemingly boundless energy. His wife's cousin, John Esten Cooke, left a vivid description of Stuart: "a gallant figure. . . . The gray coat buttoned to the chin; the light French sabre balanced by the pistol in its black holster; the cavalry boots above the knee, and the brown hat with its black plume floating above bearded features, the brilliant eyes, and the huge moustache, which curled with laughter at the slightest provocation."

of the unit.• George Cary Eggleston recalled, "I have known [Sweeney] to ride with his banjo, playing and singing, even on a march which might be changed at any moment into a battle, and Stuart's laughter on such occasions was sure to be heard as an accompaniment as far as the minstrel's voice could reach."

JEBS °The song that most people heard about, which was more of a recruiting song for the cavalry than anything else, was "If You Want to Have a Good Time, Jine the Cavalry." The refrain from that song is haunting and describes the humor, the dedication, and the mission of the cavalry: "If you want to catch the devil, if you want to have fun, if you want to smell hell, jine the cavalry."•

Soon after Lee's bloody setback in September 1862 at Antietam Creek, Stuart provided another boost to Confederate morale. That October, while McClellan visited his wife a hundred miles away in Philadelphia, Stuart raided the Pennsylvania town of Chambersburg. The Northern cavalry tried to capture him, but they were no match for the Rebel horsemen. Once again, Stuart circled the one-hundred-thousand-man Army of the Potomac, riding 130 miles in three days.

CBH °This second ride around McClellan further mortified the Federals and further elated the Confederates. The effect of that ride was to place McClellan in a very precarious political situation vis-à-vis his commander, JD Abraham Lincoln.• °There were many contributing factors to McClellan's dismissal, and Stuart's second ride around his army, during which it did nothing,• was one of the last before the president finally acted.

Another result of the Chambersburg raid was that Stuart's star rose even higher, gaining even international attention. The London *Times* of October 28, 1862, declared, "Anything more daring, more gallant, and more successful than the foray of General Stuart—a Highlander by extraction—over the border of Maryland and Pennsylvania, has never been recorded." In New York City, the press clamored to know, "Who is Stuart?"

JEBS   James Ewell Brown Stuart was born on Wednesday, February 6, 1833, in Patrick County, Virginia. °He came from a large family; ten children survived. His mother was a gentle woman. She loved poetry, nature, and flowers and was a significant influence on the romantic side of her son. She was also a religious person and passed on a sense of oneness with God to Jeb at a very tender age, making religion an important part of his life. His father, Archibald, was a fun-loving, gregarious lawyer, who was involved extensively in public service. The blending of these two personalities came together in their son, creating a genial, fun-loving, and dedicated spirit.•

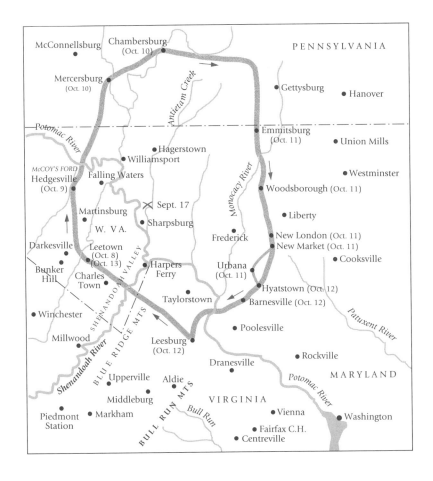

The route of Stuart's second ride around McClellan, the Chambersburg raid of October 1862

One of the keys to Stuart's success was that he surrounded himself with men who were similar to him. Johann August Heinrich Heros von Borcke (left) immigrated to America with the express purpose of fighting for the Confederacy. The six-foot-two, 250-pound giant reputedly carried the largest sword in the Confederacy. He fought in all Stuart's engagements from Second Manassas to Chancellorsville.

John Pelham of Alabama (right) resigned from West Point only a few weeks before his graduation. He was assigned to Stuart after the battle of First Manassas as a commander of horse artillery. He fought in more than sixty engagements and refined the concept of the flying battery. Pelham's artillery kept pace with Stuart's fast-moving cavalry on raids and proved adept in operations against railroads and river gunboats.

In 1850 Stuart entered West Point, where he distinguished himself as a good student and a cheerful soul. Nicknamed "Beauty," he quickly made friends, among them, Custis Lee, Robert E. Lee's oldest son. When Colonel Lee became superintendent of the academy in JEBS 1853, °Stuart became a regular visitor at the Lee home, giving him the opportunity to meet the colonel's daughters. A very close, almost father-son relationship developed between the cadet and the superintendent during that time.°

After graduation in 1854, Stuart was commissioned a second lieutenant and sent out west. There he grew his JEBS whiskers. °His first duty assignment was at Fort Leavenworth, Kansas, and his post commander was Col. Philip St. George Cooke, a cavalry officer. Stuart met one of Colonel Cooke's daughters, Flora, courted her, and soon thereafter married her.° Jeb and Flora started their family immediately. First came a daughter, little Flora, then a son, Jimmy, and later a third child, Virginia.

JEBS °Stuart was frequently away from home on patrols against marauding Indians or trying to calm the vicious outbreaks of murder and arson that occurred between the pro- and antislavery forces in the Kansas Territory.° In June 1856 he helped quell a riot staged by the abolitionist John Brown. Three years later, that chance meeting became historically significant.

GWG °History is full of coincidences, and sometimes coincidences pile on top of coincidences. A situation such as that occurred when Stuart appeared at Harpers Ferry, outside the engine house that Brown occupied in October 1859. It just happened that Stuart was in Washington presenting some ideas for improving cavalry gear. It also just happened that he was ordered to accompany Colonel Lee to Harpers Ferry to suppress Brown and the raiders. All of these things came together to place Stuart in the position where only he could identify Brown at Harpers Ferry, to place Stuart in the position where he, once again, was with Lee, his former superintendent from West Point and the man under whom he would gain great fame during the Civil War.•

JMM °IN 1862 STUART RODE around the Union army on three separate occasions. These excursions demonstrated the ineptitude of the Federal cavalry and created great esprit de corps, not only in Stuart's own cavalry, but in the Confederate population as a whole, who saw this as a spectacular exploit.•

GWG °Early in the war there was a good deal of truth in the notion that the Confederate cavalry was superior to its Northern counterpart. The Southerners were better mounted and better horsemen. Stuart knew that was the case and exploited it. In so doing, his so-called Black Horse Cavalry created terror among most Union soldiers in Virginia.•

Knowing that his men were generally better than the Yankees, Stuart focused on embarrassing his adversaries. George Cary Eggleston suggested: "His audacity was due to his sense of humor. He would laugh uproariously over the astonishment he imagined the Federal officers must feel after one of his peculiarly daring or sublimely impudent performances."

WCD °Stuart had an innate sense of fun, which was partially why he enjoyed raiding behind enemy lines. He liked being in dangerous situations, discombobulating the foe, confusing them. In August 1862, before Second Manassas, he did the same thing by having his horsemen haul logs behind their horses to create a huge dust

Perhaps the greatest personal blow Stuart suffered during the war was the death of his five-year-old daughter, Flora. When he learned of her illness, he felt helpless and told his officers, "I shall have to leave my child in the hands of God; my duty requires me here." To von Borcke he said that light blue flowers reminded him of little Flora's eyes and sunbeams recalled her hair. In the photograph above, he wears a mourning band on his left sleeve.

cloud, thus duping the Federals into thinking that there was a large body of infantry moving toward the front instead of a few horsemen dragging some trees. Deception, after all, is a part of the cavalryman's art, and Stuart played this to the fullest, not just because it was good military policy, but because the boy in him enjoyed misleading the Federals.•

Just prior to Second Manassas, Stuart suffered an embarrassment of his own. He was with his close friend and trusted scout, John S. Mosby, when a column of Union troopers caught them off guard. Mosby reported: "Two cavalrymen saw us and rode forward. When they got in pistol range, they opened fire. The firing gave the alarm and saved Stuart. He mounted his horse, bareheaded, and got away. But he left his hat!" Stuart wrote of the incident in a letter home: "My dear wife, I had a very narrow escape yesterday morning. I lost my haversack, blanket, cloak, and hat with that palmetto star. I intend to make the Yankees pay for that hat!"

Pay they did. Several days later Stuart raided Union Gen. John Pope's headquarters near Catlett's Station, CBH Virginia. °His men made a mess of the encampment, burning tents, stealing stores, and such, but Stuart retrieved Pope's uniform as partial compensation for the loss of his hat.• Stuart's men also burned a railroad bridge and captured more than half a million dollars in currency and gold. Once again, the press had a field day with Stuart's hijinks.

JMM °The Dumfries raid of December 1862 was another interesting exploit that also showed Stuart's sense of humor. Both armies had gone into winter quarters, but Stuart set out toward Washington and again—for the third time—rode around the Union army. He captured a telegraph office at a depot behind the Federal lines and sent a message to Montgomery Meigs, the Union quartermaster general in Washington, saying: "Next time I capture some of your mules, supply better mules. These are kind of worn out." That too made the newspapers, and everybody in the South got a chuckle out of it.•

The cavalryman's war, however, was not all humor, and by the end of 1862 tragedy touched Stuart both personally and professionally. In November his little Flora, then five years old, died of a fever. Stuart grieved terribly, but never in front of his men. °His wife visited him in camp, wearing black in honor of their daughter. Stuart told her in the nicest way she should not to come to camp in mourning dress. His men were very high spirited, and he needed to maintain that high spirit. They did not need to see sadness.°

JEBS

°In 1863 the harshest realities of the war struck Stuart's inner circle. One after another, he lost the men who were closest to him. John Pelham, his gifted artillerist, was killed in March 1863 at Kelly's Ford. Channing Price was killed in May 1863 at Chancellorsville. Will Farley, one of his most effective scouts, was killed in June 1863 at Brandy Station. Rooney Lee and others of his key subordinates were wounded. Heros von Borcke, wounded at Upperville in June 1863, left the scene to recuperate, and he never fought in the field again. One by one, many of the men closest to Stuart and on whom Stuart had relied both for success in combat and for comradeship away from battle were either killed or disabled, never to return.°

GWG

In combat Stuart was a consummate cavalier. One of his aides, Virginia congressman Alexander R. Boteler, noted: "Stuart himself a little in advance of us with his plumed hat in his hand, looked like an equestrian statue—both man and horse being as motionless as marble—his fine soldierly figure fully revealed in the light of the camp fires that were blazing brightly on both sides of the road, as far as the eye could reach and lighting up the foreground splendidly."

At the same time, Major General Stuart's role as a leader in the Army of Northern Virginia continued to grow. This was most evident at the battle of Chancellorsville. °One of his finest moments as a soldier was not as a cavalry commander but as commander of Stonewall Jackson's corps after Jackson had been wounded. Stuart led the Mighty Stonewall's men for the remainder of the battle of Chancellorsville on May 3–4, and he did so with great success. Stuart most likely would have been assigned to take command of the corps after Jackson's death, but he was too valuable to Lee as a cavalry commander to be assigned to the infantry.•

JMM

Regarding Stuart's performance, W. W. Blackford wrote: "Stuart has never received the credit he deserved for his conduct in the battle of Chancellorsville, for it was under him that it was mainly fought. To have led the troops to victory in a battle where the odds were more heavily against us than in any battle of the war, except Sharpsburg, displayed a military genius and heroism surpassed by few characters in history."

STUART'S ROLE IN the Gettysburg campaign has been perhaps the most enduring puzzle of the Civil War. To some extent historians have blamed him for the Rebel loss, but did the absence of Stuart's cavalry really embarrass Lee's army?

Stuart staged a grand review for Lee at Brandy Station on June 8, 1863, and was roused from his sleep the next morning by von Borcke (mounted on horseback) when eleven thousand Union cavalrymen stumbled into the Virginia cavalry camps near Culpeper, Virginia. The fight that followed was the largest cavalry engagement of the war. Although Stuart claimed a victory by remaining on the field after the Federals withdrew, the battle instilled confidence in the Union horseman.

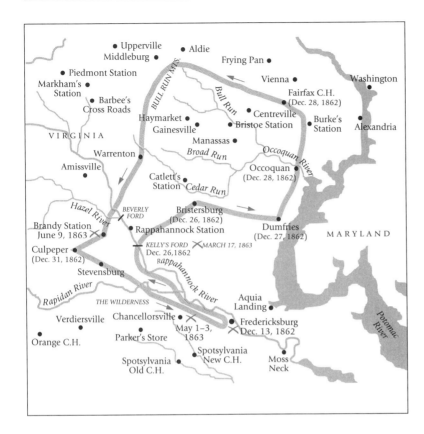

The route of Stuart's third ride around the Union army, the Dumfries raid, December 1862

On June 8, 1863, Stuart held the grandest cavalry review of the war at Brandy Station, Virginia. Lee was impressed and wrote home: "Dear Mary, I reviewed the cavalry in this section yesterday. It was a splendid sight. Stuart was in all his glory." Blackford described a few details of the review, noting: "They came by at a trot, taking the gallop a hundred yards before reaching the reviewing stand; and then the charge at full speed, yelling just as they do in a real charge, and brandishing their sabers over their heads. The effect was thrilling."

The review was something of a last hurrah, however. Some time afterward, Mosby recalled, "The spectators little imagined that the squadrons which appeared in the grand parade before the commander in chief would be in deadly combat on the same ground the next day."

The Gettysburg campaign commenced the day after the review. Lee's army was on the move, and Union Gen. Joseph Hooker wondered where it was going. On Tuesday, June 9, he ordered ten thousand Federal horsemen to flush Lee out. Instead, they found Stuart at Brandy Station.

GWG °The Federal troopers surprised Stuart early on the morning of June 9, but he reacted well and professionally. He shifted his men to the points of danger, and in the end, through hard fighting—both mounted and dismounted—his troopers won the day.•

CBH °Stuart always fought hardest when things looked the worst, and indeed the situation looked the worst at Brandy Station. He was dangerous that day, perfectly heedless of the danger around him. According to one of his troopers, he was here, there, everywhere. His rich baritone voice rang out the words of command: "Give them the saber, boys! Give them the saber, boys!"•

Sensational accounts of the battle made newspaper headlines, but the Southern press also criticized Stuart, reporting that he had been caught by surprise. Stuart was outraged and on June 12, 1863, wrote: "The papers are in error, as usual, about the whole transaction. It was no surprise. The enemy's movement was known, and he was defeated. The *Richmond Examiner* of the twelfth lies from beginning to end." Yet the papers had not mentioned that, contrary to their performances in the past, the Yankee cavalrymen were no longer an inferior foe.

JEBS °After Brandy Station, the Confederates acknowledged that they had always known that the Federals could fight, but now they could ride *and* fight. For the first time the Union cavalry had battled the Confederate cavalry to a stalemate and had walked off the battlefield rather than flee from CBH it.• °The encounter at Brandy Station had provided the individual Federal cavalry trooper with an opportunity to redeem himself on the field of battle, and he did.•

During the next two weeks, Union troopers under Gen. Alfred Pleasonton attacked Stuart time and again, trying to penetrate his screen along the Blue JD Ridge Mountains. °Stuart's mission

Stuart's effects are preserved in the Museum of the Confederacy in Richmond.

was to block two gaps in the mountain range—Ashby's Gap and Snicker's Gap—and Pleasonton's mission was to take those gaps, reconnoiter the valley, and report on Lee's army.•

The tenacious Federal effort climaxed with a five-day battle that stretched among the towns of Aldie, Middleburg, and Upperville. Stuart stubbornly held the mountain gaps, screening Lee's advance from prying Union eyes. Tee Edmonds recorded in her diary on June 21, 1863: "The Yankees are advancing rapidly. Stuart's retreat was so near us we returned in order to see the bear at a nearer view. Little did we imagine our quiet piece of country would be turned into a whirl of excitement and the battleground of two contending cavalry forces. Now and then, a volume of smoke and boom from the cannon gives the Yanks a salute, but they only advance this side of Upperville."

JMM

°Stuart's cavalry effectively screened the Confederate movement north in the Shenandoah Valley. Once the Army of Northern Virginia was safely in Maryland and on its way into Pennsylvania, Lee gave discretionary orders to Stuart to raid the Union rear.• His orders of June 23 stated: "General, you will be able to judge whether you

Screened by an early morning mist, Union Brig. Gen. John Buford's division splashed across Beverly Ford and surprised the pickets of Brig. Gen. William E. "Grumble" Jones's Confederate brigade. The camp was quickly overrun and 150 prisoners taken before Jones could withdraw toward Brandy Station and regroup.

Stuart realized that the Federal cavalry had developed to the point that it was nearly on an equal footing with his own horsemen. He now faced his greatest challenge of the war. Lee and the Army of Northern Virginia were moving north, crossing the Potomac yet again. It was Stuart's task to screen the movement of the army, to keep his counterparts from detecting the migration of Southerners into Maryland and Pennsylvania. Once that was accomplished, he was to join the army and provide intelligence on the whereabouts of the Federals. In the first instance, Stuart succeeded admirably; in the second, he was thwarted by false information and an irresistible prize. As a result, he was not in a position to prevent the collision of the two armies at Gettysburg.

can pass around their army without hindrance, doing them all the damage you can. After crossing the river, you must move on and feel the right of [Gen. Richard] Ewell's troops, collecting information, provisions, etc. Be watchful and circumspect in all your movements."

Stuart left for Pennsylvania on Thursday, June 25, but his plan to cut through the Union army at Thoroughfare Gap was detoured by a large column of passing infantry. The delay cost him two days. He finally crossed the Potomac River on June 28, near Rockville, Maryland. There he discovered a train of Union supply wagons. Because Lee had specifically ordered him to collect provisions for the invading army, °on June 28 Stuart seized the wagons.

When he turned the wagons north, however, in less than half a day it became apparent that his progress had been slowed significantly from forty miles a day to twenty. To the invading Confederates, time was of the essence.*

JEBS   °If there was any fault to Stuart's ride toward Gettysburg, it was in capturing and keeping the 120 supply wagons that slowed his advance to about two miles per hour. After the war, when Stuart was heavily criticized for seizing the supply wagons, Confederate Gen. Jubal Early pointed out that it would have been difficult to turn down 120 wagons when there were a lot of hungry Confederates ahead who needed the food and supplies in those wagons.*

On Tuesday, June 30, Stuart arrived in Hanover, Pennsylvania, where he was further delayed by a force of Union horsemen. W. W. Blackford recalled: "We met Kilpatrick's division of cavalry and had a hot affair with them. We were just opposite Gettysburg, and if we could have made our way direct, the fifteen miles of distance to that place would have passed that day."

The Union cavalry dogged Stuart's every move, forcing him farther north. It was not until Thursday, July 2, that Stuart reached Gettysburg. By then, the battle was in its second day.

CBH   °It has been said that when Stuart finally presented himself to Lee on July 2, that Lee said, "Well, General Stuart, you are here at last." There is no evidence that GWG those were Lee's words, however.* °Yet there is no question that Lee dealt quite harshly with Stuart in terms of

While Stuart's cavalry was not present at Gettysburg, Lee was not without cavalry. Both Richard S. Ewell (left) and William E. "Grumble" Jones (right) commanded horsemen and were with Lee. Maj. Henry B. McClellan, cousin to the Federal general and an aide on Stuart's staff, pointed out, "It was not the want of cavalry [at Gettysburg] that General Lee bewailed, for he had enough of it had it been properly used. It was the absence of Stuart himself that he felt so keenly."

their close relationship. He had never spoken to Stuart the way he did on July 2, but no one knows precisely what he said, even though it is known that the tenor of the conversation was strong.•

The controversy of Stuart and Gettysburg was not a question of the absence of Confederate cavalry. Before the battle began, Lee had two brigades of cavalry with him. One was under William E. "Grumble" Jones, a talented outpost officer, and the other was led by Beverly Robertson, but neither man held Lee's trust to the JEBS extent that Stuart did. °What Lee lacked at Gettysburg from an intelligence-gathering perspective was the support and discernment of his trusted lieutenant, Stuart. He missed the man.• To that extent, Mosby later commented: "Now, the essence of the complaint against Stuart is that the cavalry, the eyes of an army, were improperly absent. It was the personality of Stuart that was needed, not cavalry."

JD °After General Lee's death, two sides formed in the controversy over who was to blame for the defeat at Gettysburg. General Lee was above reproach, so someone had failed him. One group blamed James Longstreet for being recalcitrant; the other blamed Stuart for being late. There is no evidence to lay blame on either man. Today most people recall the words of Gen. George E. Pickett, who said, "I thought the Yankees had something to do with it."•

AFTER GETTYSBURG THE battered Rebel Army of Northern Virginia lived off the wagons that Stuart had captured. The freight fed the men, and the wheels carried the wounded. During Lee's perilous retreat, Stuart hit the Federals like lightning, protecting the army until it could recross the swollen Potomac River into Virginia.

JEBS °Stuart continued to maintain a positive spirit. He was obviously, along with many other Southerners, disheartened over the defeat at Gettysburg, but he did not let that interfere with his desire to continue to perform in an exemplary fashion.•

GWG °His behavior in the campaign and subsequent to Gettysburg showed that he was a professional soldier in

While Federal Gen. Joseph Hooker had botched his head-to-head meeting with Lee at Chancellorsville in May 1863, perhaps his greatest contribution in frustrating Lee's plans in Pennsylvania was in sending his cavalry after Stuart the next month. The resulting battle of Brandy Station embarrassed Stuart, and the confident Union cavalry challenged him throughout the time his cavalry screened Lee's movement into the North.

For honor's sake Stuart performed superbly during Lee's retreat from Pennsylvania, but the constant combat of June and early July also exhausted him. His cavalry was blunted on July 3 and had to fight its way through the Catoctin Mountains on July 5 and through Hagerstown on July 6. He began screening the army's crossing of the Potomac on July 7, and for the next seven days he juggled his position across western Maryland to protect Lee's infantry. His horsemen skirmished daily with Federal cavalry, such as John Buford's brigade depicted at left.

the best sense of the word. He was able to get beyond disappointments and to put aside criticisms, although they clearly upset him. He focused instead on getting his job done.*

Through the fall and winter of 1863, Stuart remained vigilant, his cavalry dangerous, but the tide of the war changed in 1864. Ulysses S. Grant pounded Lee in the Wilderness, and a new Union cavalry chief came to face Stuart—Maj. Gen. Philip Sheridan.

GWG °Sheridan was anxious to hurt Stuart and the Confederate cavalry, but George Gordon Meade, who commanded the Army of the Potomac under Grant's overall direction, was reluctant to approve the mission. A fiery confrontation flared between the two. In the end, Grant intervened and supported Sheridan, his protégé. With Grant's blessing, Sheridan went off to raid Richmond with ten thousand horsemen.*

BP °The fact that Sheridan specifically wanted to take on and vanquish Stuart demonstrated the extent to which Stuart had become a symbol to both sides.* Outnumbered three to one, the Confederate cavalry commander met the Union charge.

WCD °Stuart's job was to stop Sheridan. Two years earlier he could have brushed any Federal cavalry aside like dust from his jacket, but now the situation was desperate. The two forces met at Yellow Tavern. There Stuart's

The facade of the jaunty cavalier gave way to a weary man on horseback, and glimpses of Stuart's dark side emerged, revealing his inability to cope with anything less than unqualified success. His reports on Brandy Station and Gettysburg reflect a man incapable of acknowledging his shortcomings. He dealt with failure by denying it, becoming an ironic victim of his own successes.

This photograph may have been taken by Julian Vannerson or George Cook. It conveys a somewhat less flamboyant Stuart than most other photographs and paintings. After Gettysburg the war was going badly for the South and every element of its military. While Stuart continued to fight well, he also faced serious problems. He was losing the men on whom he had depended during the glorious days of success; they were falling in combat and none were there to take their places. Supplies were low, horses and weapons were scarce, and the enemy seemed to increase steadily in number. Stuart was also distracted by sporadic criticisms and felt compelled to defend himself, or more specifically, to exonerate himself.

penchant for being a frontline commander betrayed him, and his lucky star fell.•

JD   °Sheridan never entered Richmond; Stuart had, for all intents and purposes, prevented that. During the battle, the Confederate commander was at the forefront of his men as he had been in most engagements, but

JEBS this time he was a little too close.• °He was shot by a dismounted Michigan cavalryman. His last words as he left the battlefield were very poignant. As he saw some of his men, disorganized and moving back, he propped himself up and said: "Go back! Go back! And do your duty, as I have done mine, and our country will be safe. Go back! Go back! I had rather die than be whipped."•

Maj. Gen. James Ewell Brown Stuart was mortally wounded on Wednesday, May 11, 1864. He died in Richmond the next evening. On a dismal, rainy Friday the thirteenth, Grant's cannons joined a chorus of heavenly thunder as the cavalryman was laid to rest.

On May 20, 1864, Lee addressed the army, saying: "The commanding general announces to the army with heartfelt sorrow the death of Maj. Gen. J. E. B. Stuart. The mysterious hand of an all-wise God has removed him from the scene of his usefulness and fame. To his comrades in arms, he has left the proud recollection of his deeds and the inspiring influence of his example."

GWG °Stuart remains and always will remain one of the great romantic figures of the Civil War. Beyond that, he was a compelling symbol and a gifted professional sol-

WCD dier.• °It's unfortunate that his lasting place in American history is as a romantic hero, the beau ideal, because there was more to him than that. Stuart was a brave man, but wars are full of brave men. Stuart was a dashing man, but the Civil War particularly was full of dashing men. Most of all, Stuart was an effective man and an innovator. He combined the gathering of intelligence and the masking of his army's movements with destruction and sabotage behind enemy lines. In some ways, Stuart did far more than cavalry had ever done before, and in some ways he presaged the mechanized and airborne warfare in the wars to come. He deserves to be remembered as an effective, imaginative soldier and not just as the man with a feather in his hat.•

Blackford closed his reminiscence of Stuart with the statement: "I can close my eyes and bring him before me as vividly as though he were there in life. General Stuart had his weaknesses—who has not?—but a braver, truer, or purer man than he never lived." Cooke commented in *Wearing of the Gray:* "To the old soldiers of Stuart, there is a melancholy pleasure in recalling the gay scenes amid which he moved, the exploits which he performed, the hard work he did. He is gone, but even in memory, it is something to again follow his feather."

Jeb Stuart was just thirty-one years old when he was mortally wounded at Yellow Tavern. Some say that he died at the right time, when the Confederacy still held a glimmer of hope for victory. To think anyone should die so young is hard to fathom, but his destiny ensured that his name would live on forever.

George Meade was skeptical of Philip Sheridan's boast that he could thrash Stuart's cavalry easily, but he authorized the mission when U. S. Grant voiced confidence in his feisty cavalry commander. Ten thousand Federal troopers found Stuart at Yellow Tavern, an abandoned stagecoach inn six miles from Richmond. They fought all afternoon, but while Stuart defended his capital city, Sheridan's target was Stuart. Around four o'clock, Stuart was shot by a dismounted Michigan trooper; he died in Richmond the next day and was buried in Hollywood Cemetery. The minor engagement cost the South its greatest cavalry leader. The loss was so great that Lee commented, "I can scarcely think of him without weeping."

THE BOY GENERALS

The Civil WAR PRODUCED nearly one thousand generals. Some were veterans of the Mexican War fifteen years before. Others were well-connected martinets with no combat experience. Yet unique to the American Civil War was an elite group of generals for whom war was a rite of passage.

BP °All wars are to a certain extent wars for young men, but in this war, more than any other war this country has ever fought, young men—many in their twenties and early thirties—found themselves in command of, not only regiments, but brigades, divisions, **WCD** corps, and even armies.• °Suddenly young men who were, in some cases, barely shaving were commanding hundreds or thousands of men, often men old enough to be their fathers. Command under those conditions called for special reserves, for special abilities, for a special character on the part of men who, by and large, customarily were not yet old enough to have developed those qualities.•

Some of the most controversial and celebrated figures of the Civil War became generals well before the age of thirty. Their legacies defy their youth, and their youth was flush with ambition. "We certainly have a tremendous task before us," twenty-five-year-old Confederate Gen. Stephen Dodson Ramseur observed. "A task which will test our manhood and will entitle those of us who perform the part allotted to us the full title of heroes."

GWG °A general bears the ultimate responsibility for every aspect of the performance and well-being of his

Opposite: Galusha Pennypacker

WCD	William C. Davis
GWG	Gary W. Gallagher
DMK	D. Mark Katz
RKK	Robert K. Krick
JMM	James M. McPherson
BP	Brian Pohanka

Adelbert Ames (left) graduated fifth in the West Point class of May 1861 and served as a battery commander and as a regimental, brigade, and corps commander during almost every action in the eastern theater. He received a commission as brigadier general of volunteers in May 1863 and was brevetted a major general of volunteers and a brigadier and major general in the regular army in January 1865. He was the last surviving Civil War general when he died in 1933.

Edward Porter Alexander (center) graduated third in the West Point class of 1857. He entered Confederate service in May 1861 and was made chief of artillery for Longstreet's corps, serving in almost every battle and campaign. Alexander was promoted to brigadier in February 1864, one of three to hold that rank in the Southern artillery service.

Hugh Judson Kilpatrick (right) graduated nineteenth in the West Point class of May 1861. He rapidly rose to the rank of brigadier through the combination of influential friends and his own aggressive performance on the field. Kilpatrick's star faded at Gettysburg. He tried to redeem himself with a bold raid on Richmond that failed but saw success again during the Atlanta campaign, the March to the Sea, and the Carolina campaign.

command, from how the camps are kept, to how drill is practiced, to how supplies are distributed, to how his men perform on the battlefield. When it becomes apparent that this involves anywhere from a thousand to ten thousand men, depending on the level of command, this becomes a tremendous responsibility, especially if it is placed on the shoulders of some very young men, as was the case in the Civil War.

To lead often meant to give one's life. The nature of combat in the war—the volleys of bullets, canister ripping through the battle lines and knocking dozens of men out of the ranks, fighting at times hand to hand—called for deeds of almost sacrificial bravery on the part of the officers. Those men led from the front, not from the back. In doing so, many of those boy generals were terribly wounded, not just once, but two, three, or four times, and then returned to the fighting. Many of them died while leading a charge, even when hope was against them, even when they knew their side had lost. That kind of gallantry transcended leadership.

These young men had grown up with stories of the Revolution, tales told to them by a grandfather, an uncle, or even their own father. They felt a temporal closeness to the founding of the Republic and the Revolutionary War and had a sense that they were a part of the immediacy and freshness of the noble experiment

that was the United States.• This perception was also colored by a heroic view of war.

WCD °Mark Twain once commented only half in jest that the Civil War was really the fault of Sir Walter Scott, who had written numerous romantic tales about bold cavaliers and bravery and the panoply and all the drama of war.• Scott had proclaimed, "It is wonderful what strength of purpose and boldness and energy of will are aroused by the assurance that we are doing our duty." °But Scott was not alone in this heroic view of war; it was in fact prevalent throughout almost all fictional literature in America and in the Western world at the time. As a result, there was a well-defined mid-nineteenth-century notion of what war was supposed to be like, what a soldier was supposed to be like, how he was supposed to behave, how he was supposed to react, how he was supposed to think, and how he was supposed to speak in living out that role.•

Growing up in antebellum America, the boys who would be generals shared the same romantic ideals of war, but they came from very different backgrounds. Before the war, twenty-four-year-old Brig. Gen. Nelson Miles had been a crockery clerk. During the war, his commanding officer, Gen. John C. Caldwell, noted, "I have to mention the distinguished conduct of Miles in every battle in which the brigade has been engaged. If ever a soldier earned his promotion, he has done so."

Joseph Wheeler (left) graduated nineteenth in the West Point class of 1859 and entered Confederate service as a colonel of infantry. In July 1862 he took command of the cavalry of the Army of Mississippi and headed the Confederate cavalry in the West. He was promoted to brigadier general in October 1862. Wheeler's cavalry was about the only resistance Sherman encountered during his March to the Sea.

Edwin H. Stoughton (center) graduated seventeenth in the West Point class of 1859. He left the army in 1861 and reentered it later as a colonel of volunteers. After a leave of absence following the Peninsula campaign, he was given his brigadier's star in November 1862, becoming at the time the youngest brigadier in the Union army. He is remembered for being captured in his sleep by John S. Mosby at Fairfax Court House in March 1863.

Thomas Lafayette Rosser (right) resigned from West Point two weeks before he would have graduated with the class of May 1861. He served throughout the Virginia battlefront, was promoted to brigadier general in September 1863, and then fought against one of his closest friends, George A. Custer, for most of the next year in the Shenandoah Valley.

George Armstrong Custer (above) was ranked thirty-fourth—last—in the West Point class of June 1861. Three weeks after graduation he was at Bull Run, and for the next four years he participated in every significant battle of the Army of the Potomac. Custer was fearless under fire, and eleven horses were shot from under him, but he was wounded only once. His reckless bravery attracted the attention of his commanders, including George B. McClellan, who had Custer attached to his staff during the Peninsula campaign.

Twenty-four-year-old Brig. Gen. Emory Upton had been reared on a farm in New York. He developed significant changes in army tactics that would last until the twentieth century. His frustration with the commanders around him elicited him to say: "I am disgusted with the generalship displayed. So long as I see such incompetency there is no grade in the army to which I do not aspire."

SOME OF THE boy generals had been lawyers or teachers. Others were barely out of school. The youngest Confederate general, William Paul Roberts, was from North Carolina. He was nineteen years old when the war broke out and only twenty-three when he received his star. Galusha Pennypacker was the youngest of all. He joined the Union army at age sixteen and was promoted to brigadier general at age twenty.

None of the boy generals had seen battle before the Civil War, but some had classroom training. As the war began, the U.S. Military Academy at West Point evolved into a proving ground. The young future generals in attendance there forged a bond that would outlast the cause, men like Joseph Wheeler, Thomas Rosser, Ranald Mackenzie, and Adelbert Ames. The most famous boy general of all, however, barely made it out of West Point.

Following a heroic charge at the June 1863 battle of Aldie, Virginia, Alfred Pleasonton (mounted on the right), then at the head of the Union cavalry in the East and in the midst of reorganizing it, recommended Custer's promotion from captain to brigadier general, making Custer the youngest general in the Union army up to that time. The photograph of Custer and Pleasonton at right was taken at Falmouth, Virginia, shortly after the battle at Brandy Station in June 1863 and three weeks before Pleasonton recommended Custer's promotion.

George Armstrong Custer

MAJ. JAMES HARVEY KIDD served in George Armstrong Custer's cavalry and characterized his commander as, "Brave, but not reckless; self-confident, yet modest; ready and willing to act, but regardful of human life; quick in emergencies, cool and self-possessed; we swear by him. His name is our battle cry. He can get twice the fight out of this brigade than any other man can possibly do."

WCD °The war has no better example of what went into the making of a boy general than Custer. Before the war he was a carefree, happy, fun-loving, irresponsible, pranksterish, typical young man of his age and of the time in which he lived.•

Born in Ohio in 1839, he was raised in a loving middle-class family of eleven children. At the age of ten he moved to his sister's home in Michigan. At seventeen he fell in love with Mary Holland, whose father did not approve of their romance. To rid his daughter of this lovesick suitor's influence, Holland recommended Custer in 1857 to West Point.

Of his experience at the military academy, J. H. Kidd recalled: "Custer was always in trouble with the authorities. He had more fun, gave his friends more anxiety, and came nearer to being dismissed more often than any other cadet I have ever known."

Old Curly, as he was called, graduated at the bottom of his class in June 1861. Three weeks later he was thrown into the war at the battle of Manassas. From that first battle at Bull Run to the Confederates' surrender nearly four years later, Custer was on the field in every important battle of the Army of the Potomac.

BP °The one thing he had above anything else was an almost hyperactive energy, and he translated that energy into behavior appropriate to the battlefield: dash, zeal, bravery, leadership, a sort of follow-me style. He

Custer drew the notice of McClellan following a reconnoiter and raid beyond the Chickahominy River. The commanding officer reported that Custer "was the first to cross the stream, the first to open fire upon the enemy, and one of the last to leave the field." Custer was summoned to McClellan's headquarters, reassigned to the general's staff, and promoted to captain. An aide's responsibilities included reconnoitering, delivering written and oral messages, relaying intelligence from subordinate commanders, acting as the commander's representative with units in action, and overseeing troop movements. The duty required hours in the saddle, infrequent meals, and exposure to enemy fire.

No soldier seemed as anxious to fight as Custer. In a letter to a cousin he wrote, "I would be willing, yes glad, to see a battle every day during my life." Custer's other side, however, was that of a friend who enjoyed the company of others, such as those he had known at West Point, where he had a reputation as being personable, fun-loving, and loyal and seemed the most popular man in his class. The many bottles and cups that litter the area between Custer (reclining, right) and his fellow staff officers hint at how one passed the time between assignments. Custer, however, had taken the temperance pledge while on leave in Monroe, Michigan, when his sister had confronted him after a drunken spree. He never violated his promise.

exhibited those talents early on, and his commander, George B. McClellan, approved of what he saw and placed Custer on his staff. It was under McClellan that Custer began to rise through the ranks.• "His head was always clear in danger," McClellan noted, "and he always brought me clear and intelligible reports."

WCD   °Custer demonstrated the kind of pluck, the kind of dash, and certainly the kind of theatricality that would call attention to a young lieutenant. There is no question that he tried very hard to call attention to himself.• He garnered attention from his appearance and through his exploits, even vowing not to cut his hair until the North had won the war. In 1862 he was the first Union officer to scout the enemy from a balloon.

Custer had his critics, but he defended his actions emphatically, saying: "I am not impetuous or impulsive. I resent that. Everything I've ever done has been the result of the study that I have made of imaginary military situations that might arise."

Cavalry commander Alfred Pleasonton took an interest in Custer, and the young officer noted, "I do not believe a father could love his son more than General Pleasonton loves me." Under Pleasonton, the

WCD twenty-three-year-old was promoted °from captain, not to major or lieutenant colonel or colonel, but to brigadier general. He was jumped four grades over many men who were much older, who had much more seniority, and who were higher in rank.• Custer took command of his cavalry brigade in 1863, just in time to lead them at Gettysburg.

JMM   °On the afternoon of July 3, three miles east of the main Gettysburg battlefield, the cavalries of the two armies clashed for several hours. The immediate outcome was that the Federal cavalry halted the advance of Jeb Stuart's cavalry, and one of the principal events in that clash was a headlong charge commanded by none other than Custer. That action completely blunted the Confederate advance and turned the tide in favor of a Union victory on that field, which was a subordinate part of the larger Union victory at the battle of Gettysburg.•

Apart from his performance in the saddle, Custer's battlefield presence was larger than life, and he showed _{DMK} that in the way in which he dressed, °wearing uniforms that were interesting and out of the ordinary. They were reflections of the personality who wore them. Certainly not regulation, his uniforms took on something of the flair of European cavaliers. Custer was extremely proud that he was a general, and he was extremely proud of the uniforms he wore. That pride placed him in front of many cameras, making him one of the most photographed men of the nineteenth century.•

Custer's sense of personal pride was met with either _{WCD} adulation or scorn. °He was one of those individuals who were either loved or hated. He either excited envy and resentment because of his cockiness and his braggadocio, or he invited adulation and almost worship. He certainly elicited a great deal of loyalty from some of the men who served under him, but no small number of his soldiers hated him because he was an extremely harsh disciplinarian and because he was a

Just prior to his promotion to major general, Custer posed one last time as a brigadier, wearing the simple blue tunic with gold-star shoulder straps and the double row of buttons befitting his rank. His regular uniform, however, was a suit of black velvet, trimmed with gold lace, and a navy blue shirt turned down over the collar of his black jacket and set off by a brilliant crimson necktie. While this costume made him an easy target on the field, Custer maintained that he wanted his men to see him in combat and be reassured by his presence in the front line.

With great caution, balloons were used as observation platforms during the Peninsula campaign. Because professional "aeronauts" were not accurate in their reports of enemy positions, a few adventurous officers were drafted for this purpose. Custer was among the first to be assigned as an observer, and the accuracy of his information impressed his commander, Gen. W. F. "Baldy" Smith, sufficiently so that he was sent aloft repeatedly, particularly before sunrise and after sunset. "I had the finest view I ever had in my life [and] could see both armies at once," he wrote to his parents. During a flight on May 3, 1862, Custer detected the Confederate withdrawal from Yorktown and, after reporting the pullout, joined in the pursuit led by Winfield Scott Hancock.

bit of a martinet. Others realized that some of the glory given to Custer very naturally rubbed off on those who served with him. No one, however, was indifferent to him.•

BP

°Custer was ideally suited to the cavalry. All the spirit that he had and the daring that he exhibited infused his men, who had once been laughingstocks, with a confidence that they could outfight the Rebels. When Custer rode to the front of his troops in his gaudy outfit with the gold braid and the big floppy collar, when he waved the huge sword that he carried and spurred his horse forward, they knew they were going to follow him. While he did dress to impress, he was more than just a colorful uniform. He did not just dress like a cavalier, he fought like a cavalier.•

DMK

°The press loved Custer and gave him the status of a celebrity. *Harper's Weekly* often carried illustrations of Custer—setting him off appropriately with his long, flowing blond hair—and emphasized his battlefield successes. He was considered one of the most attractive men of the nineteenth century. Women adored him. He loved to flirt with women and later let his wife know that sometimes they had flirted back.•

By 1863 Custer had fallen in love again, this time with his future wife, Elizabeth Bacon. "I read him in all my books," she wrote. "When I take in the book heroes,

Following the rout of the Confederate army at Cedar Creek, Custer was dispatched to Washington to present the captured Southern battle flags to Secretary of War Edwin Stanton. The parade of flags along Pennsylvania Avenue was met with enthusiastic cheers, waving hats, and fluttering handkerchiefs. "Washington has not had many such sensations," the Washington Star *announced. "The soldiers in the city were jubilant, and when they met Custer in the street, would give him a hug; and some of the old soldiers would kiss [his] hand." The action at Cedar Creek had closed forever the Shenandoah Valley to the Confederacy, and a grateful secretary took the occasion to announce Custer's promotion to major general. Alfred R. Waud sketched the ceremony for* Harper's Weekly.

there comes dashing in with them my life hero, my dear boy general. Every man seems so ordinary beside my own particular star."

WCD   °If the qualities demonstrated by Custer were indeed archetypal for most of the boy generals, then it followed that he should continue to act in the same manner after his promotion to brigadier, demonstrating unquestionable bravery and a sense of flamboyance and maintaining magnificent connections. Custer stayed well connected to the end of the war. When General Pleasonton's star declined, Custer quickly became the protégé of Gen. Philip Sheridan, who eventually recommended Custer's promotion to major general. He was the youngest major general in American history and has remained the youngest in the history of the armed forces.• Sheridan praised him, saying, "Custer is the ablest man in the cavalry corps."

JMM   °Sheridan came to depend on Custer more and more. He utilized Custer's division as a kind of shock troops for his cavalry. In a number of battles, especially in Sheridan's Shenandoah Valley campaign in the summer and fall of 1864, most notably at Cedar Creek on October 19,

Twenty-five-year-old George A. Custer (left) had not finished moving his division into position near Appomattox when a Confederate officer approached with a flag of truce. Custer was not present at the meeting between Grant and Lee, but some reports place him on the porch of the surrender house, others visiting old friends in the Confederate ranks.

Custer posed with his wife, Elizabeth, and his brother, Tom, shortly after the war (right). He had met Libbie during a furlough in Monroe, Michigan. After several communications with her father, in which he pointed out his vow of temperance, Custer and Libbie were married on February 9, 1864. After a short honeymoon, the groom returned to his brigade. Following the surrender ceremony at Appomattox, Philip Sheridan, Custer's commander, purchased the pine table used by Grant and presented it to Custer as a gift for Libbie along with a note, which said, "There is scarcely an individual in our service who has contributed more to bring about this desirable result than your gallant husband."

1864, Custer's division carried out shock-troop tactics that completely broke the Confederates' left and forced them to retreat, reeling up the Shenandoah Valley in the third and most decisive defeat of Jubal Early's Confederate force in the Shenandoah Valley.•

Capt. George B. Sanford, one of Custer's men, observed: "Brave as a lion himself, [Custer] seemed never for a moment to imagine that any soldier in his command would hesitate to follow him even to the death. And indeed he had reason to be firm in this belief."

Perhaps the most famous example of Custer's flamboyance came on his last day of the war. Lee's army had surrendered in April 1865. On May 18 the Army of the Potomac marched in parade down Washington's Pennsylvania Avenue for the Grand Review. Custer arrived on his horse, Don Juan.

WCD   °It was certainly a joyous affair, but the review also had a solemn bit of military pomp and ceremony—until Custer appeared. Just coincidentally, as he passed in front of the reviewing stand, he lost control of his horse. The animal was spooked and took off at a gallop. To regain control Custer galloped at full tilt down Pennsylvania Avenue to the adoring adulation and cheers of the crowd. Later he maintained this had been an accident. It probably was not. The conspicuousness of the episode was another example of Custer's panache, taking advantage of a last opportunity to swagger for a crowd at the end of the war.•

Galusha Pennypacker did not have a military background when war began in April 1861. He was only sixteen years old when he enlisted in a ninety-day regiment and served as a quartermaster sergeant. At age seventeen Pennypacker raised a regiment and was commissioned its captain. After service in Florida and the Carolinas, he was attached to Benjamin Butler's Army of the James and participated in the siege of Petersburg. A brigade commander, he was wounded four times.

Galusha Pennypacker

IN 1861 THE AVERAGE age of a general was just less than forty years. By 1865 the youngest general was twenty. As the war aged, its generals became younger.

WCD   °It is a measure of how unique these boy generals are to the Civil War that Galusha Pennypacker, who became a brigadier general in the Union army just short of his twenty-first birthday, was not old enough to vote for the president who made him a general. Pennypacker remains to this day the youngest general officer in the history of the U.S. Army.•

Pennypacker participated in both assaults on North Carolina's Fort Fisher, the first under Benjamin Butler in December 1864, the second under Alfred H. Terry in January 1865. Terry called Pennypacker the real hero of Fort Fisher, noting that his demonstration of courage under fire inspired his men to breach the defenses and subdue the fort's garrison. Severely wounded during the assault, Pennypacker was hospitalized for ten months. His general's star came on April 28, 1865, a month before his twenty-first birthday.

He was born near Valley Forge, Pennsylvania. His grandfather had fought in the Revolutionary War, and his father had served in the Mexican War. Pennypacker began his military career as a sixteen-year-old lieutenant. He was soon promoted to major, then colonel. By age nineteen he was in charge of a regiment. In 1863 Gen. Alfred Terry, his commanding general, remarked, "[Pennypacker] is a most excellent and deserving officer. He will make his mark in the service."

BP   °Despite his youth, Pennypacker was highly regarded by his superiors. He proved his gallantry in February 1865 at Fort Fisher on the North Carolina coast. Pennypacker had formerly commanded the Ninety-seventh Pennsylvania, and he maintained that connection, that bond with those men, many of whom were twice his age. When he saw the regiment falter as it charged the ramparts of Fort Fisher, when he saw the entire color guard, the men around the flag, cut down and the flag go down, he ran forward and grabbed up the flag of his old regiment and led the charge up the rampart. He was terribly wounded and fell with the flag.° Lying in the sand, Pennypacker said to the men attending him: "I know I cannot live with such a wound, but I want you to tell the general that when I fell, the two leading flags on those ramparts were my regiments'. We have the fort."

BP   °He was not expected to survive his wounds. General Terry, in command of the assault on Fort Fisher, said

Stephen Dodson Ramseur graduated fourteenth in the West Point class of 1860. He joined the Confederate service as an artillery officer and served at Yorktown. During the Seven Days' battles, he led an infantry regiment until he was wounded at Malvern Hill. Ramseur was made a brigadier following Antietam and fought at Chancellorsville and Spotslyvania before moving into the Shenandoah Valley, where he was made a major general on the day following his twenty-seventh birthday.

that Pennypacker was the true hero of the fight. With his health still uncertain during the last months of the war, twenty-year-old Pennypacker was promoted on February 18, 1865, to brigadier general.° He was hospitalized at Fort Monroe for ten months and later received the Medal of Honor.

After the war he briefly left the army, returning to serve in the occupation of the South during Reconstruction and was later posted to the frontier. He retired from the army in 1883 and died a bachelor in Philadelphia in 1916.

Stephen Dodson Ramseur

EARLY IN THE war the North had held to the army's established procedures for promotion, basing any advancement on a soldier's years of experience. The South, however, recognized immediately the need for skillful commanders, regardless of age. Stephen Dodson Ramseur had attended West Point, graduating a year before Custer.

RKK   °Ramseur was a brilliant young man, popular in almost every circle. He possessed that intangible quality that makes people willing to follow another. He repeatedly displayed his prowess on the battlefield.°

After commanding an artillery unit during the first year of the war, Ramseur was made a colonel of the Forty-ninth North Carolina Infantry. In taking command of the Forty-ninth in 1862, he recalled, "They cheered for me. And to tell you the truth, I feel that we will make a name for ourselves the state may yet be proud of."

GWG   °Ramseur's temperament perfectly suited the Army of Northern Virginia. Like Robert E. Lee and Stonewall Jackson, who were his idols, Ramseur was aggressive, willing to follow up any advantage, and always eager to engage the enemy. He was audacious and pugnacious.° His superiors noticed Ramseur's out-in-front style, and on Lee's recommendation, the twenty-five-year-old colonel was promoted to brigadier general.

RKK   °There were slightly more than fifty brigades in the Army of Northern Virginia, and Ramseur's became one of the three or four best. That brigade, although it was not as famous as the West Texas Brigade or the Stonewall Brigade, ranked among the most successful. Of course, that accomplishment was a reflection of the leader who crafted it, led it, and turned it to his will.•

Brigadier General Ramseur's greatest day came on May 12, 1864, at the bloody battle of Spotsylvania. °It was one of the greatest moments of peril in the history of the Army of Northern Virginia. Ramseur's brigade was one of the first to enter that fight. It helped close a break in the Confederate line and then maintained its position through several long hours of hard fighting, through the rest of that seemingly endless day.•

In his report afterward, Ramseur acknowledged his men, saying, "To the gallant officers and patriotic men of my little brigade, the country owes much of the successful charge, which I believe turned the fortune of the day at that point, in our favor."

°His reward for this performance was promotion to major general one day past his twenty-seventh birthday (he had been a brigadier at the age of twenty-five). Ramseur completed his career in the Shenandoah

Ramseur learned the night before the battle of Cedar Creek that his wife had just given birth to their daughter. That morning he wore a white rose on his uniform in her honor. While trying to rally his troops near Miller's Mill, he was wounded critically, with both lungs punctured. The ambulance that was removing him from the area was captured by one of Custer's patrols. Seeing that his friend from West Point days was grievously injured, Custer had Ramseur taken to Belle Grove, Sheridan's headquarters.

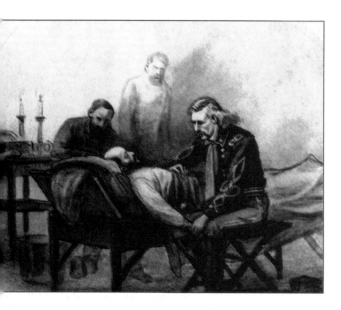

Throughout the night Custer and Henry DuPont, another graduate of the military academy, stayed at the bedside of their wounded West Point brother. As word spread, other acquaintances from the academy came to pay their respects. While he lay dying, Ramseur asked that Custer snip off a lock of his dark hair to send to his wife of less than one year. His last words to his colleague from Michigan were, "Armstrong, I knew if I fell into your hands, you would treat me kindly."

Valley campaign under Jubal Early in the fall of 1864, where he showed great aptitude as a division leader.•

Fewer than five months after his promotion to major general, Ramseur was mortally wounded at the battle of Cedar Creek, Virginia. He was captured and taken behind enemy lines. Surrounded by old West Point friends, including Custer, Ramseur died.

★　★　★

YOUNG MEN BECAME leaders based mostly on skill and merit, but political favors could help, and family connections were even better. Twenty-five-year-old Brig. Gen. William Henry Seward Jr. was the son of Lincoln's secretary of state. In the South there were two young generals named Lee.

Fitzhugh Lee

BP °FITZHUGH LEE WAS made a general at the age of twenty-six. He was a nephew of Robert E. Lee, but in many ways he was the almost perfect opposite of his uncle. Whereas Robert E. Lee was quiet, dignified, and austere, Fitz Lee was a portly, rollicking, swashbuckling, fun-loving character.•

GWG °Lee participated in most of the activities of Jeb Stuart's cavalry in the Army of Northern Virginia, from the Seven Days' campaign through the Gettysburg campaign. He served well, and in the late summer of 1863, when the Southern cavalry was expanded and new divisions were created, he was promoted to major general and given command of one of the new divisions.•

Regardless of how well Fitz Lee merited promotion, some criticized the hint of nepotism. One such detractor, Thomas R. Arcart, declared cynically, "I confess that I was a little annoyed this morning at the announcement of the promotion of Fitzhugh Lee. I suppose in a few days we'll see the balance of the Lees promoted also."

Fitzhugh Lee (left) graduated forty-fifth in the West Point class of 1856 after almost being expelled for misconduct by his uncle, Robert E. Lee, then superintendent of the academy. Fitzhugh Lee was badly wounded on the frontier and returned to the academy in 1861 as an assistant instructor of tactics, but that was short-lived when he resigned his commission and offered his services to the Confederacy. Had he not been R. E. Lee's nephew, Fitzhugh Lee would still be remembered as one of the youngest and most capable commanders in the Confederate cavalry with services rendered at Antietam, Chancellorsville, and Gettysburg. Severely wounded at Winchester in 1864, he remained out of action until the last months of the war.

William Henry Fitzhugh "Rooney" Lee (right) was R. E. Lee's second son and a graduate of Harvard. He served a brief two-year stint in the prewar army but resigned in 1859 to farm the Custis ancestral plantation at White House, Virginia. With the advent of the war he enlisted and was assigned to the cavalry in western Virginia. He proved to be an exceptional brigade commander at South Mountain (after which he received his brigadier's star), Fredericksburg, Chancellorsville, and Brandy Station until he was captured by Federal troopers in June 1863 and forced to sit out the war for nine months. Returning to action in April 1864, he was promoted to major general and given additional responsibilities as attrition thinned the ranks of the Confederate command structure. Both men were with R. E. Lee at Appomattox.

Rooney Lee

Robert E. Lee's second son, William Henry Fitzhugh Lee—nicknamed Rooney—was also a cavalry brigadier. °It was no exaggeration to describe him as a great hulking presence. One man who saw him described Rooney Lee as being too large to be a man but too small to be a horse. There was a good bit of opposition or resentment or jealousy elsewhere in the army at the promotion of so many Virginia officers, especially when a number of Lees were promoted. Like Fitzhugh Lee, Rooney Lee was a capable young officer in the cavalry service.°

°He played a conspicuous part in the battle of Brandy Station, the largest cavalry battle of the war, with nearly twenty thousand mounted men on the field. Rooney Lee anchored the left side of the Confederate line, and his brigade suffered the highest casualties of any Confederate brigade on the field. Lee himself was wounded. He fell into Union hands shortly thereafter and spent the better part of a year in Northern prisons.°

Micah Jenkins

Boy generals on both sides shared one quality: ambition. That was especially true of twenty-six-year-old Confederate Brig. Gen. Micah Jenkins. °He had been

GWG

Micah Jenkins was a graduate of South Carolina's Military Academy in 1854 and founded a military school of his own in 1855. He was elected colonel of the Fifth South Carolina Infantry, which held the far right side of the Confederate line at First Manassas, and then organized and led the Palmetto Sharpshooters on the peninsula. James Longstreet held Jenkins in high regard as a troop commander and was not disappointed with his performances during the Peninsula campaign and at Cedar Mountain, Second Manassas, Fredericksburg, Chattanooga, and Knoxville. After Jenkins received his brigadier's star in July 1862, he campaigned hard and ferociously for a second star, sometimes drawing the ire of his men for his exceptional ambition. In an eerie parallel with the mortal wounding of Stonewall Jackson at Chancellorsville, almost a year to the date and very close to the same spot, Jenkins was riding with Longstreet's staff during the battle of the Wilderness when they fell under friendly fire that knocked Longstreet out of the war for six months and killed several officers in the party, including Jenkins.

born on Edisto Island, South Carolina, and his father was a prominent and powerful landowner. Jenkins was able to attend the South Carolina Military Academy in Charleston, now known as The Citadel. Graduated first in his class, he was fascinated with military life, tactics, and training. While still a very young man, he and a fellow graduate, Asbury Coward, founded what was called the King's Mountain Military Academy. Jenkins was there when the war began.•

°He started the war with a higher rank than most of the young men who became generals during the Civil War. He did well in the early fighting of the war, especially on the Virginia peninsula and during the Seven Days' battles. He worked with the Palmetto Sharpshooters, and his reward was promotion to brigadier general in July 1862, just after the completion of the Seven Days' campaign.•

RKK

°For much of the rest of the war, Jenkins expended most of his energy, effort, time, and concern earning promotion to major general. His ambition was so naked, in fact, that of all Confederate officers of any rank, none have half as many negative comments on record from their subordinates about crass and graceless ambition as Jenkins.• One soldier went so far as to say, "Jenkins would walk forty miles on the skulls of his men to make major general."

As ambitious as he was, young Jenkins never made it to major general. During the battle of the Wilderness, he was with a group of officers riding with Gen. James Longstreet when they were struck by friendly fire. Longstreet was wounded, but Jenkins was killed.

Nelson Appleton Miles

BP

°OCCASIONALLY A BOY general arose who had no real military training to speak of, yet his ambition and skill allowed him to rise high in the army. Such a man was Nelson Appleton Miles.•

Miles was working as a clerk in Boston when the war broke out. He recruited a hundred men for a local regiment, but he was considered too young for command. After serving in the Peninsula campaign, Miles was made lieutenant colonel of a New York unit, then colonel. In

December 1862 he was with the army at Fredericksburg. As the battle wore on, the Union advance stalled. Wave after wave of Federal soldiers crumbled before the famous stone wall at Marye's Heights.

BP °As these men were being slaughtered on that field, Miles concluded that a bayonet charge would carry the position. He wanted desperately to lead that charge, but he knew that he needed more troops to be successful. At that moment he was struck in the throat, the bullet exiting behind his ear. The injury, however, did not stop him. He held the wound together with his hands, returned down the hill to try to find Gen. Oliver O. Howard, his superior officer, to urge him to make another attack.° Miles collapsed before he could lead the suicidal charge, and General Howard commented, "He was determined either to be killed or promoted."

Miles survived Fredericksburg and went on to win the Medal of Honor for valor at Chancellorsville, where he was again wounded. He finally received his promotion to brigadier at age twenty-four and to major general at age twenty-five. Gen. Francis Barlow, a colleague, noted: "[Miles] has a remarkable talent for fighting battles. The sound of cannon clears his head and strengthens his nerves."

Francis Channing Barlow

ANOTHER YOUNG COMMANDER, Francis Channing Barlow,
BP was °one of the boy generals who saw war as hellish and thought that the Union army was incredibly incompetent and mismanaged. He was a tremendous leader of men in battle and a shining example of a bright young man with potential who turned himself into a consummate soldier.°

He enlisted as a private at the beginning of the war but was promoted to colonel when he reenlisted in August 1861. Barlow served in the Peninsula campaign and was seriously wounded at Antietam, after which he was promoted to brigadier general.

Barlow took his brigade to Chancellorsville and Gettysburg. During the battle on the Pennsylvania countryside, he was temporarily paralyzed by a bullet and left

Nelson Appleton Miles had no formal military education prior to the war but worked in a Boston crockery store by day and attended school by night. With the outbreak of the Civil War, he recruited one hundred volunteers for the Twenty-second Massachusetts Regiment and was himself commissioned a captain of infantry. Miles's superiors believed he was too young to command at age twenty-two, and so he was attached to O. O. Howard's staff during the Peninsula campaign. He saw action at Fredericksburg, Chancellorsville (where he was awarded the Medal of Honor), the Wilderness, Spotsylvania, and Petersburg and was wounded on four separate occasions. After the war Miles was made custodian of the imprisoned Jefferson Davis and, following the reorganization of the army in 1866, continued his military career in the West.

Francis Channing Barlow (far left) was known as a boy general more for his clean-shaven appearance than for his youth. He graduated from Harvard in 1855 and was practicing law in New York when the war broke out. Barlow enlisted for ninety days as soon as the call went out for troops and then reenlisted with the rank of lieutenant colonel. He survived the Peninsula campaign but was wounded at Antietam, where he earned his brigadier's star. His brigade was driven from the field at Chancellorsville by Stonewall Jackson's celebrated flank attack, and at Gettysburg he was left on the field at the end of the first day, temporarily paralyzed. When he did return to the front it was as a divisional commander under Winfield Scott Hancock (center). He enjoyed his greatest successes in uniform at Spotsylvania and Sayler's Creek.

for dead. He received medical treatment through the auspices of Confederate officers, and he rejoined the army as U. S. Grant began the last campaign of the war.

The high point of his career may have been in May 1865 at the Mule Shoe and the Bloody Angle at Spotsylvania when his brigade captured more than three thousand prisoners, including two generals, and thirty regimental colors. His last action was at Sayler's Creek in April 1865, and he was promoted to major general in May.

At the dedication of the Barlow statue at Gettysburg, Nelson Miles observed: "He was utterly devoid of the sensation of fear, constantly aggressive, and intensely earnest in the discharge of all duties. Under the most depressing circumstances he was never without hope or fortitude."

Emory Upton

BP °THE ONE BOY general who had the greatest lasting effect on the U.S. Army was Emory Upton. He was not one of those officers who did what he did out of any sense of boyish adventure. Upton was a student of the art of

WCD war.• °He was in some ways the antithesis of Custer. In the long run, he was perhaps the more productive, perhaps the more capable, but he was certainly less flamboyant. In subordinate roles on the battlefield, Upton repeatedly showed himself to be a capable, competent, and calm commander under fire.•

BP °He served as a battery commander in the terrible battles of the Seven Days as McClellan tried and failed to take Richmond. He served at Antietam. He said that he had read about the dead falling in heaps, but he had never seen anything like that until Antietam, where he saw whole ranks fall together. The tremendous loss of life led Upton to ponder the lessons that could be learned from the example of these terrible slaughters. How could the Union maximize its abilities, its skills?•

WCD At Spotsylvania, Upton devised and implemented a new attack formation. The effectiveness of his innovation led to his promotion to brigadier general. °Such a refinement in tactics may not have taken great brilliance to accomplish, but on the battlefield, more or less on the spur of the moment, to see the problem in front of him and to devise an innovative solution marked Upton as a man of merit. It showed that he was resourceful and adaptable, and those two elements made him successful.•

Upton was intolerant of what he considered battlefield ignorance. His frustration peaked a month after his promotion, when three hundred of his men were killed in a single battle. On June 4, 1864, Upton voiced his anxiety, commenting: "We are now at Cold Harbor since June 1. On that day we had a murderous engagement. Our loss was very heavy and to no purpose. Thousands of lives might have been spared by the exercise of a little skill."

WCD He was promoted to major general at the age of twenty-five, but at the end of the war his military career had just begun. °In his later years, as a high-ranking officer in the post–Civil War army, Upton, more than any other man, was responsible for reorganizing the army into the shape that it essentially holds today.• Having served in artillery, infantry, and cavalry, he successfully revised the army manuals for all three branches.

BP °He worked tirelessly at tactics. Unfortunately, his health began to fail; some say he had a sinus tumor, others contend it was a brain tumor. He was also haunted by the loss of his young wife to tuberculosis. Ultimately, he committed suicide in his quarters at the Presidio in San Francisco. His death was both a terrible human tragedy and a great loss to the U.S. Army.•

★ ★ ★

GWG °THE CIVIL WAR affected the lives of these young generals in very dramatic ways. It brought them to a level of renown and responsibility far greater than they would

Emory Upton (above) graduated eighth in the West Point class of May 1861 but held the reputation of being the class genius. Gifted with an ability to see solutions before most people saw problems, he was promoted quickly, making general in May 1864. Serving in the West in the last months of the war, he was the first Union commander to defeat Nathan Bedford Forrest.

After the war (below) Upton was placed on the board of examiners at West Point. He married and took his wife with him when he was sent overseas to study European tactics. Her health was frail, however, and she died soon after he returned in 1870 to become commandant of cadets at the military academy. He grieved for her the rest of his life. Upton spent the next decade writing profusely on tactics and the three branches of the army before health problems led him to take his own life in 1881.

Nelson Miles (above) played a significant role in the Indian wars and in 1895 became general in chief of the U.S. army. He died in 1925, the last of the full-rank major generals of the Civil War.

The battle of the Little Big Horn (below) in June 1876 marked the end of George Custer's career and the beginning of the Custer legend.

have achieved in the normal course of affairs. It also served as the great focal point, the great defining moment of their lives. Most of them looked back repeatedly through the rest of their careers on what they had done and where they had been during the Civil War.* Many of the boy generals stayed with the military after the war.

George Armstrong Custer found more fame for his exploits on the western frontier. He died at the head of the Seventh Cavalry in 1876 when he encountered a superior force of Sioux and Cheyenne at the battle of the Little Big Horn. He was buried at West Point.

Nelson Miles also went west. °One of the preeminent examples of the boy generals, he concluded his career, not only with the reputation of being a famous Indian fighter, but in command of the entire army. In 1895 he was made general in chief, and at his retirement in 1903 he was the army's highest-ranking officer—all without the benefit of a West Point education.*

A few of the boy generals went on to lead in the Spanish-American War in 1898. °By coincidence all had been cavalrymen—Fitzhugh Lee, Joseph Wheeler,

Several former Civil War generals took up arms again during the Spanish-American War. Interestingly, some of them had worn gray and been cavalrymen during the previous conflict. Fitzhugh Lee's staff in Cuba is pictured at left, with Lee seated second from the left. He had been consul-general in Cuba on the eve of the war and was commissioned a major general of volunteers by William McKinley when war broke out.

The exploits of Joseph Wheeler (below) in the Civil War's western theater were second only to those of Nathan Bedford Forrest. After the war he practiced law and then served eight terms in the U.S. House of Representatives. When hostilities broke out between Spain and the United States, Wheeler was made a major general of volunteers and commanded the cavalry division on the Santiago expedition and took part in the battle of San Juan Hill. He was sent to the Philippines in command of a brigade and returned to the United States in 1900 as a brigadier of the regular army.

Thomas Rosser—all former Confederates now wearing U.S. uniforms. There are several stories about Wheeler, particularly one in which he shouted for his men to charge the "damn Yankees" as he was leading them against a Spanish position in Cuba.•

Adelbert Ames was the last surviving Civil War general. He won the Medal of Honor for bravery at the battle of First Bull Run. As a young brigadier, he commanded troops at Gettysburg. He died in 1933 at the age of ninety-eight.

In some ways, the boy generals grew up with the country. °In a way, they were emblematic of that raw sense of exuberance, excitement, adventure, and all the other things that go into a definition of youth that the country felt as a whole. The three million men who went into the armies felt it from 1861 to 1865 to one degree or another. The boy generals are representative of both the romanticism and the reality of the time in which they lived and the events through which they passed.•

Youth is the time of life marked by growth and development. Caught in the fire of war and destruction, these boy generals struggled to mature with the nation itself. By remembering them, their lives were not all wasted—their youth was spent on freedom.

WCD

THE UNION CAVALRY AND PHILIP SHERIDAN

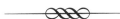

In the FIRST TWO YEARS of the Civil War, the Union cavalry proved mostly ineffective against its Confederate counterpart. Without quality horses or proper training, Federal riders endured humiliation and devastation on the battlefield and faced confident Rebels whose horsemanship was second nature. It took hard work, organization, and visionary leadership to turn the Union cavalry's early failure into ultimate victory.

One of the most decisive moments for the Federal horsemen occurred during Maj. Gen. Philip H. Sheridan's 1864 campaign in the Shenandoah Valley. Although his cavalry had improved, he noted: "I knew that I was strong, yet I deemed it necessary to be very cautious. With the presidential election impending, the authorities in Washington impressed upon me that the defeat of my army might be followed by the overthrow of the party in power. Under circumstances such as these, I could not afford to risk a disaster."

On October 19, 1864, the battle of Cedar Creek proved to be a defining moment for the Union, its cavalry, and its tenacious leader, Sheridan. The Rebels launched a massive attack at dawn, shocking and overwhelming the sleeping Federal army.

PAH °Returning from a Washington conference, Sheridan was at Winchester, fourteen miles from his army. Over breakfast, he and his staff thought they heard the rumble of cannon. They decided to head back to the army immediately.°

ECB	Edwin C. Bearss
WCD	William C. Davis
PAH	Paul A. Hutton
EGL	Edward G. Longacre
BP	Brian Pohanka

At Cedar Creek, Virginia, on the morning of October 19, 1864, five Confederate divisions attacked Sheridan's Army of the Shenandoah, taking them by surprise and wrecking two of his three corps. Sheridan was in Winchester, twelve miles away, returning from a Washington conference, when he heard the rumble of artillery in the distance. Racing to the sound of battle, he encountered a steady stream of retreating Union soldiers. He cursed and cajoled them into returning with him. By noon his troops had reformed their lines, and the diminutive Sheridan rode the length of it, evoking cheers and instilling a determination to retake their camps.

After an hour's ride, the Federal commander saw his worst fears realized. He recalled, "There burst upon our view the appalling spectacle of a panic-stricken army—hundreds of slightly wounded men, throngs of others unhurt but utterly demoralized, and baggage-wagons by the score, all pressing to the rear in hopeless confusion."

BP °Sheridan raced to the scene of the action, outdistancing his escort and all but two staff officers.• "I was sure the troops had confidence in me," he recounted. "I thought I ought to try now to restore their broken ranks."

One of Sheridan's staff officers, Maj. George A. Forsyth, remembered: "One glance at the eager face and familiar black horse, and they knew him. And starting to their feet, they swung their caps around their heads and broke into cheers as he passed beyond them."

PAH °To show his men that he was there, Sheridan took his personal guidon and, with his staff reluctantly following, crossed between the Union and Confederate lines, galloping the whole length. The men began to chant his name, and then they charged. The cavalry opened the Confederate flanks, and the Southern force was shattered. The Confederate dream of retaking the Shenandoah was over.•

BP °By his example, by his bravery, by his very voice, Sheridan so galvanized his men that he literally turned defeat into victory.° That morning Sheridan and his cavalry achieved success at a crucial time for Abraham Lincoln. °With the election of 1864 only two and a half weeks away, a resounding Confederate victory might not have been followed by Lincoln's landslide reelection.° A grateful president thanked his general, saying, "With great pleasure, I tender to you and your brave army the thanks of the nation, and my own personal admiration and gratitude, . . . especially for the splendid work of October 19, 1864."

ECB

In 1861, however, Lincoln had little praise for his cavalry or its leaders. °At the start of the war the Federal cavalry was clearly inferior to the Confederate. By and large, Northerners were not the horsemen that Southerners were. Many enlistees were city boys from the streets of New York, Philadelphia, and Boston.° Capt. Frederick C. Newhall of the Third Pennsylvania Cavalry commented about the men training for his command: "Many of them showed much more fear of their horses than they ever did afterward of the enemy. The wild fumbling after mane or saddle strap are a lasting source of amusement."

BP

°Conversely, many Southerners seemed to have been born in the saddle. To a large degree this was because the prewar South was a land of few good roads and very little in the way of public transportation. Southerners had to learn how to ride to do anything or to get anywhere.°

EGL

°Compounding this Federal handicap, the Union procurement system for acquiring horses was plagued by incompetent or criminal or unscrupulous contractors.° In addition to the lack of good horses and riders, the Union army also lacked competent leadership.

WCD

°Because it had been built around the Regular U.S. Army, the Northern army was hamstrung by the existing prewar structure. Men who had risen in rank according to the old rules of seniority were now in their fifties, some even in their sixties, commanding an arm of the service—the cavalry—that called for younger men, men with spirit and ambition.° The fact that this was not

BP

At four o'clock that afternoon of October 19, two hundred Union buglers sounded the charge and Sheridan's men moved against Jubal Early's Confederates. The general rode a second mount, Breckinridge—which had been captured at Winchester from the Southern general of the same name—and joined his men at the crest of a small hill, waiting only for George Custer's cavalry to join him. Neither side held an advantage until the Federals broke the left flank of the enemy line and then rolled down the line until the Confederates retreated. It was a personal triumph for Sheridan as well as a national one.

There were only six regiments of cavalry, dragoons, and mounted riflemen in the army prior to the war. They were posted on the frontier, charged with controlling the Native American population, protecting settlements, and guarding the western trail routes. Cavalry was viewed as a useful tool, but only as a servant to the army, not as a combat unit in itself. The general staff (right) also believed that improved weapons were rendering cavalry obsolete. Thus, when the first call for volunteers went out in the North, general in chief Winfield Scott authorized only one additional cavalry regiment.

seen as a problem further exacerbated the situation. The War Department did not understand that the war was going to require a significant cavalry force. Lacking a vision of the wartime possibilities for mounted troops, the high command perceived cavalry as too expensive to maintain.

At Bull Run, the first major conflict of the war, the Federal leaders lacked a firm grasp of cavalry's role in combat and failed to make good use of their horsemen. Basically, cavalry was used to guard the artillery and infantry units along the left flank of the army. It saw almost no action in the fighting until it had to hold the Union line while the infantry retreated in panic.

On the other hand, the Confederate army made maximum use of its cavalry, much of it commanded by Col. James Ewell Brown Stuart, whose troopers smashed into the Federal line late that afternoon and turned the battle in favor of the Confederacy. One of the commanding generals on the scene, Gen. Joseph E. Johnston, pointed to the quality of leadership at the head of this cavalry, noting: "J. E. B. Stuart is a rare man, wonderfully endowed by nature with the qualities necessary for an officer of cavalry. Calm, firm, acute, active, and enterprising."

After Bull Run, the reputation of the Confederate cavalry was greatly enlarged through the tales told by the defeated Union soldiers in Washington. Capt.

James H. Stephenson observed: "These men astonished the crowd of eager listeners with some of the most marvelous stories of the prowess of the Rebels. The Black Horse Cavalry were like demons mounted upon fiery dragons, and their swords fearful to think of."

In the aftermath of the defeat, the War Department acted to expand the cavalry, issuing a call for thousands of volunteers. As the rosters filled, however, the problem of leadership arose. A succession of leaders followed, but there were no quick solutions.

EGL °**THE POPULAR CONCEPTION** of the cavalryman was that he was a kind of knight-errant, something out of the pages of Sir Walter Scott—a soldier who would fight the war in a refined and exalted way. In 1861 that sort of image drew hordes of young men into the Union cavalry, but most of those recruits were not cavalry material.•

BP °Some joined the cavalry thinking that they would rather ride than walk from the beginning of the war to its conclusion. They quickly learned that the demands of the cavalry service were in many ways greater than that of the infantry. In the cavalry, the first thing each trooper did was to feed, water, and groom his horse. The infantry could loaf and socialize, but the cavalry

By the end of 1861, the shortsightedness of the old army had been corrected, and eighty-two volunteer cavalry regiments were in the process of enrollment and outfitting. Shortages of horses were so great and the demand so sudden that mammoth depots, like the one pictured below, were required to house and train the mounts. In the early years of the war, unscrupulous speculators did a thriving business in providing Lincoln's army with blind and otherwise unhealthy horses.

George Stoneman, a member of the West Point class of 1842 and a veteran of the Mexican and Indian Wars, was named chief of cavalry by George B. McClellan. Stoneman, however, acted more as an administrator than a tactical commander. As a result, the cavalry came to be, in the words of one Pennsylvania trooper, "for the most part scattered about and used as escorts, strikers, dog-robbers and orderlies for all the generals and their numerous staff officers from the highest in rank down to the second lieutenants."

worked constantly. In that division of the army, horses came first, men second.•

Life in the cavalry was not only exhausting, but the training and tactics were complex and time consuming. EGL °At the start of the war conventional wisdom held that it took two years to develop a fully rounded cavalryman. Horse soldiers first had to get acquainted with their animals and learn how to use them in battle. Second, they had to learn to fight in unison and in formation.• Pvt. Lucian P. Waters of the Eleventh New York Cavalry complained: "The cavalry tactics are ten times more difficult to learn than those of the infantry. The wheeling into columns and platoons are very difficult to thoroughly commit to memory."

To command the Union's growing ranks in 1861, Lincoln pinned his hopes on George B. McClellan, an aspiring general who looked every bit a dashing cavalier. BP °McClellan had an affinity for the cavalry, having adapted the standard-issue saddle from a European model. Because of his studies of European military systems, he should have been able to use his cavalry more effectively, but he did not.• He ignored the tactical wisdom of utilizing cavalry as a massive strike force. Nor did he explore any other ways to utilize that arm of the service.

Capt. Hampton S. Thomas of the First Pennsylvania Cavalry recalled, "Those who served will remember that from the fall of 1861 to the summer of 1862 the cavalry were, for the most part scattered about and used as escorts, strikers, dog-robbers and orderlies for all the generals and their numerous staff officers."

WCD °Cavalry has several basic functions. First and foremost, it is the eyes and ears of an army. It is supposed to be out in advance of an advancing army, bringing back information on enemy whereabouts, numbers, movements, and if possible, enemy intentions. At the same time, cavalry should perform some raiding functions in the enemy's rear when feasible—disrupting communications, destroying telegraph lines, tearing up railroads, burning supply dumps, and so on. Finally, cavalry also has to act as a screen behind which a friendly army can move unseen.•

The lackluster performance of the Federal cavalry pointed to deficient training, substandard mounts, and poor utilization. There was no esprit de corps. Units were spread throughout the army and used largely as escorts and messengers. Meanwhile, the Southern cavalry had coalesced into an effective combat force with an impact much greater than its size suggested.

The reins of McClellan's cavalry were first held by Maj. Gen. George Stoneman, but he proved a poor

BP choice. °His medical record revealed that he suffered from a severe case of hemorrhoids for much of the war, which might explain his ill temper.•

In March 1862 McClellan launched his Peninsula campaign with the goal of taking Richmond. He failed to make use of his cavalry effectively, and the bold cavalry action of the campaign belonged to Stuart, who led his horsemen on a one-hundred-mile ride around McClellan's army. First Lt. Asa B. Isham of the Seventh Michigan Cavalry recalled, "The Rebels, possessing a cavalry force operating en masse, swept along McClellan's lines with impunity, destroying stores and transportation, without let or hindrance from the scattered bands of Union cavalry."

WCD °When Lincoln was forced to replace McClellan in the fall of 1862, his decision was not based solely on McClellan's faults on the battlefield but included his failure to produce a cavalry that could contend with the Confederate horsemen.•

Despite numerous setbacks, the seeds of the cavalry's imminent glory were now being planted. Reorganization was the first step. Second Lt. Edward B. Tobie of the First Maine Cavalry commented: "The scattered commands were gathered together and the cavalry was organized into brigades and divisions, the whole forming a corps. The cavalryman's prospects

Among the Federal cavalry's more brilliant early commanders was John Buford (above). An 1848 graduate of West Point, Buford had served in the old army dragoons and had been posted on the frontier. With a reputation as one of the army's most talented and experienced cavalry officers, he was relegated to a desk in Washington. Perhaps one of John Pope's most significant contributions during his brief tenure as an army commander was his assigning Buford a field command.

brightened. He began to feel there was a chance for him yet."

In addition, dynamic new leaders began emerging, men who understood the tactical role of the cavalry. Among them was John Buford. Released from a desk job, he was given command of a cavalry division. BP °Buford was probably the single finest Union cavalry commander of the war prior to Sheridan.• Col. J. H. Kidd of the Sixth Michigan Cavalry recalled: "Buford was rightly called 'Old Reliable.' Not because of his age, but for the reason that he rarely, if ever, failed to be in the right place at the right moment. Solid, rather than showy, not spectacular, but sure. His courage and ability were both conspicuous."

In 1862 Buford was not yet in position to make a big impact on the struggling cavalry. General Stoneman, after several failures, was replaced by Alfred Pleasonton, an ambitious, politically motivated, headline-grabbing PAH commander. °He looked like a cavalryman—dashing, polished top boots, aggressive—and was a good judge of character. The latter was perhaps his greatest contribution to the evolution of the Federal cavalry.•

Alfred Pleasonton (right, seated at the right) succeeded Stoneman as head of the Federal cavalry in June 1863 and instituted a massive reorganization. An 1844 graduate of West Point, he was vain, headline-hungry, and political, but he had an eye for talent and quickly marked several of his junior officers for command potential. One of these was George Custer (right, seated on the left).

BP °Just prior to Gettysburg he promoted three of his staff officers, three young captains, to the rank of brigadier general over several senior officers. These three were Wesley Merritt, Elon Farnsworth, and George Armstrong Custer—all of whom would play an important role in the Gettysburg campaign and, in the case of Merritt and Custer, beyond the end of the war.°

By 1863 THE FORTUNES of the Union cavalry had begun to change. The Federal riders were becoming battle tested, and the Union had learned how to acquire better horses and superior weapons. With leaders who could finally marshal those elements together, the cavalry was ready to challenge its Confederate counterpart. Capt. Willard F. Glazier of the Second New York Cavalry suggested, "The Rebel cavalry under Jeb Stuart has long

The charge of the Eighth Pennsylvania Cavalry at Chancellorsville was one of the few instances in which mounted cavalry attacked massed infantry. Having ridden between a Confederate skirmish line and a larger body of infantry, the Federal horsemen had little choice but to draw sabers and charge. As gallant as the charge was, the incident was of minor significance to the course of the battle. The sudden appearance of Union cavalry in their midst, however, put many Confederates on alert for additional cavalry. That evening Southern muskets cut down Stonewall Jackson, mistaking his reconnaissance party for Yankee cavalry.

One of the turning points of the day-long battle at Brandy Station occurred when the Thirty-fifth Battalion of Virginia Cavalry, known as the Gray Comanches, charged Union artillery ensconced on Fleetwood Hill. The guns were won at the cost of approximately one hundred Virginians; Fleetwood Hill fell back to the Southerners and the Federal cavalry withdrew. Although the Northern horsemen had performed well at Brandy Station, Pleasonton was criticized for not winning the battle and lost favor with his superiors.

Judson Kilpatrick was an ambitious division commander whose recklessness on the battlefield earned him the nickname "Kilcavalry." He had glimpsed success at Brandy Station, but at Gettysburg he ordered a disastrous charge on the third day. To save face—and possibly ensure a postwar political career—he planned a raid on Richmond, but Kilpatrick failed to execute the plan and withdrew on the outskirts of the city. In the last year of the war he served under William T. Sherman, who called him a "hell of a damned fool" but praised his bravery in battle.

been organized into an efficient body, which, at times, has sneered at our attempts to match them, and yet they have been made to feel, on some occasions, that we are a growing power."

In the spring of 1863 the Union was concerned over a rumored Confederate invasion of the North. In response °Gen. Joseph Hooker ordered Pleasonton to engage Stuart's cavalry, which he knew to be in the vicinity of Culpeper, Virginia. In the Union's first attempt to unleash its cavalry en masse, the ambitious Pleasonton led a mounted force of eleven thousand men across the Rappahannock River and struck at Stuart's forces, taking the Confederate cavalier by surprise.•

The ensuing battle of Brandy Station formed on Fleetwood Hill and Yew Ridge, with thousands of mounted troopers fighting saber to saber and stirrup to stirrup. Second Lt. Edward P. Tobie of the First Maine Cavalry recalled, "Now opened before us, and of which we were a part, a scene of the grandest description. The whole plain was one vast field of intense, earnest action. It was a scene to be witnessed but once in a lifetime, and one worth all the risks of battle to witness."

The Confederate veterans of the battle also sang its praises. W. W. Blackford, a staff officer to Stuart, recounted: "It was what we read of in the days of chivalry. Acres and acres of horsemen sparkling with sabers, dotted with brilliant bits of color when their flags danced above them. Hurled against each other full speed and meeting with a shock that made the earth tremble."

°Brandy Station, besides being the largest cavalry engagement ever waged in North America, was the great watershed in the history of the cavalry in the East. The Union cavalry may not have won the day in decisive fashion, but it inflicted heavy losses on Stuart's horsemen and its pride rose. Pleasonton's men were gaining a reputation as fighters. They had mastered their horses, their tactics, and they now gained a sense of confidence in the face of their greatest adversary— Stuart himself.•

Because the battle was not a decisive Union victory, Pleasonton's leadership was criticized. Capt. Charles Francis Adams of the First Massachusetts Cavalry quipped, "I am sure a good cavalry officer would have whipped Stuart out his boots, but Pleasonton is not and never will be that."

Kilpatrick's division always looked good on paper. His camps, however, reflected his own lack of discipline and orderliness. This photograph of his headquarters in Stevensburg, Virginia, in March 1864 shows Kilpatrick (in the doorway) with his staff, his mother-in-law, and a cousin. Although he never drank, he was not guilty of excessive morality. His headquarters were frequented by women of questionable virtue, and some even wore uniforms so as to not be obvious.

As commander of the Army of the Potomac, George Meade made no secret of his lack of faith in horse soldiers. He was adamantly opposed to Philip Sheridan's proposal to use the Federal cavalry as an independent command. Meade took the matter to Grant, who, to his chagrin, authorized Sheridan's scheme.

One of the most critical aspects of maintaining an efficient cavalry was the care and maintenance of horses. There were no stables in the field, thus the Federals devised a mobile black-smith unit that traveled with the mounted regiments.

WCD

°Perhaps Pleasonton's greatest contribution to the Yankee cavalry was to identify Custer and ensure his promotion from a midlevel, obscure officer to brigadier general. In Custer he had an aggressive, alert, dashing, daring, colorful, occasionally irresponsible but irrepressibly enthusiastic brigade commander who later rose to division command under Sheridan.° Custer remembered: "Oh, could you have but seen some of the charges that were made. While thinking of them, I cannot but exclaim, 'Glorious war!'"

At Brandy Station, Custer was still a captain, but he displayed the bravery and tactical skill that distinguished him as a great cavalryman throughout the war. On the field near Fleetwood Hill, Custer recalled: "After ordering the men to draw their sabers, I informed them that we were surrounded, and all we had to do was open a way with our sabers. They showed their determination by giving three hearty cheers. Simultaneously, both regiments moved forward to the attack. The enemy, without waiting to receive the onset, broke and fled."

Another hero of Brandy Station was Capt. Wesley Merritt, who shortly afterward was given his brigadier's star. Col. James H. Kidd of the Sixth Michigan Cavalry described him, noting that "modesty which fitted him like a glove, charming manners, the demeanor of a gen-

Sheridan replaced Pleasonton as cavalry commander when Grant was elevated to general in chief of the Union army. Sheridan was an unimpressive little man, five feet five inches tall, with a large, bullet-shaped head and coarse black hair that some said appeared to have been painted on. Lincoln, not particularly admired physically himself, described him as "a brown, chunky little chap, with a long body, short legs, not enough neck to hang him, and such long arms that if his ankles itch he can scratch them without stooping." Grant, the pragmatic realist, heard one too many comments about Sheridan's stature and warned, "You will find him big enough for the purpose before we get through with him." Later, Lincoln wrote Sheridan: "When this particular war began, I thought a cavalryman should be at least six feet four inches high, but I have changed my mind. Five feet four will do in a pinch."

tleman, and cool but fearless bearing in action were his distinguishing characteristics."

Merritt and Custer went on to fight valiantly at Gettysburg, but the first bright moment for the Union cavalry at Gettysburg was under the hand of Brig. Gen. John Buford. He was a Kentuckian, a Southerner—with relatives fighting for the Confederacy—and a West Pointer. Prior to the war he had served on the frontier. It was said that he had been offered a commission in the Confederate army at the start of the war, and he had torn up the letter, thrown it on the floor, and said, "I will live and die under the flag of the Union." In 1863 Col. Charles S. Wainwright, an artillery officer, observed, "Buford was straightforward, honest, conscientious, full of good common sense, and always to be relied on in an emergency."

EGL °Buford determined the site of the battle of Gettysburg, securing high ground west of the town for the
PAH Union army.• °Although the battle is not known as a cavalry engagement, cavalry played a critical role in the course of the action. Colliding with Confederates on the first day of battle, Buford's men held the Southerners at bay until the rest of the Army of the Potomac arrived. His men, armed with rapid-firing carbines, dismounted and demonstrated exceptional firepower so

With Sheridan at its head, the Federal cavalry had all the pieces in place to become the irresistible force that had heretofore been the prerogative of Stuart's cavalry. Stuart was gone, though, as were many of the Confederate cavalry leaders who had paid for their bravery. In Sheridan, Grant had found a ruthless, relentless commander whose prime assets were a fixed determination and a jugular instinct. Competent subordinates had also risen to fill critical spots in the command structure of the cavalry. From left to right, Henry E. Davies, David M. Gregg, James H. Wilson, Alfred T. A. Torbet, and Wesley Merritt surround Sheridan in this picture taken during the summer of 1864. Chief of staff James Forsyth sits slightly behind the group.

that the Confederates believed they were facing far more men than they did.•

WCD °By late 1863 more and more Yankee horsemen were being equipped with Spencer carbines, an efficient, effective, reliable, and simple repeating rifle that could fire up to six or seven shots in relatively rapid succession. It was not with just a wry sense of humor that the Confederates quipped that the Spencer carbine was loaded on Sunday and fired all week.•

In contrast to men like Buford, Custer, and Merritt, there was one Union cavalryman whose actions and character prompted much controversy—Gen. Judson Kilpatrick. To his credit, he was completely fearless, and on many occasions he contributed to cavalry victories, ECB but he was a merciless commander. °He drove his men hard and broke down their horses. He was daring, which was ancillary to his tremendous ego, and he had a reputation as a womanizer.•

BP °Kilpatrick's wife had died midway in the war, and he also lost a young child. These emotional experiences, combined with the horrors of war, may have destroyed any sense of personal restraint. He spent much of the rest of the war accompanied by a succes-

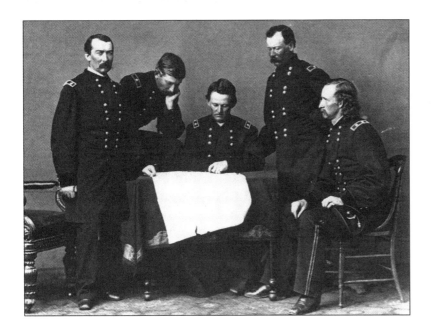

Custer joined his colleagues for this sitting, and while the photographer urged them to scrutinize the map, Sheridan had his own pose in mind. From left to right, they are Sheridan, James Forsyth, Merritt, Thomas Devin, and Custer. In the late summer and fall of 1864 Grant ordered his cavalry to rid the Shenandoah Valley of Confederate forces and to destroy all supplies that might aid the enemy. Sheridan's greatest adversary would be John S. Mosby, and the Gray Ghost frustrated him like no one had before.

sion of mistresses who became accessories to his headquarters. Sometimes the women would wear soldier's clothing so they could pass as young officers at a distance.

Because he was so reckless and was so wont to charge into action without reconnoitering or even considering it, Kilpatrick became known among the Union cavalry-men as "Kilcavalry."• °He wanted to make a name for himself, and he felt the only way to do that was through aggressive, offensive action.

At Gettysburg he directed one of his brigade commanders—young, recently promoted Elon Farnsworth—to lead a mounted attack against Confederates ensconced behind stone walls and large boulders along the Confederate right. The terrain was totally inappropriate for a cavalry attack, and Farnsworth realized this and tried to convince Kilpatrick of the futility of the attack.• Kilpatrick refused to rescind the order, questioning Farnsworth's courage in the process. With his honor at stake, the young brigadier led the doomed cavalry charge and was killed along with many of his men.

There were other tragedies for the riders in blue, including the loss of Buford, who died of typhus five months after the victory at Gettysburg. Despite these

Custer was Sheridan's favorite lieutenant. The two men shared several character traits, but none more essential than a relentless determination to succeed. Sheridan once told Grant that there was no other officer in the cavalry in whom he had greater confidence than Custer.

troubles, the Union cavalry continued to mature and ride toward greater glory.

THE EXPERIENCE AND confidence gained during the Gettysburg campaign carried the Federal riders to the end of the war. Capt. Charles W. Ford of the First Maine Cavalry observed: "During the early days of the war, the cavalry were constantly humiliated by insinuations and aspersions cast upon them by other branches of our own army. How many times have you heard the sarcastic remark: Whoever saw a dead cavalrymen? They had no defense then. They need none now."

Ironically, one of the last hurdles was not from the ranks of the enemy but from within. The problem lay with Union Gen. George Gordon Meade, the senior commander of the Army of the Potomac, the main Union army of the eastern theater. Meade had little use for cavalry. He had previously had a falling out with Pleasonton, who also had ambitious plans for the Union horsemen. °Pleasonton had wanted to use his men as an independent wing, but he was never allowed to do so. When U. S. Grant was given command of the Union armies, it became clear that he wanted his own man—Sheridan—in command of the cavalry. Pleasonton's previous squabbles with headquarters made it easy for Grant to remove him. So the man who had done so much to reorganize the cavalry gave way to the one who would take the cavalry to its greatest victories.•

Like Pleasonton, Sheridan wanted his cavalry to act independently of the main army and, like Pleasonton, he encountered resistance from Meade. He noted, "General Meade deemed cavalry fit for little more than guard and picket duty and wanted to know what would protect the transportation trains and artillery reserve, cover the front of moving infantry columns, and secure his flank from intrusion if my policy were pursued."

The new cavalry commander was just five feet five inches tall. While still a cadet at West Point, the feisty Sheridan had once nearly bayoneted an overbearing sergeant. As an officer he had made a name for himself under Grant in the western theater of the war.

Now, "Little Phil," as he was sometimes called, refused to let Meade hold his riders back. He continued to argue his point but made little headway with his superior, observing: "General Meade would hardly listen to my proposition. He was filled with the prejudices that, from the beginning of the war, had pervaded the army regarding the importance and usefulness of cavalry."

PAH °Sheridan continued to press for an independent command. With his cavalry free to act on its own, he proposed to engage and defeat Stuart and end Confederate dominance from the saddle. Meade took the matter to Grant, hoping to be relieved of this recalcitrant cavalryman from the West, this upstart, this Ohio farm boy. Grant, however, was receptive to Sheridan's proposal and approved the plan.•

Organizationally, Sheridan retained all of Pleasonton's appointments, most notably Custer, Merritt, and James H. Wilson. All three men were in their twenties and came to be known as boy generals.

BP °Wilson was another key figure in the resurgence of the Union cavalry. He knew that the success of the cavalry was to a great extent dependent on the quality of horses, and he personally saw to it that the horses acquired for the service were purchased at a fair price and that they were quality animals.• Sheridan recognized Wilson for his talent and placed him in the field as a cavalry commander.

Although Wilson eventually fell from Sheridan's favor, he went on to redeem himself in the last year of

EGL the war in the West °when he led the largest and, tactically, the most successful cavalry raid in American history. This massive raid to Selma, Alabama, included the capture of numerous fortified towns and thousands of Confederate prisoners and destroyed goods worth millions of dollars to the Confederacy. Wilson's cavalry concluded its wartime service with the capture of the fugitive Confederate president, Jefferson Davis.•

In the meantime, Custer and Merritt continued with Sheridan through the end of the war. Having made it this far together, the pair developed a rivalry that benefited the Union. Col. James H. Kidd of the Sixth Michigan Cavalry observed: "In the association

James H. Wilson disappointed Sheridan during the Yellow Tavern encounter with Stuart's cavalry, and his performance improved only marginally in the Shenandoah Valley. When Grant requested a cavalry commander for Sherman's cavalry, Sheridan had little problem in dispatching Wilson, who distinguished himself in the last year of the war by defeating Nathan Bedford Forrest and capturing Jefferson Davis.

The Shenandoah Valley had twice been used as a corridor for the invasion of the North, and its farms had kept the Confederate army supplied with food. The terrain favored mounted troops that could operate on good roads and fight on the cultivated fields. Sheridan took an army of forty thousand into the Valley and advanced cautiously, probing and skirmishing with Jubal Early's twelve thousand Confederates during August 1864. Gradually, Sheridan made progress, mostly by attrition. While Early's Southerners fell back, Mosby's Rangers harassed the Federals relentlessly. Within the parameters of the larger conflict between Sheridan and Early, this smaller, deadlier, unforgiving conflict simmered.

of the two under the same command there was strength, for each was in a sort the complement of the other. Unlike in temperament and appearance and in their style of fighting."

Merritt served Sheridan well, but it was Custer with whom Sheridan developed the closer bond, °even friendship. "If there was any romance or poetry in war," said Sheridan, "Custer could develop it." Hard-bitten, pragmatic, without the slightest trace of romanticism, Sheridan nevertheless admired Custer, especially his dash and flare, but he particularly respected the fact that Custer was as tenacious, as persevering as Sheridan himself.•

The Union cavalry was now complete. It featured a dynamic group of leaders, support from the top, proper horses, and a corps of riders who had finally gained sufficient experience to outride the Rebels.

In the spring of 1864 Sheridan and twelve thousand cavalrymen launched a raid on Richmond to flush out Stuart. At Yellow Tavern, one of Custer's men mortally wounded Stuart, leading Sheridan to report: "Under him, the cavalry of Lee's army had been nurtured but had acquired such prestige that it thought itself well nigh invincible. Indeed, in the early years of the war, it had proved to be so. This was now dispelled by the successful march we had made in Lee's rear, and the removal of Stuart at Yellow Tavern had inflicted a blow from which entire recovery was impossible."

PAH

BP   °Grant began to realize the many abilities that Sheridan possessed. He had commanded infantry throughout the war. He then took the Federal cavalry that had once been a laughingstock and made it into an effective strike force. Grant began to wonder what would happen if Sheridan headed a force of infantry and the bulk of the cavalry in the East as an independent command with the goal of clearing all Confederate forces from the Shenandoah Valley.•

EGL   °The Valley was known as the breadbasket of the Confederacy because of the foodstuffs and forage it supplied to Southern forces. Sheridan decided if he were going to win the battle of the Shenandoah, he was going to have to strip it of all its provisions so that the South could not profit from them.• The campaign came to be known as "the Burning." Capt. George N. Bliss of the First Rhode Island Cavalry recalled, "On the 17th day of August, 1864, orders were issued for the destruction of all the wheat and hay south of the line from Millwood to Winchester and Pettycoat Gap in the Valley of the Shenandoah, Virginia, and for the seizure of all mules, horses, and cattle that might be useful to the army."

PAH   °Sheridan's actions presaged the age of total war. He felt that for armies alone to fight was but a duel, and he said that war was far more terrible. War must be brought to the people. The population must feel the

While the Federal cavalry flourished in combat, its success also meant that one of the longtime duties of cavalry continued as well, namely, the conveyance of prisoners of war from the field to the rear.

sting of it. If they were impoverished, then they would force their government to plead for peace; thus to Sheridan the torch was as important a weapon as the sword.• When his army departed from the Valley in late 1864, it left no crops in the field awaiting harvest.

IN 1865 GEN. Joshua Lawrence Chamberlain wrote: "We had a taste of General Sheridan's fighting style, and we liked it. He transfuses into his subordinates the vitality and energy of his purpose, transforms them into part of his own mind and will. He shows the power of a commander."

°Like Buford and Pleasonton, Sheridan also employed cavalry effectively as dismounted skirmishers. His troopers became mobile infantry, and equipped with rapid-firing weapons, they could deliver significant firepower on the battlefield. He also used cavalry en masse, noting that ten thousand horsemen crashing into an enemy line could bring about enormous confusion and create opportunities for the infantry.•

°In April 1865, during the last campaign, Sheridan's army acted as Grant's shock troops, prying Robert E. Lee and the Army of Northern Virginia away from heavily fortified Petersburg. On April 1, 1865, a battle occurred at Five Forks that came to be known as "the Waterloo of the Confederacy."•

°Five Forks was not just a victory for Sheridan's cavalry; his infantry was involved as well. He succeeded on the battlefield because of the high degree of mobility achieved through the combined operations of cavalry and infantry. Together they created a lightning strike. Before Lee could move sufficient troops to Five Forks, Sheridan's cavalry arrived, took it, and held it for the infantry. The loss of the vital intersection forced Lee to abandon Petersburg.•

Sheridan engineered the first decisive victory for the Federals in the Valley at the third battle of Winchester. One soldier described the affair as "the hardest days fight i ever saw," but the men in the ranks recognized their commander's role in the victory. "They simply believed he was going to win," a staff officer wrote, "and every man apparently was determined to be on hand and see him do it." James Kidd of the Sixth Michigan Cavalry observed that Sheridan "was the only general of that war who knew how to make cavalry and infantry supplement each other in battle."

PAH

BP

WCD

Sheridan, standing with his sword, and his staff were photographed just prior to the Shenandoah campaign, which some have described as the beginning of the end for the Confederacy. The battle of Cedar Creek ended the major action in the valley, and both commands began returning troops to Petersburg. Sheridan, however, kept most of his cavalry in the area until March 1865. After a last engagement at Waynesborough, he joined Grant for the final weeks of the war.

There was little doubt the Union could not have achieved this kind of success without Little Phil. He demanded the utmost from his men, sometimes beyond human endurance. °By his voice and by his example, Sheridan had an amazing power of leadership over men in battle that made them at least attempt to do the impossible. One example occurred at Five Forks, where an infantryman had been shot through the jugular vein and fallen. Sheridan rode up to him and said, "Get up, my man. You're not hurt at all." The man stood up, took three steps, then collapsed dead.•

That quality of command was certainly an inspiration to his top leaders, including Merritt and Custer, as they put further pressure on Lee's army during the last months of the war. °Merritt, despite the rivalry with Custer, consistently used Custer as his leading strike force. Custer's men were always out in front, and Custer was always out in front of his men.•

°With the fall of Petersburg in early April 1865, the defense of the Southern capital, Richmond, was rendered untenable, and the Confederates abandoned the city. On the morning of April 3, 1865, Union troops walked in unopposed and occupied the town.•

°During the last desperate week of battle between Richmond and Appomattox, as the Confederates

The postwar years for Little Phil included command of the Military Division of the Gulf and assignment as commander of the Fifth Military District (Texas and Louisiana) during Reconstruction. His harsh policies in the latter role, however, led to his removal after six months. He was assigned to the West, where cavalry fought the Cheyenne, Apache, Kiowa, Comanche, Sioux, and other tribes in what Sherman called "at best an inglorious war." In 1870 Sheridan briefly toured Europe as an observer of the Franco-Prussian War, after which he told Grant, "I saw no new military principles developed, whether of strategy or grand tactics." He succeeded Sherman as general in chief in 1884, but found the position powerless.

ECB   retreated, they were harassed repeatedly by the Federal cavalry.• °As dawn broke on April 9, Lee learned that Union cavalry had captured his supply trains at Appomattox. Lee met with his officers, and they decided to make one more attempt at breaking out,• but the Rebels' last efforts were in vain. Almost mercifully, Custer and his riders moved in quickly to cut off Lee's retreat.

ECB   °Sheridan's cavalry held the Confederates at bay long enough for the Union infantry to advance. Lee, on learning this, said: "I have no other alternative. I must go seek General Grant. I would rather die a thousand deaths."•

Lee surrendered to Grant in the home of Wilmer McLean, a local farmer who had volunteered his house for the occasion. The top generals from both sides hurried to be present at the historic event. Most succeeded, but °Custer was unable to gain entrance into the little parlor. Numerous period illustrations to the contrary,

BP

he watched the surrender from the porch. Sheridan, however, purchased from the owner one of the tables on which the surrender was written out and presented it to Custer, his favorite subordinate,• commenting, "I know of no one whose efforts have contributed more to this happy result."

As Sheridan praised Custer, his most valued horseman, so Grant acknowledged Sheridan, the victorious leader of the Union cavalry, noting, "I believe General Sheridan has no superior as a general, either living or dead, and perhaps not an equal."

WCD   °Part of Sheridan's greatness as a general was the fact that he achieved a oneness of mind with his commander, Grant, and great as his ego was, Sheridan never let it get in the way of his mission to carry out his commander's orders.

That last week of the war was the prime week for cavalry of the entire war. It was what the Union cavalrymen had been training for and waiting for

In the summer of 1887, Sheridan was photographed at Nonquitt, Massachusetts, with his family. From left to right, they are his daughter-in-law (seated), his daughter Irene (on the steps), his son Michael (standing), his son Philip Jr. (on the steps), his wife, Irene (seated in the center), his daughters Louise and Mary (on the steps), and the general. He had been diagnosed with heart disease, and like Grant, he wanted to compose his memoirs before he died. On August 5, 1888, the day after he had completed reading the proofs from his publisher, he suffered a heart attack and died.

since 1861.* Under Gen. Philip Sheridan's leadership, the Union cavalry's ultimate dominance was a dramatic turnaround. The Federal horsemen overcame years of mistakes, indecision, and self-doubt, defeating a formidable enemy at its own game. The magnitude of the Union cavalry's contribution toward bringing the war to a conclusion would never be forgotten.

WILLIAM TECUMSEH SHERMAN

War is ALL HELL, GEN. William Tecumseh Sherman was alleged to have said. It was not an excuse but a simple definition of the strategic thought of a man highly regarded by half the nation and despised by the other half. As a liberator and as a destroyer, he became one of the most controversial generals on either side of the Civil War. By war's end, his epic March to the Sea had gained him heroic status in the North and satanic status in the South for he had made good on his promise to make Georgia howl. As a practitioner of total war, he warned: "You cannot qualify war in harsher terms than I will. War is cruelty, and you cannot refine it. The crueler it is, the sooner it will be over."

By the fall of 1864, when his troops marched triumphantly into Atlanta, Sherman had become a major power broker and a towering military presence. His Atlanta victory electrified and inspired the Northern populace, assured the reelection of Abraham Lincoln, and represented a huge step in bringing the South to its knees. Yet even before the smoke had cleared, Sherman, the relentless warrior, was already preparing his next move—a dramatic march of destruction across Georgia to the sea.

It had been a long road to hero status for him. Just five years earlier this man who now swayed presidential elections and galvanized the population had been a self-described failure and had once said: "I am doomed to be a vagabond. I look upon myself as a dead cock in the pit not worthy of further notice."

WCD	William C. Davis
WEE	William E. Erquitt
DE	David Evans
PAH	Paul A. Hutton
JFM	John F. Marszalek
CN	Chris Nelson

The marriage of the irreligious Sherman in 1850 to his intensely pious Roman Catholic foster sister Ellen Ewing was difficult and loud. Because of his military duties, they spent as much time apart as they did together and maintained an angry correspondence throughout. Despite their difficulties, following his breakdown during the first year of the war, she devoted all her energies to promoting his career. The couple had seven children, but two died during the war. All of them had red hair like their father. Standing with Ellen in this postwar photograph is her fourth child, Thomas, named for her father.

He was one of those rare men—a warrior like Ulysses S. Grant—who only find themselves in times of war. Ironically, the two men, both from Ohio, had known each other before the war, at a time when they were both struggling. °Sherman had seen Grant in Saint Louis during Grant's lowest time. His face dirty, his clothing disheveled, Grant was hauling wood for a living. This seemed to Sherman the consequence of what happened when officers left the army, that they could not function in the civilian world.•

PAH

Sherman seemed almost to have been born a warrior. °His father, Charles, chose the name Tecumseh for his son from his admiration for the great Shawnee war leader, one of the most prominent Native Americans of his time. He felt there was no greater way to express this admiration than to bestow that name on his son.•

WCD

With the death of his impoverished natural father, nine-year-old Tecumseh was adopted by the rich and powerful Thomas Ewing, a future U.S. senator from Ohio. To Ewing, Tecumseh needed a Christian name, so he called the boy William.

°Sherman, however, was always an outsider. He always had so much to prove, and throughout his life, trying to please the towering figure of his stepfather was his greatest goal.•

PAH

In 1836 he entered West Point, graduating four years later, sixth in his class. The military seemed to appeal to his exaggerated need for order. Yet for the next twenty years, both in and out of the military, he led a rocky, insecure existence.

°Sherman was an unlucky officer because he failed to get what were, for ambitious young men, the right assignments. He missed the war with Mexico entirely— the great proving ground that launched the careers and reputations of the men who were destined to take com-

WCD

mand from the beginning of the Civil War. Sherman was relegated to sideshow assignments in the South and in the far West in California. His poor postings were one of the reasons he did not stay in the military.•

Out of the military and in the business world, he was bright, competent, and conscientious, but he always seemed to be in the wrong place at the wrong time. He also now had a wife and family to support, having married his foster sister Ellen.

WCD °He was approaching middle age, and he still was nowhere. He had made no fortune, he had enjoyed no success, and this played tremendously on his mind.• Drifting from job to job, by 1859 the senator's son was reduced to living in a humble house in Kansas. His fortunes improved though, and as the war approached, he was working happily as the civilian superintendent of the newly founded Louisiana State Seminary of Learning and Military Academy.

JFM °Perhaps the greatest irony in Sherman's life is the fact that he had a deep affection for southerners. His experiences in the South and in making acquaintances throughout the region, particularly in Louisiana, helped him to enjoy being with southerners and to enjoy life in the South.•

In February 1861, when it became apparent to him that the South would be going to war, he decided to

Recently graduated from West Point in 1840, Sherman (above) spent most of his early career in the South, and his experiences and acquaintances there had a profound influence on the rest of his life. While he found most of his duties to be boring, he thoroughly enjoyed the security a military career offered. When he married, began a family, and accepted a posting to San Francisco, however, he was frustrated by his inability to earn a sufficient living.

In 1853 Sherman resigned his captaincy to take up banking. When the bank failed, he moved his family to Fort Leavenworth, Kansas, and opened a law and real estate office. Unsuccessful in either venture, he drifted from job to job while living in this rough cabin in 1859 (left).

Sherman discovered an aptitude for drawing while at West Point, and no pastime proved more enjoyable for him in the service than painting. At Fort Moultrie in the early 1840s he produced landscapes and portraits, often becoming engrossed in his work and finding it painful to lay down the brush. Later in life he would draw occasional sketches, but he never painted again with the intensity he knew at Moultrie. In Kansas, separated from his family while he searched for financial security, he began drawing pictures for his children, such as this bird in 1859.

leave the seminary and head north. The secession of the southern states offended his most cherished beliefs of the Union—obedience to the law and a sense of order. °When it came time to leave, he stood before his corps of cadets and bade them a tearful farewell. Placing his hand over his heart as he left, he said, "You are all here."•

After the war began, Sherman entered the fray. He served first in the debacle at Bull Run, then he went to Kentucky where old demons and insecurities caught up with him. He faced allegations of insanity, depression, and more. °Isolated in Kentucky, he saw that the Union effort was disorganized. His own sense of helplessness added to his frustrations and brought on a terrible depression. In introspection he saw a situation similar to that of his prewar years, which were characterized as nothing but failure. Feeling inadequate and depressed, he contemplated suicide. Afterward, he told friends that had it not been for his children, he believed he would have taken his life.•

Having fallen to his deepest emotional depth, Sherman seemed to find himself. In February 1862 he was given a new command, head of the Department of Cairo, headquartered at Paducah, Kentucky. The change also brought him together with Grant. At Shiloh in April 1862, the great warrior began to emerge, prompting the *Cincinnati Gazette* to report, "He dashed along the line, encouraging his troops everywhere by his presence, and exposing his own life with the same freedom with which he demanded they offer theirs."

War seemed to give Sherman purpose where before there had been none. He seemed to evolve, °finding the one thing that he was truly good at was leading men in battle, a trait unusable in peacetime. Prior to the war he had been a good student, had applied himself well, and had been a hard worker, but he had been unfocused. In some ways he was too smart for his own good. It was only with the coming of the war that he found the right path.•

From Shiloh, along with Grant, he went to victories at Vicksburg and then Chattanooga. His brilliant planning and capture of Atlanta placed him at the forefront of Civil War commanders, with Grant, Robert E. Lee, and Stonewall Jackson. Men were now willing to follow him anywhere, and that was just where he intended to take them.

AS MILITARY THEORY, the March to the Sea was a grim discipline. As military innovation, it made Sherman a major prophet of modern warfare. By carrying out this plan, he helped usher in the concept of total war in America.

DE The Atlanta into which Sherman marched was a war-torn prize. °One of his officers observed that it was a used-up town by the time it was captured by Union forces in September 1864. The city had undergone more than a month of siege, enduring daily bombardments, sometimes receiving as many as three thousand shells in a twenty-four-hour period. John Bell Hood, commander of the Confederate Army of Tennessee and entrusted with Atlanta's defense, did not help matters when he abandoned the city on the night of September 2. Rather than leave munitions to resupply Sherman's army, he blew up an ordnance train and caused even more damage to the town's industrial region.•

Sherman took little time to gloat over his Atlanta victory. His mind was already elsewhere, concentrating on

With maps of his greatest accomplishments behind him, Sherman posed in this postwar photograph above with his son Tom. After the fall of Vicksburg in 1863, Sherman's army encamped about twenty miles from the river town. Ellen and four of the children came to visit him there, including six-year-old Tommy who became the focal point of a small incident. A Confederate was visiting the camp under a flag of truce and struck up a conversation with the boy. Articulating a six-year-old's pride in his dad's work, Tommy said, "Father can whip you fellows every time." The Southerner asked how the boy could be so sure, and Tommy proceeded to enumerate the strengths and locations of Sherman's soldiers.

The July 22, 1864, battle of Atlanta gave way to the bombardment of the city, with Sherman closely supervising the siege (left), but the loss of the last railroad out of town on August 25 led the Confederates to abandon the city.

Sherman's army was not responsible entirely for the destruction in and around Atlanta. The Georgia Central tracks above (left) are littered with the debris of a Confederate ordnance train that was destroyed by the Southerners to prevent its capture.

The photograph of Sherman's wagon trains beginning to stockpile supplies (above right) was taken with the great symbol of Atlanta, the car shed of the Western and Atlantic Railroad, in the background. The fall of Atlanta was a blow to Southern morale, a much-needed lift for Northern spirits, and carried some weight with the electorate in sweeping Lincoln back into office for a second term.

DE

the march. He evidently had been pondering it for some time, probably °before he left Chattanooga in April 1864. As he was leaving, someone reportedly asked him what his ultimate objective was, and he muttered something about saltwater.•

The idea for a military campaign like the March to the Sea was the result of Sherman's lifetime of observation, thought, and study about warfare itself. The objective of the march was basic and simple. "They [the Southerners] cannot be made to love us," Sherman said, "but they may be made to fear us."

JFM

°He came to see that the war was not just a battle between armies, it was a campaign between societies. Over a period of time he fashioned the idea that rather than hurl his army at another in pitched battle, he should attack the Southern mind. If he could march an army through the very center of the Confederacy, doing all kinds of destruction, showing the people that their army could not protect them, then he would have broken the Southern will and brought the war closer to an end.•

His planning of the march was meticulous, and his
CN eye for detail amazing. °He did not just loose his army
on the road to Savannah, he studied census records. He
knew what and how much food Georgia produced
county by county, and he planned his route accordingly.•

Attacking both civilian and military targets was part
DE of his theory of no-holds-barred total war. °There was
an infrastructure behind an army and behind a society,
and this was what Sherman wanted to root out when he
marched across Georgia. He wanted to destroy factories,
tear up railroads, and eliminate foodstuffs. He was
determined to wage a campaign of economic terrorism
by destroying not only the South's will to fight, but also
its means to fight.•

Sherman was not the first to practice total war.
Other armies had attacked civilian populations, but
Sherman's march was more methodical and daring
DE and placed a high premium on isolation. °He had to
cut his supply lines and abandon his base before he
could plunge into the heart of the Southern Confederacy. Everything his army needed—provisions, ammunition, food—would either have to be carried by his
soldiers or in wagons. Once begun, there would be no
turning back.•

Several major problems had to be addressed before
he could turn his eyes to the Atlantic. One involved
what to do with his battle-of-Atlanta adversary, Hood,
and the marauding Army of Tennessee. The last thing
Sherman wanted to do was to spread out his army
chasing Hood all over the South. At this point, luck
came into play when Hood made one of the greatest
military blunders of the war. The Confederate commander abandoned his campaign in Georgia and
moved his own march westward toward Tennessee.
WEE °The people of Georgia felt that Hood had abandoned
them, and rightfully so, for he had. Their army left
them at the mercy of Sherman, whose cavalry had a
free range of operation from fifty to a hundred miles
south of Atlanta.•

Sherman was elated by the news of Hood's movement to Tennessee. "If he will go to the Ohio River, I will
give him rations. My business is down south," he said.

SHERMAN.

FALL OF ATLANTA.

Brilliant Strategic Movement
of the Union Commander.

HOOD HOODWINKED.

A BATTLE FOUGHT NEAR EAST POINT

GENERAL HARDEE KILLED.

The Rebels Assisting
Sherman's Plans.

*The headlines of a Northern newspaper
sketch out the primary stories of the
fall of Atlanta, although the news of
Confederate Gen. William J. Hardee's
death was greatly exaggerated. At the
end of the campaign, Sherman noted,
"The rebels have lost, beside the important city of Atlanta and stores, at least
five hundred dead, two thousand five
hundred wounded, and three thousand
prisoners. . . . If that is not success I
don't know what is."*

Sherman's senior officers during the last year of the war comprised, from left to right, Oliver O. Howard, John A. Logan, William B. Hazen, Sherman, Jefferson C. Davis, Henry W. Slocum, Joseph A. Mower, and Frank Blair.

John Bell Hood opposed Sherman in the latter weeks of the Atlanta campaign. After withdrawing from the city, he took his Army of Tennessee north to harass Sherman's supply lines and draw him out of Georgia, but Sherman was not impressed. He was beginning to implement his plans for a march to the sea. If Hood abandoned Georgia for Tennessee, that only made his plans more feasible.

Another problem was convincing Lincoln and Grant that the maneuver was militarily sound. °Sherman had to do a good bit of negotiating. What it finally came down to was Grant's sense of trust in Sherman. Somewhat concerned with Hood and the Army of Tennessee, he wired Sherman, "If there is any way of getting at Hood's army, I would prefer that, but I must trust your own judgment." Secretary of War Edwin M. Stanton added the approval of the War Department, which included Lincoln's tacit approval.•

Sherman was so sure of his plan that he even wrote Grant a personal note brimming with confidence, even cockiness: "If you can whip Lee, and I can march to the Atlantic, I think Uncle Abe will give us twenty days' leave of absence to see the young folks."

On the verge of the march, Sherman issued his controversial order to evacuate Atlanta. °He had wanted to make Atlanta into a garrison town, but he had an army to feed and maintain. At the same time he did not want to have the responsibility of feeding a civilian population, and he forcefully expelled all but about fifty families from the city.•

The stage was now set, but a few remaining details had to be addressed. All trains were sent back to Chattanooga, and the rails were torn up. In the last act of isolating his army, he even cut the telegraph wires—

some say because he did not want any messages to come through from Washington telling him to stop the march, nor did he want any messages getting out concerning where he was going or what he was doing. Before severing communication, in his last communication with Grant, Sherman once again emphasized the march's purpose and his confidence: "If the North can march an army right through the South, it is proof positive that the North can prevail. . . . I will not attempt to send couriers back, but trust to the Richmond papers to keep you well advised. I can make this march and make Georgia howl!"

THE MAN WHO believed war was all hell created his own inferno on November 15 when the torch was put to Atlanta. This act brought the curtain up on the March to the Sea and stunned the South with its heartlessness. Maj. Henry Hitchcock observed: "Immense and raging fires light up whole heavens. First, bursts of smoke, dense, black volumes, then tongues of flame, then huge waves of fire roll up into the sky. Presently, the skeletons of great warehouses stand out in relief against sheets of roaring, blazing, furious flames."

The conqueror of Atlanta had facilitated the best news of the Union war effort in several months. His decision to avoid a headlong clash had magnified his success: his armies had kept a large Confederate force occupied and inflicted heavy losses, he had outmaneuvered two of the best generals the Confederacy had to offer, and he had captured Atlanta, one of the gate cities of the South and a major railroad and manufacturing center.

With Atlanta in his possession and
Hood's army posing no immediate
danger, Sherman's troops relaxed. He
even suggested that Georgia might
pull out of the war. He posed with his
staff at one of the Atlanta forts. They
are, from left to right, aide L. M.
Dayton, medical director E. D. Kittoe,
commissary officer A. Beckwith, chief
engineer Orlando M. Poe, chief of
artillery William F. Barry, W. Warner,
J. E. Marshall, Sherman, chief of ordnance T. G. Baylor, G. W. Nichols,
inspector general C. Ewing, and an
unidentified major.

In truth, Sherman had not ordered the whole city lev-
eled, only primary manufacturing and military targets.
The fire, however, spread quickly into some civilian sec-
tors, and the memory of seeing Atlanta ablaze under the
Yankee torch was one many Southerners would never
forget or forgive. They felt the very heart was burned out
of this beautiful jewel of the South. One Atlanta citizen
decried, "Hell has laid her egg, and right here it hatched."

The following morning, with the city still blazing
behind them, Sherman and his army of sixty-two thousand men turned eastward toward the Atlantic and
began the march. On the outskirts of town, Sherman
turned and looked back. "Behind us lay Atlanta smoldering in ruins, the black smoke rising high in the air
and hanging like a pall. The day is extremely beautiful,
and an unusual feeling of exhilaration seems to pervade
all minds, a feeling of something to come," he recorded.

The army marched in secret. None of them knew
that their final destination was Savannah, approximately 275 miles away. F. Y. Hedley of the Thirty-
second Illinois groused: "We were about to march out
into the great unknown. It was a voyage upon untried
waters, beyond which might lie no shore. Those who
would fall would leave their bones in a strange and
unfriendly land forever."

WCD °Savannah was Sherman's goal for very good reasons. It would take the city out of the war as a blockade-running port, and the direct route to Savannah from Atlanta took Sherman's army through the heartland of Georgia—the granary, the breadbasket of that deep part of the southeastern South that provided so much of what kept Confederate soldiers fed and fighting.•

It was a young, tough, confident army that the commander fielded. One Southern woman, Lizzie Perkins, recalled, "They told us they were going to play 'smash' with the Confederacy. Just going to sweep it out in one lick."

Sherman's Army of Georgia moved quickly and stealthily, foraging off the land. Foraging was necessary because the army could not carry enough supplies to sustain it. Along the way military, industrial, and psychological targets were priorities, and railroad targets were particularly prized and drew special treatment.

DE °The Federals would take crowbars, tools, fence rails, whatever was handy, and pry the crossties from the

Rather than chase Hood's Army of Tennessee back over the route he had just completed in seizing Atlanta, Sherman chose to use his army in a grand raid across Georgia that he believed would demoralize the South. He sent troops to Nashville and supplies and unfit soldiers to Chattanooga. Then he had the railroad between Atlanta and Chattanooga destroyed, thus eliminating a need to protect supply lines. On November 14 a lean, campaign-hardened army of sixty-two thousand gathered in Atlanta (left). They also amassed three thousand cattle, twenty-five hundred wagons, six hundred ambulances, sixty-five field pieces, and seventeen thousand horses and mules.

While they could abandon Atlanta, the Federals could not leave anything behind that might be useful to the Confederates, particularly anything having to do with the railroads. Thus the work of destruction began, and Sherman's men became experts at their task. In the left photograph above, Union soldiers placed rails over a bonfire, after which the rails were bent. In the photograph to the right above, rails and locomotive parts are piled next to the fire, awaiting their fate.

railway beds. They would use these to set bonfires across which they would then lay individual rails. Twenty or thirty minutes later the center of these rails would be red hot, and troops would take the rails by the ends and wrap them around trees or telegraph poles on the right-of-ways, forming contrivances that they called "Sherman's bow ties" or "Sherman's hairpins."•

The march itself was a model of speed and efficiency using a two-wing approach. °By dividing his army into two wings, with two columns within each wing, Sherman made maximum use of Georgia's limited road system. There was less congestion, and traffic moved freely on the roads. The formation also spread the army across a sixty-mile-wide front.•

One officer described the Georgia countryside across which the army traveled as "a garden." With abundant foodstuffs available, Sherman's order to forage liberally has been debated ever since. The vagueness of this order allowed for substantial abuse. °Soldiers came to joke about the latitude of this license as they would go through houses along the way, despite orders to the contrary, and remove the silver plate, break dishes, cut paintings from their frames, smash pianos, steal money—if there was any—and generally pillage. This they said was foraging "liberally."•

Southerners charged that Sherman only winked at the wrongdoings. °He did not do anything about this, however, because these men were doing precisely what he wanted to do in this march: They were terrorizing

358

Sherman instructed his corps commanders in the art of destroying railroads in detail: "Let the destruction be so thorough that not a rail or tie can be used again." His method, which he innovated, was to use railroad ties to fire the rails and then twist the rails with a grapple hook his engineers had designed, which made them impossible to straighten without milling machinery. Often the misshappened rails were buried, but a variation on the procedure was to wrap the softened rails around trees—the legendary Sherman neckties. Many of these continued to litter the Georgia countryside for years following the war.

the countryside, which fit into what needed to be done. If people had been shot or raped, he would have taken firm action to punish the crime, but the destruction of property and the appropriation of food did not bother him.• One Union soldier boasted: "We had a gay old campaign, destroyed all we could not eat. Burned their cotton and gins, spilled their sorghum, burned and twisted their railroads, and raised hell generally."

WEE °In most instances, these soldiers were operating miles away from any of their commanders' influence or supervision, and the temptations were great. Normal Christian men with high morals would not normally do some of the things that they did, but they were caught up in this, and a great deal of temptation was more than the average soldier could stand. He had to get involved, and he seemed to feel that this was his opportunity to punish the South.•

The worst of Sherman's raiders were called "bum-
DE mers." °Unlike the foragers, who operated under the command of an officer and returned to the column each night, bummers just went out on their own. They

went where they wanted and did what they pleased. They wreaked havoc wherever they went and created the image that dominates the popular conception of the March to the Sea, namely its being a very violent undertaking by lawless men.• "Like demons they rushed in. Like famished wolves they come breaking locks and whatever is in their way," Dolly Sumner Lunt Birge charged.

JFM Yet even with this element of lawlessness, horrendous crimes like rape and murder were rare. °Very few people were killed or even injured. The most amazing fact is that there were few instances of rape. The best evidence held that there were possibly two rapes during the entire time.•

CN The one thing that did escalate the degree of destruction though was the sight of Union soldiers recently liberated from Southern prison camps. °Prisoners who had escaped from the Confederate prisons at Andersonville and near Millen looked like walking corpses to

The army that marched across Georgia was composed of rough, battle-toughened western fighters who had survived Shiloh and Chickamauga. "In my judgment," Sherman said, they were "the most magnificent army in existence." Many of his soldiers came to agree with him that destroying and plundering were necessary actions for punishing the enemy and ending the war. It was also a lot better than charging entrenched troops.

The Union army had learned to carry instant communication with it, and the War Department depended on telegraph lines to stay informed of the actions of its armies. During the march, however, the only news of Sherman's army came via the Confederate press, which never failed to report that the Federals in Georgia were on the verge of annihilation. When Lincoln voiced his concerns about Sherman's silence, Grant repeated his steadfast confidence that his general would appear in Savannah as he planned.

Sherman's men. They had never seen anything like the emaciated skeletons who found them on the Georgia countryside. The only comparable scene would not occur for another eighty years, the liberation of the Nazi concentration camps. The Federals were outraged by what they saw. Sherman was infuriated. From that point on, the burning and looting became almost indiscriminate.• The march was only half over, and there were still one hundred miles of Georgia ahead left to waste.

OF ALL THE groups affected most by the march, probably Southern women felt the strongest hatred toward the Yankees. Sherman's brand of total war brought Northern armies marching right up to their doorsteps and beyond.

WCD °Naturally, Sherman would be the focal point for the worst venom, the worst hatred, the worst animosity the Confederate women, especially in Georgia, could feel. As his men marched through Georgia, they drew every kind of insult and epithet that could be thrown at them.• "I doubt if history affords a parallel to the deep and bitter enmity of the women of the South. No one who sees them and hears, but must feel the intensity of their hate," noted Sherman.

One woman described Sherman as a huge octopus who stretched out his long arms and gathered everything in, leaving behind only ruin and desolation. His men were considered as nothing more than a bunch of murdering, thieving monsters. Mary Chesnut, the great diarist of the war, recorded, "Darkest of all Decembers

At the beginning of the march, orders were given that the army would forage "liberally" on the countryside, soldiers were not to enter the dwellings of any inhabitants, and only officers could order the destruction of property, but that was limited to areas of guerrilla activity. Designated foragers set out each day to acquire sufficient food for the army. Nevertheless, Sherman's "bummers" quickly became villains to the people of Georgia. Each man took his task seriously and proved ingenious in acquiring food, livestock, and whatever personal belongings he fancied. Rarely did they injure anyone or burn houses, but they did pick them clean and leave a trail of destruction behind them.

ever my life has known, sitting here by the embers, stunned, helpless, alone."

The women spoke of retaliation. One Georgia woman promised, "Our men will fight you as long as they live, and these boys will fight you when they grow up!"

Sherman saw it differently. The march was a police action. The Southerners were lawbreakers who had started the war. He would finish it, and they would step back in line. "To those who submit to rightful authority, all gentleness and forbearance, but to petulant and persistent Seccessionists, why death is mercy! And the quicker he or she is disposed of, the better," he said.

While he is commonly thought to have said, "War is hell," what Sherman actually said was a bit more complex. °He did say, "War is cruelty," and later, in the postwar years, he said, "There is many a boy here today who looks on war as all glory, but boys, it is all hell." That phrase was popularized and transformed into "War is hell." To say the least, many Georgians knew firsthand that war was hell for them.•

Although Sherman felt that his wartime actions were right, he did feel some remorse about the way Southern children felt about him. "They are taught to curse my name, and each night thousands kneel in

WEE

prayer and beseech the Almighty to consign me to perdition," he lamented.

While Southerners may have hated Sherman, his men idolized him. He became "Uncle Billy" to many of his troops. °He would sit on a stump with several enlisted men and share a cigar and chat, telling old stories. This kind of thing endeared a commander. He was not one of those ivory tower, greatly distant men with pretty sashes and flashy swords that men saw but never knew. The men in Sherman's army could get to know Sherman somewhat. He was not a spit-and-polish soldier. He was no martinet, and partly because of that, the men fighting under him had a tremendous respect for him and a kind of filial affection. This was a powerful bond between the two, and a powerful tool for him to use as a weapon of war when he had to take those men into battle.•

Sherman chose to avoid sending major portions of his troops into Macon and Augusta, but one objective he could not pass up was Milledgeville, the Georgia capital. The Federals entered the town shortly after Gov. Joe Brown had fled for his life. Claiming the capital, the Northerners held a mock session of the legislature, rescinded Georgia's ordinance of secession, and warmed themselves with bonfires made of Confederate money.

With Hood's army fighting in Tennessee, Sherman marched across Georgia almost unopposed. The only confrontation of note happened at Griswoldville, ten miles from Macon, where Sherman's right wing went up against a determined unit of Georgia militia.

°After the battle, as the Federals secured the field, they found that they had been fighting young boys and old men. These grizzled Union veterans were shocked at first, and then they realized how desperate the Confederacy had to be if this was all that was left to oppose them.•

An immediate result of Sherman's march was the emancipation of thousands of slaves. In gratitude for their freedom, they laid provisions, information, and adoration at Sherman's feet. They also created a huge problem. With nowhere else to go, legions of them

WCD

JFM

As the army roamed toward Savannah, some of what it encountered angered the men and generated a spirit of vindictiveness. They heard tales of hound dogs being used to chase down fugitive slaves and escaped Union prisoners, and so they shot almost every dog they saw to prevent its being used for those purposes again. At Millen, Georgia, they were incensed when they came across an open pen used to confine captured Federals and several hundred unmarked graves. Escaped prisoners from Andersonville, such as the soldier below, also told horror stories. All of this increased the army's desire to punish the Confederates, military and civilian.

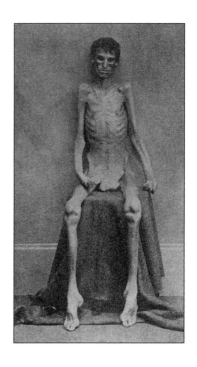

Throughout the march, slaves welcomed the army enthusiastically. They acted as spies and gave directions, which Sherman appreciated and found to be far more reliable than information received from Southern whites. At the same time, he discouraged them from following the army and chose not to impress any in his service. Thousands of them followed anyway, such as the wagonload of refugees pictured at right. Their presence worried Sherman and his officers, who wondered if they could find sufficient food to maintain the army and the slaves, too.

Perhaps the most controversial moment of the march occurred at Ebenezer Creek on December 9. The Fourteenth Corps under Jefferson C. Davis (below) was being pursued by Confederate cavalry. When Davis's men completed the crossing, they immediately removed the pontoon bridges they had used, stranding hundreds of former slaves. Fearing that they might be slaughtered by the Confederates, the slaves panicked and tried to swim across the creek. An indeterminate number drowned, despite the aid of many of Davis's soldiers.

began to follow the army. They were not welcome, and the situation led to tragedy.

JFM °As the army approached Ebenezer Creek, pontoon bridges were erected for a portion of the army to get across. Confederate cavalry under Joseph Wheeler, one of the few viable units in the state, was closing on the Federals. The Union commander at the scene, a man with the improbable name of Jefferson C. Davis—no relation to the Confederate president—who had no love for slaves, immediately pulled up the pontoon bridges as soon as his men had crossed. The slaves were left on the other bank of the creek, knowing that the Confederate cavalry was coming and fearing that they might be attacked. In their panic they dove into the swollen creek to try to swim to the opposite bank and safety. Large numbers were drowned as a result, despite the fact that many Union soldiers tried to help them across. This incident precipitated an enormous controversy and has been cited as an example of Sherman's personal animosity toward black people.° Sherman, however, was not responsible for this tragedy, but it probably did not cause him any distress either.

WEE °Sherman most definitely was a racist, and that was evident in his letters to his wife, Ellen, in which he on many occasions degraded blacks, saying that they were not capable of holding any position of authority and

The goal of Sherman's march was Savannah, a Southern port city untouched by the ravages of war. By early December 1864 his army was poised before it, ready to make contact with the Union fleet and reestablish its supply lines. Food had been plentiful along the way, but the marsh area around Savannah offered only alligators and rice. A long siege would be disastrous for a hungry army, and so Sherman chose to storm Fort McAllister to the south of the city, which would allow the fleet to supply him. The assault took only fifteen minutes, and he lost eleven men. With a secure supply line established, he could lay siege to Savannah and would have had he not received instructions from Grant ordering him to rush his soldiers to Petersburg.

claiming that it took two of his soldiers to handle just one black soldier. He also decried their lack of proficiency in any field, and on and on.•

In Washington, Lincoln—cut off from the march— waited. Would Sherman deliver Georgia to him as promised, or would the South rise from the ashes in Savannah as it had so many times before and prolong the war? For their part, the Southern papers reported that Sherman was on the verge of annihilation. Much of the time the president was not aware of where Sherman was. In December 1864, when Sen. John Sherman approached him regarding news of his brother, Lincoln answered: "We have heard nothing from him. We know what hole he went in, but we don't know what hole he will come out of."

SHERMAN'S ARMY HAD marched more than 250 miles virtually unopposed, but as they neared the ocean and the fixed defenses of Savannah, he knew the opposition would be more formidable. Not only would they have to contend with a highly competent Confederate leader in Lt. Gen. William Hardee, who was charged with the defense of the city, his army also faced a new problem—supply.

JFM The Savannah area was mostly marshland, producing, in the words of one soldier, "nothing . . . but alligators in the swamp and rice in sheaves in the fields." The rich farmland was far behind now, so unlike the early weeks of

365

Sherman determined to take Savannah before Grant's transports arrived to move his men to Virginia. His opponent was William J. Hardee, who refused to surrender. The Federal commander positioned his troops around the city, but left one route of escape open for the Confederates. On the evening of December 20, 1864, Hardee took advantage of Sherman's generosity and abandoned the city. The Federals began occupying the city without firing a shot. Meanwhile, Sherman convinced Grant that he could march to Virginia in the same time it would take to move by ship, and he also noted that his men would be in better shape from the overland march than they would be after being crammed onto transports.

the march across Georgia, the army was now hard pressed to find food, especially since it had to focus on taking up positions around the well-entrenched coastal city.*

The supply problems could be solved if contact were made with the Federal fleet that was waiting for Sherman off the coast. Standing between him and the fleet, however, was Confederate Fort McAllister on the

DE Ogeechee River. °McAllister controlled traffic on the river, and Sherman needed access to the Ogeechee to communicate with the fleet.*

Brig. Gen. William Hazen was chosen to lead the assault on the fort. His men had been recruited by Sherman himself when the unit had been formed in Paducah, Kentucky, and had served under him at Shiloh and Vicksburg. Hazen's troops advanced on the fort in the face of artillery and small-arms fire. They charged across

DE ground laced with land mines, °encountered abatis, and swarmed across a ditch, about fifteen feet deep and seven feet across, packed with more abatis. They quickly scaled the parapets and subdued the garrison after brief but fierce hand-to-hand combat. The entire assault lasted fifteen minutes and cost eleven Federal lives and eighty wounded. In possession of the fort, the army was not long in drawing supplies from the fleet.*

Brimming with confidence, Sherman turned his attention to Savannah. Since leaving Atlanta, everything had gone according to his way. Then a letter arrived from

WCD Grant °instructing him to put his army on transports and bring them to Virginia to join him in the effort to finally capture Lee's army, and with it Petersburg and Richmond.˙ Grant stated, "I have concluded that the most important operation toward closing the rebellion will be to close out Lee and his army." It was the worst possible news. If Sherman acted on Grant's order immediately, there would be no time to take the city, but then he realized it would take time for the transport ships to arrive. While he waited, he could proceed with his original plan.

Taking Savannah would not be easy, and it could be very costly. Suffering heavy casualties after the stupendously successful march, however, was the last thing he wanted. Before committing his army to combat, he CN decided to try to intimidate Hardee, °sending him a message threatening to burn the town unless Hardee surrendered. News of the march had certainly preceded him, so Sherman referred to it as part of his bluff.˙ Hardee, however, refused to be intimidated, so Sherman laid plans to besiege the city.

While the Federals took up positions around Savannah, the Confederate commander began having second thoughts about defending the city. His troops numbered less then ten thousand, compared to Sherman's sixty-two thousand. With the odds against him, he began looking for a way out.

WCD °He had maintained an escape route by having his men build a pontoon bridge across the river that would allow him to evacuate Savannah before the city

In February 1865 Sherman's army moved into South Carolina, with one wing threatening Augusta and Columbia and the other threatening Columbia and Charleston. Confederate defenses were scattered and uncoordinated, because the Southerners were unsure of Sherman's objective. Columbia was abandoned on February 16 and Charleston on February 17. Charleston, the cradle of secession, had been pounded for most of the war. The scaffolding around the circular church in the photograph below (left) towers over the devastated city. The Mills House hotel (below right) was once the home of P. G. T. Beauregard, until it fell under the guns of the Federal navy.

Sherman was pleased with his successful march because the devastation had brought the war closer to completion and because he had achieved military success without excessive casualties. He was a national hero, one of the military stars of the Union war effort, and he had rocked the Confederacy to its core.

and his garrison could be taken. Hardee's rationale was that the loss of the city was inevitable, but the loss of the city and his ten thousand men would be foolish. He probably was ready to evacuate at a moment's notice.•

Some say that Sherman allowed this bridge to be built because he wanted Hardee to give up the city without a DE fight. °He had gone to Hilton Head Island, South Carolina, to confer with another general about the siege on Savannah. During his absence, late in the evening of December 20, Hardee began his evacuation of the city. His entire command was safely in South Carolina by daylight the next morning. The Union troops heard them crossing the pontoon bridge and they were close enough to have interfered, but no orders were given.•

Before leaving the city, the Confederates laid waste to their navy yard and torched one of their own ironclads. Savannah was Sherman's for the taking.

From South Carolina he moved unimpeded into North Carolina. After engagements at Averasborough and Bentonville, Joseph E. Johnston— recently returned to command— requested a meeting with Sherman on April 17 at the James Bennett house (right) in Durham Station, near Raleigh.

DE °Since Sherman was not on the scene to give any orders, there may have been an unspoken understanding between him and his officers that if the Rebel army tried to leave, it would be more expedient simply to let it go. It was never noted whether this bloodless victory was of Sherman's choos-

WEE ing or simply a stroke of fate.• °The evacuation of Savannah might best be compared to two bullies in a schoolyard—one scared, and the other glad of it.•

On Christmas Eve 1864, Lincoln received a wire from Sherman: "I beg to present you as a Christmas gift the city of Savannah. With 150 heavy guns and plenty of ammunition and also about 25,000 bales of cotton." The march was over, but Sherman's legacy lived on.

WCD °Sherman's March to the Sea made him one of the great commanders of history, and in the North, of course, he was viewed as a great hero, a great conqueror. It had been a triumphal procession from Atlanta to the sea. Songs were sung, stories were written, pictures were painted—Sherman was the hero of the hour.

Upon Grant's inauguration as president in 1869, Sherman became a full general and general in chief of the army— a post he held for thirteen years.

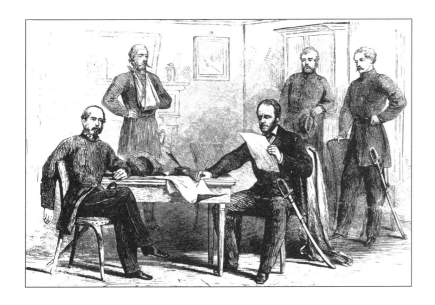

Contrary to the ferocious image generated during the march across Georgia and the Carolinas campaign, Sherman negotiated lenient terms for the surrender of Johnston's army. Some of these, however, intruded on matters of civil policy, and officials in Washington immediately rejected the agreement and criticized Sherman. On April 26 Johnston and Sherman met again and agreed to terms limited to military matters. Grant conveyed approval to these terms, and on May 3 Johnston's army laid down its arms.

On the other hand, what Sherman's March to the Sea did for his reputation in Southern eyes is exactly what one would have expected. If there were any Antichrist, if there were any Satan on earth in 1864 in the South, it was William T. Sherman.•

During the March to the Sea, Sherman had isolated his troops so much that in the North they were calling it the lost army, yet when he finally "came out of his hole," as Lincoln said, and marched triumphantly into Savannah, he had placed the Federals much closer to total victory. The march had changed the war, and it also changed warfare forever.

Grant reconsidered his earlier proposal of having Sherman's army brought to Virginia by sea, and Sherman chose to march up the coast, believing that he could permanently sever all supply lines to Richmond and Petersburg in the process. Along the route, his troops continued to destroy property and forage liberally. Confederate forces under William Hardee and Joseph E. Johnston—who had replaced Hood as commander of the Army of Tennessee—failed to impede their progress. Eight days after Lee surrendered to Grant, Johnston met with Sherman to discuss surrender terms.

Sherman's postwar career included command of the Division of the Mississippi, military assistance to

During Grant's first presidential campaign, he took both Sherman (far right) and Philip Sheridan (second from the left) with him on a western tour. The three dominated the highest level of army command from the time Grant became general in chief on March 9, 1864, until Sheridan died in the same post on August 5, 1888.

the construction of the transcontinental railroad, and campaigning during the Indian wars. In July 1866, when Grant was promoted to full general, Sherman was posted to Washington to take temporary command of the army; following Grant's inauguration as president in 1868, Sherman was made a full general and general in chief of the army. In 1872 the Republican Party tried to nominate him as a presidential candidate, but forever wary of politicans and politics in general, he refused to be drafted, saying: "If nominated I will not accept; if elected I will not serve." He published his memoirs in 1875 and retired from the army in 1883. Sherman moved to New York City in 1886, where he died in 1891. One of his pallbearers was Joseph E. Johnston.

Sherman died in New York on Valentine's Day 1891 and was honored on February 19 with a huge procession. Observers could only recall Grant's funeral five years earlier as an equal event. The body was taken by train to Saint Louis, where the funeral cortege rivaled that in New York. In Calvary Cemetery, Father Tom Sherman, the general's son, conducted the grave-site ceremony.

NATHAN BEDFORD FORREST

Nathan BEDFORD FORREST
was untutored in war. On the battlefield he relied solely
on intuition, and his self-taught tactics made him one
of the most fearsome and feared men for any Federal to
come up against during the years between 1861 and
1865. He was a hero to the poor Southern white man
and a symbol of what the Confederacy was willing to
do to win. While Sherman had defined war as hell, Forrest was more specific, saying, "War means fighting, and
fighting means killing."

He was known as "the Wizard of the Saddle" and
reputed to have killed more than thirty Union soldiers in
hand-to-hand combat and to have had twenty-nine
horses shot from beneath him. From the moment he first
took command of a cavalry battalion in 1862, Forrest ter-
rorized the Federals and continued to do so throughout
the war. He was a constant threat wherever he went, and
it was rare when Union Maj. Gen. William Tecumseh
Sherman did not refer to him as "that devil Forrest."

JMM °He was a large man with a colorful personality.
What set him apart from his colleagues—especially in
the western theater of the war—was his fearlessness.
Forrest was a violent man with a fierce temper, and he
struggled with his temper for most of his life. He
thought nothing of killing other men and in fact was
proud of it.°

A masterful tactician, Forrest consistently outmaneuvered his adversaries and exploited every opportunity to
confuse and deceive his opponents. While a sense of
professional respect and even old school ties colored

ECB	Edwin C. Bearss
JMM	James M. McPherson
BP	Brian Pohanka
WJR	William J. Rasp
WS	Wiley Sword
BSW	Brian S. Wills

After a whirlwind courtship, Forrest married Mary Ann Montgomery on September 25, 1845. In 1846 she gave birth to a son, William Montgomery, and in 1847 to a daughter, Frances A., whom they called Fanny. Mother and daughter were photographed together (above). In 1852 Forrest moved the family to Memphis, a boom-town on its way to becoming the inland slave-trading capital of the Southwest. While his business as a slave trader prospered, six-year-old Fanny died on June 26, 1854, possibly of typhoid fever. The notice of her funeral (below) appeared in one of the Memphis newspapers.

funeral Notice.

The friends and acquaintances of N. B. FORREST, are requested to attend the funeral of his daughter **FANNY ANN**, from the residence of her father, on Adams Street, this afternoon, at 5 o'clock

TUESDAY, JUNE 27, 1854.

BP

ECB

BSW

the interchange between most Confederate and Federal leaders, Forrest stood fast against the hated Yankees—even when the war was all but lost. In his words, the conflict was "War to the knife—knife to the hilt."

Forrest's greatest victory occurred near the war's end when he clashed in June 1864 with Federal forces under Maj. Gen. Samuel D. Sturgis at the battle at Brice's Cross Roads in Mississippi. °It was one of the most one-sided victories of the Civil War, and the fact that Forrest, out-numbered as he was, gained the victory is certainly the preeminent example of Forrest as a tactician and a bat-tlefield commander.•

The confrontation at Brice's Cross Roads was the result of Sherman's concern for the protection of his army as it plowed into Georgia in pursuit of the Con-federate Army of Tennessee. °Forrest, Sherman said, was the only cavalryman, North or South, whom he feared, and he ordered Sturgis to search out and destroy For-rest's command. Sturgis, a West Point graduate of the class of 1846, marched from the Memphis area on June 2 with eighty-five hundred men—a division of cavalry, a division of infantry, and twenty-two cannon. Forrest, meanwhile, was moving toward Middle Tennessee to strike at Sherman's lone railway supply line.•

While he was advancing on the Tennessee railroad, Forrest learned of Sturgis's advance. Before dawn on June 10, 1864, he formulated a plan to meet the Feder-als head-on.

°He knew that the Federals had been on the march for a week and that several miles of their route con-sisted of deep, boggy landscape. Additionally, the road they would have to use had been badly cut up by a week's rain. While the rain had subsided on June 10, the humidity was still high. In Mississippi the combination of heat and humidity greatly limited an individual's ability to move, and Forrest knew that he could use the natural elements as weapons against the Federals.•

When the two forces met, Forrest's situation appeared dire. Of his forty-eight hundred troops and twelve guns, only one eight-hundred-man brigade was on the field. As Forrest predicted, however, the long march had exhausted the Union soldiers.

By midday the two sides were locked in fierce
ECB combat. °Forrest's men fought dismounted. Each man
carried two Colt Navy revolvers rather than a saber, and
they proved more effective in hand-to-hand combat
than the Federals did with sabers. One of the combat-
ants later said, "So close was this struggle that guns,
once fired, were not reloaded but used as clubs while
the two lines struggled with the ferocity of wild beasts."

Forrest ordered his head of artillery, Maj. John W.
Morton Jr., to move his guns—without either cavalry or
infantry support—within two hundred yards of the
ECB Union lines• and "Give 'em hell." °Meanwhile, he sent a
brigade under Col. Tyree H. Bell wheeling around the
Union left while another force under Brig. Gen. Abram
Buford moved around the Union right—the classic
double envelopment. The Union line collapsed.• Utterly
routed, the Federals fled with the Confederates close
behind, firing on their enemy at will.

In the panic of the rout, as Col. Edward Bouton
proposed to act as rear guard, a flustered Sturgis said:
"For God's sake, if Mr. Forrest will let me alone I will
let him alone. You have done all you could and more
than was expected of you, and now all you can do is
save yourselves."

BP °By the end of the day, Sturgis had lost half his force,
fourteen of his twenty-two field pieces, and his supply
wagons, and his demoralized force was in utter retreat.
Forrest, however, was not the type of commander who

Fifteen-year-old William followed his father into battle and served by his side for four years. At Shiloh, Forrest was briefly distracted from the action by news that his son was missing; Willie and two peers eventually appeared with fifteen Union prisoners. After the war, Willie served in his father's businesses and finally became a quietly successful railroad and levee contractor. He did not attend Confederate reunions after his father's death, nor did he discuss the war in which he had been wounded three times. He died after a stroke in 1908 as he sat in a Memphis audience of the stage adaptation of Thomas Dixon's The Clansman. *This 1862 photograph is the earliest known image of William.*

In the mid-1840s slaves were fast becoming the single most valuable commodity in the agricultural South. The value of a plantation's slaves came to be greater than that of the planta-tion itself and its produce, livestock, and accessories. The route of the trade tended to move from the more settled eastern South to the frontier wilder-nesses of Mississippi, Louisiana, Arkansas, and Texas. Notoriously high prices were paid in the markets of Louisiana and Memphis.

Slaves were bought and sold through auctions. When buyers came, the slaves were displayed and inspected in much the same way that livestock was purchased. Sales frequently made no allowance for maintaining slave families. Forrest claimed that he tried to keep families together and that there were some people to whom he would not sell slaves because they had reputations as cruel masters. This sketch of a slave auction was made from life by Eyre Crowe in 1853.

The first commercial mention of Forrest's name was as a partner of the Hernando-based slave trader S. S. Jones. In 1852 he joined the firm of Forrest and Jones, and in 1853 he was briefly the junior partner of the well-established Memphis slave trader Byrd Hill. In 1855 he founded his own business with Josiah Maples, but the firm came to be embroiled in a lawsuit that cooled Forrest's interest in partnerships. From 1856 to 1858 Forrest apparently worked as the head of his own business, acquiring agricultural holdings that would make his slave dealings more profitable. JMM A bill of sale from Hill and Forrest below bears the latter's signature and guarantee that the slaves thus purchased were sound, healthy, and sensible.

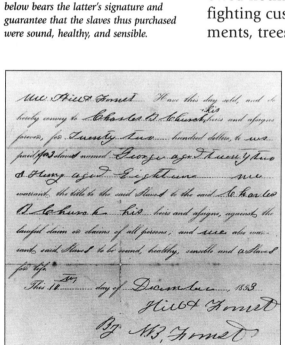

stopped when the battle was won. He pursued every adversary until he himself was stopped. That single-minded ruthlessness kept his men in pursuit of Sturgis's Federals, and the poor, befuddled, routed Yankee army was all but ridden into the ground as it was chased back to Memphis.•

The battle of Brice's Cross Roads illustrates some of the tactics Forrest employed throughout the war. Because he was successful, his strategies were adopted by field commanders on both sides. °Forrest's tactics owed nothing to textbooks and more to the Indian-fighting customs of the woodlands. In those engagements, trees were used for cover, a force advanced by rushes, and deception, decoys, rapid mobility, and swift transitions from mounted to dismounted fighting characterized action. While Forrest had no firsthand experience in Indian warfare, he had lived on the frontier and had quickly adapted to that kind of fighting.•

Forrest's impressive military achievements earned him noteworthy distinctions. He was the only man on either side to enlist as a private and earn the rank of lieutenant general. Yet all of his accomplishments were not enough to earn him a place at the top of the Confederacy's leadership.

Shortly after their marriage, Forrest and Mary Ann moved into this house in Hernando, Mississippi. Although not large, it was above average by southwestern frontier standands. Near the center of town, it combined two log cabins constructed side by side, then covered with clapboards to form a single house with two chimneys. Forrest purchased it two or three weeks after his uncle had been killed, paying three hundred dollars for the lot on March 28, 1845.

WS   °Time after time Forrest won victories and accomplished things that nobody believed he could. Nevertheless, he was always regarded with a degree of suspicion by the leaders of the Confederacy. While they acknowledged that he knew how to fight and could fight well, they believed he was unreliable for important high-command assignment because he was not sufficiently trained and disciplined in the manner of a West Point–educated officer.•

FORREST NEVER HAD the opportunity to attend West Point. In fact, he had only six months of formal education to his credit. At times his semi-literacy presented problems for those who had to decipher his directives. Aware of his literary shortcomings and sometimes embarrassed by his lack of education, Forrest would

WJR °have his adjutants write and sign his letters for him. Maj. Charles W. Anderson, one of his adjutants, later recalled a moment in conversation with Forrest when the general looked down at the pen in the major's hand and said, "I don't look at a pen that I don't think of a snake."•

The kind of life into which Forrest was born did not lend itself to a formal education. He was born on July 13, 1821, in Chapel Hill, Tennessee, the oldest son in a family of nine children. Survival was no mean accomplishment in that time and place. Two of his brothers

Just prior to the war Forrest had this photograph taken in Memphis by W. E. Craver. He was forty years old, a successful real estate and slave broker, and a city councilman. Tennessee seceded from the Union on June 8, 1861; Forrest, his son, and his brother enlisted in Capt. Josiah White's Tennessee Mounted Rifles on June 14.

and all three of his sisters died early of typhoid fever. Nor did Bedford, as he was called, survive peacefully. A neighbor noted that whether at play or while being disciplined, he could yell louder than any other child in the area.

Life was harsh in this rugged backwoods country. It
JMM became harsher when Forrest's father died and °sixteen-year-old Bedford had to become the head of the family. The frontier was violent; life itself was a struggle against nature and, in some instances, against people. There he learned that only the strongest and the most aggressive would prevail and would succeed in life.•

When he was twenty Bedford left his family and moved to Hernando, Mississippi, to seek his fortune. By the time he was twenty-one he had killed his first man,
BSW avenging the murder of his uncle. °This was not unusual on the frontier where there was little regard for the law and a person had to address the wrongs committed against him. Violence was the most basic solution to these problems. In the context of that life, Forrest's act was not so particularly brutal as it was a basic, commonsense approach to any problem.•

Killing his first man was not the only significant event that occurred in the life of Forrest in 1842, however.
ECB °He also met and married Mary Ann Montgomery, the daughter of a Presbyterian preacher. She was with her mother, and the two were going to church when their buggy broke down in the middle of a stream. Some of the local young men were laughing at the mother and daughter stranded in midstream when Forrest rode up, dismounted, waded out to the buggy, and rescued Mary Ann and her mother. He then proceeded to thrash the people who had been making fun of the two women. Within six weeks he and Mary Ann were married.• The couple had two children, a boy, William Montgomery,

The battle at Brice's Cross Roads was perhaps the most perfectly planned engagement of Forrest's career. There the self-taught Forrest, pitted against West Point–trained Samuel D. Sturgis, drubbed the Federals and chased them back to Memphis. Sturgis was acting under orders from William T. Sherman to engage Forrest and prevent him from pestering the Federal supply lines into Georgia. When that mission failed at Brice's Cross Roads, Sherman petitioned the War Department to "go out and follow Forrest to the death, if it cost 10,000 lives and breaks the treasury. There will never be peace in Tennessee till Forrest is dead."

The victory at Brice's Cross Roads ele-vated Forrest in the eyes of several Confederate leaders, particularly those from Georgia whose state was being invaded by Sherman. When they peti-tioned Richmond for Forrest's reassign-ment to harass the Federal supply line, Jefferson Davis refused, believing that the removal of Forrest would effec-tively capitulate the war in the West. Ultimately, the Southern high com-mand failed to believe that Forrest was worthy of its trust. He was regarded only as a bold partisan raider, and Brice's Cross Roads was but another successful raid. This shortsighted view of Forrest denied the Confederates in Georgia the one man whose rapid and lethal style might have frustrated Sherman's advance on Atlanta.

and a girl, Frances. His daughter died a victim of disease at the age of six.

BSW　°Having been raised with very little money, Forrest wanted to accumulate wealth so that his family would not have to endure the hardships he had survived.° In 1851 he decided to move the family to Memphis to seek his fortune as a planter.

WS　°He saw that the basis for becoming a successful planter was to have a good labor force, and that led him into the slave trade. Forrest became a slave trader, not out of any malicious intent toward blacks, but because BSW they were a means to an end.° °Finding success as a busi-nessman before the Civil War, he made probably as much money as anyone could make as a planter.° By 1860 Forrest owned three thousand acres of land, valued at $190,000, and he had forty-two slaves; his personal estate was valued at $90,000. At age thirty-nine, he had become one of the wealthiest men in the South.

While slave trading had made him rich, he was not WS known to mistreat his slaves. °Forrest felt that slaves were property to be protected, and whipped or mis-treated slaves were generally unacceptable to prospective purchasers.° Over time slave traders have been depicted as social outcasts, but Forrest's career belies this stereo-type. His wealth was his passport to social esteem. In 1855 he was even elected a city alderman in Memphis.

BP　°Forrest had quite a few strikes against him in prewar southern society. Because of his lack of education, his

Perhaps the greatest testimony to Forrest's effectiveness came from Samuel Sturgis (below) as he pulled back from the battle at the crossroads: "For God's sake, if Mr. Forrest will let me alone I will let him alone!"

Forrest's first significant battle was at Fort Donelson, near Dover, Tennessee. A Federal force under U. S. Grant had succeeded in taking Fort Henry, ten miles to the west, and had taken position around Donelson in February 1862. The Confederates decided that Donelson was lost and their best course of action was to fight their way out and fall back on Nashville. Despite heavy sleet and snow, Forrest led his cavalry in sweeping Union soldiers from three roads that could have been used to evacuate the fort, but his commanders deemed the hour to be late and ordered him to pull back to the fort. At the end of the day, Forrest had lost one horse and his overcoat bore fifteen bullet holes.

uncouth way of expressing himself, his slang, his poor diction, and his inability to read and write, he could have been viewed as what southerners called "white trash." Yet Forrest managed to transcend his upbringing and his lack of education and became a powerful member of the community. That kind of will power, determination, and grit enabled him to achieve significant goals throughout his life, and these same strengths brought him victory after victory on the battlefield.•

On June 8, 1861, Tennessee seceded from the Union. Six days later Forrest signed on with the Tennessee Mounted Rifles in °Dr. Josiah S. White's office. At six foot two, hair beginning to turn with flecks of gray, steel gray eyes, and powerfully built, he enlisted as a private in Captain White's company.•

Forrest did not remain a private for long. He used his money to equip a cavalry battalion, composed of about six hundred men, and was promoted to lieutenant colonel. The *Memphis Avalanche* of July 24, 1861, observed: "No better man could have been selected for such a duty of known courage and indomitable perseverance. He is a man for the times."

The first significant military action of his career took place in late December 1861 at Sacramento, Kentucky. There Forrest employed the guerrilla tactics that would make him legendary, and he fought side by side with his men, applying his standing rule of combat: "Forward men, and mix with them."

He operated independently of the larger army and by his own sense of honor. This earned Forrest success, but it also brought disdain. °There was a kind of professional brotherhood among the West Pointers who were in charge of most of the principal armies on both sides of the Civil War. They had known each other at West Point, and many of them had known each other in Mexico where they had fought fifteen years earlier as junior officers. Forrest was not a part of that brotherhood, so he did not operate in conjunction with it. He operated by his own rules and sometimes made up the rules as he went along.°

IN FEBRUARY 1862, Colonel Forrest found himself in Tennessee at Fort Donelson on the Cumberland River as part of a Confederate force under the command of Brig. Gen. John B. Floyd and with Brig. Gen. Gideon J. Pillow and Brig. Gen. Simon B. Buckner. Union Gen. Ulysses S. Grant had successfully marched on Fort Henry and was then deploying around Donelson.

ECB   °On February 14, in below-freezing weather, Union gunboats joined the Federal forces surrounding the fort and began shelling the Confederate position. Southern artillery returned the fire, striking all the ships in the small ironclad flotilla and forcing them to withdraw. Despite the success of his artillerists, Floyd decided that his position at Donelson was untenable and that his force should attempt to break through the Federal lines.

Early the next morning the Confederates attacked and slowly pressed the Union forces back. The route to Nashville was open, but inexplicably Pillow ordered a withdrawal. Grant seized the initiative,° and the Federals regained the ground lost earlier.

That night Floyd decided to surrender the fort. Forrest was the lone dissenting voice. He said,

A midnight war council on February 15 of the four Confederate generals inside Donelson concluded that the Federals were being reinforced and that the enemy had taken back whatever gains the Confederates had made in the day's fighting. They decided to surrender, but Forrest announced that he had not come to Donelson to surrender. With the permission of the generals, he led about five hundred of his cavalry and a number of men from different units out by a flooded road (below) while Simon Buckner (above) inquired what terms Grant would offer for the fort's surrender.

At the battle of Shiloh on April 6, 1862, Forrest joined the fight at the part of the field that later came to be known as the Hornets' Nest. He charged the Federal position but bogged down forty yards short of his objective. B. F. Cheatham's troops, however, had followed Forrest's cavalry and succeeded in taking a portion of the Union line. Forrest's men moved off to join other troops engaging a division at the center of the Hornets' Nest and then moved to a hill overlooking Pittsburg Landing when nightfall ended the fighting. That evening Forrest scouted the Northern camp and saw reinforcements arrive, but his report was discounted by his commanders. In the morning, the reinforced Federals pushed the Confederates back; Forrest's cavalry covered the retreat.

"These people are talking about surrendering, but I'm going out of this place before they do or bust hell wide open."

WS   Giving up was not part of Forrest's makeup. °Here was a situation where the bungling and incompetence of the Confederate commanders had turned a favorable situation toward the prospect of surrender, and Forrest absolutely refused to allow that to happen to his com- ECB mand if at all possible.° °While thirteen thousand Confederates laid down their weapons, Forrest and his cavalry of about five hundred escaped by a flooded road.°

Forrest's determined action at Fort Donelson earned him recognition. His actions following the battle of Shiloh, Tennessee, two months later in April 1862 cemented his reputation. While screening the Confederate retreat from the battlefield, Forrest clashed with the pursuing Union column led by Gen. William Tecumseh BSW Sherman at a place called Fallen Timbers. °Forrest took a relatively small group of men and attacked Sherman, forcing the Federals to deploy and giving the Confederate army more time to escape.

In characteristic style, he rode out in advance of his men• and was quickly surrounded by Sherman's Federals. As he turned to shoot his way out, °he was seriously wounded. Forrest reached down, grabbed his assailant by the collar, pulled him up behind him to protect him from being shot by anybody else, and galloped away with him.• He threw the man off when he was no longer in danger.

The legend of Forrest was born. The bullet wound required two operations and knocked Forrest out of action for several weeks. He used his convalescence to recruit additional troops, placing an advertisement in the *Memphis Appeal,* promising, "Come on, boys, if you want a heap of fun and to kill some Yankees."

In June, Forrest assumed command of a mounted brigade of fourteen hundred men. In July his aggressive tactics and the threat of not taking prisoners bluffed the enemy at Murfreesboro, Tennessee. There the commander surrendered his twelve-hundred-man garrison and $250,000 in Union property. Forrest had reportedly ordered, "Whenever you see anything blue, shoot at it, and do all you can to keep up the scare."

This was not the only time deception worked for Forrest. It was also the key to his success against Col. Abel Streight as Forrest pursued him through the mountains of northern Alabama in the late spring of 1863. °When the two forces finally faced each other, Forrest was at the

Braxton Bragg won his greatest victory at Chickamauga on September 20, 1863, but then failed to capitalize on it. The Union army under William S. Rosecrans pulled back to Lee and Gordon's Mills (left) and then retreated to Chattanooga. The only Confederate force to press the pursuit was Forrest's cavalry; Bragg was in no hurry to follow the Federals, which allowed Rosecrans to regroup in Tennessee. Forrest was ordered to prevent reinforcements from arriving from Knoxville, but he annoyed Bragg by pursuing a Union detachment that was being sent for just that purpose. As a result, Bragg ordered Forrest to relinquish most of his troops to Joseph Wheeler for a raid on Rosecrans. With no troops to command, Forrest took a brief leave and contemplated resigning his commission when orders arrived from Bragg placing him under Wheeler's command.

Infuriated by the actions of Bragg (above), Forrest went to the general's Missionary Ridge headquarters and verbally accosted him. Listing a series of grievances, he announced that he would no longer obey Bragg's orders and even threatened him, saying, "If you ever again try to interfere with me or cross my path it will be at the peril of your life." He demanded a transfer, which Bragg passed on to Richmond. It was approved by Jefferson Davis after the president traveled to Bragg's headquarters to quell a mutiny among his generals.

There is no more controversial event in Forrest's career than his assault on Fort Pillow. The debate continues whether the affair in April 1864 was a massacre or a normal military action. Forrest's failure to control his men's unbridled fury toward primarily African-American and Tennessee Unionist troops constitutes the blackest mark on his record.

ECB head of a force of six hundred men and Streight had fifteen hundred. The two met under a flag of truce, and Forrest stood so that Streight could see troops and artillery marching around a nearby hill. This prompted the Federal to ask how many men Forrest had with him, and Forrest answered by claiming to have enough to handle the situation.° °Streight was half-convinced that he was outnumbered and so he surrendered his force.° When the deception was exposed, Forrest was alleged to have said, "Ah, Colonel, all's fair in love and war, you know."

WJR °If he could use intimidation or bluff, Forrest would. It was a tactic that all soldiers wanted to use but did not have the courage to try.° Forrest not only intimidated the enemy, but also not a few Confederates. His own troops feared his explosive temper, as did some of his commanding officers. At one moment the mercurial Forrest could be a soft-spoken gentleman and the next—usually in the face of a perceived challenge—an overbearing bully of homicidal rage, capable of anything.

JMM °Braxton Bragg was a case in point. Following the battle of Chickamauga in September 1863, Bragg failed to follow up his victory by pushing on and attacking the Union forces again at Chattanooga before they could regroup. Forrest lost his temper° and threatened Bragg, saying, "You have played the part of a damn scoundrel,

and are a coward, and if you were any part of a man I would slap your jaws and force you to resent it. . . . I say to you that if you ever again try to interfere with me or cross my path it will be at the peril of your life." Forrest never served under Bragg again nor was his insubordination punished. °Bragg knew that Forrest would have no compunction about killing him, so Bragg let the matter drop.°

Two weeks after his outburst Forrest met with Confederate President Jefferson Davis and obtained his consent to transfer to the West. There Forrest would be free to operate in and around Union lines in northern Mississippi and western Tennessee.

FORREST WAS EQUALLY successful in his new area of operation. In his memoirs, Sherman wrote: "I wanted to destroy General Forrest who was constantly threatening Memphis and the river above as well as our route to supplies in Middle Tennessee. In this we failed utterly."

Forrest was awesome in ability and unorthodox in his behavior. For him winning was everything, and war was not the place to be a gentleman. Earning the animosity of his Union enemies paid a high dividend, and Forrest was promoted to major general in December 1863. Major General Forrest, however, is not remembered for the success he achieved in the first quarter of 1864. Rather his notoriety stems from the massacre that occurred on April 12 at Fort Pillow, Tennessee.

°Originally a Confederate fort, Fort Pillow was one of several forts on the Mississippi River established early in the war to protect the flow of supplies on the river. In the spring of 1864 it was garrisoned by about six hundred Federals, including three hundred blacks, most of whom were former slaves, and three hundred whites, all of whom were Tennessee Unionists.

In a four-page letter written to his sister, Achilles V. Clark of Forrest's command suggested that the affair at Fort Pillow was brought about when the Federal troops refused to surrender the fort. "Our men were so exasperated by the Yankee's threats of no quarter that they gave but little. The slaughter was awful—Words cannot describe the scene. . . . I with several others tried to stop the butchery and at one point had partially succeeded—but Gen. Forrest ordered them shot down like dogs and the carnage continued. Finally our men became sick of blood and the firing ceased."

Forrest seemingly was adept with any weapon in either hand. Accounts of him in combat contain reports of his using rifles, revolvers, and sabers effectively. In hand-to-hand fighting, there were few Federals who could match the pistols carried by Forrest's men. This 1851 Colt Navy pistol was used by Forrest himself.

Forrest and most of his men were enraged by the use of black troops against them,• and the idea that some Tennesseans sided with the Union was equally

BP repugnant. °These Yankee Tennesseans had been dubbed by Forrest's men "homegrown Yanks," and they had no small amount of contempt for these—in their view—turncoats.•

Within five hours his men had worked their way close to the fort. Forrest issued his usual demand for the Federals' surrender, promising fair treatment and adding, "Should my demand be refused, I cannot be responsible for the fate of your command."

BP °As negotiations progressed between the lines, the Confederates worked still closer to the fort.• Finally the Federals refused to surrender, and Forrest gave the order for his men to charge. Significantly, Forrest did not lead the assault as was his custom.

WS °There was minimal fighting before the fort was breached, but the Confederate troops randomly went about shooting up the garrison, many of whom were trying to surrender.• One Confederate sergeant recalled: "The poor, deluded Negroes would run up to our men, fall upon their knees and with uplifted hands scream for mercy, but they were ordered to their feet and then shot down. The white men fared little better."

Another Confederate soldier recounted a similar

JMM story. °He had no agenda, no ax to grind, and he admired Forrest. He said that he tried to stop the slaughter but Forrest came up and said, "No, no. Shoot them down like dogs."•

BP   °All the rage that possessed these Southern soldiers at the sight of other Tennesseans in blue uniforms and, worst of all in their minds, blacks in blue uniforms came to the surface. Whether Forrest ordered it or not, and that is still debated, he certainly watched as the slaughter went on. The kindest thing that can be said is that he lost control of his men. By the time the shooting stopped, hundreds of Union soldiers had been killed, many of them after they had surrendered.•

Many Northerners believed that Forrest ordered the massacre. A congressional committee that investigated

JMM   the incident reached that same conclusion. °The only thing Forrest said about it was in his official report on the capture in which he said something to the effect that the action would be a lesson to the North that black troops could not stand up against Southerners. He admitted that a great many blacks had been killed, but his report claimed that they had been killed in the battle or while they were trying to run away. It was clear from the evidence, however, that others were shot

In February 1864, William Sooy Smith led 7,000 Federal horsemen on a large-scale raid into Mississippi that was to link up with another raiding force led by Sherman. Smith's troopers were late, arriving at Okolona, Mississippi, and began the job of wrecking the railroad there. When Smith realized he had missed the opportunity to join Sherman, he retraced his line of march back to Memphis. Forrest's cavalry of 2,500 men slammed into the Federals on February 22, but Smith's troopers withstood several assaults. Forrest's younger brother, Jeffrey, was killed leading one of the assaults, and an enraged Forrest led the following charge against the center of the Union line, which broke and scattered. The Yanks reformed, and Forrest charged alone into them. Col. Robert McCulloch brought his troopers up to join their commander. The Federals fell back, and Forrest charged again. The fighting turned to hand-to-hand, and the Northerners withdrew to Memphis, disheartened and panic-stricken.

In September 1864 Forrest staged a daring raid on Memphis with the goal of freeing prisoners from Irving Prison and capturing three generals: R. P. Buckland, who commanded the Memphis garrison; Stephen A. Hurlbut, former commander of the West Tennessee District; and Cadwallader C. Washburn, the current West Tennessee district commander. Although he succeeded in none of these goals, he did capture four hundred prisoners with whom he bargained for supplies from Washburn.

deliberately as they tried to surrender. Confederate soldiers flatly refused to take them prisoner.°

BSW Most historians doubt Forrest planned the taking of Fort Pillow to be a massacre but believe he did little to stop the slaughter once it started. °If Forrest were upset at what happened at Fort Pillow, he was upset because he lost control, not because of what happened. If Forrest had remorse, it was because he had to answer charges, not because of what had happened. His men did what they thought he would have wanted them to do, whether he actually ordered them to do it or not.°

After the Fort Pillow incident Forrest went on to score his greatest victory at Brice's Cross Roads in June 1864. In frustration, Sherman recommended: "Follow Forrest to the death if it costs ten thousand lives and breaks the [Federal] treasury. There will be no peace in Tennessee till Forrest is dead."

Forrest continued to wreak havoc against Union forces, but the situation of the Confederacy had become so dire that no number of daring cavalry raids could alter the inevitable. By the beginning of 1865 it was clear to Forrest that the war was lost. He fought his final battle on April 2 in Selma, Alabama. Having intercepted information regarding Forrest's position and planned movements, Union Gen. James H. Wilson crushed his command.

BP °Just as Forrest had used dismounted cavalry to fight so effectively earlier in the war, now Wilson did the same thing, but Wilson's cavalrymen were armed with

seven-shot Spencers, probably the best weapon of the war. They charged the defenses of Selma and everywhere broke through. It was now Forrest who had to try to cut his way out, and he did, although he was very nearly killed doing so.• As Wilson moved on, the remnants of Forrest's cavalry were regrouping when news arrived of Lee's surrender at Appomattox.

On May 9, Forrest issued a farewell address to his men, saying: "That we are beaten is a self-evident fact. Any further resistance on our part would be justly regarded as a [height] of folly. . . . You have been good soldiers; you can be good citizens. Obey the laws, preserve your honor, and the government to which you have surrendered can afford to be, and will be, magnanimous." It was perhaps the most conciliatory Confederate message of its kind.

Forrest was promoted to brigadier general on July 21, 1862, following his capture of a Union garrison at Murfreesboro, Tennessee. He was appointed a major general on December 4, 1863, after thwarting a Federal attempt to seize the railroad between Chattanooga and Atlanta. On February 28, 1865, Forrest was promoted to lieutenant general after John Bell Hood's ill-fated Tennessee campaign. This hand-sewn gilt collar insignia was removed from Forrest's uniform by his family prior to his burial.

AFTER THE WAR Forrest quickly evolved into a forward-looking businessman rather than a backward-looking autocrat. He said: "I did all in my power to break up the government but I found it a useless undertaking and I now resolve to stand by the government as earnestly and honestly as I fought it. I'm also aware that I am at

During four years of war, twenty-nine horses were alleged to have been shot from under Forrest, and he claimed to have killed a man for each horse lost. After the war, a group of Union soldiers approached his home and were attacked by his old warhorse, King Philip, who rushed at their blue uniforms and tried to bite them. As they defended themselves, one of Forrest's servants ran out to protect the horse. In the subsequent conversation with the general, one of the officers of the party said that he now understood how Forrest had achieved his remarkable war record: "Your negroes fight for you, and your horses fight for you."

Forrest returned to Memphis after the war. While many viewed him as an unreformed Rebel or looked to him for leadership in resisting Reconstruction, he wanted only to return to business.

There is little doubt that Forrest played some role in the Ku Klux Klan, although he called for its dissolution when he saw that its terror campaign had little effect. This night rider was captured and then posed for his captors.

this moment regarded in large communities of the North with abhorrence as a detestable monster, ruthless and swift to take life."

At the war's end Forrest returned to his cotton plantation to resume his life as a planter. He also became involved in more ominous Reconstruction activities. He joined the Ku Klux Klan and is reputed to have been its grand wizard, although he never admitted it. In many ways the Klan was a continuation of Confederate guerrilla operations. Now, however, they were being carried out against political efforts to reconstruct the South rather than military efforts to defeat it.

The Klan's purpose was to intimidate Republican voters and Republican leaders and, secondarily, to control the black population that had been granted political rights in the South. So the Klan became a night-riding organization that would abduct individual Republican leaders, black and white, and flog them or sometimes shoot them.

Through the Klan Forrest was able to use whatever means he deemed necessary—violence or intimidation, the very things he had done on the frontier—to maintain the South as he wanted it, as a place where white supremacy retained control and power. If the radicals wanted to change it, then he was willing to fight them as he had done during the war.

While he never acknowledged being its leader, Forrest did claim that he ordered the Klan's dissolution in 1869. It became apparent that the federal government planned to use military force to subdue the Klan, which over time had become more violent than even Forrest could tolerate. He withdrew from the Klan. The last eight years of his life he repeatedly criticized and scorned the violent racial animosities and oppressions practiced by the Klan.

Two years later Congress set up a committee to investigate Klan violence. The committee had considerable circumstantial evidence that Forrest was involved with the Klan, at least for a time in the West Tennessee area, so he was subpoenaed to testify. He, of course, denied any knowledge of or involvement with the Klan.

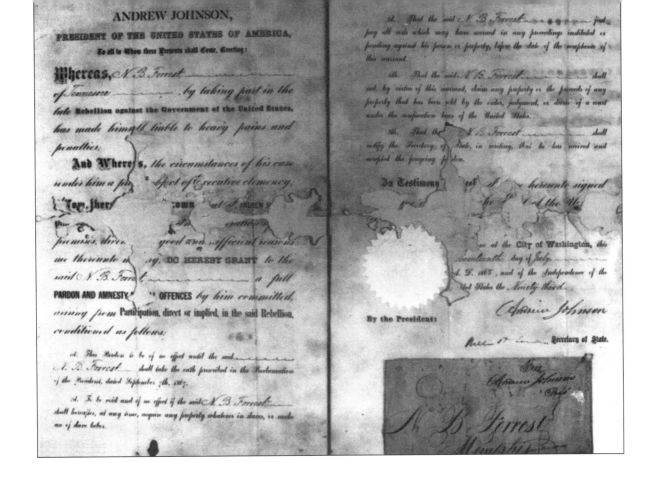

Forrest's business ventures floundered after the war. In 1867 he became president of the Planter's Insurance Company, but the following year he filed for bankruptcy. Because of his role in the Confederacy, Forrest was stripped of his rights as a U.S. citizen. In the summer of 1868 those rights were restored, and he was pardoned by President Andrew Johnson. For six years following his pardon, he served as president of the Selma, Marion, and Memphis Railroad, but in 1874 he resigned from the debt-ridden company. Plagued by ill health and huge debts, Forrest lay dying in Memphis on October 29, 1877.

One of the last men to call on him was Jefferson Davis, but the ailing cavalryman hardly recognized the former president of the Confederacy. At about seven o'clock that night, Forrest uttered his last words. Unlike Stonewall Jackson, Robert E. Lee, and others in the pantheon of Civil War heroes, he did not refer to a scene of distant battle. Characteristically, his last words were a command: "Call my wife."

At war's end Forrest was anxious for a presidential pardon. Because he had been a high-ranking Confederate officer and had owned property before the war that was worth more than twenty thousand dollars, he had to apply directly to the president. The greatest obstacle was the legacy of the Fort Pillow massacre; however, he found influential friends to intercede for him with Andrew Johnson, whose lame duck administration had nothing to lose by granting it.

He was eulogized throughout the country by both friend and foe. Sherman called him "the most remarkable man" the war produced, with "a genius for strategy which was original and . . . to me incomprehensible. . . . He seemed always to know what I was doing or intended to do, while I . . . could never . . . form any satisfactory idea of what he was trying to accomplish."

Forrest found other admirers on the European continent following a magazine profile written by General Viscount Wolseley, retired commander of Great Britain's army. He pointed out that Forrest was more a leader of mounted infantry than cavalry, describing them as dragoons who used horses to reach an objective and dismounted to fight a pitched battle rather than make one or two charges through the enemy. Regarding Forrest's lack of formal military education, he noted, "[Forrest's] operations . . . seem as if designed by a military professor, so thoroughly are the tactics . . . in accordance with common sense and business principles."

Today there are a variety of opinions concerning the overall accomplishments of the man known as the Wizard of the Saddle. Professionally, he is considered the greatest American cavalryman of all time. In the face of superior numbers, he attacked and seized the initiative, which, once gained, he pursued relentlessly. The man who had so little education is now studied by soldiers as part of their military training.

WJR Personally, °he was either admired or despised. He had many admirable qualities: his genius, his instinctiveness, his intelligence, his coolness on the battlefield. Yet he also had many damnable qualities.• °To women he was probably the quintessential southern gentleman, but to anyone whom he considered an inferior he could be violent or even deadly.• °At the very least he was a man who should be respected for what he did in the context of nineteenth-

BSW

WS

The financial well-being Forrest had known before the war remained only a memory. He returned to his plantation with seven former Union officers as partners and had little trouble in hiring laborers, but when he pursued more lucrative projects, such as the insurance business and a Memphis paving project, they failed. In 1868 he filed for bankruptcy in the district court in Memphis; the U.S. marshal's warrant reproduced here indicates that the former general owed debts in excess of $150,000.

Forrest went through many postwar business ventures, but his most exhausting was that as chief executive officer of the Selma, Marion, and Memphis Railroad. He supervised every phase of the construction, maintenance, and daily operation of the line, but he conducted business as he had everything else in his life—according to his own headstrong, independent way. He sold bonds like the one reproduced here to finance construction. The line was marred by occasional accidents, slow construction progress, and a generally weak financial condition. In 1873 poor cash flow halted construction, and in 1874 hard economic times forced him to relinquish control of the railroad.

century America. He should not be judged entirely by today's standards because he most certainly was a product of the time and era in which he lived.•

Most Southern generals rose to legendary status on the merits of their high ideals, unflinching morality, and impeccable behavior, but alongside Lee, Jackson, and Longstreet, there was the less polished, more rugged Nathan Bedford Forrest. He became the mythical figure for the proud Rebels who never gave up the cause. What they failed to perceive is that, rather than looking back at the Old South, Forrest had glimpsed and placed his hope in the New South.

JOHN S. MOSBY

Few CIVIL WAR figures are more colorful and mysterious than John S. Mosby. As commander
of an irregular group of Confederate partisans known as
Mosby's Rangers, he wreaked havoc behind enemy lines
during the last half of the war. His men struck swiftly
and ferociously, routing Federal cavalry, disrupting communications, appropriating supplies, then vanishing
into a sympathetic section of northern Virginia called
Mosby's Confederacy. Never caught, never surrendered,
Mosby earned grudging respect from his foes, honor
among his friends, and an enduring legend as the Gray
Ghost of the Confederacy.

Many Southerners sang Mosby's praises. Gen. Jeb
Stuart said: "John S. Mosby has for a long time attracted
the attention of his generals by his boldness, skill, and
success. . . . None knew his daring enterprise and
dashing heroism better than those foul invaders."
Robert E. Lee succinctly noted, "Hurrah for Mosby!"

Northerners damned him as a dangerous foe. Col.
Charles Russell Lowell of the Second Massachusetts
Cavalry, the unit that probably pursued Mosby's Rangers
more than any other, stated, "Mosby . . . is an old rat
and has a great many holes." Philip Sheridan voiced
similar frustrations, saying, "Mosby has annoyed me
considerably." Those vexations were so great that
Ulysses S. Grant ordered, "Where any of Mosby's men
are caught, hang them without trial."

Fifteen men formed the first incarnation of Mosby's
Rangers. Within twenty-eight months that unit had
become a battalion of guerrillas working behind the

WCD	William C. Davis
JD	John Divine
BP	Brian Pohanka
JDW	Jeffry D. Wert

Mosby (left) attended the University of Virginia until he killed a man in 1853. He was sentenced to a year's incarceration, but family influence secured a pardon from the governor. During the nine months that he did serve, Mosby began the study of law and continued his training in the office of the prosecutor who had convicted him.

He was admitted to the bar and opened a practice in Howardsville, where he met Pauline Clarke (right). The couple was married December 30, 1857, in a Roman Catholic ceremony in Nashville, Tennessee.

lines in Northern Virginia and one of the most renowned combat units of the Civil War. The partisan rangers struck almost daily, in daylight and in darkness, at outposts, pickets, wagon trains, detachments of troops, headquarters, and railroads. They attacked without warning and then disappeared, fighting with a bravado that evoked both fear and hatred in their opponents. By the end of the war they stood unvanquished. All operations directed against them had failed. When the principal armies of the South capitulated, Mosby disbanded his men rather than surrender. One ranger, John Munson, recalled, "Every affair in which Mosby and his men figured had in it something novel, something romantic, something which is worth the telling." Mosby himself confessed, "The true secret was that it was a fascinating life, and its attractions far more than counterbalanced its hardships and dangers."

Throughout the unit's existence recruits appeared regularly, attracted by the glamour and success of partisan action, the lack of regulations and routine found in the regular army, the opportunity to stay near their homes, and the acquisition of plunder, which was divided equally among the men. They were largely Virginians and Marylanders, and those who failed to adapt to Mosby's discipline and standards were sent on to Lee's Army of Northern Virginia.

While there were several partisan units at one time, the only unit to serve consistently from its inception to the cessation of hostilities was Mosby's, and the one defining component of that command was Mosby him-

WCD self. °The Civil War could not have happened at a better time for him, as indeed it did for many of the men who became its prominent leaders and its lasting legends.

JDW Mosby and the war were meant for each other.• °He was a remarkable warrior, and one who no one suspected would be one of the most famous Confederates of the war when it began in 1861.•

JD There were three elements to his success: °he struck fast and hard, he had the loyalty of his men, and he

BP ruled with an iron hand.• °While it is possible to overemphasize his effect on the course of the war, nonetheless, Mosby was the stuff of romance and an outstanding soldier.•

He was born on December 6, 1833, in Powhatan County, Virginia. His father and mother, Alfred and Virginia Mosby, were native Virginians, as was his grandfa-

WCD ther who had fought in the Revolutionary War. °Despite his diminutive stature he was feisty, and his early record bears that out.•

At the age of nineteen, while a student at the University of Virginia, Mosby shot a man. It was not quite self-defense, but neither was it unwarranted. As a result, Mosby was expelled from school, convicted of unlawful shooting, and jailed for nine months. While there he studied law, and when he was released he became a successful country lawyer.

In 1854 he met Pauline Clark, the daughter of a Kentucky congressman. They married and by 1861 had two children. When the war came, Mosby was twenty-seven years old.

JDW °He was undoubtedly a reluctant soldier. He was not trained to fight, but when the time came, when Virginia seceded, Mosby went.• His first six months of service were under Col. William E. "Grumble" Jones, a respected outpost officer. Those around Private Mosby, however, generously described him as disinterested. William W. Blackford, a member of Jeb Stuart's staff, recalled: "He was rather a slouchy rider, and did not

As a part of the Virginia cavalry, Mosby was under Jeb Stuart's command. Ordered to scout the Manassas battlefield, he found that he had an aptitude for this work. He quickly came to Stuart's attention, who attached Mosby to his staff. The first significant service he performed was a reconnaissance of the Union army during the Peninsula campaign. He returned with the suggestion that Stuart could ride completely around the Federals. Four days later Stuart led twelve hundred men on a four-day raid that gave him an instant reputation. Mosby rode at the head of the column, scouting the roads in advance of Stuart's cavalry.

seem to take any interest in military duties. . . . [W]e all thought he was rather an indifferent soldier."

Mosby was not fond of routine camp life; he preferred assignment to the outposts. From the summer of 1861 through the spring of 1862 he served along the picket line and also scouted. Jones was impressed with the quiet Mosby and installed him as a staff adjutant, but Mosby was not enamored with those new duties. He garnered occasional scouting assignments and caught the eye of General Stuart.

WCD °Stuart was the force behind the making of Mosby. He recognized the young man's ability as an intelligence gatherer. He saw that Mosby was successful at getting behind Yankee lines, getting close enough to Union encampments to note the movements of men and matériel, and returning with the information. Mosby's reports were accurate and timely, he was quick at what he did, and he was as good a scout as Stuart had.•

In June 1862, while Gen. George B. McClellan's Army of the Potomac was marching up the Virginia Peninsula toward Richmond, Mosby brought Stuart a report that changed the course of the war. He had scouted and found that the entire Union body—all one hundred thousand men—could be circled by cavalry in a matter of days. With Lee's approval, Stuart made the spectacular raid with Mosby in the forefront, scouting for Federal units.

To his wife on June 16, 1862, Mosby wrote: "My dearest Pauline, I returned yesterday with General Stuart from the grandest scout of the war. I not only helped to execute it, but was the first one who conceived and demonstrated that it was practicable. Everybody says it was the greatest feat of the war. I never enjoyed myself so much in my life."

JDW °Stuart's ride around McClellan in June 1862 undoubtedly embarrassed McClellan, a man of enormous ego, and it embarrassed the Lincoln administration. In the end it helped lead to McClellan's dismissal.•

The exploit stirred Mosby to request permission to lead a partisan command. In July Stuart balked, but around Christmastime 1862 Mosby pressed again and Stuart consented. On January 1, 1863, Mosby began his partisan ranger career. Stuart knew his scout had been called to partisan life, so to the Confederate faithful of Northern Virginia, he wrote a glowing introduction: "You are all such good Southern people through this section. I think you deserve some protection, so I shall leave Captain Mosby with a few men to take care of you. I want you to do all you can for him. He is a great favorite of mine and a brave soldier, and if my judgment does not err, we shall soon hear something surprising from him."

For the next two and a half years Mosby did not disappoint. His rangers harassed the enemy with deadly impunity while living off Union spoils and the sympathy of the population.

Mosby and his men enjoyed the hospitality of many families throughout the region, and among them was a young
JDW diarist, Tee Edmonds. °In her early twenties, she lived on her family's plantation, Belle Grove, with her mother, Betsey, and her brother Clement. Their home served as a safe place for Mosby's men, and Tee documented the rangers' actions in her diary.• She noted, "The arrival of Mosby's men is like bright sunshine after dark clouds."

Sometime during the winter of 1862 Mosby proposed that a small, independent force could wreak havoc behind enemy lines. Stuart gave him nine men and left them in Loudoun County when the cavalry left for winter quarters near Fredericksburg. At the time Mosby had no plans to organize a partisan command, but the nine-man detail was the beginning of twenty-eight months of raids, ambushes, and attacks against any Union forces that entered a small area that came to be known as Mosby's Confederacy. Five of Mosby's Rangers posed below.

Mosby's most notorious action occurred on March 8, 1863, when he raided the headquarters of Union Col. Sir Percy Wyndham (above). The Britisher had called Mosby a horse thief, and nothing spurred the Virginian to action more than a personalized foe.

Wyndham was away, so Mosby seized Brig. Gen. Edwin H. Stoughton from his bed in the Gunnell House (below), along with two captains, thirty enlisted men, and fifty-eight horses without firing a shot or losing a man.

JDW °Mosby's Confederacy, as it was called during the war, primarily embraced the two counties of Fauquier WCD and Loudoun.• °It was a dense, somewhat wooded tangle, and, to the enemy, a very confusing area.• Mosby himself drew the borders from Snicker's Gap in the Blue Ridge Mountains south to Manassas Gap, then east along some old railroad tracks to the plains, up the crease of the Bull Run Mountains to Aldie, and then back to Snicker's Gap.

WCD °The people of Mosby's Confederacy were over-whelmingly pro-Virginia, pro-Confederacy, and there-fore pro-Mosby. They opened their homes, silos, barns, hayricks, and cellars to Mosby's men, and they fed and hid them. Without this informal civilian volunteer infrastructure, Mosby could not have operated. With the people behind him, he was able to achieve great things.•

Mosby's first great achievement came in March 1863. After a series of successful raids around Washington, he had drawn the ire of a British soldier of fortune, Col. Sir JDW Percy Wyndham, who °charged Mosby with being a horse thief. Mosby of course resented the allegation and decided to capture the Englishman. On the night of March 8, 1863, he gathered twenty-nine of his men, virtually his entire command at the time. From scouting reports he had learned that he could cross the Union lines and reach Fairfax Court House, the site of Wyndham's headquarters, with little opposition. Once there, however, they discov-ered that Wyndham was in Washington, but Brig. Gen. Edwin Stoughton, whose infantry brigade was camped around Fairfax Court House, was in town.•

Twenty-three-year-old Stoughton was a West Point graduate with a reputation as a drinker and a womanizer. That Sunday night he had hosted a cham-JDW pagne party. °Mosby found him sound asleep and, according to Mosby, pulled the covers back, lifted Stoughton's nightshirt, and spanked him with the broad side of his sword. Stoughton bolted upright in bed, and Mosby asked, "Do you know Mosby?"

Stoughton groggily replied, "Yes, have you captured him?" "No," Mosby answered, "but he has captured you." From that moment on, Mosby was one of the most famous soldiers in America.•

WCD BY CAPTURING A Yankee general from his sleep, two captains, thirty privates, and fifty horses, Mosby covered himself with glory. °The news was played up in both Northern and Southern newspapers. Mosby found that he had a large following in the Northern press, as did several Confederate officers, but Mosby was probably the only Confederate officer below the rank of general who was widely known in the North, because his exploits found a readership.•

In Richmond he was ordained a Southern knight and officially commissioned a major by General Lee's order. In Washington, Mosby became so feared that each night soldiers took the wooden planks off the bridge connecting Virginia to the capital so Mosby would not kidnap Lincoln.

JDW °Mosby delighted in the perception that the Federal government feared him. He welcomed anything that brought him fame or attention. When he saw the news story reporting that planks were removed regularly from the bridge out of fear of him, he must have been amused.•

Lincoln saw the humor in it, too. Regarding the Stoughton raid, he said, "I don't mind the loss of the brigadier as much as the horses. I can make a much better general in five minutes, but the horses cost $125 apiece."

Despite his notoriety, Mosby continued to capture prisoners, horses, arms, and supplies. He cut telegraph lines and picked off stray messengers, patrols, and stragglers. With each phantomlike strike, frustration turned to hatred in the soldiers whose unlucky duty it was to chase him. Sometimes Mosby ambushed his pursuers, and always he eluded capture. Out of fear and

Mosby's tactics were simple: to fight meant to attack, and success was contingent on surprise. When the signal was given, the rangers charged en masse, firing Colt pistols, with Mosby in the midst of it all. The combat was measured in minutes. If the fight went against them, then each man found his own way out of the engagement.

The rangers were a viable partisan command because of their ability to disappear, to blend in with the people of the countryside. There were no camps, no headquarters in the traditional sense. Instead, Mosby's command depended on safe houses, homes that took in one or two of the rangers and their horses in return for supplies gathered from the raids. When Federal raiding parties threatened these homes, the rangers took to the woods in which they constructed huts like the one above or "shebangs," a pole structure covered with limbs.

frustration, the Union commanders called him a murderous coward who avoided a fair fight. That perception changed on April Fools Day 1863, following an encounter at Miskel's farm in Loudoun County.

°The entire affair was a mistake on Mosby's part. He had ridden into a potential trap, camping at Miskel's farm at the junction of Broad Run and the Potomac.• The next morning the rangers awoke to the charge of the First Vermont Cavalry, which outnumbered them three to one. °From the Federal perspective, Mosby's men were trapped. The bluecoats charged into the barnyard with sabers and pistols against men armed only with pistols.•

Ranger John Munson recalled: "Mosby at once mounted, and the Mosby yell—to which no person has yet been able to do full justice—rose on the wings of that memorable morning." °The commander of the Union detachment was shot and killed immediately. The front element was broken by the gunfire of Mosby's men, and then Mosby shouted for a counterattack. They turned what looked like sure defeat into a stunning victory and then chased some of the Federals for miles. The Union army—and the First Vermont was a good unit—learned that it had a formidable foe in Mosby.•

The fight at Miskel's farm very nearly ended Mosby's rangers. A group of seventy rangers and Mosby had spent the night in the barn; they were awakened the next morning by charging Federal cavalry. The massed firing of the rangers stopped the attackers, and then Mosby led his men in a charge that scattered the Union horseman.

JD   °Mosby too learned a lesson: never camp in a place with only one entrance. He also learned that he had several reliable lieutenants under him.• Tee Edmonds recalled: "I was walking in the garden, and seeing a string of rebels coming down, I soon discovered the plumed fellow at the gate. I knew then it was our squad returning. Up they came after having a rough, tough time with the Yanks, who got them in rather a tight spot. However, all returned safe and sound."

When news spread of the fight at Miskel's farm, men WCD flocked to join Mosby's Rangers. °During the course of the war, more than a thousand men at one time or another served with him. They had to follow orders, and they had to be excellent horsemen. By and large, they JD were very young.• °They rode as if they had been born to the saddle. Many had been hunters most of their lives, having learned the skill from their fathers. They were WCD daredevils,• °but they also had to be discreet. They had to guard what they said, and above all they had to follow orders, because Mosby could be an iron disciplinarian.•

At least nineteen hundred men served in Mosby's command from January 1863 to April 1865, but he rarely gathered more than three hundred at a time for a mission—a larger group would have been more easily detected. Virginians overwhelmingly filled the ranks, with Marylanders providing the second largest contingent, attracted by the proximity of the battalion to their homes and the glamorous reputation of the rangers. Some recruits came from Canada, England, Scotland, and Ireland. Others were Northerners from New York, New Jersey, and Pennsylvania. In explaining why so many came from such distances to join him, Mosby said, "The true secret was that it was a fascinating life and its attractions far more than counterbalanced its hardships and dangers."

The portrait of Mosby charging into action with a plumed hat and scarlet-lined cape by Louis Mathieu Didier Guillaume is largely artistic license. While the rangers were "a lot of dandies" by their own admission, the garish uniforms and hats with ostrich feathers and gold braid were reserved for special occasions that might attract impressionable young women. Mosby dressed colorfully when he was called to Lee's headquarters, probably to make an impression on his commander and on the regular Confederate troops. In combat the rangers wore something gray, plain jackets and pants that were typical of Confederate cavalrymen.

JDW °Mosby was not what most people would call a warrior. He was five seven or five eight and weighed no JD more than 128 pounds.° °Just about every man in his organization could have bested him in a rough-and-tumble fight, but his greatest asset was his eyes. Several people mentioned that he could stare a hole through a person. Once he gave a man a stern look, that man obeyed.° His eyes were blue, luminous, piercing. When Mosby's eyes flashed, remarked John Esten Cooke, a member of Stuart's staff, they "might have induced the opinion that there was something in the man, if only it had an opportunity to 'come out.'" "When he spoke," ranger John Munson added, "[his eyes] flashed the punctuations of his sentences."

JDW °The popular image of Mosby's Rangers was of men with plumed hats and capes, particularly red-lined capes. As one of his men said, "We were a lot of dandies."° Their uniforms, however, generally meant "something gray"—plain jackets and pants comparable to those of a Confederate cavalryman. The trimmings, the braid and the capes, were reserved for special occasions—portraits, dances, or events that tended to attract young impressionable women. Vanity, however, gave way to practicality, and all knew that red-lined capes made conspicuous targets in the field.

Two items were indispensable to the rangers: horses and pistols. If a prospective recruit could not provide his own horse, he was not allowed to join the rangers. Each man had at least two mounts, and many had more. They maintained their supply of horses from the local farms, an area well known for the quality of its horses, and from the capture of Union mounts.

Regarding their armament, each man carried pistols, the ideal weapon for the type of combat in which they engaged, and a few carried carbines. Mosby considered the saber an outdated weapon and useless in cavalry fighting. He boasted: "My men were as little impressed by a body of cavalry charging them with sabers as though they had been armed with cornstalks. My command reached the highest point of efficiency as cavalry because they were well armed with two six shooters. I think we did more than any other body of men to give the Colt pistol its great reputation. We did not pay for them, but the U.S. Government did."

While the Colt was not a particularly accurate weapon and had a tendency to shoot high, the rangers practiced frequently and were decent marksmen. John Munson remembered: "It was no uncommon thing for one of our men to gallop by a tree at full tilt and put three bullets into its trunk in succession. This sort of shooting left the enemy with a good many empty saddles after an engagement."

JD °Many Federal units that engaged Mosby's men thought the devil himself had hit them. When a swarm of screaming young men suddenly appeared in their midst, firing pistols and riding through them like daredevils, the disciplined Union soldiers often broke in panic.• Just as quickly as they struck, the rangers would disappear.

WCD °The men who enlisted to fight with Mosby knew the people and the landscape around them, placing them in perfect position after a raid to melt into the terrain or into the night. On issuing a call, they could be brought together again to rendezvous at a certain point for a given task, which made them extremely difficult for the Federals to track down or apprehend. Mosby was gifted with a genius for that kind of warfare.• He explained: "My men had no camps. . . . They would scatter for safety and gather at my call like Children of the Mist."

ON JUNE 10, 1863, six months after becoming a partisan ranger, Mosby formally organized the Forty-third Battalion of Virginia Cavalry. It was very nearly a shortlived command.

JDW °Mosby's wife, Pauline, was visiting him at the time, staying at the home of James and Elizabeth Hathaway, and Mosby had joined her there.• On the evening of

The rangers carried pistols, which were ideal for the type of combat in which they engaged. Some carried carbines, but there was only one story of a ranger using a saber, and that was to prod a Yankee from beneath a wagon. To a man, they used the six-shot, single action .44 caliber Army Colt revolver, which they acquired from captured Federal cavalrymen. They wore a brace of pistols in two holsters, and many also had a pair in saddle holsters and additional loaded cylinders stored for rapid reloads.

At the right is the first of a series of three paintings depicting the Berryville raid of August 13, 1864, which was Mosby's first action against Philip Sheridan. In this opening scene, one of Mosby's scouts, John S. Russell, informed him that a Federal wagon train was on the turnpike between Harpers Ferry and Winchester. Mosby is on horseback on the right, with his staff officers behind him—Samuel Chapman, J. Richard Sowers, A. G. Babcock, and Thomas Booker.

One of the chroniclers of Mosby's Rangers was twenty-three-year-old Amanda Virginia "Tee" Edmonds (below). The Edmonds family's farm, Belle Grove, served as a refuge for several of Mosby's men. Her diary provides an account of the battlefield feats of the rangers, noting card games, meals, flirtations, dances, horseplay, and infatuations. Several rangers found their brides in Mosby's Confederacy.

June 11 they had unexpected visitors in the form of a Yankee patrol. °The Union cavalrymen entered the house with questions about Mosby, and they began to search the residence room by room.•

Capt. William H. Boyd of the First New York Cavalry reported: "Every nook from basement to attic was explored, but Mosby had left a few minutes before we reached the place. We found Mrs. Mosby in no pleasant humor because the slumbers of herself and her husband had been broken by Yankee cavalry. Mrs. Mosby is decidedly handsome and converses with more than ordinary intelligence, but is very unkindly disposed toward Northerners."

°When the Union soldiers had entered the Hathaway house, Mosby had exited through a window and climbed onto a limb of a nearby walnut tree. He clung there as the Federals searched his room, questioned Pauline, and walked beneath him. When they left, he crawled back into the house and went to bed again with Pauline.•

°Chasing Mosby was extremely frustrating work, and anyone who ever tried to catch the Gray Ghost found that the task was an almost impossible feat.• Col. Charles Russell Lowell of the Second Massachusetts Cavalry wrote: "I do not fancy the duty here, serving against bushwhackers. It brings me in contact with too many citizens,

The third painting in the Berryville raid trio (left) depicts the return from the raid. The rangers had seized about two hundred cattle, one hundred wagons, as many as six hundred horses and mules, and two hundred prisoners. In the wagons they found rations for themselves and their mounts and several fiddles, but no one saw a paymaster's chest containing $112,000. After removing whatever valuable supplies they found, the wagons were torched. Mosby's men were in high spirits as they returned, and the fiddles were used to entertain the group. The men divided the horses among themselves, and Mosby sent the cattle and mules to Richmond. A half-hour after leaving the scene, the First Rhode Island arrived and extinguished the fires, saving the paymaster's chest in the process.

BP and sometimes with mothers and children." °Lowell had once referred to Mosby as an old rat with a good many holes. His frustration was that Mosby's "holes" were in fact the sympathies of the local population.•

After his narrow escape, Mosby lay low. With Lee moving through the Shenandoah toward Pennsylvania and the Union army shadowing his march just east of the Blue Ridge, too many Yankee soldiers were in Mosby's Confederacy. Once again, though, Stuart called on Mosby to scout for him.

JDW °Ironically, it was Mosby's information that helped sway Stuart in June 1863 to get permission from Lee to ride around the Federal army in the midstages of the Gettysburg campaign.• Mosby told Stuart his best route to Pennsylvania was through a break in the Union column at Thoroughfare Gap.

JDW °Unfortunately, Mosby's intelligence was dated, and he had not seen all the elements of the army in the march at that time.• Stuart found the gap had closed and was forced to detour around the Union flank. The error cost him two days, and thus his cavalry arrived late for the battle of Gettysburg. While many criticized Stuart for his late arrival, Mosby defended him to his grave.

As quickly as the battle of Gettysburg changed Confederate fortunes, so the luck of Mosby's Rangers changed. In August 1863 Mosby was seriously wounded, shot in the thigh and the groin. He was disabled for nearly a month. °During that time he turned command over to his subordinates, and there is evidence that discipline was lax whenever Mosby was away. It was his personality that held the command together.•

Mosby returned in the fall, organized two new companies in the battalion, and renewed the business of harassing the Union rear. By the end of his first year as a partisan commander, he had suffered casualties but few real defeats. With the dawn of a new year, fate dealt Mosby a cruel hand.

°The worst defeat suffered by Mosby's Rangers during the war occurred on the bitterly cold night of January 10, 1864, at Loudoun Heights, the mountain above Harpers Ferry, Virginia. Mosby's men had learned that they could attack the camp of the First Maryland Cavalry, Potomac Home Brigade—known as Cole's Cavalry after their commander, Maj. Henry A. Cole. This Union command operated from a base camp on the heights and had opposed Mosby's Rangers in earlier operations.•

Mosby was at the head of a column of one hundred men. He deployed a squad of ten men to seize the camp's headquarters, but at the critical moment when the squad moved on its target, Mosby's main body mistook it for a Federal party that had discovered the Confederates. The confusion ruined Mosby's surprise, and Cole's Cavalry mounted a crushing counterattack.

°In the action on Loudoun Heights Mosby lost four men killed and four mortally wounded. Most critically, Mosby lost First Lt. William Thomas Turner, known as "Fighting Tom" to the rangers, and Capt. William E. "Billy" Smith. At that time, Smith and Turner were regarded as the two most efficient officers in the battalion—the first to go into battle and the last to leave.•

Wagon trains were regular targets. On July 13, 1863, Mosby reported to Stuart that he had captured 29 sutler's wagons near Fairfax, along with 100 prisoners and 140 horses. The wagons were loaded with food, tobacco, cloth, cutlery, illegal alcohol, newspapers, and books. Instead of destroying the wagons, Mosby redirected them to Middleburg, but the Second Massachusetts Cavalry pursued the rangers and overtook the slow-moving convoy at Aldie. The outnumbered rangers had little choice but to abandon the booty and flee. One of them groaned that with the 29 wagons they could have opened the first department store in Mosby's Confederacy.

As George Meade pursued Lee following the battle of Gettysburg, the Federals occupied most of Mosby's operating theater, disrupting his pattern of activity for the next two months. He responded by initiating a wagon campaign against Meade's army. Sometimes the seized goods were shared with the escorts that were captured with the wagons, sometimes the wagons were recaptured. Lee voiced his only criticism of Mosby during this campaign, seeing no military reason for it. Mosby's losses were higher than normal, perhaps due to the fact that the same cavalry that had recaptured the wagons at Aldie consistently pursued Mosby's Rangers in this campaign. When Mosby was wounded and out of action for almost a month, the campaign continued, but mostly out of a quest for plunder. Harper's depicted the recapture of one of Meade's supply trains (left).

Tee Edmonds recalled: "Oh, the sad intelligence the remaining portions of Mosby's command bring back. The attack made last night near Harpers Ferry came out with the loss of two of his best men. Truly, the suffering of the South will never end." Mosby himself reported: "My loss was severe; more so in the worth than the number of the slain. Among those who fell were two of the noblest and bravest officers of this army, who thus sealed a life of devotion and of sacrifice to the cause they loved."

THE DEBACLE OF Loudoun Heights devastated Mosby and his men. More than any other skirmish it ended all the romantic notions of war and became the terrible harbinger of coming cruelties. The year 1864 would be long, bloody, and bitter for Mosby's Rangers.

That winter Mosby suspended most ranger operations. In March, Grant became commander of the Union army. Then came May and the death of Stuart at Yellow Tavern. Lee had lost the eyes of his army, and Mosby had lost his best friend in the war.

°The two were close, and Stuart's death, as Mosby said in his memoirs, was a crushing blow to him:• "After General Lee lost Stuart, he had no chief of cavalry. No one was there who could bend the bow of Ulysses." Following Stuart's death, Mosby began report-

WCD

The Hathaway home (right) was the site of another Mosby legend. Informed that he would be staying there with his wife, cavalrymen of the First New York searched the house. All they found were James and Elizabeth Hathaway, Pauline Mosby, and a pair of spurs belonging to Mosby. James Hathaway was arrested and the Federals departed. Meanwhile, in the upstairs bedroom, Pauline opened the window and her husband crawled back inside. Upon the arrival of the New Yorkers, he had dressed and climbed out on a limb of a large walnut tree next to the house. From his perch he had seen his wife interrogated and watched the troopers who had not entered the house as they searched the grounds for him, not once looking up.

ing directly to Lee, the only commander of a unit below corps level to do so.

WCD   In August 1864 °Sheridan came into the Valley of Virginia with a mandate to clear it of all Southern forces and to eliminate it as the granary of the Confederacy and as an invasion route for Rebel armies. He excelled in this task, and it was apparent at the outset that he did not regard Mosby as a threat. He quickly learned, however, that Mosby, while his command was small in numbers, was strong in the Valley.•

On a sweltering August morning, just six days after Sheridan had arrived in the Shenandoah, Mosby attacked Sheridan's supply wagons. In the rocky, rolling meadows near Berryville, Virginia, he burned eighty wagons carrying rations for the Federal cavalry. Known as "the Berryville wagon raid" to the rangers, the action infuriated Sheridan, who ordered immediate reprisals.

JDW   °Sheridan's troops carried out their orders to destroy as much as they could, and in August and September they destroyed crops and burned barns. In retaliation, when Mosby's men captured barn burners, they summarily executed them. Sheridan reported these things to Grant, and Grant responded: "The families of most of Mosby's men are known and can be collected. I think they should be taken and kept at Fort McHenry, or some secure place, as hostages for the good conduct of

Mosby and his men. Where any of Mosby's men are caught hang them without trial."•

Shortly after sending his reply to Sheridan, Grant sent a second telegram in which he suggested: "If you can possibly spare a division of cavalry, send them through Loudoun County, to destroy and carry off the crops, animals, negroes, and all men under fifty years of age capable of bearing arms. In this way you will get many of Mosby's men."

Evidently Sheridan did not convey Grant's orders to hang Mosby's men to his commanders. While he was frustrated by Mosby's actions, he knew that reprisals would be met with reprisals and Mosby could execute more of his men than he could of Mosby's.

°The Federals now viewed Mosby as a very dangerous man. There were substantiated stories of his being personally involved in combat and in killing men by his own hand, and that vested him with an aspect of fear that not every enemy leader commanded.•

On September 14 Mosby's willingness to engage the enemy resulted in another wound. During his two-week

When Sheridan moved into the Shenandoah Valley, Mosby threw all his men and resources into any operation that would frustrate the Federals. He had six companies, a steady source of recruits, and skilled and experienced officers. Thus he could divide his force into two or three attack groups, which extended his theater of operations and allowed him to threaten Sheridan's communications. Sheridan, however, was focused on Jubal Early's army, but knowing that he could not overlook Mosby, he authorized a special one-hundred-man unit under Capt. Richard Blazer to emulate Mosby's tactics and eliminate the rangers. After one month's operation Blazer's scouts had ambushed a small unit of rangers and wounded Mosby.

On September 23, 1864, while Mosby recuperated from yet another wound, the rangers stumbled into two divisions of Sheridan's cavalry. A whirlwind of action swarmed around them, and each man fought his way out as best he could. None were killed, but the Federals, who did have casualties, captured six. One of the dead was Lt. Charles McMaster, but before he died he reported that he had been shot after surrendering; the six rangers were executed.

Mosby took thirty Union prisoners and had them draw lots from a hat until he had singled out seven men. Four were to be shot and three hanged. Only the three who were to be hanged died. Of the four who were to be shot, two escaped and two were wounded. Mosby wrote Sheridan, promising that he had only avenged his men's executions and that he would treat future prisoners in the same manner in which Sheridan treated his.

absence, ranger Sam Chapman led the partisans. On September 23, while searching for targets of opportunity in the Shenandoah, the rangers accidentally charged the rear of Sheridan's cavalry. °The Federals countercharged and scattered the rangers, turning the action into a running gunfight primarily south and east of Front Royal. During the fighting, Lt. Charles McMaster of the Second U.S. Cavalry was unhorsed.• Before the Federals could rally, McMaster received a fatal head wound.

°In the Confederate version of the attack as submitted by Chapman, McMaster was fighting on foot at the time he was shot. The Federal version argued that McMaster had surrendered and was killed afterward.•

°Six of Mosby's men were captured during the melee. When McMaster's comrades found him, he was still conscious and he said that he had been shot after he had surrendered.• His dying testimony infused Sheridan's cavalry with a vengeance that they swiftly delivered to Mosby's men.

°Tensions had been building between these two commands, and they came to a tragic climax in the streets of Front Royal that day.• Tee Edmonds recalled: "Six of our dear soldiers were captured at Front Royal and were brutally shot. Two of them hung. Poor Tom Anderson met his sad fate there. They pinned a card on his body that said, 'This would be the fate of all Mosby's guerrillas caught hereafter.' Oh, will the grief and mourning of our dear ones never be subdued."

JDW °Mosby was back with his command on September 30 and learned the details of the incident. When he had the opportunity, he rode to Front Royal and ascertained from the townspeople that George Custer had given the order to execute the captured rangers.

Custer, however, had not ordered the executions of Mosby's men even though years after the war Mosby still maintained he was the culprit. If Custer had anything to do with it, he probably concurred in the order, but the person who ordered the action was Gen. Alfred T. A. Torbert.°

BP °The executions seem to have been a haphazard affair. At one point, Torbert was involved in ordering the executions of two of the men. In other cases, it was most likely a decision made on the spot by junior officers. Col. Charles Russell Lowell was present as were Torbert, Custer, and Wesley Merritt.°

On October 5, 1864, Colonel Lowell lamented: "I was sorry enough the other day that my brigade should have had a part in the hanging and shooting of some of Mosby's men. I believe that some punishment was deserved, but I hardly think we were within the laws of war, and any violation of them opens the door for all sorts of barbarity."

The rangers wanted quick revenge, but instead Mosby focused on the war effort. Sheridan was attempting to

Confident of victory in the Shenandoah, Sheridan sent Wesley Merritt's cavalry into the Valley from the Blue Ridge to the Alleghenies, destroying barns, mills, crops, and livestock. The systematic destruction persisted for three days and left the region a barren wasteland. Residents of the Valley remembered it for generations as "the Burning." Throughout the raid, Mosby's Rangers prowled the fringes of the Union squadrons. They could do little but capture or shoot barn burners. Their best retribution was a series of raids that achieved minimal results.

JDW

In response to Mosby's report on his activities of the first half of 1863, Lee responded, "I am much gratified by the activity and skill you have displayed, and desire to express my thanks to yourself and the brave officers and men of your command for the valuable services rendered to the country. The smallness of your loss, in comparison with the damage inflicted upon the enemy, is creditable to your own judgment and to the intelligence and courage of those who executed your orders."

When Sheridan attempted to use the railroad to move men and matériel closer to Grant in Petersburg, Mosby responded by harassing his work details, wrecking sections of track, and derailing locomotives. One such derailment netted $173,000, which the rangers divided, although Mosby took none. The Federals abandoned the railroad project when Sheridan proved victorious in a last clash with Early's Confederates at Cedar Creek in October.

rebuild the Manassas Gap Railroad, which trespassed on Mosby's Confederacy. Mosby was not going to allow that to happen. He staged another spectacular raid.

JDW

°In October, Mosby and eighty men derailed a Baltimore and Ohio train outside Harpers Ferry and captured $173,000. It was called "the greenback raid."• Every man on the raid received $2,100, though Mosby took none. Again he had embarrassed Sheridan, but that same day a seventh ranger was hanged. Mosby decided it was time to stop the bloodbath, so he wrote on October 29, 1864, to General Lee with grim intentions: "It is my purpose to hang an equal number of Custer's men whenever I capture them." Lee approved, and by November 6 Mosby held thirty of Custer's men.

JDW

°The thirty Union prisoners were placed in a line along Goose Creek, which flowed through Rectortown. Mosby, interestingly, stood back; he wanted little part in this. A hat was passed around with slips of paper in it. Seven slips were marked, and whoever pulled out a marked slip would be one of the seven to be executed.• Among the unlucky seven was a teenage drummer boy. Mosby spared him and ordered the others to draw again.

°Mosby ordered three of them hanged, as three of his men had been hanged, and four of them shot. None of the rangers wanted to execute the Federals, but they followed orders. Of the seven condemned men, however, only three died.• Two were shot and lived, two others escaped, but three were hanged. Just as the

Union hangmen had left a note on Mosby's dead, Mosby's men pinned a note to the hanging bodies of the Union dead, which read: "These men have been hung in retaliation for an equal number of Colonel Mosby's men hung by order of General Custer, at Front Royal. Measure for measure."

Mosby was not disappointed when he heard that four had lived. They would carry the grim story back to Sheridan's army, and they did.

DAYS AFTER HIS retaliation, Mosby wrote to Sheridan explaining his actions and requesting an end to the cycle of violence. He said, "Hereafter any prisoners falling into my hands will be treated with the kindness due to their condition, unless some new act of barbarity shall compel me reluctantly to adopt a course of policy repulsive to humanity."

BP   °In a sense, Mosby called Sheridan's bluff because he had retaliated. He made it quite clear by the note that was left with the bodies that at this point he considered the matter closed in an eye-for-an-eye resolution. Nonetheless, Sheridan was enraged and all the more

JD   determined to vanquish Mosby• °and began to burn everything in the Valley.•

For four days in November, Sheridan's cavalry set fire to Mosby's Confederacy. They called it "the burning

WCD   raid," but it did not stop Mosby. °In the end, Sheridan had failed. It was his one great failure of the war.•

In December 1864 Mosby was gravely wounded and rumors of his death circulated for weeks. Then in February 1865 he appeared in Richmond. Although weak and gaunt, he received a hero's welcome.

WCD   °In some ways he was the last hero, and that was the part he continued to play when he delayed so long in capitulating. Mosby must have been dreadfully torn during the last months of the war. He was an intelligent man; he had to know the South was doomed.•

JDW   °Mosby, however, refused to surrender. He had tried to negotiate terms of surrender, but in the end he could not. On April 21, 1865, twelve days after Lee had surrendered to Grant at Appomattox and a week after John Wilkes Booth had assassinated Lincoln, Mosby gathered

The slight twenty-eight-year-old who had entered the war as a disinterested soldier had paid a price for his tenacity in the Valley. Wounded five times, he carried one bullet for the rest of his life. In February 1865 in Richmond, almost recovered from his fifth wound, he wore a full, sandy-colored beard and mustache (above).

By April he was gaunt and the full weight of the actions of the three previous years were apparent in his face (below).

as many men of his command together as he could summon to Salem, Virginia, which is called Marshall today. There in a field, each company—there were eight companies by this time—formed in ranks, and Mosby officially disbanded the Forty-third Battalion of the Virginia Cavalry.* He said: "Soldiers! I have summoned you together for the last time. The vision we have cherished of a free and independent country, has vanished, and that country, is now the spoil of a conqueror. I disband your organization in preference to surrendering it to our enemies. I am now no longer your commander. After association of more than two eventful years, I part from you with a just pride, in the fame of your achievements, and grateful recollections of your generous kindness to myself. And now at this moment of bidding you a final adieu accept the assurance of my unchanging confidence and regard. Farewell!"

Tee Edmonds recorded on April 21, 1865: "Oh, Mosby, the Confederacy can claim thee no more. We cherish thy great adoration for our cause, and the love which we give thy fame shall be seared in our memory."

There were many ranger reunions in the years after the war. They passed resolutions, held parades, answered roll calls, planned fund-raisers for memorials, and shared memories. Mosby avoided them, except for one in 1895.

After disbanding the battalion, Mosby ventured south to find Joseph E. Johnston's army, but when he learned that Johnston had surrendered to William Tecumseh Sherman, he abandoned any thought of continuing the struggle. With a five-thousand-dollar reward for his capture, he went into hiding in the area around Lynchburg, Virginia, until he was paroled two months later by Grant. He returned to civilian life as a lawyer. Remarkably, he became a Republican, and in 1868 he supported Grant for president.

Through the waning years of the nineteenth century there would be many ranger reunions, but Mosby attended only one. At the 1895 reunion Mosby said, "Life cannot afford a more bitter cup than the one I drained when we parted at Salem, nor any higher reward of ambition than that I received as Commander of the Forty-third Virginia Battalion of Cavalry."

John S. Mosby died May 30, 1916, at the age of eighty-two. In his memoirs, he summoned words from the classics to explain his sanguine devotion to a lost cause: "It is paradoxical but true that the Confederate cause was lost at Bull Run. Yet the victory reflected on those who won it all the glory that was Greece and the grandeur that was Rome . . . and no matter now what men speculate as to what might have been, cold must be the heart that can read that glorious record and not feel sympathy with suns that set."

After the war Mosby returned to his law practice. His family grew to four sons and four daughters, but he lost one son in 1873, and then he lost Pauline and a second son in 1876. He joined the Republican Party, offending many friends, but making a new friend of U. S. Grant, who appointed him as consul to Hong Kong. During other Republican administrations he was given a post in the General Land Office and made an assistant attorney in the Department of Justice. Mosby wrote extensively about the war years when he returned to his practice. He died in 1916 at the age of eighty-two.

JOSHUA LAWRENCE CHAMBERLAIN

He seemed AN UNLIKELY candidate to become a military hero. Soft-spoken, philosophical, deeply religious, Joshua Lawrence Chamberlain was a bookish college professor in Maine when the Civil War broke out. In July 1863, on a rocky slope overlooking the Gettysburg battlefield, this quiet academic proved that a man of the pen could be just as mighty with the sword.

On the critical second day of the battle of Gettysburg, this college professor on sabbatical and in command of a volunteer regiment found himself defending the hill known as Little Round Top. Afterward he recalled: "The edge of conflict swayed to and fro, now one party, then the other having the contested ground. The heroic energy of my officers could avail no more. It was too evident that we could maintain the defensive no longer."

PAH °Chamberlain was in the most dangerous place at the most trying time, with the fate of the battle and, by JST extension, the fate of the Union in the balance.° °It was a moment in which a critical decision had to be made. Unorthodox action was required, and an unorthodox man came to make the decision.° "My thought was running deep," he explained. "As a last desperate resort I ordered a charge. The inspiration of a noble cause enables men to do things they did not dream themselves capable of before."

For his role in the defense of Little Round Top, Chamberlain was awarded the Medal of Honor and a permanent niche in the pantheon of U.S. history, much to the surprise of those who thought him little more than an ivory-tower intellectual.

CMC	Chris M. Calkins
WCD	William C. Davis
GWG	Gary W. Gallagher
PAH	Paul A. Hutton
JMM	James M. McPherson
JCO	Julia Colvin Oehmig
BP	Brian Pohanka
JST	James S. Trulock

Chamberlain's father, Joshua Chamberlain Jr. (left), was an industrious farmer from Brewer, Maine, who held several civil offices and was an officer in the militia. A man of few words, and direct ones at that, he instilled in his children a belief in action over words, but his sternness was balanced by a devotion to their happiness and well-being.

His first son was named Lawrence Joshua Chamberlain after the War of 1812 naval hero James Lawrence, whose dying words were, "Don't give up the ship." As an adult, Chamberlain chose the sequence, Joshua Lawrence. He pursued an academic profession, and at the outbreak of the war, Chamberlain (right) was a professor of modern languages at Bowdoin College.

Following Chamberlain's appointment to the colonelcy of the Twentieth Maine Infantry, Josiah Drummond, the state's attorney general, wrote incredulously: "My dear governor, have you appointed Chamberlain colonel of the Twentieth? His old classmates here say you have been deceived, that C is nothing at all. That is the universal expression of those who know him."

PAH °Certainly it was thought that a college professor would be the last to lead men into battle. Chamberlain seemed soft, effete, too lost in intellectual pursuits to be a man of action, but in fact he was just the opposite.° °He became an ideal example of the citizen soldier, the schoolteacher who was not a man of war, but who, when a crisis arose, went forward into battle and became great at it.°

WCD

BP °Chamberlain was an idealist in the truest sense, and the Civil War was a war fought by idealists, by people who believed in something. Whether Federal or Confederate, a soldier in the Civil War was someone who was willing to give everything for a belief.° "We know not of the future and cannot plan for it much," Chamberlain wrote, "but we may cherish such thoughts and such ideals and dream such dreams of lofty purpose that we can determine and know what manner of men we will be whenever and wherever the hour strikes that calls to noble action."

The lofty dreams and high ideals that were to guide Chamberlain throughout his life had their roots in rugged Down East Maine, a region defined by the Puritan values of the earliest immigrants to New England. °This background bred people with firm dedication to principle, to duty, and to a sense of fulfilling God's will in their own lives by doing the best they could with the talents God had given to them.•

JMM

°Puritans had a reputation of rigidity. There was a time when young Chamberlain and his father were plowing a field. They came across a rock in the field, and his father looked down at him and said, "Move it." He asked how, and his father said, "Move it, that's how. Do it."• That became the solution for a thousand problems and an order of action for life.

JCO

°His father had wanted him to be a soldier; his mother preferred that he be a minister, a more noble ambition she thought, especially during peacetime. Chamberlain did not particularly care to do either,• observing: "Both alike offered but little scope and freedom. They bound a man by rules and precedence and petty despotisms and swamped his personality."

JCO

Setting his sights instead on a missionary career, he decided to study theology. He wanted to attend Bowdoin College in Brunswick, Maine, but was unschooled in one

In choosing his career, Chamberlain decided to prepare at Bowdoin College, but admission stipulated a knowledge of Greek and Latin, which he lacked. He prepared a space in the attic of his parents' home, and for a year he followed a rigorous schedule of study until he emerged with the requirement satisfied.

421

JST important entrance requirement—Greek. °In the way that he had learned from his father about single-mindedness and singleness of purpose, he set off a place for himself in the attic of his home.• Less than a year later he emerged from his attic having taught himself Greek and ready to begin his career as a Bowdoin College student.

"The first two years in college were on the whole a pretty severe experience," he recalled. "Hard study had to be done to acquire good habits of work. Well remembered are those weary nights when some problem would be given out for the next morning's demonstration over which a pale student sat staring at the words until the stars were lost in the flush of dawn." There was more to college life than just relentless study, however; there was a minister's daughter at the First Parish Church, Frances Caroline Adams, known to her friends as Fannie. She was bright, flirtatious, and will-

JST ful, but Chamberlain found her enchanting, and °he fell in love with her.• "I know in whom all my highest hopes and dearest joys are centered. I know in whom my whole heart can rest sweetly and surely. Fannie, dear Fannie, only tell me that you do love me as I do love you," he wrote.

JCO °Fannie was a complex person. She had been born to a prominent Boston family, but when she was very young her family gave her away to live with a relative in Maine, the Reverend George Adams. Having been given away like that as a young child, Fannie had difficulties trusting other people, much less loving

JST another person.• °This limited trust was characteristic throughout their life together, but Chamberlain may never have understood that part of his relationship with his wife.•

During Chamberlain's Bowdoin years there was another woman who had a profound influence on his

GWG destiny. Harriet Beecher Stowe, the wife of °Calvin Stowe, one of his professors, was writing *Uncle Tom's Cabin* at that time. She would host reading groups with some of the Bowdoin students and read them passages from her novel. It was a kind of indoctrination for Chamberlain into the great issue of slavery,

Harriet Beecher Stowe moved to Bowdoin in 1851 with her husband, Calvin, a professor of natural and revealed theology. On Saturday nights she hosted readings in their home on Federal Street, the highlight of which was her presentation of the latest installment of her writing before it was sent to the National Era, *an abolitionist newspaper. The work was called* Uncle Tom's Cabin, *and Chamberlain was not immune to its dramatic and emotional style.*

and he developed very strong feelings on the question,• stating emphatically, "Slavery and freedom cannot live together."

IN 1861 CHAMBERLAIN had a secure position as a professor at Bowdoin College, had married Fannie, had fathered two children, and had bought a home in Brunswick. Life seemed predictable and settled, but the outbreak of war changed all that.

PAH   °Chamberlain had every reason and every excuse to avoid going to war, but he was determined to go because, to him, it was the right thing to do. One had to play one's part• in this struggle of ideals.

JCO   °He wrote the governor and asked what he could do. Meanwhile, the college learned of his offer and was not happy with the prospect of losing Chamberlain. He was young and brilliant, an up-and-coming professor in their ranks, so he was offered the chairmanship of the department of modern languages and a two-year European sabbatical. He accepted the sabbatical, but rather than go to Europe he went to war.•

In his letter to Gov. Israel Washburn, Chamberlain said, "I have always been interested in military matters and what I do not know in that line I know how to learn." Washburn offered him the colonelcy of a new volunteer regiment, the Twentieth Maine, but Chamberlain declined the position in favor of the

BP   number-two spot, lieutenant colonel. °Although he

In 1851 Chamberlain became the choir conductor in the First Parish Church, and the pastor's daughter, Frances Caroline Adams (left), often played the church organ for the choir. Chamberlain fell in love with her, and they were married on December 7, 1855. The Chamberlains had three children, but one son lived only a few hours. Grace Dupree (center) was born in 1856, and Harold Wyllys (right) in 1858. The photographs of the children date from 1862.

Adelbert Ames, the first colonel of the Twentieth Maine and a West Pointer from the class of May 1861, had been wounded at the battle of First Bull Run and received the Medal of Honor for his actions that day. He had seen duty around the Washington defenses and on the Virginia Peninsula, but his military service to that time had been as an artillery officer, not as a commander of raw recruits. He found an eager officer in Chamberlain and developed a high opinion of his executive officer.

aspired to command, he knew that he had a great deal to learn about the military, and it was a wise move on his part.•

The colonelcy of the Twentieth was extended to West Point graduate and veteran of the battle of First Bull Run, Adelbert Ames. °When he first reviewed the soldiers of the Twentieth, he despaired that they would ever be combat ready. Passing a rather paunchy man standing round-shouldered in line, he shouted, "For God's sake, man, draw up your bowels!"• Ames was an impatient man who knew that his superiors would be judging him by the performance of his regiment, and his preferred method of instruction was bellowing, yelling, and dressing down any offenders of military decorum. It was the time-honored method of martial instruction to which Ames added his own incendiary temper.

°The volunteers who made up the Twentieth Maine were rugged men. Some of them were lumberman from the Aroostook wilderness. They were also lobstermen, fishermen, and sailors. To function as soldiers they needed discipline, and they received that from Ames. In exchange, a downright hatred for Ames developed• among the regiment.

That hatred was shared by Chamberlain's younger brother, Tom, then an enlisted man in the regiment, who groused: "Colonel A. takes the men out to drill and he will damn them up hill and down. I tell you he is about as savage a man you ever saw. I swear the men will shoot him the first battle we are in."

Nonetheless, °Ames succeeded in making these ragtag and bobtail civilians into a fighting instrument.• Under his watchful eye, Chamberlain too began to learn the art of soldiering, °bringing his typically diligent approach to his being a soldier. He read military manuals assiduously. He sought out West Pointers among his comrades in the Army of the Potomac and asked them to set up the equivalent of study groups so that Chamberlain and others who were new to the military could learn from these men who were soldiers.• He wrote home: "I study I tell you every military work I can find and it is no small labor to master the evolutions of a battalion and brigade. I am bound to understand everything."

How effective these lessons were would soon be apparent in September 1862 when the Twentieth Maine was assigned to the Fifth Corps of the Army of the Potomac and ordered north to head off the Army of Northern Virginia's invasion of Maryland. °Marching toward Antietam, the Twentieth Maine experienced its first taste of what war was about. There had been heavy fighting in three gaps along the crest of South Mountain. The dead Confederates had yet to be buried and lay where they had fallen along the ridge crest, behind stone walls, and around the trees.•

The sight of the dead was unsettling to the men from Maine. Chamberlain was no exception and recorded his thoughts: "I saw him sitting there gently reclined against the tree, essentially old, this boy of scarcely sixteen summers. His cap had fallen to the ground on one side, his hand resting on his knee. It clasped a little testament opened at some familiar place. He wore the gray. He was my enemy, this boy. He was dead—the boy, my enemy—but I shall see him forever."

The Twentieth Maine had been held in reserve at the September 17, 1862, battle of Antietam, but on December 13 it was moved into the line at Fredericksburg. There it charged the stone wall at Marye's Heights but could do nothing more than trade places with another regiment in the icy mud of the hillside. The order to fall back almost did not reach them when the army withdrew from the town and pulled back across the Rappahannock.

Chamberlain and the Twentieth Maine were held back from the fighting at Antietam. They would spend the rest of that fall honing their military skills.

A friendship and camaraderie developed between Ames and Chamberlain, and the men of the regiment grew to appreciate their lieutenant colonel. Meanwhile, they waited impatiently for the Union army to make its next tragic move—Fredericksburg.

°For any new regiment there could not have been a worse battle to be its first action than Fredericksburg. It was a campaign and a battle that were poorly planned and executed even worse.• The Federals launched the offensive on December 13, 1862, via pontoon bridges across the Rappahannock River. Fighting from house to

On the second day at Gettysburg, Chamberlain, now commanding the Twentieth, was ordered to hold the extreme left of the Union line. His men repelled several Confederate assaults. With heavy casualties and his ammunition almost exhausted, Chamberlain ordered his men to charge the Southerners. A desperate maneuver, it succeeded in finishing the fight for Little Round Top. The Twentieth Maine took four hundred prisoners, one of whom surrendered his sword with one hand while trying to fire his pistol at Chamberlain with the other.

WCD

house through the town, they came upon the strongest Confederate position of the war—the stone wall at Marye's Heights.

BP °Wave after wave of Federal soldiers advanced on the nearly impregnable position, and rank after rank were mowed down. They did all they could to take the heights that day but° never crossed the wall.

JST °From across the river, Chamberlain had watched the initial attacks literally in tears, witnessing what appeared to be the sacrificial deaths of so many men.° Around three o'clock that afternoon the Twentieth was moved toward the action, crossing the river and advancing through the town. Chamberlain was standing with Ames when the order to advance on the heights came. The colonel glanced at the enemy batteries above them and swore to his second-in-command, "God help us now! Take care of the right wing!" Turning to the men, he yelled, "Forward the Twentieth!"

Chamberlain recalled, "We were directed straight forward, toward the left of the futile advance we had seen so fearfully cut down. The air was thick with the flying, bursting shells, whooping solid shot. On we pushed up slopes slippery with blood." As the skies darkened the Twentieth was moved to the front to relieve a regiment that had stalled before the stone wall.

JMM °They had to stay on the field through that freezing night and all through the next day. It was a gruesome experience for Chamberlain because the only cover that some of them could find was the dead bodies of Union soldiers who had been killed in the previous attacks.° "The living and the dead were alike to me," Chamberlain remembered. "I slept though my ears were filled with the cries and groans of the wounded and the ghastly faces of the dead almost made a wall around me. We lay there hearing the dismal thud of bullets into the dead flesh of our lifesaving bulwarks."

This photograph was taken by A. H. Messinger at the U.S. General Hospital in Annapolis, Maryland, sometime after Gettysburg. It is the only known image of Chamberlain as a full colonel or wearing a corps badge. For his actions on Little Round Top he received the Medal of Honor. Immediately following the unlikely charge, he moved his depleted regiment to the summit of Big Round Top to prevent its falling into Confederate hands.

Wounded six times during the war, Chamberlain suffered his worst wound during the siege at Petersburg. On June 18, 1864, a unified assault was ordered against the Confederate line, with Chamberlain's brigade in the lead. During the charge, at the front of his men, he half-turned toward his line and motioned to the left with his saber when he was hit in the right hip by a minié ball. He believed he had been mortally wounded, but his former surgeon from the Twentieth Maine operated on him throughout the night, repairing the damage done by the ball. Chamberlain suffered from the wound for the rest of his life.

The Twentieth stayed on the field the next day and then fell back to the town. Around midnight they were moved back toward the front and began digging in. As Chamberlain inspected his line, he came across a soldier digging in, but facing the wrong way—he was a Confederate. Careful that his voice did not give him away, Chamberlain used his best southern accent to assure the man and then hastened back to his own line. He arrived in time to meet a staff officer who ordered the Twentieth back across the river.

The battle of Fredericksburg had been the Twentieth Maine's baptism by fire, and the men had proved themselves admirably. In the spring of 1863 Ames was promoted to general of another brigade, and Chamberlain became colonel of the Twentieth Maine. His chance to prove himself in his new rank came on a hot July day in Pennsylvania.

Chamberlain needed eight months to recuperate from his wound. When he returned to the front, the army was still at Petersburg. He returned, however, as a brigadier general, given the first and only battlefield promotion since Congress had granted that power to U. S. Grant. In his absence, the regiments of his brigade had seen limited action, the most significant of which had been aimed at eliminating Robert E. Lee's supply lines. The picture at left was taken at Fort Sedgwick after the siege.

BY THE SPRING of 1863 Chamberlain the college professor had completed the transition to Chamberlain the soldier. "No danger and no hardship ever makes me wish to get back to that college life again," he wrote. "I can't breathe when I think of those last two years. Why I would spend my whole life campaigning rather than endure that again." °In the camps of the Union army he found an excitement and a new camaraderie that he had never known before. He came into his own, and he knew it would be difficult to return to the old life.•

After the battle of Chancellorsville he wrote to his six-year-old daughter, Grace: "My dear little Daisy, there has been a big battle and we had a great many men killed or wounded. We shall try it again soon and see if we cannot make those Rebels behave better."

On July 1, 1863, the Fifth Corps was ordered to proceed with all haste to the Pennsylvania town of Gettysburg. °The Union had very nearly lost the battle on that first day. Now as the second day was dawning, both sides knew this would be a decisive engagement.•

°The key part of the Union line ran from Cemetery Hill along Cemetery Ridge to the south, and Cemetery Ridge gradually ascended up Little Round Top. When the chief Union engineer, Brig. Gen. Gouverneur Warren, climbed Little Round Top on the afternoon of July 2, he was astounded to find no Federal soldiers there. The left end of the line was completely

Thomas Davee Chamberlain was thirteen years younger than his brother. He spent hours looking for Chamberlain after he learned that his brother had been wounded at the Petersburg front. When he found him and learned that the attending doctors had decided he would not survive his wounds, he brought in the surgeons who saved Chamberlain's life.

WCD vulnerable.⁺ °"Here is a place that commands the entire left half of the field, and here are Confederates coming to take it," he reported to George Gordon Meade, the Federal commander. Warren immediately scrambled to find reserves, anybody, to send up Little Round Top to hold the summit.⁺

He found Col. Strong Vincent, who rushed the Third Brigade into position. Vincent placed his regiments in a defensive line around the south spur of the hill, ending with the Twentieth Maine, commanded by Chamber-

JST lain. Surveying his deployments, °Vincent came to Chamberlain and explained that the Twentieth held the extreme left of the Union line and that a "desperate attack" was expected at any moment to turn the position. His last words to the colonel of the Twentieth Maine were, "Hold that ground at all hazards."⁺ Both

PAH men knew that °if Little Round Top fell to the Confederates, Lee would be triumphant. He would have his victory on Northern soil. Of all men, Chamberlain understood what was at stake, and he was determined to hold his ground.⁺

Almost immediately after taking position on the summit, Chamberlain recalled: "A strong fire opened at once from both sides, the enemy still advancing until they came within ten paces of our line. From that moment began a struggle fierce and bloody beyond any I have witnessed."

On July 2 the Twentieth Maine was made up of 358 men and 28 officers with a few more joining the fight

JST who had been listed as "absent sick." °Chamberlain sent Company B under Capt. Walter G. Morrill to the left to guard against a flank attack.⁺ Company B was made up mostly of men from Piscataquis County, and they were known as excellent marksmen.

Musket fire was heard on the right, gradually moving toward them until the Twentieth was engaged all along its line. As Chamberlain watched over the fighting from a place behind the line, Lt. James H. Nichols of Company K came to him with news that something odd was happening behind the enemy battle line. Moving to a higher position, Chamberlain saw a long column of Confederates advancing to his left. He could not reposition his regiment without surrendering a portion of his ground, so he moved the color guard to the left of the line and ordered his commanders to move their men to the left and maintain their fire—°he had the right wing of his regiment open into a single line, as opposed to the traditional double rank of battle, so they could cover twice as much ground.• When the Confederates—the Fifteenth Alabama under Col. William C. Oates—charged on what they thought would be the Union rear, they were surprised to see a line of Federal troops—the improvised left wing of the Twentieth Maine.

The Confederates moved within ten feet of the Federal line and withdrew and attacked again and again. A hole opened in the center of the Federal line, defended only by a lone color bearer who had planted the flag and cradled it with his left arm while he loaded and fired a borrowed musket with his right. Chamberlain ordered his brother, Tom, to repair the breach any way he could.

During a brief respite, the soldiers tended their wounded. The fighting resumed, hand to hand in some places along the line. Two hours had passed, and more than a third of the Twentieth Maine were dead or wounded. The Confederates attacked again, and the Maine men barely repulsed them.

"At times I saw around me more of the enemy than my own men," Chamberlain remembered. "Gaps, openings, swelling, closing again with convulsive energy. In the midst of this struggle our ammunition utterly failed. Half my left wing already lay on the field."

°In that desperate moment he chose to charge them in a great right wheel, with the left wing coming out first as if it were a gate on a hinge.• "The words 'Fix bayonets!' flew from man to man," Chamberlain recalled. "The click of the steel seemed to give new zeal to all. The men dashed forward with a shout."

The sudden sight of two hundred hoarsely screaming men advancing downhill

Chamberlain's gauntlets and shoulder straps. Note that the impressions from his brigadier's stars are apparent.

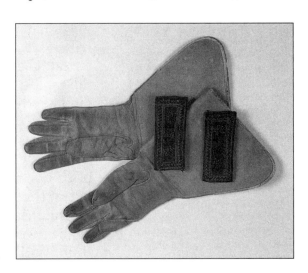

BP

JST

As part of the surrender terms approved by Grant and Lee at Appomattox, the Southern troops would have to lay down their weapons and surrender their battle flags in a ceremony to the officers appointed to receive them. Chamberlain was chosen to receive the arms, artillery, and public property. On the morning of April 12 his brigade was lined up along the road under their divisional banner highlighted by a red Maltese cross. The troops stood in place as a column headed by John B. Gordon approached. Chamberlain ordered his troops to attention, then to shoulder arms, rendering martial honor to the Confederates. Gordon responded by a salute with his sword and ordered his men to return the honors.

with fixed bayonets was enough to terrorize most courageous men, and the Fifteenth Alabama was no exception. Many raised their hands in surrender; others fled to their flank or rear. Groups were isolated and captured in whole companies. Those who had gone toward their flank had encountered the detached Company B under Morrill, who °now stood up and began firing into the flank and rear of the Confederates, creating the impression that another regiment had closed on the position.• Oates, who had lost half of his men, decided to cut his way out and ordered a retreat. The situation did not allow for an orderly withdrawal though, and the Confederate colonel recalled, "We ran like a herd of wild cattle."

°Four hundred Confederates surrendered, so many that it was difficult for the Maine men to keep track of them. Chamberlain's charge was a grand success born of desperation, but one that made this extreme left of the Union line safe.• "Our loss is terrible," Chamberlain reported, "but we are beating the Rebels as they were never beaten before. The Twentieth has immortalized itself."

432

While Little Round Top was secure, the same could not be said for Big Round Top. There was still a possibility that the Confederates would seize the high ground on the Union extreme left. It fell to Chamberlain to take the summit of the next mountain. The colonel called for the colors. "I had not the heart to order the poor fellows up," he recalled. One of his men remembered his saying: "I am going, the colors will follow me. As many of my men as feel able to do so can follow us." He then led the way in the dark as every man in the regiment fell in behind him. Aside from a few enemy patrols, which they captured, they encountered little opposition in taking the summit of Big Round Top.

BP   °Increasingly, Chamberlain viewed the war as a test, not only of the people to survive as a nation, but as a very personal test of himself. He knew that somehow he was rising to the challenge.• The most difficult part of the test, however, was yet to come when in the spring of 1864 the Fifth Corps was ordered south as part of U. S. Grant's costly and relentless push toward Richmond.

BP   °From May 1 to June 3, 1864, Grant's army lost approximately fifty thousand men. Most of his soldiers knew that they were going to die; it was just a question of when.• A literary man, Chamberlain recorded: "The Wilderness, Spotsylvania, the North Anna, Cold Harbor, unspoken, unspeakable history.

After Grant and Lee had departed, civilians and soldiers posed with stacked rifles in front of the court-house at Appomattox. During the two days that followed the surrender, the two armies intermingled as the Federals hosted the Southerners with rations they no longer needed. They traded for souvenirs, food, coffee, and clothes.

The last act of the surrendering Confederates was for the color-bearers to
furl or fold the battle flags, all of
which bore signs of the four years of
war. Nearly all were torn, with dark
splotches of blood testifying to the way
in which they had been defended.
These banners were their most precious
possessions, symbols of their valor, and
the soldiers gave them up slowly,
painfully, even kissing the fabric while
tears formed in their eyes.

Thousands upon thousands plunged straightaway into
hell-like horrors."

In mid-June Grant's wornout army arrived at Petersburg, Virginia, the main rail line to Richmond. Now
commander of the Third Brigade, Chamberlain prepared to do his part in the assault on this tactically
critical city.

JST °His brigade was about a mile in front of the rest of
the army. Surveying the expansive line of Confederate
entrenchments, Chamberlain saw a small angle in the
defensive line that would create a deadly crossfire into
GWG the attacking force.• °Orders came telling him to move
forward. Incredulous, he responded by pointing out
how exposed his brigade was:• "Circumstances lead me
to believe that the general cannot be aware of my situation. From what I can see of the enemy's lines, it is
my opinion that if an assault is to be made it should
be made by nothing less than the whole army."

JMM °There was little coordination in the Union attacks
at Petersburg, and the order came back repeating that
he was to attack. So Chamberlain did, knowing that it
was a terrible sacrifice,• but as a man of conscience
Chamberlain was at the head of his men. He said, "I
felt it was my duty to lead the charge in person and
on foot."

JCO °The Confederate fire was relentless, and the men leaned into it as if it were a storm of hail. The color-bearer next to Chamberlain was hit, and Chamberlain

JST picked up the flag.• °He had turned to urge his men on

JCO when he was struck.• °The bullet went in one hip, up around the upper thigh and lower hip area, went through his body, grazed his bladder, severed arteries,

PAH and came out the other side.• °He used his sword to prop himself up because he knew that if he fell his men would lose heart and the charge would stall. He stood there, straining, using all his willpower to stand and hold the colors and urge on his men. Finally, overcome by loss of blood, he blacked out and fell.•

He thought the wound was mortal. When stretcher-bearers came after him, Chamberlain told them to attend to the less seriously wounded. They ignored his orders and carried him from the battlefield. In a field hospital three miles behind the line, the colonel wrote his wife, saying: "I am lying mortally wounded . . . , but my mind & my heart are at peace. . . . You have been a precious wife to me. . . . Cherish the darlings. . . . Do not grieve too much for me. We shall all soon meet."

HIS DOCTORS, superior officers, and even the Northern press gave Chamberlain no hope of survival after his terrible wounding at Petersburg, but the stubborn

On the morning of May 23, 1865, Chamberlain led his division for the last time in the Grand Review of the Army of the Potomac. His only awkward moment was when a young girl ran toward him with a bouquet of flowers and startled his horse. After riding past the reviewing stand, at the invitation of the president, he dismounted and joined the dignitaries there. When he saw the remnants of the regiments that had charged with him on the day he had been wounded at Petersburg, he broke protocol by returning their salute.

Yankee from Maine would not only pull through, he would return to fight again.

JCO °A minié ball expands on impact and causes significant internal damage; in most cases there was little hope of survival. Chamberlain's doctors examined him and concluded that they could do nothing for him. Chamberlain himself was as sure as they were that he would not live long, but his younger brother, Tom, would not allow this. He searched for the Twentieth Maine's respected surgeon, Dr. Abner O. Shaw, and also found Dr. Morris W. Townsend of the Forty-fourth New York. They operated on him throughout the night, wondering if they were prolonging his life or his pain.° At one point they stopped, but Chamberlain urged them on, determined to live.

When Chamberlain returned home to Brunswick (below), he found that he had arrived in time for Bowdoin's commencement. A feature of the event was to be a reunion of the surviving graduates who had returned from the war. When Chamberlain learned that Grant was in nearby Portland, he invited him to attend. The general's acceptance caused much excitement, and the Chamberlains were accorded special recognition as Grant's hosts. At the commencement ceremony, the college conferred an honorary doctorate on the general in chief.

Two generals, Gouverneur Warren and Charles Griffin, recommended Chamberlain's promotion to brigadier general. Meade promptly endorsed the request. Grant had been given authority to promote officers on the field for special acts of gallantry. On June 20 he exercised that authority in Special Orders WCD Number 39. °It was perhaps ironic that Chamberlain

Chamberlain tried to resume his professorship at Bowdoin College but could not complete the full schedule of his duties. He and Fannie, living in the house pictured at left, also lost another child, seven-month-old Gertrude. Then he learned that he had been mustered out of the army, still needing surgery for his Petersburg wounds. This last situation was resolved through normal channels, correcting the deviation from policy and ensuring the necessary surgeries. Nevertheless, Chamberlain frequently lapsed into depression and restlessness until friends suggested that he pursue political office. He served four terms as governor of Maine.

finally received his brigadier's star only at a time when it was thought he would never have a chance to wear it. Later Grant told him it was the only battlefield promotion he had ever made.•

BP °That Chamberlain survived his wound was amazing, but the damage the bullet did internally was something that would cause him terrible suffering and any number of operations during the rest of his life.• He spent five months convalescing at home in Brunswick, but despite the knowledge that his wounds would never heal completely, he announced to family and friends that he planned to return to the front: "It is true that my incomplete recovery from my wounds would make a more quiet life desirable and when I think of my young and dependent family the whole strength of that motive to make the most of my life comes over me, but there is no promise of life in peace and no decree of death in war and I am so confident of the sincerity of my motives that I can trust my own life and the welfare of my family in the hands of Providence."

He returned to Petersburg on November 18, but
BP °he could not walk without terrible, excruciating pain. While he did not like it, he often had to be helped up on his horse. Yet many believe that his greatest service during the war came in those last desperate months of battle.•

Grant was making his final push to cut Lee's army off from the few remaining supply routes into Richmond, and a key Union victory came after Chamberlain led a daring charge at the battle of Quaker Road. °At the beginning of this charge a bullet passed through the neck of Chamberlain's horse, struck the general in his bridle arm, riddled his coat sleeve, and then hit him just below the heart. Fortunately, it was deflected by a brass-backed mirror and a sheaf of field orders, exiting the back of his coat and then knocking his aide out of his saddle.

Chamberlain passed out and slumped over his horse. He regained consciousness as Gen. Charles Griffin rode up and said to him, "My dear general, you are gone." Chamberlain misunderstood Griffin. He looked at his troops and saw them breaking on the flank and turned back to Griffin and said, "Yes, general, I *am* gone," and he raised his sword and began exhorting his men to turn and face the enemy.•

°He pushed ahead of his men who were falling back, trying to rally them, and suddenly he found himself inside the Confederate line, surrounded by Rebel

After he first went back to Little Round Top with Fannie in the spring of 1864, Chamberlain returned many times. In October 1889 he spoke at the dedication of the monument of Maine granite that marked the area where his regiment had fought, similar to the monument pictured below. Inscribed on the stone were the names of those men who had fallen that day, and Chamberlain never failed to imagine them as they were when he stood overlooking that site.

soldiers who lowered their muskets, crossed their bayonets, and demanded his surrender.•

Thinking fast and grateful for the faded coat he wore,
Chamberlain replied in a southern accent: "Surrender?
What's the matter with you? What do you take me for?
Don't you see those Yanks right onto us. Come along
with me and let us break 'em." He turned and waved
PAH his sword toward the Federals and °led the Rebels into
the Union lines where they were taken prisoner.•

CMC °Chamberlain successfully rallied his troops, counterattacked, and by that evening controlled the sought-
after junction of the Quaker and White Oak Roads.•
BP °His bravery at the Quaker Road won him the brevet, or
honorary, rank of major general, and he continued to
perform superbly, including the April 1 battle of Five
Forks, called the Waterloo of the Confederacy because
Lee lost a sizable portion of his remaining army there.•

CMC °It must have been an incredible sight to these Union
troops to see the Confederates running away from them
and to be capturing scores of Confederate battle flags.
They were all carried away by the enthusiasm of it and
pushed on, and Chamberlain was among them, savor-
ing the victory.•

The battle of Five Forks, however, meant tragedy as
well as triumph for Chamberlain. Years later he would
always remember one of his men, Maj. Edwin A. Glenn.
JST °He had ordered Glenn to break a small line of Confederates and had further encouraged him, saying, "If you will
break that line you shall have a colonel's commission."

From a distance he saw the war-torn banner of
Glenn's unit advance and finally pass over the position
of the Rebel defenses. He rode forward to congratulate
Glenn when he encountered two men carrying the
major on a makeshift stretcher. The men told him that
Glenn had been shot as he wrested the Rebel flag from
the rallying Southerners. The mortally wounded man
could only whisper, "General, I have carried out your
wishes." Chamberlain was utterly anguished by that
and said, "Oh, my orders. My orders were never worth
your life." It haunted him his whole life.• After the
battle he sent through the recommendation for Glenn's
brevet promotion.

*Fannie had been loving and under-
standing of Chamberlain's depression
and restlessness after returning from
the war. She had not wanted him to go
to war, and as he became involved in
postwar politics, there was less time for
the two of them to be together. Their
relationship deteriorated to the point of
her contemplating divorce in 1868, but
she took no action. She lived a reclu-
sive life, painting and tending to her
children and, in time, her grandchildren. In her old age she began to lose
her sight, and Chamberlain or Wyllys
would read to her. Fannie died in
Brunswick on October 18, 1905.*

Shortly after returning from the war, Chamberlain (second from the right) had served temporarily as president of Bowdoin College. Retiring from politics after four terms as governor in Augusta, he was unanimously elected to the college presidency in 1871, serving in that capacity until 1883. He reformed the curriculum and revised many harsh disciplinary practices that he recalled as unnecessary from his years as a student. As a fund-raiser for the college, he was tireless. Many Bowdoin students fondly recalled being interviewed in his office and study, surrounded by the artifacts of his wartime service.

JCO °After the battle of Quaker Road, a wounded Gen. Horatio G. Sickel had °said to him, "General, you have the soul of a lion and the heart of a woman." That epitomized who Chamberlain was.•

CMC After four long years the end finally occurred at Appomattox. °In the surrender terms, which were very magnanimous toward the Southern soldiers, Grant stipulated that the Southerners stack their weapons in front of the Union troops in some type of ceremony.• Out of all the officers in the army Grant chose Chamberlain to preside over the official surrender ceremonies of the Army of Northern Virginia at Appomattox.

Early on the morning of April 12, Chamberlain assembled his men at the courthouse. Watching the Confederates approach, he recalled: "Before us in proud humiliation stood the embodiment of manhood, with eyes looking level into ours, waking memories that bound us together as no other bonds. Was not such manhood to be welcomed back into a union so tested and assured."

GWG °As the Confederates came into sight, Chamberlain ordered his men to offer the marching salute by coming to shoulder arms. The Confederate general in the front of the line, Gen. John Brown Gordon, had been looking down, obviously dispirited. When he saw that he and his men were being shown a great honor by the Federals who were going to receive the surrender, he ordered his men to return the salute.•

CMC °Many of the Confederate soldiers wrote in later years that the Union troops had given them truly a soldiers' sympathy. They wept unashamedly in front of their former enemies and gave up their battle flags. Very few civil wars end this way, and this was what made the American Civil War so particularly significant and why all Americans should be proud of what Chamberlain did that day.• "We cannot look into those brave, bronzed faces," he said, "and think of hate and personal mean revenge. Whoever had misled these men, we had not. We had led them back home."

CMC °THE GRAND REVIEW of the Army of the Potomac in Washington was its last assemblage as a military organization. The units were mustered out, and the men

PAH returned to their homes.• °Chamberlain more than most understood that an incredible and unique chapter in history was coming to a close. That was the curse of being an intellectual. He knew that his greatest moments in life had been at Little Round Top and later on the road to Appomattox. Nothing throughout the rest of his life, no matter how great the honor, could ever again come close to what he had felt and experienced on those occasions.•

WCD °When Chamberlain finished with the war, it was not just the nation that had to heal, but also Chamberlain himself and, not just physically, but emotionally and spiritually.• He returned home to Brunswick in July

This photograph was taken of the Twentieth Maine reunion at Gettysburg in 1889. A quarter of a century had passed, and Chamberlain was asked to speak of the battle and those who had fallen around him that day in 1863. He was by then a speaker much in demand, invited repeatedly to various reunions. Active in many veterans organizations, Chamberlain was the Maine department commander of the Grand Army of the Republic and commander for Maine's Military Order of the Loyal Legion commandery. He also served a term as the president of the Society of the Army of the Potomac.

1865. The town seemed unnaturally quiet after the roar of the battlefields where he had earned his fame.

JCO °His ten-year wedding anniversary was in December of that year, and for their anniversary present he gave Fannie a beautiful bracelet he had designed that listed the twenty-four battles in which he had been involved.• While Fannie treasured the gift, it could not mend the rift that had grown between them during the four-year war.

In 1900 Chamberlain was appointed surveyor of the port of Portland. The position allowed him to maintain his residence in Brunswick, still serve Bowdoin College, and pursue his own interests, such as speaking, writing, and traveling. Rarely did he vary from his daily routine, always wearing a dark suit, a blue shirt with a starched collar, and a black tie. People still sought him out, and he always talked with them.

JCO °Like many veterans from many wars, Chamberlain had difficulty adjusting to home life. He had seen things that Fannie could not comprehend. They had grown apart, and by 1868 Fannie was considering divorce. They overcame their problems, however, and they were married nearly fifty years. Fannie died in 1905, and her death broke his heart.• "We pass now quickly from each other's sight," he wrote, "but I know full well that where beyond these passing scenes you will be there will be heaven."

Despite chronic pain from his Petersburg wound, Chamberlain's later years were filled with varied and productive service. He was governor of Maine for four terms and president of Bowdoin College for twelve, but by far his greatest contributions were his writings through which he sought to make his own peace with the memory of war. "Where is the reckoning for such things, and who is answerable?" he asked. "Was it God's command we heard, or His forgiveness we must forever implore? "

PAH °Few wrote so compellingly as Chamberlain, and few thought so deeply about what the war had meant and what all wars meant and why men would stand up to that incredible fire.• "There is a way of losing that is finding," he wrote. "When soul overmasters sense, when the noble and divine self overcomes the lower self, when duty and honor and love, immortal things, bid the mortal perish. It is only when a man supremely gives that he supremely finds."

BP   °He loved to talk to other veterans in the decades after the war, always making the point that they were heroes. He would say such things as "Heroism is latent in every human soul" and "Transcendence of self has immortalized you." His words were almost religious, and he became in a sense a spokesman for the religion of those who had passed through the hell of battle. •

JST   °Chamberlain returned to Gettysburg many times after the war. Little Round Top, that otherwise insignificant hill, was a focal point of his life. Among his last writings, he had noted, "I went, it is not long ago, to stand again upon that crest whose one day's crown of fire has passed into the blazon coronet of fame." When he returned, the spirits of Gettysburg rose up to him, and he felt them most poignantly • and gave that feeling expression: "In great deeds something abides. On great fields something stays. Forms change and pass; bodies disappear; but spirits linger. . . . This is the great reward of service, to give life's best for such high sake that it shall be found again unto life eternal."

On February 24, 1914, the eighty-five-year-old Chamberlain was finally delivered from the pain of the wounds he had received some fifty years earlier. For Joshua Lawrence Chamberlain the Civil War was never simply a clash between the states; it was a personal and spiritual quest to rise above human limitations, to sacrifice the body so that the soul could prevail. He left a legacy of an ordinary American who rose to feats of greatness when destiny called his name.

In his later years, Chamberlain's political career was mostly forgotten, but his war service was not. He was continually addressed as "General," although his grandchildren could only pronounce it as "Gennie," which became the name his family used for him for the rest of his life. In 1912 he wrote two magazine articles on the battles of Fredericksburg and Gettysburg, and he completed work on a manuscript that was published posthumously as The Passing of the Armies. *He helped to plan the grand reunion for the fiftieth anniversary of Gettysburg but was too ill to attend. The cumulative effects of his Petersburg wound finally brought about his death on February 24, 1914.*

Bibliography

Blackford, W. W. *War Years with Jeb Stuart.* New York: Charles Scribner, 1945. Reprint, Baton Rouge: Louisiana State University Press, 1993.

Blight, David W. *Frederick Douglass' Civil War: Keeping Faith in Jubilee.* Baton Rouge: Louisiana State University Press, 1989.

Brandt, Nat. *The Congressman Who Got Away with Murder.* Syracuse, N.Y.: Syracuse University Press, 1991.

Chamberlain, Joshua Lawrence. *The Passing of the Armies: An Account of the Final Campaign of the Army of the Potomac, Based upon Personal Reminiscences of the Fifth Army Corps.* New York: G. P. Putnam, 1915.

Chambers, Lenoir. *Stonewall Jackson.* 2 vols. New York: William Morrow and Co., 1959.

Davis, William C. *Jefferson Davis: The Man and His Hour.* New York: HarperCollins, 1991.

Dowdey, Clifford, ed. *The Wartime Papers of Robert E. Lee.* Boston: Little, Brown, 1961. Reprint, New York: Da Capo Press, 1987.

Evans, David. *Sherman's Horsemen: Union Cavalry Operations in the Atlanta Campaign.* Bloomington: Indiana University Press, 1996.

Fellman, Michael. *Citizen Sherman: A Life of William Tecumseh Sherman.* New York: Random House, 1995.

Fleming, Thomas J. *West Point: The Men and Times of the United States Military Academy.* New York: Morrow, 1969.

Freeman, Douglas Southall. *R. E. Lee: A Biography.* 4 vols. New York: Charles Scribner's Sons, 1934–35.

Gallagher, Gary W., ed. *Lee the Soldier.* Lincoln: University of Nebraska Press, 1996.

———. *Stephen D. Ramseur: Lee's Gallant General.* Chapel Hill: University of North Carolina Press, 1988.

Grant, Ulysses S. *Personal Memoirs.* 2 vols. New York: C. L. Webster, 1885.

Hassler, Warren W., Jr. *General George B. McClellan: Shield of the Union.* Baton Rouge: Louisiana State University Press, 1957. Reprint, Westport, Conn.: Greenwood Press, 1974.

Henderson, G. F. R. *Stonewall Jackson and the American Civil War.* 2 vols. New York: Longmans, Green, and Co., 1900.

Hurst, Jack. *Nathan Bedford Forrest: A Biography.* New York: Alfred A. Knopf, 1993.

Jordan, David M. *Winfield Scott Hancock: A Soldier's Life.* Bloomington: Indiana University Press, 1988.

Keen, Hugh C., and Horace Newborn. *43rd Battalion, Virginia Cavalry, Mosby's Command.* 2d ed. Lynchburg, Va.: H. E. Howard Publications, 1993.

Longacre, Edward G. *The Cavalry at Gettysburg: A Tactical Study of Mounted Operations during the Civil War's Pivotal Campaign, 9 June–1 July 1863.* Rutherford, N.J.: Fairleigh Dickinson University Press, 1986.

McFeely, William S. *Frederick Douglass.* New York: W. W. Norton, 1991.

———. *Grant: A Biography.* New York: W. W. Norton, 1981.

Marszalek, John F. *Sherman: A Soldier's Passion for Order.* New York: Free Press, 1993.

Mitchell, Adele H., ed. *The Letters of Major General James E. B. Stuart.* N.p.: Stuart-Mosby Historical Society, 1986.

Morris, Roy, Jr. *Sheridan: The Life and Wars of General Phil Sheridan.* New York: Crown Publishers, 1992.

Nesbitt, Mark. *Saber and Scapegoat: J. E. B. Stuart and the Gettysburg Controversy.* Mechanicsburg, Pa.: Stackpole Books, 1994.

Oates, Stephen B. *To Purge This Land with Blood: A Biography of John Brown.* New York: Harper & Row, 1970.

Patterson, Gerard A. *Rebels from West Point.* New York: Doubleday, 1987.

Piston, William Garrett. *Lee's Tarnished Lieutenant: James Longstreet and His Place in Southern History.* Athens: University of Georgia Press, 1987.

Sears, Stephen W. *George B. McClellan: The Young Napoleon.* New York: Ticknor & Fields, 1988.

Sergent, Mary Elizabeth. *They Lie Forgotten: The United States Military Academy, 1856–1861, Together with a Class Album for the Class of May 1861.* Middletown, N.Y.: Prior King Press, 1986.

Starr, Steven Z. *The Union Cavalry in the Civil War.* 3 vols. Baton Rouge: Louisiana State University Press, 1979–85.

Swanberg, W. A. *Sickles the Incredible.* New York: Charles Scribner's Sons, 1956.

Thomas, Emory M. *Bold Dragoon: The Life of J.E.B. Stuart.* New York: Harper & Row, 1986.

———. *Robert E. Lee: A Biography.* New York: W. W. Norton, 1995.

Trulock, Alice Rains. *In the Hands of Providence: Joshua Lawrence Chamberlain and the American Civil War.* Chapel Hill: University of North Carolina Press, 1992.

Tucker, Glenn. *Hancock the Superb.* Indianapolis: Bobbs-Merrill Co., 1960.

Urwin, Gregory J. W. *Custer Victorious: The Civil War Battles of General George Armstrong Custer.* Rutherford, N.J.: Fairleigh Dickinson University Press, 1983. Reprint, Lincoln: University of Nebraska Press, 1990.

Vandiver, Frank. *Mighty Stonewall.* New York: McGraw-Hill Book Co., 1957.

Villard, Oswald G. *John Brown, 1800–1859: A Biography Fifty Years After.* Boston: Houghton Mifflin, 1910.

Waugh, John G. *The Class of 1846: From West Point to Appomattox—Stonewall Jackson, George McClellan, and Their Brothers.* New York: Warner, 1994.

Wert, Jeffry D. *Custer: The Controversial Life of George Armstrong Custer.* New York: Simon & Schuster, 1996.

———. *General James Longstreet: The Confederacy's Most Controversial Soldier—A Biography.* New York: Simon & Schuster, 1993.

———. *Mosby's Rangers.* New York: Simon & Schuster, 1990.

Wills, Brian S. *A Battle from the Start: The Life of Nathan Bedford Forrest.* New York: HarperCollins, 1992.

Woodworth, Steven E. *Jefferson Davis and His Generals: The Failure of Confederate Command in the West.* Lawrence: University Press of Kansas, 1990.

Wyeth, John A. *That Devil Forrest: Life of General Nathan Bedford Forrest.* 1899; Reprint. Baton Rouge: Louisiana University Press, 1989.

Illustration Credits

THE SOURCES for the illustrations in this book are shown below. Credits from left to right are separated by semicolons, from top to bottom by dashes. The following abbreviations have been used throughout:

LC   Library of Congress, Washington, D.C.
NA   National Archives, Washington, D.C.
NPG   National Portrait Gallery, Washington, D.C.
USAMHI   U.S. Army Military History Institute, Carlisle, Pa.
USMA   U.S. Military Academy, West Point, N.Y.

2: Ole Peter Hansen Balling, *John Brown*, oil on canvas, NPG (NPG.74.2), Washington, D.C./Art Resource, New York. 4: Leib Image Archives (66803); Leib Image Archives (65705). 5: Harpers Ferry Historical Association (HF-154). 6: West Virginia State Archives, Boyd B. Stutler Collection. 7: West Virginia State Archives, Boyd B. Stutler Collection. 8: West Virginia State Archives, Boyd B. Stutler Collection. 10: F. O. C. Darley, *Border Ruffians Invading Kansas*, pen and ink, Yale University Art Gallery, The Mabel Brady Garvan Collection (1946.9.2063); Kansas State Historical Society (FK2.83). 11: West Virginia State Archives, Boyd B. Stutler Collection. 12: Leib Image Archives (1287-01); Collection of The New-York Historical Society (574). 13: LC (Z62-53868). 14: The Western Reserve Historical Society, Cleveland, Ohio. 15: With the permission of The Jefferson County Museum, Charles Town, W.V. 16: Harpers Ferry Historical Association. 17: Harpers Ferry Historical Association (HF-194)—West Virginia State Archives, Boyd B. Stutler Collection; Harpers Ferry Historical Association (HF-160). 18: Harpers Ferry Historical Association (HF-169)—Harpers Ferry Historical Association (HF-510). 19: Harpers Ferry Historical Association (HF-263)—Harpers Ferry Historical Association (HF-222). 20: Frank & Marie-Therese Wood Print Collections, Alexandria, Va. (#1484)—The Western Reserve Historical Society, Cleveland, Ohio. 21: Harpers Ferry Historical Association (HF-343). 22: Harpers Ferry Historical Association (HF-491). 23: Harpers Ferry Historical Association (HF-110)—The Valentine Museum, Cook Collection, Richmond, Va. 24: Harpers Ferry Historical Association (HF-103A). 25: USAMHI, MOLLUS Collection (94:4850). 26: USMA Museum. 28: USMA Library. 29: USMA Library. 30: USMA Library. 31: USMA Museum—USMA Library. 32: USMA Museum—USMA Museum. 33: USMA Museum.

34: USMA Museum. 35: USMA Museum. 36: USMA Museum. 37: LC (BA-1244)—USMA Museum. 38: USMA Library; USMA Library. 39: USMA Library. 40: USMA Museum. 41: USMA Museum. 42: USMA Museum. 43: USMA Library. 44: USMA Museum. 45: USMA Museum—USAMHI, MOLLUS Collection (45:2247). 46: USMA Museum—USMA Museum. 47: USMA Museum—Eleanor S. Brockenbrough Library, The Museum of the Confederacy, Richmond, Va., Katherine Wetzel Photo. 48: USMA Museum—USMA Museum. 49: USMA Museum. 50: USMA Museum. 51: USMA Museum—USAMHI, MOLLUS Collection (43:L2122-a). 52: John Roy Robertson, *His Excellency Jefferson Davis, Painted at the Executive Mansion, Richmond, Virginia, August, 1863*, oil on canvas, The Museum of the Confederacy, Richmond, Va., Katherine Wetzel Photo. 54: The Old Court House Museum, Vicksburg, Miss. 55: Leib Image Archives (887-08)—The Casemate Museum, Fort Monroe, Va. 56: LC. 57: The Casemate Museum, Fort Monroe, Va.—Courtesy, Special Collections Division, The University of Texas at Arlington Libraries, Arlington, Tex. 58: LC (Z62-5962). 59: Boston Athenaeum (A/B71M766/Hi.1861). 60: USMA Museum—USAMHI, MOLLUS Collection (17:804)—The Western Reserve Historical Society, Cleveland, Ohio. 61: USMA Museum—USAMHI, MOLLUS Collection (129:6647). 62: The Valentine Museum, Cook Collection, Richmond, Va.; Courtesy of Ted Yeatman. 63: Leib Image Archives (B1233)—*Harper's Weekly*. 64: LC (Z62-36285). 65: The Library of Virginia. 66: LC (Z62-107217). 67: LC (B482101-5918)—Currier & Ives, 1865. 68: *The Illustrated London News*. 69: The Casemate Museum, Fort Monroe, Va. 70: USMA Museum—USAMHI, MOLLUS Collection (113:L5849)—LC (Z62-77185). 71: USMA Museum—USAMHI, MOLLUS Collection (91:4662)—USMA Museum—USAMHI, MOLLUS Collection (74:3699-f). 72: LC (Z62-15660)—LC (Z62-8756). 73: The Library of Virginia. 74: LC (B8184-10296)—Beauvoir, The Jefferson Davis Shrine. 75: Beauvoir, The Jefferson Davis Shrine—USMA Museum—USAMHI, MOLLUS Collection (85:L4280). 76: LC (Z62-61347). 77: LC

Society (44986). **149:** *Decision at Dawn,* by Don Troiani, photograph courtesy of Historical Art Prints, Southbury, Conn. **150:** *Lee's Texans,* by Don Troiani, photograph courtesy of Historical Art Prints, Southbury, Conn. **151:** *Frank Leslie's Illustrated Newspaper.* **152:** *Illustrated London News.* **153:** Leib Image Archive (2101). **154:** LC (B8184-4153); LC (B8171-7292). **155:** *Surrender at Appomattox* by Tom Lovell © 1987, The Greenwich Workshop, Inc., courtesy of The Greenwich Workshop, Inc., Shelton, Conn. **156:** The Western Reserve Historical Society, Cleveland, Ohio; The Valentine Museum, Cook Collection, Richmond, Va.—The Valentine Museum, Cook Collection, Richmond, Va. **157:** The Western Reserve Historical Society, Cleveland, Ohio—The Museum of the Confederacy, Richmond, Va., Katherine Wetzel Photo. **158:** *General Robert E. Lee,* by Don Troiani, photograph courtesy of Historical Art Prints, Southbury, Conn. **159:** Virginia Historical Society, courtesy Washington and Lee University. **160:** Leib Image Archives (3905). **162:** LC (Z62-1286). **163:** USAMHI, MOLLUS Collection (108:5590)—USAMHI, MOLLUS Collection (43:L2110-bl). **164:** Leib Image Archives (65708); NA (165-SB-2). **165:** Leib Image Archives (65707); Leib Image Archives (73904). **166:** Frederick Douglass Historic Site (#10996-A); NPG (NPG.80.21), Washington, D.C./Art Resource, New York. **167:** University of Tennessee Library, Special Collections. **168:** LC (Z62-54395). **169:** LC (Z62-34810); LC (Lot 10615-59-H). **170:** LC (Z62-7823). **171:** Leib Image Archives (23807). **172:** NA (111-BA-11088); LC. **173:** Collection of the J. Paul Getty Museum, Malibu, California, Ezra Greenleaf Weld, Frederick Douglass, abolitionist orator, Cazenovia, New York, August 22, 1850, dauguerreotype, 2⅝" x 2⅛". **174:** Boston Athenaeum (Rare D945.3D74). **175:** Leib Image Archives (39603). **176:** LC (Z62-28483)—LC (B8171-7890). **177:** LC (Z62-1288). **178:** LC—Courtesy Moorland-Spingarn Research Center, Howard University; Courtesy Moorland-Spingarn Research Center, Howard University (#298). **179:** Courtesy Frederick Douglass Historic Site (#137). **180:** LC; Courtesy Frederick Douglass Historic Site (#10996b). **181:** Courtesy Moorland-Spingarn Research Center, Howard University. **182:** USAMHI, MOLLUS Collection (91:4686). **184:** LC (Z62-24677). **185:** LC (26-859)—USAMHI, MOLLUS Collection (87:4380). **186:** LC (Z62-14966); LC (Z62-62999). **187:** LC. **188:** LC (Z61-902). **189:** Chicago Historical Society (photograph ICHi-10533, U. S. Grant—Grant & Perkins Leather Store, Galena [Ill.], ca. 1865, photographer unknown). **190:** USMA Library (1244)—Ulysses S. Grant photograph collection of James A. Bultema. **191:** LC (Z62-3583). **192:** The Western Reserve Historical Society, Cleveland, Ohio. **193:** LC (B8184-10608). **194:** LC (BH8255-191)—Ulysses S. Grant photograph collection of James A. Bultema. **195:** Ulysses S. Grant photograph collection of James A. Bultema—The

Western Reserve Historical Society, Cleveland, Ohio. **196:** Ole Peter Hansen Balling, *Grant and His Generals,* oil on canvas, 120" x 192", NPG (NPG.66.37), Washington, D.C./Art Resource, New York. **197:** Ulysses S. Grant photograph collection of James A. Bultema—LC (B8184-B46). **198:** LC (BH83-1402). **199:** USMA Museum (#4423). **200:** USAMHI, MOLLUS Collection (44:L2154-a; 44:L2154-c; 44:L2154-d). **201:** *Peace in Union,* by Thomas Nast, courtesy The Galena/Jo Daviess County Historical Society and Museum. **202:** Ulysses S. Grant photograph collection of James A. Bultema; Ulysses S. Grant photograph collection of James A. Bultema. **203:** Ulysses S. Grant photograph collection of James A. Bultema. **204:** LC (Z62-4599)—Ulysses S. Grant photograph collection of James A. Bultema. **205:** LC. **206:** Ulysses S. Grant photograph collection of James A. Bultema—Ulysses S. Grant photograph collection of James A. Bultema; LC (Z62-38122). **207:** Ulysses S. Grant photograph collection of James A. Bultema. **208:** USAMHI, MOLLUS Collection (23:L1121). **210:** LC. **211:** The Valentine Museum, Cook Collection, Richmond, Va. **212:** LC (Z62-103596). **213:** Lloyd Ostendorf Collection, Dayton, Ohio. **214:** USAMHI, MOLLUS Collection (43:L2141). **215:** NA (111-B-514); From Clarence C. Buell and Robert U. Johnson, eds., *Battles and Leaders of the Civil War,* 4 vols. (New York: Century, 1884–88; reprint, Secaucus, N.J.: Castle, 1985), 3:80. **216:** American Heritage Engraving, Alexandria, Va. **217:** American Heritage Engraving, Alexandria, Va. **218:** American Heritage Engraving, Alexandria, Va. **219:** Frank D. Briscoe, *Charge of the Louisiana Tigers,* courtesy The Museum of the Confederacy, Richmond, Va. **220:** USAMHI, MOLLUS Collection (87:4399-3)—American Heritage Engraving, Alexandria, Va. **221:** The Collection of Jay P. Altmayer. **222:** Detail from *Decision at Dawn,* by Don Troiani, photograph courtesy of Historical Art Prints, Southbury, Conn. **223:** Courtesy of the Gettysburg National Military Battlefield Park—NA (200-CC-2288). **224:** Frank & Marie-Therese Wood Print Collections, Alexandria, Va. (#2800). **226:** Courtesy of the Gettysburg National Military Battlefield Park. **227:** LC (BH834-85). **228:** LC (Z62-103594). **229:** USMA Library. **230:** USAMHI, MOLLUS Collection (111:5726)—Courtesy, Georgia Department of Archives and History (HAL-158). **232:** Lloyd Ostendorf Collection, Dayton, Ohio. **234:** USAMHI, MOLLUS Collection (RG-100s). **235:** From Almira Hancock, *Reminiscences of Winfield Scott Hancock* (New York: C. L. Webster, 1887; reprint, Gaithersburg, Md.: Olde Soldier Books, n.d.), 90—Courtesy Security Pacific National Bank Photograph Collection/Los Angeles Public Library. **236:** USAMHI, MOLLUS Collection (23:1102). **237:** Courtesy of Brian C. Pohanka. **238:** The Western Reserve Historical Society, Cleveland, Ohio. **239:** "Camp Baxter, St. Johnsbury, Vermont, 1861, Third

344: Chicago Historical Society (ICHi-12456, photograph, Philip H. Sheridan). 345: NA (SC-83595). 346: USAMHI, MOLLUS Collection (73:L3628-ll). 348: The Archives of the University of Notre Dame. 349: The Western Reserve Historical Society, Cleveland, Ohio—The Archives of the University of Notre Dame. 350: The Archives of the University of Notre Dame. 351: The Archives of the University of Notre Dame—USAMHI, MOLLUS Collection (94:4819). 352: LC (B8184-10064); LC (B8171-2712). 354: LC (B8184-10069)—USAMHI, MOLLUS Collection (87-4394). 355: LC (B8171-3623). 356: LC (B8171-3626). 357: LC (B8171-3668). 358: LC (B8184-3630); LC (B8184-3631). 359: From Clarence C. Buell and Robert U. Johnson, eds., *Battles and Leaders of the Civil War*, 4 vols. (New York: Century, 1884–88; reprint, Secaucus, N.J.: Castle, 1985), 4:665. 360: NA (111-B-671). 361: NA (165-SB-62). 362: *Harper's Weekly*. 363: LC (B8184-5526). 364: NA (200-CC-657)—Kansas State Historical Society (B-Davis, Jefferson C.-*1). 365: LC (B8184-10236). 366: *Harper's Weekly*. 367: The Archives of the University of Notre Dame; The Archives of the University of Notre Dame. 368: LC (B8184-2017)—The Western Reserve Historical Society, Cleveland, Ohio. 369: The Archives of the University of Notre Dame—The Western Reserve Historical Society, Cleveland, Ohio. 370: National Archive (111-BA-1436). 371: The Western Reserve Historical Society, Cleveland, Ohio. 372: USAMHI, MOLLUS Collection (85:4280-tc). 374: Tennessee State Museum Collection (95.47.3), photography by June Dorman—Tennessee State Museum Collection (95.47.4), photography by June Dorman. 375: Tennessee State Museum Collection (1996.41.2), photography by June Dorman—Tennessee State Museum Collection. 376: From Frederic Bancroft, *Slave-Trading in the Old South* (Baltimore: J. H. Furst, 1931)—Tennessee State Museum Collection (93.8), photography by June Dorman. 377: Memphis and Shelby County Room, Memphis/Shelby County Public Library and Information Center (1542-C-1096)—Hendershott Museum Consultants, Inc., Little Rock, Ark. 378: From Bennett H. Young, *Confederate Wizards of the Saddle* (Boston: Chapple Publishing Co., 1914). 379: Alabama Department of Archives and History—USAMHI, MOLLUS Collection (73:L3618-b). 380: From John A. Wyeth, *That Devil Forrest: Life of General Nathan Bedford Forrest* (1899; reprint, Baton Rouge: Louisiana University Press, 1989). 381: USAMHI, MOLLUS Collection (87:4400)—From John A. Wyeth, *That Devil Forrest: Life of General Nathan Bedford Forrest* (1899; reprint, Baton Rouge: Louisiana University Press, 1989). 382: *The Illustrated American*. 383: NA (111-B-4791). 384: Confederate Memorial Hall, New Orleans, La.—*Frank Leslie's Illustrated Newspaper*. 385: Tennessee State Library and Archives. 386: Courtesy, A. Winston Rutledge, Tennessee State Museum Collection (X89.4), photography by

June Dorman. 387: *Southern Steel*, by Don Troiani, photograph courtesy of Historical Art Prints, Southbury, Conn. 388: *Harper's Weekly*. 389: Hendershott Museum Consultants, Inc., Little Rock, Ark.—From John A. Wyeth, *That Devil Forrest: Life of General Nathan Bedford Forrest* (1899; reprint, Baton Rouge: Louisiana University Press, 1989). 390: LC (Z62-10724)—From the Collection of Herb Peck. 391: Hendershott Museum Consultants, Inc., Little Rock, Ark. 392: Tennessee State Museum Collection (95.47.11), photography by June Dorman. 393: Tennessee State Museum Collection (93.86), photography by June Dorman. 394: USAMHI, MOLLUS Collection (85:L4288). 396: Manuscripts Print Collection, Special Collections Department, University of Virginia Library (10,571-a); From Adele H. Mitchell, ed., *The Letters of John S. Mosby* (n.p.: Stuart-Mosby Historical Society, 1986). 398: *Illustrated London News*. 399: The Valentine Museum, Cook Collection, Richmond, Va. 400: Leib Image Archives (20141)—Courtesy of Jim Moyer, Stuart-Mosby Historical Society. 401: *Munsey's Magazine*. 402: The Museum of the Confederacy, Richmond, Va.—*Muney's Magazine*. 403: Frank & Marie-Therese Wood Print Collections, Alexandria, Va. (#2769). 404: L. M. D. Guillaume, *Col. John Singleton Mosby*, oil on canvas, courtesy of the R. W. Norton Art Gallery, Shreveport, La. 405: The Valentine Museum, Cook Collection, Richmond, Va. 406: Jean-Adolphe Beaucé, *Scout Bringing Information to Colonel Mosby*, 1868, oil on canvas, courtesy The Museum of the Confederacy, Richmond, Va.—Courtesy of Nancy C. Baird. 407: Charles Edouard Armand-Dumaresq, *Mosby Returning from a Raid with Prisoners*, 1868, oil on canvas, courtesy The Museum of the Confederacy, Richmond, Va., Katherine Wetzel photo. 408: LC (Z62-6920). 409: LC (Z62-6235). 410: Courtesy of James Young. 411: *Ranger Mosby*, by Don Troiani, photograph courtesy of Historical Art Prints, Southbury, Conn. 412: The Western Reserve Historical Society, Cleveland, Ohio—LC (BH8301-2410). 413: The Western Reserve Historical Society, Cleveland, Ohio. 414: The Valentine Museum, Cook Collection, Richmond, Va.—USAMHI, MOLLUS Collection (30:1453). 415: The Valentine Museum, Cook Collection, Richmond, Va.—The Valentine Museum, Cook Collection, Richmond, Va. 416: Eleanor S. Brockenbrough Library, The Museum of the Confederacy, Richmond, Va. 417: The Library of Virginia. 418: Courtesy of the Pejepscot Historical Society, Brunswick, Maine (#1993.29.38). 420: Courtesy of Brewer Public Library, photograph by Brian Higgins, Brewer Historical Society; Courtesy Bowdoin College, Archives Class Photograph Albums, Hawthorne-Longfellow Library. 421: Courtesy Bowdoin College, Archives Campus Views, Hawthorne-Longfellow Library. 422: NA. 423: Courtesy of the Pejepscot Historical Society, Brunswick, Maine (1984.122.I; 1993.29.11; 1993.29.10). 424: LC, courtesy

of The Museum of the Confederacy, Richmond, Va.
425: USAMHI, MOLLUS Collection (87:4366-#5).
426: *Bayonet,* by Don Troiani, photograph courtesy of Historical Art Prints, Southbury, Conn. **427:** James C. Frasca Collections. **428:** Courtesy Joe Umble. **429:** USAMHI, MOLLUS Collection (28:L1358). **430:** Maine State Archives (#639). **431:** Courtesy of Don Troiani. **432:** *The Last Salute,* by Don Troiani, photograph courtesy of Historical Art Prints, Southbury, Conn. **433:** LC (B8171-7169). **434:** Richard Norris Brooke, *Furling the Flag,* 1872, oil on canvas, USMA Museum. **435:** USAMHI, MOLLUS Collection (75:L3719). **436:** Courtesy of the Pejepscot Historical Society, Brunswick, Maine (#1981.62.6). **437:** Courtesy of the Pejepscot Historical Society, Brunswick, Maine (#1982.82.94). **438:** USAMHI, MOLLUS Collection (49:2427). **439:** Courtesy Bowdoin College, Special Collections, Hawthorne-Longfellow Library. **440:** Courtesy of the Pejepscot Historical Society, Brunswick, Maine (#OH 1499). **441:** Collections of Maine Historical Society. **442:** Courtesy of the Pejepscot Historical Society, Brunswick, Maine (#1984.74.2). **443:** Courtesy of the Pejepscot Historical Society, Brunswick, Maine (#1984.74.3).

Index

CIVIL WAR JOURNAL

THE COMPLETE EXPERIENCE ON VIDEO FROM THE HISTORY CHANNEL

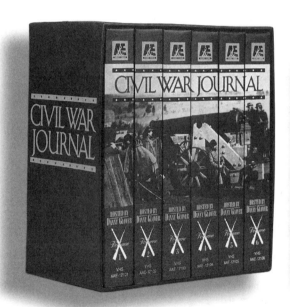

HISTORY COMES ALIVE AS PERSONAL ACCOUNTS REVEAL THE EVENTS, LEADERS AND BATTLES OF THE CIVIL WAR, INCLUDING **THE BATTLE OF ANTIETAM**, **THE BATTLE OF CHARLESTON**, **THE BATTLE OF VICKSBURG** AND MORE.